A Mission Divided

A Mission Divided

The Jesuit Presence in Zimbabwe, 1879-2021

David Harold-Barry

Published by Weaver Press, Box A1922, Avondale, Harare. 2022
<www.weaverpresszimbabwe.com>

© The Society of Jesus, PO Box UNZA 46, Lusaka, Zambia., 2022

All except the most recent photographs are taken from the Jesuit Archive, P.O. Box MP 610, Mount Pleasant, Harare. Details of the photographers have been given when these are known.

Photograph on front cover is of Fr Leonard Kennedy who planted orange trees wherever he found himself. Here he rests by 'Jacob's well' as the women draw water. Photograph on the back cover is of Fr Walter O'Connor looking bemused, Silveira House, 1961.

Typeset by Weaver Press
Cover by Danes Design, Zimbabwe
Maps by Street Savvy, Harare
Index by Rita Sephton

The author and the publishers would like to express their gratitude to The Society of Jesus, Province of Southern Africa, for their support of this publication.

All rights reserved. No part of the publication may be reproduced, stored in a retrieval system or transmitted in any form by any means – electronic, mechanical, photocopying, recording, or otherwise – without the express written permission of the publisher.

ISBN: 978-1-77922-411-8 (p/b)
ISBN: 978-1-77922-412-5 (e-pub)
ISBN: 978-1-77922-413-2 (PDF)

Contents

Introduction	xvi
1. The *Mise en Scène*	1
White missionaries and white conquerors	4
A sustained and imaginative commitment	6
Mechanics or gardeners?	7
The Jesuits	10
The Jesuits in Zimbabwe	12
Occupation or process	14
A 'degraded' people	15
Dispossessed of their land	19
A damaged environment	23
2. Ox-wagons and Mosquitoes 1878-89	26
Gonçalo da Silveira (1521-61)	26
Henri Depelchin	30
Kimberley, May 1879	35
Shoshong, July 1879	36
Tati, August 1879	37
Bulawayo, September 1879	40
Tati, January 1880	41
Umzila's, Tshamatshama, May 1880 - October 1881	43
Mweemba's, Zambia, May-October 1880	49
Mission to the Lozi, Zambia 1881	54
GuBulawayo	59
Empandeni	60
Conclusions	62
3. Putting down Roots	66
Chishawasha	66
Empandeni again	69
Embakwe	71

The first *Chimurenga*: the Ndebele and the Shona rising, 1896/97	73
The impact of the risings	77
The railways	81
Kutama (1912)	82
Driefontein	83
Gokomere	84
Schools	85

4. Growth and Questions — 89

Musami (1915)	89
The 'Jeep' years	91
The approach of war	96
6 February 1977	97
ZANLA at Musami	99
The end of the war	101
Independence	102
Mhondoro (1925)	103
Makumbe	105
Fort Victoria (Masvingo) (Gokomere), Bikita (Silveira), Macheke (Monte Cassino)	117
Wedza (Hwedza), Gwelo (Gweru), Wankie (Hwange)	119
Christian villages	122
Outstations	123
Mariannhill leaves Mashonaland	124
All Souls (1930)	127
Chikwizo, St Martin's 1960	128

5. Reaching the Zambezi — 131

Kutama (1912)	132
Marymount (1949)	133
Kariba (1957)	136
Mhangura (1958)	137
Chinhoyi (1954)	138
Karoi (1963)	138

Murombedzi (Gangarahwe, St Kizito's)(1964)	140
Banket (1964)	141
Hurungwe (St Boniface)(1968)	143
Makonde (St Rupert's) (1964)	143
Sipolilo (St Edward's) (1958); Guruve (St Joseph's) (1980)	148
Chitsungu (St Raphaels) (1964)	149
Kangaire (1970)	150
Mutorashanga (St James) (1979)	150
Alaska (St John the Evangelist) (1973)	151
Mount Darwin (Christo Mambo) (1973)	151
St Joseph's farm (1965)	152
St Albert's Mission (1962)	153
Abduction of students	154
Hedrick Mandebvu	156
Closing the school	156
Chinhoyi Rural Training Centre	157
The Diocese of Chinhoyi (1986)	159
6. Urban Tensions	**161**
Bulawayo	161
Harari (Mbare) in the early twentieth century	163
Elizabeth Musodzi	164
Charles Mzingeli	166
Mbare in the late twentieth century	168
Highfield, Dzivarasekwa and Mabvuku	170
The Cathedral in Salisbury and Campion House	171
Mount Pleasant, Mabelreign, Marlborough, Braeside and Rhodesville	172
Enkeldoorn (Chivhu) Umtali (Mutare) and Gwelo	173
(Gweru), Que Que (KweKwe) (1915), Gatooma (Kadoma) (1915) and Umvuma (Mvuma)(1921)	174
Marandellas (Marondera) (1952)	174
Bindura, (1964)	175

7. Mission and Culture — 176
- Local sisters — 180
- Local priests — 181
- Welcoming communities of Religious — 184
- Welcoming local-born Jesuits — 190
- A mischief-maker or a prophet? — 193
- Charism and culture — 195
- *Resourcement* — 199

8. A 'Dual Mission'? — 201
- St George's College — 204

9. Education for Development — 219
- St Ignatius College — 220
- St Peter's Kubatana — 233
- The School of Social Work — 238
- Silveira House — 243
- Rural credit — 256

10. Justice and War — 264
- The Catholic Commission for Justice and Peace — 267
- The Zimbabwe Project — 272
- Jesuit Refugee Service — 275
- 'Healing wounds, healing a nation' — 277
- The violent deaths of seven Jesuits — 279
- Martin Thomas (1932-77) — 285
- John Conway (1920-77) — 287
- Christopher Shepherd-Smith (1943-77) — 288
- Desmond 'Gussie' Donovan (1927-78) — 289
- Gregor Richert (1930-78) — 290
- Bernhard Lisson (1909-78) — 292
- Gerhard Pieper (1940-78) — 293

11. 'And there was much else…' — 295
- Small Christian communities — 295
- University chaplain — 297

Prisoners	300
People living with HIV/AIDS	303
Young people on the streets	305
Shingirirayi	306
People living with disabilities	306
Abandoned babies	308
Meteorology, astronomy, entomology, apiculture and archaeology	308
Retreats	310
Education Co-ordination	312
Mukai/Vukani	316
Theological reflection	313
Communications	317
'Intellectuals'	320
Liturgy and church décor	322
Finance	325
Archives and libraries	326
Richartz House	329
12. Into the Future ...	**331**
Appendix: Jesuit Foundations in Southern Africa 1875-2021	**339**
Acknowledgements	343
Index	**345**

David Harold-Barry is a Jesuit priest from Ireland who has spent fifty-five years in Zimbabwe, the first fourteen in Rhodesia. He spent twenty-five years at Silveira House, a Leadership Training and Development Centre, where he had ample opportunity to witness the frustration of people both before and after independence. The reasons were different, but the underlying structures that caused the frustration were the same.

Besides writing a column in *The Zimbabwean* and producing two books, one about the Jesuits killed in the war and the other a collection of essays on the situation in Zimbabwe at the turn of the century, he has also been engaged in training young Jesuits, giving retreats, working in prisons and starting a community of l'Arche for people living with intellectual disabilities.

Avant-propos

When Aston Chichester was new in Southern Rhodesia, he was taken for a drive by Henry Seed to see a rural mission. Simon Taonyei, a catechist, was also in the car. They came to a 'gate' or barrier across the road for cattle, constructed of branches and bushes. Seed, frustrated as to how to proceed, drove straight through the obstacle saying, 'they'll soon rebuild it'. Chichester stopped him and got out of the car and carefully reconstructed the barrier. Seed's reaction is not recorded but Taoneyi said later, 'I knew from that moment he was the right man to be our bishop'.

Dedication

To the members of the new Jesuit Province of Southern Africa (established 2021) and all those with whom we work in the evolving task which started in 1879 with the founding of the Zambezi Mission.

1

Introduction

I set out to enter a wood with well-trodden paths, only to discover I was in a forest, dense and *sans frontiers*. It is the story of a mission, the Zambezi Mission, but what strikes the inquirer is the individual Jesuit. Everywhere you turn you find someone using his initiative and his strength to start a work and push the boundaries. The basic tool of the early Jesuits in the interior of southern Africa was their boots.[1] Constantly exploring the opportunities they had in the first hundred years, they founded eighty works that ranged from mission stations, parishes, schools and colleges to social centres, houses of study, seminaries and even an observatory. Beyond all this, there was a multitude of outstations. Everywhere these works involved building and planting. It is a story of blending the skills of the many Jesuit brothers,[2] in brickwork, stonework, engineering, plumbing, carpentry, ironwork, printing, gardening, agriculture and so forth, with the planning, preaching, teaching and pastoral activities of the Jesuit priests with whom they lived, worked and formed one community. The variety of aptitudes was vast but the cohesiveness of focus was equally impressive. One cannot delve into the boxes in the Jesuit archives or listen to the accounts of older Jesuits without a sense

---

1   I write this on the day we celebrate S. Pierre Favre, first companion of Ignatius who died exhausted at the age of forty in 1546. He had walked the roads of Europe 'without a spare tunic' for years; from Paris to Rome, to Cologne, to Lisbon and Ignatius wanted him to go to Ethiopia.

2   When we say, Jesuit, we mean either a brother or a priest – the latter being a man ordained for that particular ministry in the Church.

of awe. Jesuits are good at sizing each other up or exasperating each other with their different temperaments, but this does not preclude standing back and thinking about all that was achieved. Irenaeus, in the second century, was in no doubt about who was behind all this.

> God is man's glory, but it is man who receives the effect of God's activity, who is the recipient of all God's wisdom and power.³

Anthropology and sociology have established themselves as respectable disciplines for academic study but the word 'missiology' sounds like a mongrel trying to ingratiate itself into a pack of purebred German shepherd dogs. Jesuit Francis Rea quotes S. C. Neill, a former Professor of Missions and Ecumenical Theology at the University of Hamburg, as saying, 'The study of missions has remained marginal and only grudgingly accepted. In at least one German faculty the professor of missiology is continually re-elected as dean by his colleagues, presumably on the grounds that he has nothing important to do.'⁴ The trouble seems to be that the sources are suspect: they are 'propaganda' in the sense of being written to edify the reader and open his wallet, they are composed without reference to the general context of the time and they come from a western point of view that does not interact with the cultures in which the missionaries operated.

Rea, writing in 1970, believed this criticism had some weight, but 'it shows a surprising oversight of the vast amount of published material dealing with missions in the period following the Reformation'. Among other examples, he refers to the 'reprinted *Jesuit Relations* of North America (1611-1791), whose value, wrote Parkman, assuredly no friend to Roman Catholicism, it is impossible to exaggerate'.⁵ Probing whether equivalent nineteenth-century sources existed, Rea believes they did: in the journals of the missionaries. These were primarily intended for their eyes alone and were likely to describe what they saw and understood, without any underlying edifying intent. When we add to the journals the vast correspondence of the missionaries of all churches 'there appear to be reasonable resources for the study of missionary history as an

---

3   *Against the Heresies*, Bk 3, 20, 2-3.
4   W. F. Rea, 'Christian Missions in Central Africa 1560-1890 and modern Missiology', *Rhodesian History* 3, p. 1. See JAZ, Box 348/6.
5   Rea, p. 4.

academic discipline as suggested by Neill'.[6]

The question a missiologist has to face is the one arising out of the almost complete failure, in human terms, of missionary activity up to the time of the 'breaking open' (Rea) of Central African society with the coming of the Europeans. Up to then, 'the society was almost impervious to missionary influence'.[7] (This was true not only of Christian missionaries but also of Muslim ones.) Rea quotes Michael Gelfand, Professor of Medicine at the University of Rhodesia, who studied and wrote a great deal about the local people of Zimbabwe. Do the people have a religion, Gelfand asked, one that satisfies them, comforts them in time of stress and maintains their culture and traditions intact. 'There is no doubt', he wrote, that they do. It is one which provides them 'with a sense of security and hope in a hard and cruel world'.[8]

We are now more aware of this world-view of the people of Central Africa than the Jesuits could have been at the time they gathered in Grahamstown in April 1879 and set out on their mission. They were men of their time and shared the general ignorance, and prejudices, of outsiders about Africa. The idea that the people had a religion of their own that satisfied and nurtured them would probably have been incomprehensible. And maybe, even after 140 years, those from outside are yet to understand. The more I, an outsider myself, probe the story of the part of Africa where I have spent my life, the less I understand. But that is not important. What is essential is that the main actors in this drama, battered and bruised by history as they are, do.

-o0o-

From its earliest days the Society of Jesus has kept records. Some of these were among the first written accounts of lands that had no previous tradition of writing their history, such as Canada, referred to already, and Mozambique.[9] Ignatius of Loyola, the founder of the

---

6   Ibid. p. 6.
7   Ibid. p. 9.
8   M. Gelfand, M, *African Crucible* (Cape Town: Juta, 1968) p.2. Quoted in Rea, p. 9.
9   The Portuguese government in the seventeenth century relied on the Jesuits for reports as they received little information of value from their own officials on the ground. In fact these officials were acting as though they were independent of Lisbon and the viceroy sent a Jesuit to inform the king that he was in danger of losing Mozambique entirely. An historian, writing in 1916, concluded that Jesuit

Society, insisted Jesuits write letters describing their experiences and reflections. These letters were to inform

- him, Ignatius, about what his men were doing and how he could help them and plan for the future;
- other Jesuits, especially those in training, about what the Society was doing and so to encourage them and get them thinking about their future mission. The founding documents of the Society only gave the broad aims of our mission and we often did not know what we were going to do until we started doing it! Ignatius himself learnt the Society's mission by what he found her doing. The great example of this was the schools. They were no plans to open schools when the Society was formed in 1540, yet before the first decade was over, they were heavily involved in this work;10
- the wider society about the work of the Jesuits and so interest them in becoming involved either by joining in or by materially supporting the work;
- and pre-empt the hostility of many who were hostile to the Jesuits and all they were doing.

So, in undertaking this work of describing the life and work of Jesuits in Zimbabwe, this writer both draws on, and, maybe, contributes to, this tradition. The situation today is quite different to what it was even fifty years ago when he was a student, to say nothing of five hundred years ago when Ignatius set out on 'this (new) life'.[11] Whatever Jesuits do now is up there on the screen, the day or even within the hour that it is done. The reason for writing our story is to record how we got to where we are now, in the hope that it will help us discern where we want to be tomorrow.

---

reports were: 'The clearest, best written, and far the most interesting documents now in existence on the country ... Compared to the ordinary state papers, they are as polished marble to unhewn stone.' G. M. Theal, *History of South Africa*, Vol. 1:p. 442. (London: George Allen & Unwin, 1915).

10 The first school was started in Messina in 1548.

11 'How will you be able to endure this life for the seventy years you have yet to live?' This question came to Ignatius once he had left his home at Loyola and he saw it as a temptation to be overcome. *The Autobiography of St Ignatius*, Chapter 2.

1

The *Mise en Scène*[1]

We must be gardeners and not mechanics in our approach to world affairs.

George Kennan

Twenty years from now the Jesuits, the Society of Jesus, will celebrate the quincentenary of their founding. Throughout their almost 500-year existence, their story has been told mainly by Jesuits, but the past thirty years has seen a surge of interest by others, drawn by the Jesuits' particular way of proceeding, as well as their achievements and failures.[2] This hopeful 'sign of the times' alerts us to the bridging of the gap between faith and culture that has made steady progress since the mid-twentieth century. No longer does the long shadow of the early Christian writer Tertullian intimidate us with his mocking, 'What has Athens to do with Jerusalem?' implying the answer 'nothing'. Today we would say, 'everything'. In fact, we live in a time of opening of

---

1   The setting.
2   See for example, Ines G. Županov, *Disputed Mission: Jesuit Experiments and Brahmanical Knowledge in Seventeenth-Century India* (New York: Oxford University Press, 1999); *Missionary Tropics, Jesuit Frontier in India (16th-17th century)* (Ann Arbor, MI: University of Michigan Press, 2005); and most recently, as editor, *The Oxford Handbook of the Jesuits* (New York: Oxford University Press, 2019). Leonardo Cohen, besides writing a number of articles and book-chapters, is the author of *The Missionary Strategies of the Jesuits in Ethiopia (1555–1632)* (Wiesbaden: Harrassowitz Verlag, 2009). Andreu Martinez d'Alòs-Moner is author of *Envoys of a Human God: The Jesuit Mission to Christian Ethiopia, 1557-1632* (Leiden/Boston: Brill, 2015).

doors to people and ideas, and this process is accelerating.

The Jesuits in the late nineteenth century came to southern Africa with attitudes closer to Tertullian than to Darwin. It is understandable in their context, as has already been mentioned in the introduction, but it contributed to a problem in the twentieth century. The missionaries of all churches discovered no way, with the exception of medicine,[3] of connecting with the people among who they had come. They had some respect for traditional herbs and roots and could see their effectiveness. Reciprocally, the people they lived among quickly came to appreciate European medicine. But this meeting point was of limited application.

They studied the language and learnt something of the traditional customs and religion of the people but they found no entry point into their minds and hearts. In fact, they even held that there was no basis to build on. They had to start from scratch. The London Missionary Society arrived many decades before the Jesuits and the Anglicans, but they all held similar views. We saw in the introduction how Africa was content and secure in its beliefs. Why should they change? That security had to be 'broken open', often violently, always exhaustively.

But, in conforming to this view, had the Jesuits of the late nineteenth century forgotten the instructions of Ignatius to his companions going to Ethiopia in the sixteenth? They were to 'proceed *con dolcezza*, sweetly, not forcing people to abandon their former customs. … Proceed with gentleness and avoid treating the people with duress … Tolerate what you can, unless prejudicial to the faith and minor abuses should not be initially challenged …'[4] Perhaps the sixteenth century was more leisurely and the nineteenth more urgent. Explorers, in the intervening years, were content to live and let live[5] but those who followed them two centuries later had a mission and it provoked resistance. Local rulers were set against education. It seems they had an intuition that it would undermine their own authority, and they were probably right. But the most glaring gap was

---

3   M. Gelfand, 'Medicine and the Christian Missions in Rhodesia, 1857-1930', in J.A. Dachs (ed.) *Christianity South of the Zambezi* (Gwelo: Mambo Press, 1973) pp. 114 ff.

4   Quoted in F. Mkenda, **Mission for Everyone** (Nairobi: Paulines, 2013), p. 52.

5   'We should live for ever in a salutary state of peace with one another.' S. van der Stel, 'Journal of his Expedition to Namaqualand 1685-6', in Eric Axelson, **South African Explorers** (Oxford: Oxford University Press, 1954), p. 50.

in religion. The missionaries, at that time, were unable to enter deeply into the religious beliefs and practices of the people. Peter Hatendi, later Anglican Bishop of Mashonaland, wrote in 1973,

> ... the Shona would admit that they had not heard of Jesus Christ until the coming of the missionary; but (they knew) the one true God manifested himself as Creator, 'Sustainer', the 'Holy Other'. God was at work among the Shona preparing them to welcome Christ. Therefore an unbiased search for things true, noble, virtuous, just, pure and lovely in Shona culture would yield surprising results. Without these jewels Shona culture could not last the vicissitudes of time. ... (For example), there is no fundamental difference between praying to the dead and praying to saints. The Shona know that the ancestors have no power to help them independently of God. The conclusion is drawn that the Shona have many true ideas about life which God has taught them indirectly and by intuition before the Christian missionaries came. In this way God has prepared them to receive the Good News of the Gospel. ... The missionary should take what he finds in vogue seriously and then offer it respectfully to Christ. The commission to 'go and make disciples of all nations' does not authorise a missionary to ignore or destroy the foundation which God himself has laid, for the grace of God takes nature for granted.[6]

But no one thought in the 1880s as Hatendi did in the 1970s. Catholic missionaries, in particular, nervously emerging from the triple experience of Reformation, Enlightenment and Revolution, were ill-equipped to explore sympathetically the culture and religion of the people. So, there was no dialogue. The Christian faith was taught as something coming from outside. They were decades away, in thought and in time, from Pope Paul VI's address at Kampala in 1969:

> The expression, that is, the language and mode of manifesting this one Faith, may be manifold; hence, it may be original, suited to the tongue, the style, the character, the genius, and the culture, of the one who professes this one Faith. From this point of view, a certain pluralism is not only legitimate, but desirable.

---
6 J. P. Hatendi, 'Shona Marriage and the Christian Churches', in J.A. Dachs, op. cit., p. 146.

> An adaptation of the Christian life in the fields of pastoral, ritual, didactic and spiritual activities is not only possible, it is even favoured by the Church. The liturgical renewal is a living example of this. And in this sense, you may, and you must, have an African Christianity. Indeed, you possess human values and characteristic forms of culture which can rise up to perfection such as to find in Christianity, and for Christianity, a true superior fullness, and prove to be capable of richness of expression, all its own, and genuinely African.[7]

They also seemed unaware of Pope Gregory the Great's instruction to Augustine in 596 when he sent him to England. These instructions were quoted by Roberto de Nobili, an Italian Jesuit who in the early seventeenth century persuaded the Church authorities that the customs he allowed in India were civil, not religious, and he proved this by citations from Hindu books of which the people who stood in judgement over him were ignorant. De Nobili clinched the matter by showing that the church had always adapted her method to the culture and customs of the peoples she evangelised. He quoted the Acts (chapters 15 and 16) before citing Gregory:

> The temples of the idols of that nation [England] ought not to be destroyed. Let holy water be sprinkled in the said temples ... for if these temples are well built, it is requisite that they be converted from the worship of the devil to the service of the true God, so that the nation seeing that their temples are not destroyed ... may the more familiarly resort to the places to which they have been accustomed.[8]

White missionaries and white conquerors

The approach of the Jesuit missionaries of the late nineteenth century would have been understandable, and the transition to a new way of thinking not seriously damaging, if there had not been a further shadow over their mission. This was their mutual relationship with the whites who settled in 1890, defeated the Ndebele in a war in 1893 and suppressed the risings of both the Shona and the Ndebele

---

7 Paul VI, Homily at the conclusion of the Symposium of the Bishops of Africa, Kampala, 31 July 1969.

8 J.C. Houpert, *A South Indian Mission: The Madura Catholic Mission from 1535 to 1935* (Trichinopoly: St. Joseph's Industrial School Press, 1937), p. 42.

in 1896/7. White power brought an uneasy peace. The indigenous people were subjugated and had no choice other than to co-operate with their conquerors. The older generation did so reluctantly, the younger saw opportunities in the new economy. A gradual process developed where the missionaries became inextricably linked with the Rhodesian project. They relied on the administration – railways, grants to schools and clinics and the 'law and order' – which the whites initiated. And the administration appreciated the efforts of the missionaries to accustom the people to settled, in contrast to nomadic, living, and to work. The missionaries, whether they knew it or not, prepared people for employment in the European economy and helped them in their transition from their homes, first to the European farms and mines and then to the towns.

This too would be understandable, but unfortunately it drew the missionaries ever deeper into the white hegemony, so that when the people began to stir and demand 'imperial citizenship' in the 1930s the missionaries, in general, shared white apprehensions. Thirty years later, when the nationalist struggle had found its feet, the Catholic Church was so compromised that the bishops' statements and letters denouncing the government's racial policies sounded hollow. This is explained concisely by Timothy McLoughlin:

> From the time of the white pioneers and gifts of land by Rhodes to the early missionaries, the policy of most churches has been to identify themselves with their institutions. Christian activity has long been measured in terms of baptisms, education within the structure of a western system, hospitals and dispensaries. In these circumstances, the Catholic Church regarded them as the accepted and ready means of fulfilling the Church's conception of its mission. But now it finds itself caught between two stools.[9]

The Church herself was divided and while she gave heroic witness during the war of liberation there were many of her members who sympathised with the Rhodesian government. Dieter Scholz, writing in 1972, quoted Swiss Bethlehem missionary Fr Albert Plangger:

> The bishops recognised as a basic weakness of their arguments the fact that legally institutionalised injustices had 'for far too long

---

9   T. McLoughlin, 'Teaching the Laity: Some Problems of the Christian Churches in Rhodesia', in J.A. Dachs, op. cit., p. 195.

been allowed to exist without protest as if they were inevitable' (Plangger, 62). Consequently, 'nothing but confusion prevails in this realm of thought here in Central Africa, with the result that grave injustices are inflicted and prolonged on whole groups of people: family life is disrupted, the liberty of the individual is needlessly constrained, uninstructed masses are confused about what is their duty and what is their due, and legislators themselves ... enact measures so ill-considered and immature that they make a mockery of justice itself.'[10]

Scholz, in 1973, commented, 'If, therefore, many European Catholics today oppose their bishops for what they have said, a good number of African Catholics criticise the same bishops for not having done what they have said'.[11] Scholz goes on to make the eminently sensible suggestion that the Church should embark on a policy of 'deliberate integration' in all its institutions. But it was too late. By the 1970s it would have been almost impossible for the Church to disentangle herself from the skewed practices she had grown used to over decades.

A sustained and imaginative commitment

If all this looks like a bleak summary of the mission of the Catholic Church in Zimbabwe in general, and of the Jesuits in particular, it has to be seen in the context of the devoted, imaginative and sustained efforts of missionaries, men and women, and all the people with whom they laboured over the past 140 years. The account that follows details a multitude of initiatives forged in the midst of huge difficulties, misunderstandings and frustrations. The Jesuits faced difficulties in procuring supplies, in transport, in sickness, loneliness and sometimes hostility. They were dedicated men and happy to be engaged in sowing a seed that would one day blossom. In recounting their story, I have tried to keep these two poles in balance; their dedication and hard work and the limitations of their witness, which we have to admit. They were not the principal agents of the tragedy that unfurled after independence but, with hindsight, we can say they did not see it

---

10 D. Scholz, 'The Catholic Church and the Race Conflict in Rhodesia', in J.A. Dachs, op. cit., p. 199, quoting A. Plangger, *Rhodesia – The Moral Issue* (Gwelo: Mambo Press, 1968), pp. 62, 24.
11 Scholz, op cit., p. 202.

coming – as perhaps they might have done had they read 'the signs of the times' more intensely.

Time has a kind way of healing all hurts and the Catholic Church, along with other Christians, has now 'moved on' and, at the time of writing, sometimes speaks out, Jeremiah-like,[12] on the issues of today. The legacy of a 'dual mission', which this study will have to describe, is already beginning to fade like the footprints on the shore before an incoming tide. But we have to confess our complicity in this dual mission and recognise that it weakened our witness. Perhaps, if we had had the wisdom of Gandhi and the courage of Romero, we might have been able to contribute with more authority to the avoidance of the desperate situation in which our country finds itself today. As Jesuits and as Church, we want to learn the lessons of history and avoid falling into similar dual mentalities.

Mechanics or gardeners?

Besides the Church's attitude to the external political context she found herself in, there was her approach to the internal life of the Christians she welcomed as her members.

A diversion can throw some light on this even if it cannot explain it. After the Second World War the Soviet Union expanded its influence into the newly liberated countries of eastern Europe and imposed a new form of control in place of Hitler's. The Americans did not know how to respond. They did not want a new war but they had to do something. This chapter begins with a quotation from George F. Kennan who was a long-time American diplomat in Moscow and knew and loved the Russian people. He understood that they had always felt threatened and wanted to expand their influence in order to feel secure. Kennan wrote a famous 'long telegram' to his superiors in Washington proposing that the Americans display their power but hold back from any threat of action.

Later, Kennan explained his thinking,

---

[12] For example, Jeremiah 26, 'The Lord says this: if you do not listen to me … this temple will be like Shiloh, and this city will be desolate and uninhabited.' On 14 August 2020, the Catholic Church in Zimbabwe issued a ringing statement, calling on the government to engage with the citizens in tackling the problems the country faces with openness and honesty. The letter, unlike many before it, had an impact at least for a while and the government took notice. Other churches and organisations of civil society came out in support of the bishops.

We must be gardeners and not mechanics in our approach to world affairs. We must realize that we did not create the forces by which this process operates. We must learn to take these forces for what they are and to induce them to work with us with understanding and sympathy, not trying to force growth by mechanical means, not tearing the plants up by the roots when they fail to behave as we wish them to. We do not need to insist that change in the camp of our adversaries can come only by violence.[13]

But has the Church followed this eminently wise advice in her own exercise of authority towards her members? Have we 'taken these forces for what they are and induced them to work with us?' In her long history, our Church started well. When Paul insisted that the Gentiles who became Christians were not to be obliged to follow Jewish ways,[14] he won a hearing among the elders in Jerusalem. But later, in the interests of unity, conformity with the Roman language and practices were imposed on all new Christians in the western Church.[15] The Celts, for instance, had to bow to Rome on the date of Easter. There were instances where Rome conceded pluralism, as with the Slavs in the ninth century at the time of Cyril and Methodius, and the Chinese in the seventeenth with the imaginative approach to their rites by Mateo Ricci. But even with this later example, nervousness in Rome led to a return to the default position and the rites were condemned in 1703.

Were the Jesuits of the late nineteenth and early twentieth century gardeners or mechanics? Where do they fit into a spectrum of pursuing indigenisation on the one hand and insisting on conformity on the other? A minute but significant indication of their attitude was the request of Fr Henri Depelchin in his letter from Bulawayo to Fr Alfred Weld[16] in Rome in 1880, 'to obtain for me the power

---

13 G.F. Kennan, *Realities of American Foreign Policy* (Princeton: Princeton University Press, 1954).

14 Acts of the Apostles 15:28. There were members of the Pharisees who had become Christians and they wanted to insist that gentiles should be circumcised and instructed to keep the law of Moses.

15 Something similar happened among the Eastern Orthodox, although there the language was Greek.

16 Alfred Weld (1823-90) was English and became novice master and then provincial and later assistant to Fr General and was with him when they were driven out of Rome in 1870 by the new Italian government and they settled in Fiesole near Florence.

from Propaganda to dispense from having the light before the Blessed Sacrament as there is no oil in this country'.[17] We may smile at his scruple but we have to understand his mindset. I am old enough to remember the care for details prevalent in the pre-Vatican II Church; it may strike us today as excessive but at that time it was a way of sticking to time-honoured traditions originating in Rome to which the universal church adhered as a way of living in practice the unity with the pope that we professed in words.

Indigenous means home-grown, native to this place. Every culture develops its own character and when another culture arrives the new culture, if it is powerful, has to choose. It can,

i. crush the culture it finds and force people to adapt to its ways, (the mechanic);

ii. ignore the culture it finds and develop a separate and parallel culture with minimal interaction with the local people, (separation for the sake of 'peace');

iii. adapt its own culture to the culture it finds in its new habitat and blend its ways with the 'host' for mutual benefit[18] (the gardener).

The Jesuits did not choose one of these options. They chose all three. There were customs they condemned, such as polygamy and – perhaps more seriously – witchcraft. They welcomed the destruction of the Ndebele kingdom which they saw as cruel and hostile, holding its people in constant fear. Second, while the mission stations were in the midst of the people the 'Fathers' house', which included the brothers, was a world away from how the people lived. Their diet was different and so was their language. But third, it was certainly mission policy to root the faith in the local people, their culture and traditions, in so far as they understood them, and initiatives were taken to achieve this.

We can call it a muddle or a series of compromises. But the Jesuits succeeded in playing a key role in establishing the Church. If we understand what has happened, perhaps we will be in a better position to move forward with a clearer idea of where we are going. After failures and frustrations, they succeeded in establishing missions and parishes, schools and a university, hospitals and clinics, social

---

17 Gelfand, p. 220.

18 Growing up in Ireland I remember our history teacher telling us the Norman invaders in the twelfth century 'became more Irish than the Irish themselves'.

centres and communication networks – in a word, the framework that enabled the gospel to reach the ears and hearts of people.

But who were they – the Jesuits?

The Jesuits

The Society of Jesus is one of the communities of men and women that have arisen in the two-thousand-year history of the Catholic Church. It is a community of men,[19] priests and brothers, founded by Ignatius of Loyola, of northern Spain, and his eight companions in Rome in 1540. Ignatius was born into the Spanish nobility in 1491 and was conventionally brought up within the chivalric order and with military training. Scant attention was paid to the educational milieu (the Renaissance) that influenced the culture of the time. Wounded in a battle with the French at Pamplona in 1521, Loyola endured tortuous operations on his leg and was forced to lie quiet for months while he recovered. He looked for books, but there were few available except *The Life of Christ* by Ludolph of Saxony and a collection of saints' lives known as *The Golden Legend*, written in the thirteenth century by Jacopo de Voragine, a Dominican.

Nonetheless, his reading had a profound effect on him and he began to be aware of the different movements in his heart – some prompting him to return to his old ways, others, ever more strongly, moving him to a whole new way of life. When he was well enough, he left his home and became what he called 'a pilgrim', setting out physically for Jerusalem and interiorly on a painful journey into his own heart to discover what God really wanted of him. He began to study and he moved from Alcalà to Salamanca in Spain and eventually to Paris, where he gathered companions and introduced them to what he had discovered and had condensed into a small book he called *Spiritual Exercises*.

They formed a group of friends bound together but still unclear of their future. They thought of going to Jerusalem and spending their lives there 'among the infidels'. They went to Venice with this in mind but turmoil in the eastern Mediterranean blocked their way. Instead of disbanding, this setback only reinforced their conviction that they

---

19 Under immense pressure from the most powerful people at the time, Ignatius did admit a woman, the daughter of the emperor Charles V, but the experiment did not work! The Mary Ward Sisters, who quite recently became officially known as the Congregation of Jesus, follow the Jesuit constitutions and way of life.

should start some form of community and serve the Church under the Pope. So they went to Rome, which now became their 'Jerusalem', and offered themselves to Pope Paul III, an enlightened man. There was strong opposition to their plans from some cardinals in Rome and Paul moved discreetly to develop enough of a consensus to allow him to officially approve them in September 1540.

The rest, as they say, is history. The Jesuits grew in numbers and in engagements in many parts of Europe and beyond, reaching India and Japan before their first decade was over. They flourished in China and South America for a century and a half. Their efforts in north America ended in martyrdom for virtually all the early French Jesuits in the mid-seventeenth century. A storm arose in the eighteenth century: a combination of the confidence generated by the Enlightenment, a resentment at the still considerable political power of the Church and the over-confidence – not to say hubris – of the Jesuits led to enormous pressure on the papacy to suppress them. Clement XIII held out and played for time but Clement XIV buckled under the pressure of the Bourbon[20] courts which threatened to follow the example of Henry VIII of England, in the 1530s, and break with Rome altogether. He signed the decree of suppression in 1773.

The Jesuits were no more, but many in Europe knew the pope's hand had been forced and slowly a groundswell developed towards their restoration, starting in, of all places, Russia. Catherine II (the Great) never accepted the suppression and told the Jesuits to continue as normal in the Russian Empire, which then included parts of Poland and Lithuania, largely Catholic lands. Tentative steps followed in other parts of Europe and when a novitiate[21] was opened in Parma in 1794, Pius VI decided he did not know about it. By this time Europe was aflame with war anyway and the Bourbons had other things on their minds. In 1801, the Russian Czar requested official recognition of the Society of Jesus in Russia and the pope granted his request. The final step was taken by Pius VII in 1814 when, in a ceremony in Rome marked by deep emotion, the Society of Jesus was restored throughout the world.

---

20 A number of the European monarchs were related to one another in an extended family known by this name.

21 A house where people aspiring to be Jesuits are welcomed and introduced to the Jesuit way of life.

But there was no question of going back to the *status quo ante*. The Jesuits had to tread carefully. Resentment against them as the perceived opponents of the Enlightenment did not die just because they were restored and, in some way, vindicated. The tussle was particularly fierce in France where the Church and the champions of secular rationalism played out their battle with one another in passionate terms over decades. It was like a long-drawn-out football match where each side periodically scores; the outcome was in doubt until well into the twentieth century when each side learnt to live with the other in peace. The papacy was on the back foot throughout the nineteenth century and saw no option but to resist any advance of 'liberalism', which it saw as the virus that, in the French Revolution and its Napoleonic aftermath, had threatened to undermine all established order. But paradoxically, as the Catholic Church dug herself in behind this redoubt, she also enjoyed a new flowering of missionary activity in every corner of the planet.

And the Jesuits – who had spent much energy in the first decades after their restoration putting their own house in order – soon joined in this movement of renewed missionary outreach. So, when Vicar Apostolic (Bishop) Ricards of the Eastern Cape approached the Jesuit General Superior in Rome, Pieter Beckx, in 1873 for help, he was pushing at an open door.

The Jesuits in Zimbabwe

In telling the story of the Jesuits in Zimbabwe, I have in mind, not only the considerations already mentioned, but some words of Pope Francis which have become a leitmotiv of his papacy:

> A constant tension exists between fullness and limitation. Fullness evokes the desire for complete possession, while limitation is a wall set before us. Broadly speaking, 'time' has to do with fullness as an expression of the horizon which constantly opens before us, while each individual moment has to do with limitation as an expression of enclosure. People live poised between each individual moment and the greater, brighter horizon of the utopian future as a final cause which draws us to itself. Here we see a first principle for progress in building a people; time is greater than space.
>
> This principle enables us to work slowly but surely, without

being obsessed with immediate results ... Giving priority to time means being concerned with initiating processes rather than possessing spaces.[22]

This tension echoes the earlier one of the gardener and the mechanic.

The initial desire of the Jesuits in 1877, when they hatched the great plan to go into the interior of Africa, was to 'occupy space' before the Protestants got there! (Actually, they were there already, long before the Jesuits.) It was not a time for ecumenism and mutual co-operation among the churches. On the contrary, they were in an only slightly less unseemly competition than the colonial powers who were pegging out vast spaces of the continent for occupation. It is easy to make this comment, but the missionaries to Africa in the nineteenth century felt they had no other option but to begin by 'occupying space'. They did not have the advantage of Jesuit missionaries in earlier centuries to India, Japan and China who worked among people living in cities and who had written texts and developed systems of communication. In those countries it was easier to develop processes. This was true too for Paul at the beginning of the Christian era. Despite all the opposition and physical suffering he met with, he was dealing with a settled society and, even more importantly, an established religion on which the gospel was founded. Jesus came to 'fulfil' something that was there already in a much more immediately accessible way than Hatendi implies above. Startling as it was, the decision of the Council of Jerusalem, to drop nearly all Jewish customs was not particularly difficult. They too were pushing on an open door and the Christians of Antioch 'were delighted'.[23]

No such consoling task awaited the Jesuits who made their way across the Limpopo River in 1879. Ten years of frustration, malaria and death lay before them. There was an established religion but, though they made some effort to understand it, they quickly came to the conclusion that it did not provide a basis on which to build. Their theological mindset was not open to think of 'processes'. They were preoccupied with occupying space. In a moment of mawkish humour, a disconsolate Fr Salvatore Blanca wrote from Old Tati after he had buried his companion, Fr Charles Fuchs, in 1880, 'his

---
22 *Evangelii Gaudium*, ##222-3.
23 Acts of the Apostles, 15:31.

tomb is the only place we can say as yet we have truly occupied' in this country.[24]

We did eventually 'occupy space' – lots of it. So the question returns: what about processes? How have we contributed to the transformation of people and society? This question, already introduced, won't go away and the present writer is acutely aware of it. He spent twenty-five years ostensibly engaged in helping to create transformative processes, only to wonder at the end what he – there has to be personal responsibility no matter how much one shelters under the plural 'we' – achieved.

Occupation or process

The mechanic occupies space in the sense that he fixes things there and then. There is no ambiguity: if the fixing was done properly the thing will work. The gardeners on the other hand follow all the processes they know have the best chance of success, but they cannot be sure. The Rhodesians were good at occupying spaces. They developed and administered the area between the Limpopo River and Lake Tanganyika, but it did not occur to them to do the hard work of putting in place processes that would lead to a smooth handover when independence came. They did not want to or, to be fair to them, could not imagine the future. They resisted it, and when control was eventually wrested from them the new people, the inheritors of the land, were untrained in the skills of managing what was now a modern economy. Frustration and resentment grew and those with the skills left and the new owners floundered or took short cuts, intent on their own gain and ignoring the plight of most of the people. I was one of those who were deeply moved by the raising of the multi-coloured flag of independence at Rufaro Stadium on the night of 17 April 1980. Robert Mugabe had visited Silveira House, where I was at the time, a number of times after his release from prison in late 1974 and his flight to Mozambique in April 1975. He spoke to us of his desire for a just society based on Christian Socialism. So, in 1980 when he 'occupied' Ian Smith's old residence, we expected his government would set in motion 'processes' that would lead to this new society. He spoke about it at the time,

> I urge you, whether you are black or white, to join me in a new

---
24 Letters and Notices, Vol. XIII, pp. 188/9.

> pledge to forget our grim past, forgive and forget, join hands in a new amity, and together as Zimbabweans, trample upon racialism, tribalism, and regionalism, and work to reconstruct and rehabilitate our society as we reinvigorate our economic machinery... Let us constitute a oneness derived from our common objectives and total commitment to build a great Zimbabwe that will be the pride of all Africa. Let us deepen our sense of belonging and engender a common interest that knows no race, colour, or creed. Let us truly become Zimbabweans with a single loyalty. [25]

More than forty years later, we are still waiting for the processes that would fulfil these aspirations.

Occupying space is the easy bit. Countless times in the last forty years we have seen people rejoice to become a minister or other high government official. Their joy is often not because they are now in a position to transform society but because they can now milk it for their own advantage. It is more difficult to do the hard work of slowly putting in place the stones that will eventually become the building we want. Jesus had a hard time with his friends. They wanted to see this new kingdom now. They did not want to go to Jerusalem to confront the rotten core in their society. They resisted in every way they could.

Perhaps it is naïve to expect people to be highly motivated and serve the good of others and not feather their own nest. But the Church loses credibility if it is seen to be concerned with its own survival and not engaged in the struggle for justice. This book is about Jesuits, and I am one of them. If we cannot 'lose our life' in trying to establish life-giving processes we are really failing to do what we were founded to do.

A 'degraded' people

The missionary endeavour in Zimbabwe over the past 130 years has been great and we can celebrate it. But we have to admit that from the beginning there was the drag anchor of a 'dual mission', already referred to and which we will examine again in Chapter 8. We never decided what our attitude was to the colonial government in terms of

---

[25] 'Mugabe's Independence speech was one of conciliation and inclusion', *Financial Times*, 9 September 2009; I am grateful to Roger Riddell for drawing my attention to this.

their segregationist policies and we will see, in Chapter 10, how we never had a unified attitude towards the liberation war. It is hard to bite the hand that feeds you. As already mentioned, the government provided many benefits but it also held an attitude honed over many decades by the settlers in South Africa and the Protestant missionaries who preceded the Jesuits. While at times praising the people among whom they ministered, their predecessors constantly reverted to a default position of describing the people as savage and degraded. This attitude as, Anthony Chennells points out,[26] served their fundraising efforts in Britain where the crowds, who came to hear the returning missionaries in Exeter Hall in London, were more likely to contribute to a vision of their country battling to bring light to a dark continent than one finding an ordered society ready to receive the benefits of the empire if presented in a respectful way. The prevailing view was summed up in an article on Africa in *The Church Missionary Atlas* of 1857, which commenced with the words,

> Africa has been described as one universal den of desolation, misery and crime, and certainly of all divisions on the globe, it has always had an unfortunate eminence in degradation, wretchedness and woe.

In quoting this passage, Chennells comments, 'That a responsible history could, in 1899, quote such a remark and add, that "these old words need little modification today," shows how vital this myth of Africa was'.[27]

This is the narrative Britain, and Europe, wanted to believe. Though kinder judgements surfaced from time to time, this was the default position which could infect anyone who turned their attention to Africa. Chennells goes on to show how the great Protestant missionary, Robert Moffat, was at first impressed by Mzilikazi, King of the Ndebele, and developed a close, even warm, relationship with him. But later, even Moffat reverts to the dominant view: 'I am among a people living in Egyptian darkness, in beastly degradation, everything in their political economy is opposed to the will of God.'[28] Chennells

---

26 A. Chennells, 'The Image of the Ndebele in the Nineteenth-Century Missionary Tradition', in M. Bourdillon (ed.) *Christianity South of the Zambezi* (Gwelo: Mambo Press,1977), p. 43.
27 Op. cit., p. 47.
28 Op. cit., p. 53.

also quotes the High Church Anglican, Bishop Knight Bruce: 'No one who has not had any dealing with heathen natives would credit what a repulsive degradation of humanity they are ...'[29] And Francois Coillard: 'The treacherous and cruel character of the Matabele is well known ... The atrocities which form their past-time and delight defy all description'.[30] The bleaker and tougher the challenges, the more appealing it was to those who came to hear the missionaries' appeals in England for support.

Chennells is speaking mainly about the Protestant missionaries who came to southern Africa long before the Jesuits, but he goes on to show how the Jesuits fell into this world view and their letters and reports are, in his view, only slightly less harsh. The English among the Jesuits who are quoted – Weld and Law – both give nuanced versions of the dominant view. Weld does not accept 'the black races give little hope of fruit owing to its inherent vices ... Judgements of the black races are too often formed from witnessing the results of generations of hard treatment of all those corrupting influences that belong to a state of slavery.' But he does go on to use that injurious word, 'degradation' about them.[31] Law wrote of some Ndebele warriors he met as, 'fine, civil, quite gentlemanly young fellows full of cheerfulness and fun',[32] perhaps implying that this was somehow surprising. Croonenberghs is more crude:

> Before coming here, ancient and modern accounts had made me foresee the aridity and unfruitfulness of this African land; but I acknowledge I was far from having a true idea of the reality. Picture to yourself a people given to idleness, plunged, drowned in sloth and all the disorders that follow from it, almost without any idea of the Divinity, or any notion of right and wrong, and whose every custom, every institution, is diametrically opposed to the morality of the Gospel. ... This people seem to have no real notion of the Deity. [33]

To enhance the context, a further diversion may be permitted. The Irish too were once seen as a 'degraded' people. Fleeing their

---
29 Op. cit., p. 60.
30 Op. cit., p. 58.
31 Op. cit., p. 62.
32 Op. cit., pp. 61,62.
33 To his family, 11 January, 1880, Letters and Notices, Vol. 14, pp. 303, 305.

country for much the same reasons as modern migrants flee theirs, they landed in America in the mid-nineteenth century malnourished and diseased. They were not welcome. 'No Irish need apply' appeared on posters advertising jobs. The English had, over centuries, created a myth of Irish people as lazy and shiftless, and their Catholic faith made them suspect as closet rebels. Edmund Spenser, the Elizabethan poet who could write moving spiritual canticles,[34] in his work *A View of the Present State of Irelande* (1596), discussed plans to subjugate Ireland. He believed that 'Ireland is a diseased portion of the State and it must first be cured and reformed, before it could be in a position to appreciate the good sound laws and blessings of the nation'. Spenser categorises the 'evils' of the Irish people as its laws, customs and religion. These three elements work together in creating a disruptive and degraded people. One example given is the 'Brehon law' which, for example, deals with murder by imposing an *éraic*, or fine, on the murderer's whole family, something akin to legal procedures traditional in parts of Africa. This particularly horrified Spenser, in whose view a murderer should die for his act.

Spenser held his views with the same fervour as the nineteenth century civilisers of Africa. To him and to them all that was visible was 'degradation'. Like the missionary in Tahiti in the South Pacific whom Chennells quotes, 'they were ready to dismiss as evil what was unfamiliar in the culture among which they found themselves'.[35] Because they were not – to use the words of Margaret Thatcher – 'one of us' they must somehow be in competition with us or at least a latent threat to our survival. This was certainly the opinion of the white settlers in Zimbabwe who, in the early decades of their presence, came to see the blacks, who were entering the economy in a big way, as a threat. And, since the missionaries had started schools and trained many of these blacks in a variety of skills and crafts, the settlers viewed the missionaries with suspicion. Once again the Jesuit attitude was seen as ambivalent. They accepted the benefits of the white establishment while assiduously working to improve the lives of black people who would inevitably struggle to overthrow it.

In 1968, we had a school strike at St Ignatius College. This

---

34 'So let us love, deare love, lyke as we ought / Love is the lesson which the Lord has taught', *Easter*. Spenser clearly did not think this applied to the Irish!
35 Chennells, op. cit., p. 45.

completely baffled me as it was an event totally outside my experience or expectation. The students put on, I have to say in hindsight, an impressive display of passive aggression. Teaching became impossible and they all had to be sent home and reapply. But I wondered then, and I still wonder now more than fifty years later, why we, as a Jesuit community, never sat down to reflect on the broader frame of why this happened. There were immediate reasons; nationalist fighters had infiltrated the country and attacked a farm and had been captured and, despite the Queen's pardon, executed. And there were local issues of food and discipline. But I do not think any of these would have carried sufficient weight if there was not also an unconscious resentment about the continued white resistance to African independence. We were an identifiable target and carried some of the responsibility. Perhaps they sensed this. In one of my history classes a young man – some students were well over twenty years of age in secondary schools in those days – asked a question which I have never forgotten: 'Why did you take our land?' I was immediately defensive, I (who had stepped off a plane into the African sunshine less than twelve months before) had not taken his land. But, of course, he meant the plural 'you'. We, whites, took their land.

Dispossessed of their land

Coenraad Brand, who lectured in Sociology at the University of Zimbabwe for many years and whose grandfather, A.A. Louw, founded the Dutch Reformed Morgenster Mission, tells the story of Louw's request to the BSAC Administrator, Leander Starr Jameson, for more land for the mission. 'How much do you need, Mr Louw?' 'We could use another 6,000 morgen.'[36] 'You can have it.'[37] The ease with which African land was given away is frightening, even today more than one hundred years later. Brand helps us enter deeper into the reaction of people to the presence of well-meaning whites when he quotes Lawrence Vambe, who grew up on Chishawasha and who saw it as a little 'theocratic empire':

> I knew that the church, both temporal and spiritual, held the whip-hand in all the tribal affairs of the VaShawasha people in

---

36 One morgen = 0.8 hectare or two acres.
37 C. Brand, 'African Nationalists and the Missionaries in Rhodesia', in M.F.C. Bourdillon, op. cit., p. 70.

the Mission; it could, if it so wished, toss out of its lands any man, woman or family at any time and for no reason at all ... the church owned the VaShawasha people; its influence over everyone was overpowering. Like the air we breathed, the church was everywhere, as much as the loud peals of the bell which rang out continually each day and was heard for miles around, as in the authority of its dogmatic but largely mystifying teaching.[38]

Vambe, who died in 2019 aged 102, opened his celebrated book, *An Ill-Fated People*, with a story of a rapid church wedding in Chishawasha before the Jesuits at the mission discovered that Josephine was pregnant. In view of the church's hold on the people a 'verbal scuffle' had ensued among the elders about what to do. Her husband, Martin, though also a Christian, had scoffed at the idea of a rushed wedding. They had both fulfilled all the customs tradition laid down for marriage and in the eyes of the community were man and wife. But if they did not have a wedding there was a fear that the whole family might be expelled from the mission land.[39] They had the wedding.

Vambe uses this incident like a grenade to blow up any complacency we might have that the reception of Christianity by the people of Zimbabwe was a smooth process. He gives us a passionate account of how the whites used their military power to subdue the people from 1890 and trample on their freedom, dignity and sense of self-worth. The settlers were only momentarily checked by the risings in the mid-1890s before resuming, with greater determination, their plan to take from the people their land and their mines and make the locals labourers on their own property. Vambe gives a psychological as well as a political history of what this meant as he viewed events growing up in Chishawasha and listened to the accounts told again and again by the elders.

The missionaries were caught between their appreciation of the order and infrastructure the settler presence gave them, enabling them to pursue their task of preaching the gospel in word and action, and their indignation at the cruelty and racialism of the settlers which always implied the local people were inferior. They

---

38 L. Vambe, *An Ill-fated People* (London: Heinemann, 1972), p .14, quoted in Brand, op. cit., p. 72.
39 Vambe, p. 10.

did not arm themselves with the understanding they could have had which, as described in Vambe's book, published in 1972 around fifty years after Josephine's wedding, would have opened their eyes. Even the Ndebele, when they pushed their way north after the *Mfecane*,[40] were so impressed by the Shona religious beliefs that they adopted them in the cult of *Mwari*, God, who they called *Mlimo*, at the Matopos shrine.

The missionaries did not explore deeply into Shona beliefs and customs. If they had done so they would have found reasons for proceeding slowly, as Loyola had counselled his men to do. It is true that in Ethiopia the Jesuits were among Christians, but *mutatis mutandis*[41] the principle stands. For example – and this is a question that has agonised the church in Africa for generations – Josephine and Martin, in Vambe's account, fulfilled all that custom required and were considered to be married in the eyes of the people. But the theologians of the church saw, in the possibility of a break-up of the marriage that would also be acceptable by custom, a barrier to the indissolubility of marriage which was and is a cornerstone to the church's reaching on marriage. Today we have surmounted this question because virtually every country in the world recognises the right of couples to divorce. We have shifted the onus of indissolubility from being an external legal framework, formerly almost impossible to break through, to an internal subjective responsibility on the couple based on their faith. Formerly, we did not trust people to work ceaselessly to make their marriage work without an external buttress. Today we have a more optimistic view of the human person: given all the information, formation and inspiration they need, individuals helped by their faith can build permanent relationships without the fear of external structures which hem them in.

And Vambe gives further examples. The church wanted an abrupt end to polygamy without considering the social results which he lists as prostitution, adultery, insecurity and loneliness. Monogamy is the 'good news' of the Church's mission since it enshrines the mutual intimacy between two people and enables them to grow in a sense of

---

40 An explosion, when the Zulu empire under Tshaka could not hold together any longer and a succession of different groups (tribes) broke away and migrated north.
41 Despite the different circumstances.

self-worth and love. But to impose it all at once with disdain for what it replaces is to substitute candles for electricity in a power-cut. You end up in a situation worse than what was there before.

Vambe gives an even riskier case, the *Mashave* dances, 'this extravaganza of song and dance,

> was enough to excite mass hysteria and to produce a great variety of physical and psychological emotions which must have had the cathartic result of relieving individual and as well as group tensions. Certainly while they were reliving their past in this way, the white man and his crazy oppressive world might well have been on the moon for all they cared.[42]

The key phrase here is 'relieving individual and as well as group tensions'. The *Mashave* dances provided this relief in the days before soccer and, according to Vambe, about as harmless. At the time of writing I was invited to participate in the annual commemoration at the beginning of November of All Saints and All Souls at Chishawasha, and as I looked around the people gathered there, I recalled and understood Vambe's words:

> Every honest African will say that the Christian Church has failed as a symbol of peace, understanding and brotherhood … and needs to re-examine its position very seriously. It has failed because it has not been able to influence the heart and mind of the European in that unfortunate country into accepting his fellow African citizen as a full human being, a child of the same God that the white Rhodesian believes in and prays to in his churches. It has not been able to change the structure of our system which rests firmly and unashamedly on race and colour and therefore consigns the African to a permanent position of inferiority… If a society has to depend for its survival solely on machine guns, rather than on its attractions of freedom, justice and the enduring foundations of respect and loyalty between its people then it is clear that its architects have failed to subscribe to the values on which western Christian civilisation was founded.[43]

---

42 Vambe, p. 181.
43 Vambe, p. 234.

A damaged environment

We might say this was all written a long time ago and that we have moved on. But have we? Gerhard Lohfink, one time professor of New Testament exegesis at the University of Tübingen, says sin has consequences:

> If I simply say, 'God forgives everything on condition that I acknowledge my guilt', the reality is too quickly covered up. The consequences of sin are not really taken seriously. Sin does not just vanish in the air, even when it is forgiven, because sin does not end with the sinner. It has consequences. It always has a social dimension. Every sin embeds itself in human community, corrupts a part of the world and creates a damaged environment.[44]

This is an apt description of Zimbabwe today. The consequences of the options of our predecessors are embedded in our society. The personalities have changed but the environment has remained the same. As the Irish poet, W.B. Yeats, wrote in 1914:

> HURRAH for revolution and more cannon-shot!
> A beggar upon horseback lashes a beggar on foot.
> Hurrah for revolution and cannon come again!
> The beggars have changed places, but the lash goes on.[45]

This is the wretched legacy of white Rhodesia and the Church is also responsible. Fidelis Mukonori laments,

> Whatever existed in Zimbabwe before the colonists came was effectively erased. Ours was a culture whose history lived in the spoken word, in songs, dances, tales passed from father to son and mother to daughter.
>
> The only things that remain of that old world now are tattered fragments. The people of Zimbabwe, orphans of a cruel colonial agenda, live now with a severe amnesia of their own past and heritage. People must learn empathy and try and set aside the story of civilisation spreading through a wild and lawless land. This is the only way to see it from the other side. An empire came, stole the land, killed the people, and made their descendants live as lower

---

44 G. Lohfink, *Jesus of Nazareth, What He Wanted, Who He Was* (Collegeville MN: Liturgical Press, 2012), p. 265.
45 *Collected Poems of W.B. Yeats* (London: Macmillan and Co., 1950) p.358.

forms of life for over a century.[46]

While there were great achievements and heroic commitments by individuals and groups, the fundamental direction of the white and Christian presence in Zimbabwe from 1890 was compromised from the start. Doris Lessing, in *The Grass is Singing*, describes the attitudes of a settler towards a young white man just out from England:

> When old settlers say, 'one has to understand the country', what they mean is, 'you have to get used to our ideas about the native'. They are saying in effect, 'Learn our ideas, or otherwise get out: we don't want you.' Most of these young men were brought up with vague ideas about equality. They were shocked, for the first week or two, by the way natives were treated. They were revolted a hundred times a day by the casual way they were spoken of, as if they were so many cattle; or by a blow, or a look. They had been prepared to treat them as human beings. But they could not stand out against the society they were joining. It did not take them long to change. It was hard, of course, becoming as bad oneself. But it was not very long that they thought of it as 'bad'. And anyway, what had one's ideas amounted to? Abstract ideas about decency and good will, that was all; merely abstract ideas. When it came to the point, one never had contact with natives, except in the master-servant relationship. One never knew them in their own lives, as human beings. A few months, and these sensitive decent young men had coarsened to suit the hard, arid, sun-drenched country they had come to. And they had grown a new manner to match their thickened sunburnt limbs and toughened bodies.[47]

Lessing was writing about a young white man who came out from the UK to try his luck, but her words have a relevance for any white man coming from Europe – including missionaries.

By the time the Church woke up to the situation in the 1970s it was too late. The words of Lord Goodman, who accompanied Sir Alec Douglas Home in the final failed attempt of the British to wrest concessions from Ian Smith in the early 1970s, could equally be applied to the Church: 'The terms of settlement (proposed) were not a sell-out. The African had been sold out long before … during the long years of British colonial

---

46 F. Mukonori, *Man in the Middle: A Memoir* (Harare: The House of Books, 2017), p. 264.
47 D. Lessing, *The Grass is Singing* (London: Flamingo, 1994), p. 18.

administration, which, notwithstanding our reserved powers, accepted discriminatory legislation. … it is against this background of constant moral capitulation … that the terms we negotiated … have to be set'.[48]

Vambe felt the tension of the ideals the Church proclaimed and the reality on the ground in his own person. He was deeply embedded in his own roots in Chishawasha and appreciated the culture and traditions of the VaShawasha society into which he was born. But he felt drawn to the Christian message by the example of the priests, and particularly the Dominican sisters at the mission who educated him. He even explored his vocation to become a priest spending three years at the new seminary founded by Bishop Aston Chichester, an hour's walk from his home in Mashonganyika village.

This tension is still there today and may explain why the Catholic Church in Zimbabwe is far less developed than in some neighbouring countries. Numbers are not everything, but they are something. In the DR Congo, Catholics make up 50 per cent of the population and in Zambia 21 per cent. In Zimbabwe the proportion is 7 per cent.[49] Maybe the statistics point to the white alien influence being much stronger south of the Zambezi. If it is true that the high-sounding words of the Congress of Berlin (1884), about defending the rights of the local people when the colonisers carved up the continent for themselves, 'have as much meaning as rosary beads wound round the knife of a murderer' (Vambe p. 84), there was little chance that the Christian gospel would be welcomed warmly. The defeat of the Shona and the Ndebele in the 1890s destroyed the self-respect of blacks and degraded the whites. The implications of both these judgements of Vambe were played out in the twentieth century and have not been resolved to this day.

---

48 Quoted in M. Meredith. *The Past is Another Country* (London: Andre Deutsch, 1979), p. 84.
49 *The World Fact Book* (New York: Skyhorse Publishers, 2021).

2

Ox-wagons and Mosquitoes 1879-89

'I don't think I could despair, even if I tried.'[1]

The 'scramble' for Africa, the high-water mark of which was the 1884 Conference of Berlin, has already been mentioned as has the less aggressive, but equally urgent, competition unfolding among the different Christian churches for space to preach the gospel, each according to their tradition. When Catholic Bishop James Ricards of the Eastern Cape turned his attention to the interior, this was his motivation.

Gonçalo da Silveira (1521-61)

Interest in the interior of the subcontinent did not begin with Ricards. Three centuries earlier Gonçalo da Silveira was the first Jesuit to enter what is now Zimbabwe. He joined the Society in Portugal when it was only three years old, in 1543, and was ordained two years later. People were 'fast-tracked' in those days. (Jerome Nadal, one of Ignatius' closest companions thought four months was long enough for the novitiate.[2]) Gonçalo quickly made a name for himself as a preacher in Portugal but he wanted to go to India as a missionary. In 1556, he was appointed provincial of Goa by Ignatius and set out on 30 March with nine companions, seven for Ethiopia and two for India. They

---

1 Augustus Law's final words in his journal at Mzila's, quoted in W. Bangert, *A History of the Society of Jesus* (Institute of Jesuit Sources, 1986), p. 475.
2 John W. O'Malley, *The First Jesuits* (Cambridge, MA: Harvard University Press, 1995), p. 362.

reached Mozambique after three months at sea on 25 July and arrived six weeks later in Goa, where he was welcomed by the sixty Jesuits who lived there. There were already about a hundred Jesuits working in India and beyond in the east.[3]

Full of energy and idealism, rather than prudence and patience, he criticised the governor for not employing Christians. He did much to establish the Inquisition[4] in Goa and 'obtained' a statement from a Nestorian bishop renouncing heresy.[5] On a visit to Cochin, an anonymous letter was left in the alms box criticising Silveira for speaking out against new Christians, that is, Jews or Muslims recently baptised. The Jewish converts wanted to keep some of their practices. At first Silveira wanted to say nothing, but, urged on by a 'nobleman', he was persuaded to support an investigation which led to the arrest of fifteen people with the idea that they be tried before the Inquisition. The governor was totally against this action but such was the overlap of Church and civil authority in Portugal and its overseas territories that he had to tread carefully. In the end Silveira preached about it 'with so much fervour and zeal that put all in awe, so that they were all sent to the Holy Inquisition in Portugal where some were burned and others made to wear sack cloth'.[6] Silveira had clearly not read the instructions of Ignatius to his fellow missionaries destined for Ethiopia, quoted earlier, where he told them to '… proceed with gentleness and avoid treating the people with duress…'[7] Four hundred years later Fr Buehlmann was to write, 'A convert from paganism … should continue to recognise the relative legitimacy of African religion and should be allowed to share in the expression of it within a certain setting, just as the Apostles continued to visit the synagogue, but

---

3 Francisco Correia, *The Venerable Fr Gonçalo da Silveira* (Jesuit Province of Zimbabwe Mozambique, 2020), p .21.

4 The Inquisition was a system of Church courts, independent of the civil courts, started in France in the thirteenth century to try suspected heretics and extended to other countries over succeeding centuries. They could condemn convicted people to harsh punishments, even death. They were abolished in the nineteenth century.

5 Correia, op. cit., p. 23.

6 Allesandro Valignano, who would later be the renowned superior of the Jesuits in the East and who promoted with great discretion the development of the missions in Japan and China. Quoted in Correia, op. cit., p. 24.

7 Festo Mkenda SJ, *A Mission for Everyone. A Story of the Jesuits in Eastern Africa, 1555-2012* (Nairobi: Paulines Publications Africa, 2013), p. 52.

celebrated their own Eucharist over and above that.'[8]

After three years, Fr General Diego Lainez, relieved Silveira of the post of provincial – it seems it was a relief to Goa too – and Silveira offered himself, and was accepted, for a new mission in Mozambique. They left Goa on 5 January, 1560 and reached Mozambique Island on 4 February. A week later, although he was offered a place on the governor's ship which happened to be going to Sofala, Silveira and two Jesuit companions chose to go in a smaller boat 'because he was in a hurry'. In the event the governor arrived in ten days whereas Silveira took twenty-seven days and arrived ill and exhausted. But his companion, Fr Andre Fernandes, was well enough to precede him to Tongue[9] where King Gamba was friendly to the Portuguese and open to the Christian faith. When Silveira arrived, he found the king had given them a free hand and within seven weeks they baptised 400 people. He left Fernandes there and went back to Mozambique Island[10] to prepare for his journey inland. Correia writes that Fernandes later recorded, 'after the first enthusiasm of their reception into the Church… the deepening of the faith did not happen as he (Fernandes) had expected … (and) he soon felt the emptiness around him'. He stayed there but was very ill at times, suffering greatly and almost dying of hunger.[11] He eventually returned to India.

Meanwhile Silveira reached Mozambique Island and within a short time left in a *pinnace*, a small boat for navigating shallow water often carried on a larger one, for his inland journey. Correia's account describes him as travelling up the Cuama River but seemingly this was a local name for the Zambezi. The boat was big enough for Silveira to curtain off an area so that he could do an eight-day retreat while others rowed! He was preparing for the great moment of his life. On reaching Sena he stayed there with the Portuguese for two months, teaching and baptising about 500 people, mainly the slaves, and sorting out marriages for the Portuguese.

Silveira arrived at the residence of Negomo Mupunzaguto, the

---

8   W. Buehlmann, 'The Church of Africa from the Council of Jerusalem to Vatican II', *Concilium*, (3)2, pp. 20-30.
9   Perhaps 50 km inland from Inhambane on the coast, which is 400 km south of Sofala.
10 A further 1,000 km north of Sofala on the coast. A small island, it would later give its name to the while country.
11 Correia, op. cit., p. 31.

Monomotapa, on 26 December 1560, and was offered women, gold, land and cattle. He refused all these and instead shared with the king a picture of Mary, the mother of Jesus, using the title Mother of God. The king asked for the picture and Correia records the tradition that the lady appeared to the king 'for five or six nights'. The king wanted to know more and Silveira embarked on a course of instruction for twenty-five days after which he baptised the king and his mother and about 300 of the people.

His success aroused the concern of the Muslim traders with whom the Portuguese had a working relationship. It was now tipping the balance in favour of the Portuguese and the Muslims persuaded the king to do away with Silveira. Stan Mudenge also sees a push-back from those at the court who saw Silveira as threatening their traditional religious beliefs and who, as a result, sided with the Muslims.[12] The king was young and as yet inexperienced and there was also a threat from a rival, called Cheputo, King of Sofala. For these reasons the king gave way and agreed to the elimination of Silveira.

He was strangled on the night of the 15 March 1561 and his body was thrown into the Musengezi River. J Mutero Chirenje is cited by Correia[13] as an historian who sees Silveira as placing himself between, on the one hand, the Shona traditional religion which accounted for all aspects of life, spiritual and social and, on the other, Christianity which arrogantly disqualifies other religious experiences as devoid of meaning.

The picture of Silveira that emerges is of a devout man, full of passion for his mission in Portugal, India and Africa. He was celebrated as the first martyr of southern Africa and a substantial life of him was written by Nicholas Godigne in 1612.[14] But he comes across as indiscreet and unwilling or unable to see other points of view. He was a man in a hurry who could not appreciate that others might not share his motivation and he was not prepared to take the time to allow

---

12 Mudenge, S, *A Political History of Munhumutapa c.1400-1902* (Harare: Zimbabwe Publishing House, 1988). Quoted in Correia, op. cit., p. 37.

13 Mutero Chirenje, 'Portuguese Priests and Soldiers in Zimbabwe, 1560-1572: The Interplay between Evangelism and Trade', *The International Journal of African Historical Studies*, 6(1), 1973, pp. 36-48, cited in Correia, op. cit., p. 45.

14 N. Godigne, *Life of Fr Gonzalves Silveira SJ.: priest who suffered martyrdom in the city of Monomotapa*. Unpublished. English translation of 1612 text by Fr James Fitzsimons. Email to the author from Fr Edward Murphy, 2021.

his message to grow gradually. He was, to use an expression we have already seen in this book, a mechanic rather than a gardener.

Correia's booklet ends with a summary of the efforts to promote the cause of Silveira for beatification. The question was raised several times over the past 450 years and a process actually started under Pope Urban VIII (1623-44). But it was soon dropped as was a further move around 1900. The information in the Jesuit General headquarters in Rome supporting such a move is, hardly surprisingly, 'not favourable'.[15]

Henri Depelchin

Three hundred years later, Ricards turned for help to the General Superior of the Society of Jesus in Rome, Fr Peter Beckx, and even went to Rome to press his case. His initiative spurred a concentrated effort led by Fr Alfred Weld, one of Beckx's assistants, whom we met in the previous chapter. Weld was inspired by the lonely death of David Livingstone at Chitambo, on Lake Bangweulu on 1 May 1873, the heroic journey of his black companions with his remains to the coast[16] and the subsequent service in Westminster Abbey in London. Weld first thought of following in Livingstone's footsteps and starting a mission in Nyasaland (Malawi) but came to the conclusion it would be too close to the Free Church Mission there. Besides, Ricards was growing more enthusiastic about Matabeleland where he learnt the ruler, Lobengula, would welcome them. The General gave him five priests and three brothers with the immediate object of taking over the already established St Aidan's College in Grahamstown which would also serve as a base for operations in the interior of the sub-continent. They sailed from England in September 1875 and assumed responsibility for St Aidan's College the following year.[17]

In 1877, Weld chose a Belgian missionary, Fr Henri Depelchin, who like Silveira had laboured in India, to lead a group that would

---

15 Correia, op. cit., p. 50.
16 Petina Gappah's *Out of Darkness Shining Light* (London: Faber & Faber, 2020) describes (fictionally for the most part) the journey of those who carried Livingstone to the coast.
17 St Aidan's had been founded twenty years earlier and it was a daunting work to take over the college. 'The students ... were of all shapes and sizes and ranged in age from seven to twenty. The oldest, Laughlin Kelly, wore a long beard. Several of the others sported moustaches. Nearly all, including the youngest, smoked and some of the seniors chewed tobacco.' F. Coleman, *The History of St Aidan's* (Institute of Social & Economic Research, Rhodes University, 1980).

penetrate the interior. Depelchin had worked for eighteen years in India and been superior of the Jesuit Mission in Calcutta. 'He had the face of a lion', Lobengula was to say of him, and, indeed, he was a man of courage and tenacity. He left India for Europe to muster men and resources for the new mission. He chose six priests and five brothers. Belgian Fr Charles Croonenberghs, though not a doctor, had gifts in applying medicine and had a reputation for healing, even the many queens of Lobengula. He also had modest gifts as an artist and drew and painted, most notably the Great Dance in Gubulawayo.[18] Br Frans de Sadeleer[19] and Br Louis de Vylder[20] were also Belgian. Frs Karl Fuchs[21] and Anton Terörde[22] were German and Br Theodore Nigg[23] came from Liechtenstein. Fr Salvatore

---

18 Charles Croonenberghs (1843-1899) spent five years in Bulawayo (1879-84) and saved the mission when Lobengula wanted to close it. Though superiors worried about his free and easy ways, he had great charm and got on well with the local people as well as the traders and travellers. Most especially he had a good relationship with King Lobengula. After he left Bulawayo, he went to America to raise money for the mission.

19 Frans de Sadeleer (1844-1921) was from Flanders and seems to have had the greatest stamina of all in the group. He was the one who accompanied Law to Umzila's and Wehl to Sofala from where he returned alone after Wehl's death. He rejoined Hedley and together they returned to Bulawayo. He was the last of the original group to leave (in 1886) and went on to spend thirteen years in the Congo (1893-1906).

20 Louis de Vylder (1841-83) was Belgian. He had fought in the papal army and was a good shot, though Depelchin did not really approve of Jesuits hunting! He bent the rule for Brothers! He had not yet made his first religious vows when the party set out for the interior and did so when they were settled at Tati. He was always cheerful and had a reputation as 'the white hunter who is always laughing'. He drowned in the Zambezi while on the mission to the Lozi in 1883.

21 Charles Fuchs (1839-1880) was German and served in the medical corps in the Franco-Prussian war. Not a healthy man, he should never have been sent on the mission. He died within five months of arrival.

22 Francis Anthony Terörde (1844-80) was German and, like Fuchs, was conscripted into the medical corps in the Franco-Prussian war. Expelled from Germany with his fellow Jesuits during Bismarck's *Kulturkampf* he completed his studies in England and was ordained in Wales. The original plan was to open the first mission in Bechuanaland (Botswana) and Terörde studied Tswana with this in mind. When Khama refused permission for a mission, Terörde went with the others to Matabeleland and finally to the Tonga country where he died, the first missionary to do so in southern Zambia.

23 Theodore Nigg (1848-91) from Liechtenstein, was less than five foot tall. He was one of those who could turn his hand to many things: tailoring, building and cooking and, as a musician, he entertained Lobengula with his piano accordion. And he was tough. When Tonga Chief Mweemba helped himself to the Jesuit goods after Terörde's death and Vervenne was too weak to prevent the thefts,

Blanca[24] and Br Pietro Paravicini[25] were from Italy. Fr Augustus Law (already at Saint Aidan's)[26] and Br Joseph Hedley[27] were English. The Limpopo River marked the southern boundary of the proposed mission and a line running east-west through Lake Bangweulu was the northern limit. Effectively the modern western boundary of Botswana, and the Indian Ocean, were the longitudinal borders.[28]

On 18 December 1878, Depelchin, accompanied by Weld, had a private audience with Pope Leo XIII who blessed a special banner of the Sacred Heart which was to become a leading symbol in the early mission and has recently been rediscovered rolled up in a cupboard.[29] Financial assistance came from Belgium, England, France, Germany, Holland and Ireland from which latter country they received the greatest support.

On 20 March 1879, Fr Weld recorded in his journal that Augustus Law had written, 'We are all together at last in Grahamstown.'[30] Law tried to forge the new group into a team, but the urgency of getting

---

Nigg arrived and confronted the chief. After a furious row, the king returned some of the goods.

24 Salvatore Blanca (1839-1916) was Sicilian. He was 'gloomy, hot-tempered and quarrelsome' and a trial to his companions. During his time at Tati he was one of those who wrote complaining letters to Rome about Depelchin which resulted in an investigation. Depelchin was exonerated but much unhappiness was caused. Blanca did receive a local Boer into the Church at Tati who twenty-five years later sold his farm at Driefontein cheaply to the Church. It later became a flourishing mission.

25 Peter Paravicini (1834-99), from Italy, had poor health and, at 45, was considered by Augustus Law, himself 46, to be too old to adapt to mission life. He spent much of his time fighting malaria.

26 Augustus Law (1833-80), grandson of the English Lord Chief Justice and nephew of a Governor General of India, entered the navy, followed his father into the Catholic Church and as a Jesuit spent three years in Guyana. He was the only one of the eleven to have some experience of Africa, having arrived in 1875 and had studied Zulu, which is akin to Ndebele.

27 Joseph Hedley (1846-1933) was born in the London dockland and joined the merchant navy before discovering his vocation to be a Jesuit. He was the last of the eleven to die – at St Beuno's in Wales in 1933.

28 Prophetically perhaps, this huge area is roughly equivalent to that of the jurisdiction proposed for the new Jesuit Province of Southern Africa established in 2021. The present writer had proposed the name, the Zambezi Province, for this in recognition of the historic links to our founders, but the proposal ran counter to the trend to harmonise acronyms for convenience of reference in the worldwide Society of Jesus.

29 It is now in the Jesuit archives in Harare.

30 Cf. Gelfand, p. 54.

on the road foreshortened his efforts and the seeds of later damaging dissension were planted. He wrote to Weld on 31 March, 'you must pray very hard that we will be able to get on (with one another) when we get to Kimberley; for things at present do not look very promising'.[31]

Depelchin wanted to develop a series of linked stations into the interior but the Anglo-Zulu war and the British defeat at Isandlhwana[32] made them feel it was unsafe to proceed directly to the country of the Matabele who were blood relations of the Zulus. They decided to avoid the Matabele lands by going west of them and heading for Shoshong in Khama's territory even though they knew that the London Missionary Society was already well entrenched there. Four wagons were purchased and equipped. Teams of fourteen oxen for each wagon were obtained and a reliable guide engaged. An emotive service was held in Grahamstown on 15 April 1879, for the mission. In his homily Bishop Ricards was moved to tears as he gave thanks for the fulfilment of his dream:

> With real eloquence he stressed the spirit of charity which in all ages has inspired the missionaries of the Catholic Church to sacrifice themselves for the salvation of souls. It was this persevering charity and self-sacrifice which was inspiring the little band of missionaries who were now leaving for the upper Zambezi. (Depelchin to Fr General Beckx, April 16, 1879).[33]

The next day the party, including Br Hedley who had been unwell for some days,[34] set out towards Kimberley.

None of them were accustomed to wagon travel and they found it difficult. Terörde records their first night:

> The jolting of the wagon as it rumbled over stock and stone rendered sleep an utter impossibility. The roof of each wagon was six feet from the floor, but the intervening space was considerably more than half filled with cases and sacks of grain and flour. On the top of these, the three occupants of the wagon lay, obtaining what rest they could. In the middle of the night a halt was called,

---

31 Gelfand, p. 63. Words in brackets added.
32 1,300 British and allied troops were killed in this battle with the Zulus on 22 January 1879.
33 Gelfand, p. 70.
34 Law to Weld, 21 April 1879, quoted in Gelfand, p. 66.

and in the early morning hours the journey resumed.[35]

They record many near accidents on route, but at the same time warm hospitality from local Boer farmers which belies the general accepted view that Afrikaners were hostile to Catholics. Law records the structure of each day.

> Our order of life is on the whole, pretty regular: 4 p.m. inspan and go on until about 9 p.m. when we outspan, light a fire and have supper. The Litanies of B.V.M. sung – *examen* – and then inspan again at about 2 or 3 a.m. and go on until sunrise – then outspan. All say Mass ... then have breakfast – various occupations etc. until 1.30, then long litanies – *Itinerarium* and *examen* – 2. Dinner, 4 outspan etc.[36]

Kimberley, May 1879

On 11 May 1879, the wagons entered Kimberley. The small Catholic community among the miners did all they could for them, contributing a substantial amount of money.[37] Depelchin then made two serious mistakes. He dismissed the guide, citing costs, and he failed to replace the draught animals, which would later be pushed to their limit and beyond.

They left Kimberley on 21 May. The journey was monotonous but they met many isolated Catholic settlers and were busy trying to learn the local languages. Augustus Law had studied Zulu and he now taught it to the others. Br Nigg's accordion propped up flagging enthusiasm. Depelchin described their halts:

> In front of our wagon the oxen are stationed, and behind the wagon to which the tents are attached is the campfire and kitchen. Br Hedley and Fr Croonenberghs erect a pyramid of twigs and sticks and the rest of us pile on pieces of dried cow's dung for

---

35 *Zambesi Mission Record* 7, p. 230.
36 Law to Weld, 21 April 1879, Gelfand, p. 66. 'long litanies' meant litany of the Saints; *Itinerarium* is a prayer for journeys found in the old Latin breviary used before the Second Vatican Council. *Examen* refers to the Ignatian practice of examination of conscience, or, better consciousness, done twice daily.
37 The Catholics organised a bazaar that raised £1,000, a considerable amount at the time. Depelchin to Notre Mère of the Assumption Convent in Grahamstown, 6 May 1879, in Gelfand, p. 76. Every contribution was appreciated, for the expenses were considerable. Depelchin put the total cost of the expedition at £4,000. The 58 oxen alone cost £696. Depelchin to Weld, 10 April 1896, in Gelfand, p. 63.

fuel. Br Nigg then sets it alight, and we soon have a fire. Brs. de Sadeleer and de Vylder, our head cooks, are all activity, and in no time our meal is ready. It is simple enough, but, thanks to the out-of-door life, and the bracing air of the veldt, appetite makes up for want of variety and lack of skill in culinary preparation. When we have finished, we sit or stand around the fire, talking over the day's adventures, and at about nine o'clock, after singing *O Sanctissima*, all but the sentinel on guard retire to rest.[38]

They then trekked down steep slopes into the Limpopo valley. Large boulders alternated with sandy tracks into which the heavy vehicles sunk. They were sharing in the experience of nineteenth-century travellers in Africa. John Campbell had written in 1813, 'As we crossed the Malalareen River, one of our wagons stuck fast in the middle of the stream in consequence of the fore wheel sinking into a hole; however, after great exertion by the Hottentots and the oxen, it was happily dragged out'.[39]

On arrival at the Limpopo on 8 July, they had to wait several days for the oxen to recover. Reaching the river provided Law with a moment of reflection:

> Three years and a half ago, Mr. Wilmot made a very fine speech ... about the Catholic Missionaries extending from St Aidan's to the Limpopo and often afterwards in jokes about this speech, (we thought) the allusion to the Limpopo nothing more than a set of eloquence and a mere flow of words. But here we are safe and sound on the banks of the Limpopo.'[40]

When they resumed their journey, they came to the famous 'Jesuit' tree marked by many previous travellers, including Livingstone, and Hedley carved a cross on it.[41] Hedley, like Law, had spent years at sea

---

38 *Letters & Notices*, 49, p. 26.
39 Eric Axelson, *South African Explorers* (London: Oxford University Press, 1954), p. 153.
40 Augustus Law to Alfred Weld, 15 July 1879. Quoted in M. Gelfand, *Gubulawayo and Beyond: letters and journals of the early Jesuit missionaries to Zambesia (1879-1887)* (New York: Barnes & Noble, 1968), p. 95.
41 Mike Main has written an account of this landmark for nineteenth-century travellers in the Limpopo valley. The name 'Jesuit' seems to have been attached because they were the ones who wrote about it and recorded that Br Hedley climbed the tree and carved a large cross there, perhaps symbolically claiming the land beyond the river for Christ. 'It has an historical specificity that allows us

before joining the Jesuits and for him this was 'hoisting the flag' on 'Occupation Day, 21 July 1879'.[42] They journeyed on, 'for six days through a dreary waste of thorn bushes, dusty and dry, almost without water and without grass'.[43]

Shoshong, July 1879

On 23 July 1879, they reached Shoshong with heavy hearts as they knew their arrival had been made known by Protestant missionaries. They met Khama, who had a huge capital (pop. 10,000), including traders and Protestant missionaries. Khama gave them a cool reception, due to the influence of the London Missionary Society. He said he had no need for additional teachers. If they were both Christians, why did they have two groups doing the same work? He suspected the presence of both would lead to conflict.[44] He even refused permission for the Jesuits to stay in Shoshong. They were allowed to camp outside the town. Depelchin was very disappointed, and made plans to move on.

Depelchin thought the British defeat of the Zulus at Ulundi on 4 July 1879, might influence Lobengula, the Ndebele king in Bulawayo, to be more accommodating and so the dejected party headed northwards on 28 July. As they travelled on, the wagons were often stuck in deep sand and the oxen were tired and many died. Their wagon drivers deserted them and they had to control these cumbersome vehicles themselves. They were short of water and there was the constant threat of wild animals.

---

readily and more vividly to form a mental picture of an evening more than 120 years ago. The certainty that the party camped at this exact spot makes it easier for us to imagine the small group of Jesuits, their wagons and exhausted oxen, the wagon hands, camp staff and servants. It is not difficult to imagine the 33-year-old Cockney Brother Joseph Hedley climbing high among the branches with his axe and we can easily think of how they must all have been feeling. They were only two weeks trek from Shoshong, where they still believed they might be able to start a mission ... It is easy to think they might have been elated, even excited at the prospects before them, literally taking the cross into the hinterland ...' 'The Jesuit Tree and Olifant's Drift', *Botswana Notes and Records*, 35, 2003.

42 *Letters and Notices*, 49, p. 55.
43 *Zambesi Mission Record*, 9, p. 305.
44 *Letters and Notices*, 64, p. 123, cited in R.S. Burrett, 'The Zambezi Mission and the residences of Good Hope and Immaculate Heart of Mary, Old Tati', *Botswana Notes and Records*, 32, p. 25.

Tati, August 1879

They reached Tati, close to the present border between Botswana and Zimbabwe, on 17 August 1879. It was then a mining and trading centre but today a forgotten, debris-strewn site sixty kilometres south-east of present-day Francistown. There were forty settlers remaining from the larger settlement a decade earlier. The Jesuits were kindly received by the traders, especially by George 'Elephant' Phillips, an agent for George Westbeech, who had a trading centre at Pandamatenga, some distance to the north-west. The Boers there were initially antagonistic to the Jesuits but slowly won over. Tati owed its development to the hunter Henry Hartley, who saw some old gold workings there. But, despite initial optimistic hopes, the goldfields were not a success and most settlers abandoned the area to seek their fortunes in the diamond mines of Kimberley.

Given its central location as a strategic supply base, Depelchin decided to found the first mission of the province there, Good Hope, as a base from which to extend further north.

> In this little abode they followed the order of the day usual in houses of their Order with a little bell summoning them at fixed hours to the exercises of community life. The brothers made a small garden in which they planted several kinds of vegetables that thrive if watered plentifully.[45]

They settled on the south bank of the Tati River and it was there that Br de Vylder made his first vows on 22 August. Up to that time they had all been in good health, but now the hardships of the journey began to be felt. Fr Croonenberghs fell ill from rheumatic fever.

One of the Boers came over to ask if it was true that Catholics worship a woman rather than God! This broke the ice and soon some were receiving Catholic instruction, and on Sundays all the Boers in residence assisted at Mass and heard the sermon in Dutch, the source of their own language, Afrikaans. At other times they would come to visit the sick man who, despite being weak, explained to them the teachings of the Catholic Church. One family, that of Jan Engelbrecht, became Catholic.

Considerable internal friction among the Jesuits surfaced at Tati when a number of traders left and with them a source of food and

---

45 *Zambesi Mission Record* 11, p. 387

medicine.⁴⁶ Letters were written to Europe, by Terörde and Blanca but mainly by Croonenberghs,⁴⁷ complaining of Depelchin's lack of leadership. They openly attacked his grand plans of ever extending forward and blamed him for the inadequate provisions and medical care. Professor R. Roberts, of the University of Zimbabwe, saw Weld as the real cause of the grand plans which hopelessly extended the Jesuits at the time.⁴⁸ Blanca made telling points about the way the wagons were overloaded and this, combined with failure to change all the oxen at once and not little by little where the old weigh on the new ones, slowed their progress.⁴⁹

Blanca enlarged on Terörde's description above about conditions in the wagons,

> In each wagon there was left, at the beginning of the journey, … a space about 1 meter 50 centimetres long, 1 meter broad and 94 centimetres high. This was the space intended for the accommodation by day and night of three persons, and that for a journey which they foresaw would last 5 or 6 months.'⁵⁰

Reading this we might wonder how people, a hundred years later, managed in the cramped conditions of a space capsule! Today we take time to foresee strains in interpersonal relations which can develop in cramped quarters. The early Jesuits made no such preparations. Space psychologist Al Holland would have approved of Law's desire that more time be spent in St Aidan's on 'bonding' before they set out. Holland describes an astronaut as saying, 'We just try to push forward information about different cultures, and we want information about our culture shared with them. So we're trying for a mutual approach there with one another'. Once astronauts are in space, however, they're on their own, Holland continues. Selecting the right mix of personalities, forging a team bond, and training about how to deal with stress, all help crews deal with interpersonal conflict themselves. When none of this works, another psychologist, Nick

---

46 Burrett, p. 30.
47 R.S. Roberts, *Journeys beyond Gubuluwayo* (Harare: Weaver Press, 2009), p. xiv, where Professor Roberts records Fr E.P. Murphy's drawing his attention to unpublished notes of Fr Patrick Lewis, Jesuit Archivist at Garnet House, Harare, on this subject.
48 Roberts, op. cit.
49 Blanca to Weld, 27 November 1879, Gelfand, p. 157.
50 Ibid., p. 161.

Kanas, says, 'astronauts sometimes resort to less desirable behaviours. Withdrawal and working more independently is a coping strategy where you don't have to deal with the other guy or girl'. Kanas adds that this can sometimes lead to more aggressive behaviour, such as being overly territorial. He also observed astronauts displacing their frustration with one another onto mission control (Blanca to Weld!) – a subconscious strategy, he says, that allows them to blow off steam without hurting their relationships with fellow crew members. Kanas suggests regular 'bull' sessions that would give teams opportunities to check in with one another and air any complaints. At the end of the day, however, Holland says 'astronauts are just normal people, which means conflict will sometimes happen. Expecting the astronauts to be perfect individuals … is completely unrealistic … We aren't looking for perfect people. In fact, if you've ever worked with someone who thinks they are perfect, you know it's not a pleasant experience.'[51]

Jesuits then, and even today, are not good at 'bull' sessions but Law put his finger on the spot when he lamented the failure to take time to 'push forward information about different cultures' before they set out. It was only later they learnt that 'Fr Blanca is a very hot-tempered man and exaggerates everything that concerns Fr Croonenberghs'.[52] And Depelchin doesn't delegate 'but takes the smallest details in his own hands[53]… and is in a state of continual worry in consequence'.[54]

The letters complaining about Depelchin were subsequently published in Europe and created uproar. A visit of enquiry, under Fr Anthony de Wit, was sent to investigate and he exonerated Depelchin. He, Depelchin, was accused of being *nimia severitate et auctoritate*, too severe and bossy, but Law denied this though he conceded he sometimes did not listen to advice. 'It came I think simply (from) his believing he was right'.[55] Weld had advised Depelchin in July 1879 to move slowly in starting new missions and insisted there should be 'nutritious and well prepared' food.[56] Fr Anthony de Wit's official investigation found that the rumours of starvation and dysentery

---

51 https://whyy.org/segments/how-do-astronauts-deal-with-conflict-in-cramped-quarters/.
52 Depelchin to Weld, 28 October 1879, Gelfand, p. 146.
53 Law to Weld, 12 November 1879, Gelfand, p. 149.
54 Ibid. p. 151.
55 Law to Weld, 20 May 1880, Gelfand, p. 322.
56 Weld to Depelchin, 1 July 1879, Gelfand, p. 92.

were exaggerated. Depelchin's confidence in his fellow Jesuits was undermined by this incident. 'I am here put down as a murderer of my companions', he wrote to Weld about the letter he had received from Fr General.[57]

In a sign that Weld knew the experience of the Jesuits in South America two centuries earlier, he wrote to De Wit, 'it is desirable to have one on each station who knows music'.[58]

Bulawayo, September 1879

The day after de Vijlder's vows Depelchin set out for Gubulawayo with Fr Law and Br de Sadeleer and they were joined later by Croonenberghs. They were delighted by the well-watered and wooded country they passed through on their way north, especially the beauty of the Matobo Hills, and arrived at the outskirts of Lobengula's capital on 2 September 1879. On 18 October, after a series of meetings with Lobengula and the exchange of many gifts, the Jesuits were allowed to stay in Matabeleland until April 1880. James Fairbairn, a trader, intervened with the king on their behalf emphasising the Jesuits' practical skills in carpentry and gun repairs. Lobengula was not interested in education for his people, and he claimed he had enough missionaries in the form of the London Missionary Society. Protestant ministers quarrelled among themselves and caused Lobengula headaches. He wanted no more of the same.

A sign of the Jesuits' confidence that they would eventually win over the king was their purchase of the house of one of the traders who wanted to withdraw south. Augustus Greite sold his dwelling for £600[59] and this became a new mission of the Sacred Heart.[60] It was a stone house with an iron stove, imported from London, a stable and an enclosed garden. They were also allowed by Lobengula to buy a large tract of land in a well-watered valley which they hoped would become a model farm offering skills in modern agriculture, blacksmithing, carpentry and wheel-wrighting. The Jesuits decided to become useful to the king and set about overhauling the royal wagon. When it was complete it caused

---

57 25 February 1880, Gelfand, p. 218.
58 Weld's diary, Suggestions for the Visitor, 24 November 1879, Gelfand, p. 157.
59 About £75,000 in today's money.
60 Burrett citing *Letters & Notices* 65, p. 192 and *Zambesi Mission Record*, 14, p. 497.

a great sensation in Gubulawayo. A week ago it appeared before the public in all its splendour. The sailcloth tent which covers it had been dextrously handled by Br Hedley (an old sailor), and Fr Croonenberghs had painted it. When Lobengula saw the device, he uttered a cry of admiration and squeezed Fr Croonenberghs hand so hard that he nearly fainted. All were in ecstasies.[61]

Given his delight, Lobengula decided to grant permanent residence confirming their acquisitions of the two properties and granting them the right to travel in his territory towards the Zambezi. The Protestants were not happy with this, but Lobengula was un-swayed by their words. In time both Christian groups learnt to tolerate and assist each other.

Br Nigg pleased the king and his court with his sewing machine, his accordion[62] and pistol that killed snakes in the town. And Croonenberghs' painting skills were also appreciated. He painted a portrait of Lobengula presiding over the Great Dance which is now housed in the National Archives of Zimbabwe. It is not particularly skilled, but it impressed Lobengula who granted Croonenberghs freedom to go almost anywhere in Gubulawayo.

But the mission was going nowhere. Lobengula decreed that no one should take up the Christian religion. It seems he felt it would undermine the basis of his state and Ndebele traditional values. The Jesuits gave medical care and grew their own food. But they could do no more except wait. The mission took a severe blow when Lobengula decided to relocate his capital in 1881 to the site of the present State Residence in Bulawayo and the old settlement was burnt down. Croonenberghs remained at the mission for five years (1879-84) where he provided a steady base for missionaries passing through or recovering from fever. He found it frustrating that he could not do more. The mission struggled on until 1887.

Tati, January 1880

Tati proved to be a fever trap and Fr Charles Fuchs, aged forty, died there on 28 January 1880. Law commented laconically, 'I suppose

---

61 ZMR 14: p. 497.
62 At the Golden Jubilee of the founding of the Hwange Diocese in 2012, I took Br Nigg's accordion, normally kept at St George's College, and played a few notes on it to the assembled crowd. Alas, the gesture caused bemusement rather than appreciation!

the German Provincial could not possibly have known the state of ill health of Fr Fuchs when he sent him on this mission – he was a perfect invalid in Europe'.[63] Edward Murphy feels it 'was a sign of the lack of scrutiny of those who had volunteered'.[64] Fr Blanca buried him and later wrote, an account of it, ending sardonically, 'his grave is, so far, the only thing of which we have definitely taken possession in these parts'. This grave, and that of his companion Fr de Wit, were soon forgotten and only rediscovered, tidied up and marked, by Rob Burrett in 1997. The mission struggled on but the damning letters sent to Europe put the whole project in jeopardy.

In 2014, Arrupe College hosted a series of events to mark the 200th anniversary of the restoration of the Society of Jesus by Pius VII. One such event was a lecture by Professor Roberts in which he mildly castigated the Jesuits for their failure to honour Henri Depelchin, the first superior of the Zambezi Mission. Depelchin laid the foundations of what, in time, became a strong Catholic presence in Rhodesia and later Zimbabwe. The Jesuit neglect of Depelchin, if that is what it is,[65] is certainly due to the failure of all his initial plans and the death of so many of the Jesuits assigned to the mission. Yet it is well to remember the huge efforts he made and his buoyant sense of optimism despite the opposition he met from many sides including his own brothers in the Society. He was meticulous in planning and was concerned about each member of his team. On reaching Bulawayo in September 1879 he wrote, 'our prospects look brilliant'.[66] As frequently happens, he was told what people thought he would like to hear and on discovering the impossibility of starting a school, let alone preaching the gospel, in Lobengula's kingdom, he eagerly grasped the favourable news about the land of the Shangaans in the east and the Lozis in the north.[67]

---

63 Law to Weld, 18 February 1880, Gelfand, p. 211.
64 E.P. Murphy, *A History of the Jesuits in Zambia: A Mission becomes a Province* (Nairobi: Paulines Publications Africa, 2003), p. 69.
65 The present writer can think of no house or work in the county named after him.
66 Depelchin to Weld, 17 September 1879, Gelfand, p. 131.
67 In response to Ray Roberts, in 2014 our province arranged for the large stone plaque to be made to both commemorate the 200th anniversary of the Restoration of the Society and to honour Depelchin and his companions.

Umzila's, Tshamatshama, May 1880 - October 1881

After many months of letters to and from Weld, Depelchin selected Fr Augustus Law, Brs Joseph Hedley and Frans de Sadeleer and a new arrival on the mission, Fr Charles Wehl, for the Shangaan mission. Law 'planned everything to the minutest detail', with one exception, wrote Professor Michael Gelfand[68] who devoted his entire distinguished life to the medical care of the people of Zimbabwe – a devotion that went far beyond the restricted field of medical science.[69] The one exception was malaria. 'The Jesuits were little concerned about this … and barely discussed the possibility of running into danger through malaria or what treatment (to take) if any members of the party contracted the disease. … Malaria proved to be the ultimate reason for the disaster that awaited this brave Englishman.'[70] I have found few references to quinine in the letters I have read of the Zambezi Mission, though one of them does record that Law was given a bottle of quinine by a Dr Cooks on 2 June 1880.[71]

Since Lobengula had, in a protracted ritual bridging the years 1879 and 1880, married the daughter of Umzila, the Shangaan Chief, Depelchin and Law at Bulawayo had many opportunities to inquire about their country. As already mentioned, the reports they received burnished their desire and they aimed to travel there with some of the guests who would be returning home after the rainy season. In the event, to Law's disappointment and suppressed annoyance, Depelchin delayed and when they did eventually set out, they were given two guides who had never been to Umzila's.[72]

---

68 Gelfand, p. 298.
69 In 1977, I brought a young man, Anthony Kanaventi, who was suffering from epilepsy to him and he, a professor of medicine at the University of Rhodesia, advised taking him to a traditional doctor. I followed his advice and took Anthony to see Simon Taoneyi's wife who lived in Chitowa, beyond Murewa. Taoneyi told me to come back with Anthony's parents, but the father refused as it was war time. We had to fall back on 'western' medicine which kept Anthony going for some time but he eventually died as a result of a major fit twelve years later. I often wonder what would have happened if the parents had gone to Chitowa.
70 Gelfand, p. 298..
71 When Fuchs died in Tati in January 1880, Law went from Bulawayo to see what he could do to help and he recommended that 'Fr Blanca and Br de Sadeleer take 'a little brandy and quinine every other day as long as the sickly season lasts.' Law to Weld, 18 February 1880, Gelfand, p. 208. Cooks' gift is recorded in Law's letter to Weld, 1 June 1880, Gelfand, p. 253, cf. next footnote.
72 Law to Weld, 1 June 1880, though the letter describes events after June 1. He

On 3 June 1880, Law, de Sadeleer, Hedley and Wehl left Gubulawayo on their fateful journey[73] with 'great hopes'.[74] They had been told it would take 'less than a month'.[75] They did not take a direct route to Umzila's but looped considerably north to take advantage of the central uplands and 'avoid the fly'. They passed by what is now the town of Rusape. On 29 June, Law wrote to de Wit that they had crossed twenty-two rivers and they were 'all safe and sound'.[76] Wehl was less sanguine:

> We were in constant want of guides to show us the way, and of men to clear the way for the wagon, and as we had to at each new village hire fresh guides and men, you can well imagine how our purses were thinned. Our journey from the Sebakwe to the Sabi took us five entire weeks, during which time we crossed eighty rivers and streams; four wagon shafts broke; six times we were forced to unload and (re)load the wagon, and we had to fell numberless trees.[77]

Worse troubles began once they crossed the Sabi River on 24 July; the river was the effective boundary between the Ndebele kingdom and the Shona chiefdoms.

There was no further word from Law for three months though various rumours filtered back to Bulawayo with alarming reports about the wagon being seized and the Jesuits being forced to struggle on to Umzila's on foot. When Law finally wrote on 27 September, he was weak with fever near Umzila's.[78] He described how the people, no longer restrained by the authority of Lobengula, seemed hostile and local chiefs delayed them with their demands and they felt they could be attacked at any time. To add to their troubles, on 6 August, Wehl, who had a habit of walking 150 yards in front of the wagon, lost his way back and three days were spent searching for him. The others thought he must have been killed and their fears of being attacked

---

refers to his annoyance in a letter to Weld of 3 March 1880, Gelfand, p. 305: 'I cannot but regret that F Depelchin let slip that fine opportunity...'
73 Ibid.
74 Ibid.
75 Depelchin to Weld, 8 April 1880, Gelfand, p. 228.
76 Gelfand, p. 324.
77 ZMR, 9, p. 467.
78 Law to de Wit, 27 September 1880, Gelfand, p. 326.

and the wagon plundered grew. Law decided they should abandon the wagon and proceed on foot. They tried to conceal their footprints by walking at a distance from each other. They struggled on for 170 miles, reaching Umzila's on 31 August 1880.

Law continued his letter describing how Umzila[79] received them kindly, gave them a hut and some food but he suggested they go back and retrieve the wagon. Neither Law nor Hedley were in a fit state to do this, so de Sadeleer went with some of the people who had accompanied them from Bulawayo. Throughout September Law and Hedley did their best to regain their strength but they gradually found they could not manage the local food. Law described their life:

> We have suffered here considerably, cooped up in a little hut – with the two king's boys, their friends coming in and going out – people continually at the door gazing at us & blocking up the little air & light that comes in thro' it - and then sickness & and the inability to often say Mass, as when many people are about, even some privacy was impossible.

Law decided to go to Umzila to ask for help and the chief gave them 'a shoulder of a small ox' and told him that he had news that Wehl was alive. But before coming to what happened to Fr Wehl, we need to conclude the story of Fr Law. He continued to hope that the wagon would soon arrive and he would go to the king (Umzila) to ask for a place to establish a mission 'wh. I fancy he will grant readily'. He now knew that the best way into the country was through Sofala and as soon as he was better, he planned to go there to replenish their supplies. On 6 October, Law added to his letter, 'Still no news of the wagon. Br Hedley and myself are getting very low. If the wagon does not arrive soon, I'm afraid we shall both die. ... If I die, please write a line to my father,

> Honble W. T. Law,
> Hampton Court Palace,
> London S.W. 1

Br Frans de Sadeleer later wrote, 'two snakes, a three-foot-long

---

79 Fr Crispen Matsilele SJ comes from Umzila's territory and tells me the chief was 'my great great grandfather.' Law and his companions would be pleased. 'The seed must die ...'

cobra and a smaller one, lived in their cabin… they fulfilled the role played by our cats in Europe and kept at bay the mice and rats visible everywhere'.[80] As they lay on the floor the two sick men encouraged one another with the memory of the Passion. On 15 October, Fr Law said his last Mass held upright by twine tied by Br Hedley. Finally, Law wrote a note on the 31 October, 'No wagon arrived yet. God's will be done. I am still between life and death … I don't know if I shall live'. He died on 25 November 1880.

Wehl later wrote an account of what happened to him.[81] On that fateful day (6 August 1880), he lost his way back to the wagon. Realising that he was lost, and that he would get even more lost if he kept wandering about aimlessly, he decided to return to Bulawayo. He slept in trees in fear of wild animals and later, when that was too cold, under blankets of grass. On 1 September, he met four people who had pity on him and took them to their home and looked after him where he lay exhausted for eighteen days. He began to hallucinate and think his saviours were planning to kill him. Eventually word of him reached a gold prospector, Robert Roxby, who came and took him to his place where Wehl stayed for five weeks until he was well enough to travel to meet de Sadeleer. The latter, on his journey to the wagon in September, had been given a letter from Wehl to Law, and de Sadeleer immediately sent word to Wehl that he was on his way to the wagon and would meet him there. De Sadeleer also had a rough time in his travels and when the two Jesuits eventually met at the wagon on the 12th or 13th of November Wehl found him critically ill.

The wagon was intact. When de Sadeleer arrived, 'Amalanga (in whose care they had left the wagon) conducted me to the wagon which we had abandoned not far from his village three months before. To my great astonishment I found our wagon exactly in the same state in which we had left it. Amalanga had had constructed all around the wagon a large and strong hedge which rendered access to it difficult to men but not to the wolves who had devoured our provisions…'[82] De Sadeleer was impressed by the attitude of Amalanga but the latter was also acting out of fear of retribution

---

80 Frans de Sadeleer, letter from Umgan in Umzila's kingdom, Roberts, p. 51.
81 *Letters & Notices*, 69, p. 141.
82 Ibid., No. 70, October 1881, p. 273.

from Umzila if he plundered the goods.[83]

Wehl and de Sadeleer then decided it was best to leave the wagon again and head for Umzila's to link up with Hedley and they walked ninety miles in four weeks, arriving on 10 December 1880 at Umgan in Umzila's territory about 200 miles from his capital. Meanwhile Hedley, knowing that Wehl was alive and fearful for his own life if he stayed any longer in Umzila's decided to set out to join up with Wehl and de Sadeleer at the wagon. The chief provided him with men to accompany him and he was so weak they had to carry him for the 45-mile journey. Wehl and de Sadeleer met Hedley on 3 January 1881 and the three proceeded to the wagon which they reached on 11 January. Frans de Sadeleer was appalled by the condition of Hedley when he saw him:

> I could not but weep, so awful was his appearance; never in my life have I seen a sick man in so pitiable a condition. His whole body was covered in inflamed swellings and ulcerations, and his wounds were gnawed by vermin; his limbs seem to have withdrawn into themselves and he seemed dazed by an excess of suffering, both physical and emotional … for five months he had not changed his clothing and it had fallen into rags … I rushed to take care of him … I laid him on our blankets, I washed him from head to foot; I bandaged his sores and anointed them with a little oil and balm; I clothed him in fresh linen. The good brother thought he was dreaming … Soon he revived (and) after a few days he was much improved.[84]

Meanwhile the Jesuits in Tati and Bulawayo waited anxiously for news and, failing to reach them by land, sent Fr Blanca by boat from Cape Town to Sofala to try to connect with Law, whom they thought was still alive. He waited for news from the interior at Inhambane until July before giving up and returning south. But at this very time Wehl and de Sadeleer were on their way to Sofala as they decided to abandon the plan to take the wagon to Umzila's. Hedley was too weak to go with them and stayed with the wagon. Twenty-five days later they reached Sofala, where they were warmly received by the commander of the fort, Captain Manuel d'Almeida. Wehl, exhausted and suffering from cerebral malaria (in Michael Gelfand's opinion)

---
83 De Sadeleer, Roberts, p. 47.
84 Ibid, p. 50.

died on 12 May 1881, and d'Almeida made sure he was buried with great honour. De Sadeleer, after buying what supplies he could carry, then set off back into the interior and re-joined Hedley at the wagon on 8 June. The two brothers then started for Gubulawayo with the wagon[85] on 28 July, going by the route they had come and arrived on 1 October 1881.

This mission to Umzila's reads like the lowest point of the whole Zambezi Mission. Another view might be that it is the highest. It was charged from the beginning with energy, high hopes and great generosity. The four Jesuits, with their guides and drivers (their co-workers), showed enormous courage and resilience. Each step of the way, described above, seemed to mount up the obstacles and disasters and the drama reaches its highest point with the lonely death of Fr Augustus Law with Br Joseph Hedley at his side. As he lay there on the floor of the hut throughout November 1880 waiting for death in a far country among people who had no idea why he had come and what he wanted, he must have gone through dark moments. Yet, as his last words in his journal, reproduced at the head of this chapter testify, he 'could not despair even if I tried.'[86] When his father at Hampton Court Palace received the letter announcing his son's death, aged forty-seven, he too would probably have had no idea of the circumstances and little understanding of what drove his son on to die in destitution in a remote corner of Africa. Law's remains were eventually exhumed by Fr Peter Prestage in 1904[87] and taken to Chishawasha, near Harare, where his brother, a soldier in the British army ironically fighting the Zulus at that very time Law was dying at Umzila's, built the finest tombstone in the cemetery.[88] Br Frans de Sadeleer concludes:

> Finally, on 1 October, we made our solemn entry into our dear residence in Gubulawayo; Fr Croonenberghs, Br Nigg and Fr de

---

85 De Wit to Notre Mère, 20 November 1881, Gelfand, p. 385.

86 Recorded by Bangert, p. 475

87 25 November 2020 was the 140th anniversary of Law's death and, since I was working on this account at the time, I conceived the idea of revisiting his first grave with Fr Shepherd Muhamba since Prestage had left fairly detailed notes of its location. In the event, they were not detailed enough. Rob Burrett had located the site but it proved to be over the border in Mozambique and, although the soldiers on the border were most co-operative, without the precise grid references they would not let us cross. At the end we had Mass on the border a short way from the place where we understood the grave to be.

88 It has a Celtic Cross. I wonder why? Law was the epitome of an Englishman!

Wit were impatiently awaiting our arrival. How can I describe the welcome given us? How happy we were, all of us, to see each other again after so much anxiety and sacrifice, after so many months gone by without news on either side. It is in moments like these especially that one feels more profoundly than ever the joy of belonging to the Society of Jesus and of being supported, assisted and consoled by brothers full of charity and devotion.[89]

Mweemba's, Zambia, May-October, 1880

Even before Law left for Umzila's at the beginning of June 1880, Depelchin, Terörde, Nigg and three new members of the mission, Fr Weisskopf, Brs Vervenne and Simonis, with the trader Alexander Walsh, a Protestant Irishman, as guide, set out from Tati for the Zambezi on 17 May. They had been traveling for an hour when they saw two horsemen coming up behind at a gallop. Alarmed, they discovered they were Fr Berghegge, another new member, and Frederick Courtney Selous bringing the teapot which they had left behind! How can one travel in the interior of Africa without a teapot?[90] They travelled up to Pandamatenga on trader 'Westbeech's road', which forms the boundary between Zimbabwe and Botswana today. Depelchin described the country through which they passed; the scant vegetation, the animals and birds and the loneliness. On 10 June, the wagon hit the trunk of tree and Walsh, their guide, was thrown under the wheel. He was badly injured and thought he would die. They spent twelve days nursing him as best they could and he recovered well enough for them to resume the journey on 22 June.

Three days later they reached Pandamatenga, where they were welcomed by a hunter called Weyer who worked for George Westbeech, a trader and hunter, and his trading partner George Blockley. Westbeech had established his base there in 1871 some distance south of the Victoria Falls.[91] He was away when the Jesuits arrived but returned within a few days. The trading station is situated in a depression at the headwaters of the Matetsi River, the area was low

---

89 15 October 1881, Roberts, p. 65.
90 Legend has it that when Fr Peter Edmonds SJ, on being sent to teach New Testament studies at Hekima College in Nairobi in 1984, discovered on his first morning at breakfast that there was no teapot, he was tempted to book the next flight home!
91 *Letters and Notices* 73, p. 186, in Burrett, p. 32.

lying and marshy, and as time was to tell it was a malarial deathbed for some of the Jesuits and other residents. Depelchin described the centre:

> A palisade of big posts of *mapani* surrounds the enclosure which has a surface area of thirty-two square meters. Within the enclosure there are six round thatched huts … oxen are kept in another enclosure, where a strong fence protects them … from lions, wolves and leopards …[92]

The Jesuits were unable to proceed immediately to the Lozi country as the Lozis were at war with one of their neighbours. They decided to make a base there and Westbeech gave them a site. They built a small wooden house and Br Vervenne began to till the land and plant wheat, potatoes and vegetables. And so they established the third mission of the province, which they called St Joseph's. But it was hardly a mission – more a staging post for the north and they responded to a suggestion of Selous that since the road to the north was blocked for the moment, they should turn east to the BaTonga on the Zambezi River. He assured them they would be welcome there. Depelchin was open to this idea as he had discovered that the French Protestant missionary, Francois Coillard, was preparing to return to the Lozi territory at the king's invitation. This would mean competition with the Protestants and Depelchin felt it would be impossible for the present to establish a Catholic presence in such circumstances.

Besides, the BaTonga chief Mweemba was based on the left (north) bank of the Zambezi and if the Jesuits could establish a base there it would open the way further east and north to Lake Bangweulu. This is eventually what happened – twenty-five years later – though there was by then no need to reach as far as Bangweulu as the White Fathers (Missionaries of Africa) were working there after coming through East Africa.

On 28 July, Depelchin, Terörde and Vervennes and sixty-three porters, guided by Blockley who had taken the place of the injured Walsh, set out for the Zambezi. This was a tsetse fly area and they could not take the oxen so they had to walk. When they reached the river, they could not obtain a crossing as the local chiefs were reluctant to provoke the Lozi king by a unilateral action of their own without

---
92 Depelchin, in Roberts, p. 105.

his permission. Also they were delayed for eight days waiting for fresh porters. Depelchin chafed at these delays as he knew the shortness of the seasons when one could travel.[93] When they could continue, they had no choice but to proceed downriver on the right bank until they reached a Tonga chief, Sitcheraba, who agreed to facilitate their crossing. But the chief, conscious of their vulnerability, increased his demands when they had half their goods on the other side of the river! While Terörde looked on in apprehension from the far bank, Depelchin tells us, 'I looked at (the chief) with a fiery gaze' and the chief quickly gave way. Even Lobengula used to be in awe of the scraggy beard and piercing eyes of Depelchin.[94]

Although they did not know it, the Jesuits were now embroiled in Tonga-Ndebele-Barotse political rivalry. Gelfand describes it in this way:

> when Law departed for Umzila's and Depelchin for the Lozi country Lobengula indicated ... there was no reason of the Jesuits to remain at Bulawayo ... it must have been difficult for him to understand that they wished to work among his powerful neighbours ... (some of) whom he looked on as his enemies and as a result he was mistrustful of their (the Jesuits') activities and only too anxious for them to leave his territory. Yet ... he listened to Croonenberghs who maintained that the Jesuits were prepared to serve him and his people and to help the sick. He was thus persuaded to give his permission for them to remain ...[95]

After crossing the river, they were only two days journey from Mweemba's and received word that the king had been informed of their coming. There had been a council meeting in which it was agreed the Jesuits would be allowed to stay and they would be given a plot to build a house. Depelchin was elated when he arrived on 9 August and later told the General that Mweemba's welcome was of 'immense importance for the Mission. ... The Zambezi is no longer an obstacle ... and Mweemba has opened the way for us ... our expedition is a real triumph and ha(s) produced incalculable results. Now we can truly

---

93 'All we can do is practise patience', Depelchin journal, Wanki, 8 August 1880, in Roberts, p. 138.
94 Depelchin to Fr General, 5 October 1880, Gelfand, p. 352, Roberts, p. 149.
95 Gelfand, op. cit, p. 43.

say that our Mission has been founded.'⁹⁶ Poor Depelchin! It is easy to understand his optimism after all he had been through and yet had to go through. But, alas, he was on the verge of painful disappointment. He failed to understand that the chief's motive for welcoming them was to bolster his own authority and discourage attacks by the Barotse or slavers from the Portuguese settlements.⁹⁷

In high spirits Depelchin set out to return to Pandamatenga on 23 August, leaving Terörde and Vervenne to establish the mission (the fourth) which they named the 'Residence of the Holy Cross'. But relations with Chief Mweemba soured when he realised that he could not extort an endless supply of goods. Both missionaries went down with fever and Fr Terörde wrote an impassioned letter on 28 August to Depelchin requesting assistance, given that Vervenne seemed near death. This message reached Depelchin at Ishabi's village on the south bank of the river where he himself was struggling to throw off a serious bout of malaria. Blockley, their guide, sent word to Pandamatenga for help and Fr Weisskopf and Br Nigg set off, on 7 September, to rescue them. When they reached Hwange, they found Depelchin in a terrible state. But worse was to come. On 15 September, they received a message from Terörde dated 9th of the month, 'I have never in my life been so broken, nor so completely exhausted ... please send us only Br Nigg but send him as quickly as possible ... I beg you please do not refuse my request'. That was Terörde's last letter. He died on 17 September, a few days before Nigg's arrival on the 20th.⁹⁸ Depelchin saw in the words, 'only Br Nigg' an awareness in the dying Terörde of the danger of exposing Fr Weisskopf to the fever and he knew Nigg could manage on his own – which he did.⁹⁹

Nigg later described the scene to Depelchin, who wrote:

> Entering our hut an appalling sight met his gaze. On a bed of rushes lay poor Br Vervennes, in the grip of feverish delirium. ... Nigg took his hand and said to him, 'Brother, do you know me?' 'Yes', he replied, 'you are Jan, the driver'. 'No, I am Br Nigg, come to take care of you'. At these words the patient regained his senses and stared fixedly at Br Nigg and, as if

---
96 Ibid.
97 Gelfand, p. 342.
98 Roberts, p. 161.
99 Loc cit.

awakening from a deep sleep, said 'Ah! Thank God. I am saved'.

Vervenne, though ill and confused, had managed to bury Terörde[100] but was unable to prevent the subsequent looting of their goods by Mweemba. An angry Br Nigg now approached the chief and demanded the return of all the looted goods. After a furious exchange some of the goods were returned and Nigg felt they should leave. A small group of porters was procured and Nigg left the mission carrying the critically ill Br Vervenne in a hammock. Most of their journey was by water, Nigg having procured the services of three small boats. Landing at Sicheraba's village they attempted the overland trip but it was evident that in their weak state they could not make it and Nigg was forced to write to Pandamatenga requesting a wagon, despite the danger from the fly. Depelchin, who had recovered sufficiently to return to Pandamatenga, dispatched Weisskopf and Mr Walsh to meet the stricken party. Both Jesuits were on the point of death and Br Nigg had lost the use of his left leg. The party finally reached Pandamatenga on 23 October 1880. Depelchin wrote to Weld, 'All our plans have been smashed to pieces and scattered to the winds like dust'.[101] Gelfand comments:

> In spite of the terrible blows that had struck these brave men, the Jesuits were not deterred. They possessed the resilience and determination so characteristic of men with this evangelical outlook. They were certain their cause would prevail in the end and were determined to carry on.[102]

---

100 At the time of the flooding of the Zambezi valley to create Lake Kariba, 'Irish Jesuits from Chikuni Mission tried to exhume the remains of Fr Terörde before the dam flooded but failed to find anything. The cross over his grave was removed and re-erected at the Catholic Church at Fumbo in the valley where it still stands today.' Fr Eddie Murphy's note in the Lusaka Jesuit archives jesuitarchlus@gmail.com.

101 10 October 1880, in Gelfand p. 359.

102 Gelfand. p. 343. Professor Michael Gelfand, a practicing Jew who had been born in South African, knew the Jesuits well and worked closely with them, especially Fr Rea, in the production of his book. He wrote more than thirty books in all and over 300 published articles and monographs. He died in 1985 and the present writer was able to attend his funeral. Robert Mugabe, then Prime Minister, was also there.

Mission to the Lozi, Zambia, 1881

Although ill himself, Depelchin decided to go to the Barotse, setting out from Pandamatenga on 5 November 1880. He hoped to make contact with some of the outlying Barotse *indunas* above the falls who could forward his message to their leader, Lewanika. The response was favourable and they were invited to return the next year, 1881. Depelchin returned to Tati, leaving Weisskopf, Vervenne and Simonis at Pandamatenga.[103]

Depelchin set out the following year with Fr Berghegge and Br de Vylder and reached Pandamatenga on 22 May 1881 where he found the residents in a shocking state of health. After rendering what assistance they could, they departed on 6 June for the Zambezi. They were delayed by a local chief at Membova from 16 to 29 June while an armed excursion of Lozi warriors went on a raid. Depelchin used the time to study the customs and to give some instructions through an interpreter who had become a catechumen.[104] Finally, on 29 June, they set out again by boat.

> Five rowers in each boat dextrously handled the long oars, and they were borne swiftly and smoothly over the waters of the broad stream. On the banks of the river, gnus, zebras and gazelles were peacefully grazing, and overhead and round about flew innumerable birds.[105]

Depelchin found the scenery invigorating; it reminded him of his years in India, especially the vegetation of the Ganges Valley. On approaching Sesheke, two gun shots announced their approach and people came down to the river to see their arrival. But then there was a six-week period of anxious waiting until local officials confirmed permission to proceed and they set out again on 17 August. The boats came to the Katima Molelo cataract.

> Before us the water descended as from step to a step of a gigantic staircase, with the impetuosity of a torrent. It seemed impossible for any boat to ascend this rampart of rock, this moving hill of waves and foam.[106]

---

103 Burrett, p. 33.
104 One preparing for Baptism.
105 ZMR 21, p 278.
106 ZMR 21, p 278.

However, after two hours most of the party were through the rapids and they camped on the banks enjoying a feast of freshly killed buffalo, shot by one of the Jesuits' travelling companions. Br de Vylder and his companions arrived the next day as they had lost their way in the channels and were confronted by four hippos. They frightened the animals by shooting in the air. Cold, wet and hungry they met some Bushmen hunters who welcomed them to their fire and supper and stayed the night with them.[107]

During the following days they ascended several more rapids before reaching Nalolo, the residence of the king's influential senior sister, on 1 September 1881. She received the Jesuits kindly and became a strong advocate for their cause. They arrived at Lealui on 6 September. Depelchin was taken with fever but he put on a brave face and they received a royal welcome the next day.

> The beating of the drums summoned the population (and) at about 08hrs the missionaries, with their interpreters, joined the assembled group. Lewanika was seated on his throne with the indunas and people in a semicircle about him at some distance. Fr Depelchin … greeting the king and took a seat by his side. … The king was pleased to see them, and promised them land to set up a mission station near his capital.[108]

Lewanika pressed the Jesuits to stay and start their mission immediately but Depelchin made a critical mistake by promising to come back the following year. When they eventually returned, they found the king had changed his mind.

The Jesuit party remained at Lealui until 13 September finalising details for their future mission. King Lewanika asked for a plough to be brought back as a gift. Once these decisions had been ratified by the *indunas* the Jesuits left, arriving back at Pandamatenga on 6 October 1881.

Depelchin felt there was still time before the rains to make another visit to Mweemba's to try to revive the prospects of the mission where Terörde had died. He reached the chief on 29 October and was well received. Mweemba apologised for what had happened previously and renewed his welcome to them. Depelchin was again elated as he felt

---

107 Roberts, p. 206.
108 Ibid., p. 242. The wording in Roberts is slightly different.

two doors were open to him north of the Zambezi.

But hope and grief marched together in this whole early phase of the Zambezi Mission. A new group of six Jesuits arrived in March 1882, among them were Prestage, Kroot, Engels and Booms. Another was Br Gerard Hooy but he was drowned in the Vaal River on 23 March. And two days earlier, at Tati, Fr de Wit died in a freak accident falling off a horse.[109] Meanwhile Depelchin was seriously injured on his return journey from the south with the new recruits when a large bag of salt fell off a wagon and landed on his leg breaking it below the knee. Luckily Fr Engels, who had served in the ambulance corps in the Franco-Prussian War, was able to reset it but the party was held up for nearly a fortnight while they allowed their leader rest and recuperation. They finally arrived back at Tati on 3 June 1882.

The combination of his injuries and the long-term effects of malaria had so weakened Depelchin that he could not make the return journey to the Lozi that year. In November 1882 he reluctantly returned to Grahamstown. Fr Francis Berghegge and Br Allen did proceed on 27 August to the Zambezi but received no permission to proceed further and had to return to Pandamatenga. Lewanika was at war with his neighbours and had no time for the foreigners.[110]

The lack of contact with the Barotse throughout 1882 undermined the mission. When two wagons loaded with provisions finally departed from Pandamatenga on 14 March 1883, in the charge of Fr Berghegge and Brs Simonis and de Vylder, failure again struck. De Vylder was drowned on 29 April, when the group were making their way through the Lusu rapids. 'A strong current forced the boat back … and there was danger of being dashed against the rocks. They jumped into the water but De Vylder jumped out on the side where the current was strongest. … Fr Berghegge gave the last absolution

---

109 He had borrowed a horse so as to accompany a Boer visitor to the Jesuit Residence to go home. On the way back he was riding one horse and leading the other while at the same time saying his breviary. Recognising its pasture the tail horse suddenly stopped and De Wit was jerked off his horse and landed breaking his neck. He was buried at Tati next to Fr Fuchs, and the present writer visited their graves both in 2004, the 125th anniversary of the founding of Tati as the first mission of the province, and again in 2017. The Bishop of Francistown, Frank Nebusah, sees Tati as the foundation of his diocese and is building a shrine there which will become a site of pilgrimage.

110 Burrett, p. 34.

as the drowning man was swept away by the current. ... it was impossible to recover his body.'[111]

On top of this, they soon discovered the change of mind of Lewanika. The lack of contact in 1882 and the Jesuits' continued contacts with Mweemba, a sworn enemy, probably turned Lewanika against them. But the weightiest reason was Westbeech's intervention in favour of the French Protestant Missionary François Coillard. Westbeech wrote in his diary, published in 1963, 'when I think that through me (the Paris Mission) is established in the country and I could have so easily settled the Jesuits in the valley ... it rather riles me'.[112] Fr Kroot, one of the recent arrivals, had a dispute with Westbeech at Pandamatenga over a piece of land and this must have soured relations.[113] Westbeech, in effect, had the key to the north and could open the way to whichever missionary group he chose. There is a final twist to this story. Westbeech became ill on his way south in 1888 and the nearest dwelling was the recently acquired Jesuit residence at Vleeschfontein. He managed to reach the mission where he was taken in and he died with a Jesuit at his bedside. [114]

The Jesuits received no help from any quarter and their goods were pilfered. They were, in effect, detained at the Barotse capital. When it was clear that no form of additional ransom could be obtained the Jesuit party was allowed to depart, arriving back at Pandamatenga on 2 October 1883, before continuing on to Tati.

The only bright point in 1882 was the establishment of a mission in the western Transvaal in a healthier area where the Jesuits could recuperate and supplies be more easily obtained. Depelchin arranged to acquire the farm, Vleeschfontein, mentioned above, for £800 from Augustus Greite, who had earlier sold them their Gubulawayo residence. Its purchase aroused controversy among the missionaries, many openly questioning Depelchin's financial sense and mental state. Kroot complained to Weld that the farm was 'bought by Mr

---

111 *Zambesi Mission Record*, 22, p. 317.
112 Gelfand, p. 407.
113 Ibid., p. 408.
114 *Zambesi Mission Record*, 3, p. 343, in Gelfand, p. 409. The story is reminiscent of the death of the Marquis of Pombal, the man who drove the Jesuits out of the Portuguese dominions in the mid-eighteenth century and pushed vigorously and successfully for their suppression. He died in 1782 attended by one of the Jesuits he had suppressed.

Greite a few years ago for £280 and now he asks from our mission £800 … on the farm there is no house, not even a tree,' and water is scarce in winter.'[115]

Faced with the combined effects of personal injury and illness, constant failure and nagging distrust from his own companions, Depelchin felt it was time to stand down and after arriving in Grahamstown he left the Zambezi Mission and went on a lecture tour of Europe to raise additional manpower and finances for the mission. He later returned to India where he continued to work successfully for some years and died in May 1900 at Darjeeling aged 78. In his place Fr Alfred Weld, who had done so much to promote the whole idea of the enterprise in the first place, was appointed Superior on 3 December 1883.

At Pandamatenga the Jesuits struggled on. Their efforts were directed towards the conversion of the many Boers and coloured hunters who were operating in the region. But there were few converts. Their impact on the local population was negligible. On 1 July 1883, Fr Weisskopf died of fever. His successor, Fr Kroot, was then ordered to move the station to the banks of the Zambezi at Tchabi but they were all too ill to comply.

At Tati, Fr Prestage had taken charge after the death of Fr de Wit in 1882 but there was little for him to do. Prestage later maintained that the loneliness of this period was his greatest teacher and he turned his hand to all manner of tasks – building, cultivation, cattle breeding, etc. He learnt the Zulu language and expanded the mission premises, digging a well some fifty-two feet deep using dynamite. He also constructed many new buildings including a chapel set a little apart from the residential quarters. Although the only Jesuit in residence, Prestage's frequent companions were Engelbrecht and Edwards. He received many guests on their way north to Matabeleland – administrators, military men, traders and many missionaries, both Catholic and Protestant. He tried to start a school and by March 1883 he recorded thirteen African and two white children. But attendance was variable and the population was too small to make the project viable.

---

115   Bartholomew Kroot to Weld 21 August 1883, Gelfand, p. 396.

Gubulawayo

At Gubulawayo matters were no better. The superior, Fr Croonenberghs, wrote:

> As long as Lo Bengula [sic] remained at old Bulawayo we had much to do, but since he left the neighbourhood is well-nigh deserted. We have kept our school open and sick people come to us. But there is no hope of conversions among the Matabele ... We have been here five years ... and not a single Matabele has dared to brave the displeasure of the King by declaring himself on our side. Yet its central position has made it worthwhile to maintain the station.[116]

It was a healthy place where sick missionaries could recover. But in December 1883 Fr Croonenberghs left Gubulawayo on route for Europe and rest. Br Allen died in February 1885 of fever and Fr Kroot in June the same year. It was decided to close both Pandamatenga and Tati. Tati was sold for £35 but Pandamatenga with the wonderful garden Vervennes had cultivated was simply abandoned.

The Jesuits gave traditional Christian names to all their houses, schools and missions well into the twentieth century but by the time the present writer arrived in the country in 1966 they had begun to use the names of the early Jesuits of the Zambezi Mission. They started, not with Depelchin or Law, but with Peter Prestage. When the time came for formalising the legal ownership of Jesuit properties in the country the province called this new entity 'The Prestage Trust'. It was a sign of the respect the Jesuits had for a man who pushed his way forward where milder souls hesitated. Gelfand considered him 'perhaps the most remarkable of the Jesuits whose vision was to stand the mission in good stead'.[117]

As only Gubulawayo remained, Prestage with Br Hedley moved there in September 1884. On one of his visits to Lobengula, the king said to Prestage, pointing to a book in his pocket, 'Do not teach that to my people, but teach them to work'. 'That is what we wish to do,' Prestage answered; 'we have come here to be useful to them'.[118] Initially nothing further came of it, but Prestage kept up pressure on

---
116 *Zambesi Mission Record,* 22, p. 319 quoted in Burrett, p. 37.
117 Gelfand, p. 427.
118 *Zambesi Mission Record,* 23, p. 353.

the king to be allowed to set up a school for the people. While religion was unacceptable the promise of practical skills such as carpentry and blacksmithing was attractive. He jokingly mentioned the kraal of Umpandeni as being a good place for a school, but again nothing happened. However, white settler encroachment was evident – 'you white men are like the chameleon', Lobengula is alleged to have said, 'he creeps up slowly step by step, then makes a pounce and seizes the fly. That will be my fate'.[119] Lobengula wanted someone of his own to be his scribe, since he no longer trusted traders and missionaries. But Prestage had to keep up the pressure and records in his journal on 18 June 1886: 'Had an interview with the King and I was told by him that all his people were perfectly free to practice what we taught them. What more could we expect?' Prestage was able to do in five months what Croonenberghs failed to do in five years. But this was partly due to Lobengula's position being considerably weakened in the mid-1880s by military disasters to his own forces, especially at Lake Ngami, as well as the threat from the white 'chameleon'. So he consented to Prestage moving to what became Empandeni Mission and gave him a free hand there.

Empandeni

Prestage was delighted, but his initial hopes were soon dashed. The new Superior of the Zambezi Mission, Fr Weld, who was based in Grahamstown, decided that the Jesuits would abandon Matabeleland. He felt that work should first be consolidated in the healthier environs of the Cape Colony before attempting to extend northward again. Accordingly, on 7 May 1886, Fr Prestage received instructions to give up the idea of Empandeni altogether. This was followed on 28 July by his recall to the Cape. At first Prestage protested by post but without success so reluctantly he left Gubulawayo on 2 December 1886, arriving in Grahamstown by mid-February 1887. Here he begged Fr Weld to be allowed to continue his work, which had only just begun to bear fruit. Prestage was clearly a persuasive man and Weld gave in to him. Prestage, accompanied by Fr Booms and Br Joseph Hedley, immediately retraced his steps to Gubulawayo, arriving on 19 May 1887.

By 18 June, Prestage had chosen the site for Empandeni Mission.

---

119 *Zambesi Mission Record*, 2, p. 356, in Gelfand, p. 433.

This 'Old Empandeni' lies some distance south of the current mission. The mission in Gubulawayo was closed. Fr Andrew Hartmann, originally from Austria, arrived at Empandeni in August 1887. A community house was built and lessons begun in the school. Fr Booms later joined them in 1888. Although there were several Ndebele attending the lessons, few were considered fully committed, especially when it came to religious studies. Most seemed afraid of retribution if they should renounce their traditional ways.

With the signing of the Rudd Concession, which pressurised Lobengula into granting mining rights in Mashonaland, over which he claimed suzerainty, to the Chartered Company Rhodes was negotiating in London, the attitudes of Lobengula and his *indunas* soured towards the few remaining settlers in Matabeleland. Most of the traders in Bulawayo fled southward to Tati, and the Jesuits decided that they would leave Empandeni for a while, appointing a caretaker to look after their property. Their departure on 13 November 1889, marks the end of the first phase of the Zambezi Mission. As the plans for a column of white settlers moving to Mashonaland developed, Frs Weld and Daignault, his successor, visited Cecil Rhodes to 'pledge their support' to use the words of Professor Roberts.[120] This phrase may rankle with us now since it seems to imply Jesuit endorsement of the colonisation of Zimbabwe in 1890. In a sense it does mean just that since the Jesuits were undoubtedly looking forward to a more stable environment in which to work and they thought the whites would provide this. But in view of the history of Zimbabwe over the past 130 years, when first the whites and then the blacks who replaced them after independence, directed the fortunes of the country to their own benefit, such a view has to be qualified. The Jesuits, as we shall see, for many decades welcomed the benefits the white administration brought. It was only in the last two decades of colonialism (the 1960s and '70s) that they and the Church as a whole found their voice to speak against the full-blown racialism that had evolved.

In 1889 this was far in the future and no eyebrows were raised when Fr Hartmann was appointed chaplain to the military column (the Pioneer Column) that thrust its way northwards by a new route, skirting Lobengula's kingdom and entering the heart of Mashona territory finally halting at present-day Harare. Other than

---

120   Roberts, p. xxxiii.

Empandeni, none of the earlier mission stations were reoccupied.

Conclusions

Despite the fact that all the other missions became part of history, they were all remembered. Thanks to the archaeological work of Rob Burrett, the graves of Fuchs and De Wit were found at Tati and Frank Nabusah SVD[121], when he was bishop of Francistown, saw the site as the primordial mission of the diocese and started the process of making it into a pilgrimage centre. The first bishop of Hwange, Ignatius Prieto SMI[122], similarly honoured the memory of the first Jesuits at Pandamatenga with a huge cross at the centenary of their coming. The bishop at the time of writing, Alberto Serrano, celebrated the golden jubilee of the founding of the diocese in 2012 with a three-day celebration which included the Jesuits – and a few notes on Br Nigg's accordion from the present writer! The Jesuit mission at Old Bulawayo is a national monument and the site of periodic celebrations by the Archdiocese. Mweemba's is now under the waters of Lake Kariba, but in 2005, for the centenary of the founding of the Catholic Church in southern Zambia, the Bishop of Monze, Emilio Patriarca, celebrated Mass on a boat on the lake over the approximate spot of the burial of Fr Anthony Terörde. And there is a monument to Br Louis De Vylder near the place where he was drowned close to the present Lusu Mission in the Western Province of Zambia. The present writer is unaware of any memorial to the Jesuits at Umzila's, though, as noted above, Law's body was later exhumed and given place of honour in the cemetery in Chishawasha, near Harare.

It is easy for one in the twenty-first century to sit in judgement over the choices made by the Jesuits of the Zambezi Mission in the 1880s. If we do so, it is simply to understand what they faced at that time and maybe, *mutatis mutandis*, to draw some conclusions.

- **Malaria.** Professor Gelfand says 'the truth is that it was the Africa fever which more than anything else contributed to the downfall of Depelchin's mission'.[123] 'It seems a paradox that, while the quinine bark was introduced to the world as a specific remedy

---

121 *Societas Verbi Divini,* the Divine Word Missionaries, founded in the Netherlands in 1875.
122 Spanish Missionary Institute, founded in Spain in 1922.
123 Gelfand, p. 22.

for malaria by the Jesuits, it was used so little by the Order in Central Africa.'[124] The Jesuits were vague about any training in management of the fever. They seemed unconcerned. This is extraordinary when we look at the list of casualties:

Date	Cause	Person	Age
28.01.1880	Malaria	Fr Charles Fuchs	40
17.09.1880	Malaria	Fr Anthony Terörde	37
25.11.1880	Malaria	Fr Augustus Law	47
12.05.1881	Malaria	Fr Charles Wehl	43
21.03.1882	Accident	Fr Anthony de Wit	59
23.03.1882	Drowned	Br Gerard Hooy	31
29.04.1883	Drowned	Br Louis de Vylder	42
01.07.1883	Malaria	Fr John Weisskopf	35
02.02.1885	Malaria	Br Alfred Allen	34
21.06.1885	Consumption	Fr Bartholomew Kroot	37
Their average age was forty years and six months			

- **Protestants**. Competition with the Protestants was a forceful motivation from the beginning and led to the expedition starting in a hurry. The Protestant missionaries were in the field well before the Jesuits in every place and their influence contributed to blocking the Jesuits in Shoshong and Lealui. One of the attractions of Umzila's was that they were not there though there were reports that they were planning to go and 'are always ready to put obstacles on our way'.[125] It was the time long before ecumenism and there is not a word in the Jesuit letters that I have come across of praise for the great Protestant missionary, Robert Moffat, who founded the mission of Kuruman in the Northern Cape in 1821, nearly sixty years before the Jesuits arrived.

- **Traders.** Hunters, explorers, miners and traders were also in the field before the Jesuits and, on balance, they helped the missionaries more than they hindered them. The Jesuits were recent arrivals and the trading posts were the only possible reference points where the Jesuits could start. We saw how these enabled them to settle in Tati and even in Bulawayo, where after a shaky start, the two

---
124 Ibid., p. 429.
125 Depelchin to Notre Mère, 12 March 1880, Gelfand, p. 222.

missionary groups learnt to co-exist. It was the renowned hunter Selous who introduced the Jesuits to Mweemba. And Westbeech, who ultimately closed the door to the Lozi kingdom, was at first welcoming.

- **Distance.** Depelchin's 'ambition was to set up in rapid succession a number of stations linked with one another throughout Central Africa, from Tati and Gubulawayo in the south to Lake Bangweulu close to the Congo border in the north and extending east to incorporate (parts of) Mozambique'.[126] Even when he had some experience of the difficulties of travel with ox-wagons on the most basic of roads he clung to this plan. He scattered his resources far too widely. Every journey took weeks, sometimes months, and his men were exhausted and prone to accidents. Yet, as mentioned, the grand plan was not so much Depelchin's as Weld's.[127] 'Depelchin did as well as any man could.'[128]

- **Politics.** It does not seem that the Jesuits understood the relationships between the power blocks in the region. We noted how Lobengula was angry at the expeditions to Umzila's and Lewanika's whom he considered his rivals or enemies, even though he had married the daughter of Umzila. He was unsure and suspicious of the Jesuits' real intentions and Croonenberghs had some difficulty in averting his anger and retaining permission to stay at Gubulawayo.

- **Economising.** The Jesuits complained that Depelchin made bad mistakes in not regularly changing the teams of oxen. It was no good replacing worn out animals with fresh oxen bit by bit as the new were inevitably dragged down by the old. Also he dismissed guides in order to save money and this too delayed them.[129]

- **Bonding.** An issue that would annoy and discourage Depelchin was the lack of unity among his men on the personal level, though they were all committed to the mission. In their hurry to leave Grahamstown they failed to spend time getting to know each other. Blanca and Croonenberghs, for example, could not get on. Depelchin complained to Weld, 'Blanca is such a passionate and vindictive man who was in such an abominable mood during the

---

126 Gelfand, p. 21.
127 Roberts, p. xiv.
128 Ibid., p. xxvii.
129 Op.cit., p. 34.

whole time of our travelling. Continually he wanted to force me to send Fr Croonenberghs to Europe …'[130] It was an age when obedience was understood to be the bond that would hold Jesuits together but we have learnt the hard way that we each have to do some inner work with ourselves if we are to live at such close quarters with others. Without this foundation obedience doesn't work.

- **The Brothers.** All the above points are, in a sense, negative. The one hugely positive reflection is the presence of our lay brothers. Every group that went out to the Zambezi Mission contained a group of brothers. Of the original team of eleven, almost half were priests and half were brothers. Law wrote to Weld: 'It is almost entirely owing to the lay brothers of this mission that we have been able so easily to get a footing here. For had we been unable to show that we cd supply some of the material wants of the people up here, it is difficult to say whether we cd have gained a footing.'[131] The brothers not only contributed much to the early pre-colonial years; they were also an integral part of the founding years after 1890.

And so the first phase of the Zambezi Mission came to an end in heroic failure. But much was learnt and the rapid development of the Jesuits' work in the succeeding decades owes a great deal to the struggles and suffering of these men who preceded them.

The plaque, inspired by the suggestion of Professor Ray Roberts, formerly of the University of Zimbabwe, that we should record visibly our reverence for the founders of the Zambezi Mission, was executed in 2014 by Mr Joseph Damson of Silveira House, Chishawasha. It was unveiled at Chishawasha Mission on 7 August 2020, by Fr Chiedza Chimhanda, last Provincial of what was the Zimbabwe Mozambique province of the Society of Jesus, to commemorate the bicentenary of the Restoration of the Society on that date in 2014.

---

130   6 October 1880, in Gelfand, p. 284.
131   12 November 1879, in Gelfand, p. 148.

3

Putting down Roots

There is a dream dreaming us.

A saying of the Kalahari people

In 1890, Alphonse Daignault, who had taken over as Zambezi Mission Superior from Alfred Weld in 1887, offered a chaplain, Austrian Fr Andrew Hartmann, for the pioneer column of soldiers, settlers and adventurers making their way into Mashonaland. They arrived on 30 September 1890 in what is now Harare. Daignault also suggested some Dominican Sisters should accompany the column and Mother Patrick and four sisters followed ten months later with Peter Prestage.[1] Dachs and Rea record the impression 'these splendid women' (in Earl Grey's words) made on the hard-edged and often prejudiced settlers.[2] They won for the Catholic Church an acceptance that the Jesuits alone would have taken a long time to achieve.

Chishawasha

As with Depelchin eleven years earlier, the Jesuits wanted a site to start a mission. It would be a base from which to reach out to people where ever they were settled and it would provide them with the means to support their work. With this in view, Hartmann, after the rainy

---

[1] Sr Paulette Curran, 'Mother Patrick Cosgrave', in J. Woods, *The Mashonaland Irish Association: A Miscellany, 1891-2019,* (Harare: Weaver Press, 2019).

[2] A. J. Dachs and W. F. Rea SJ, *The Catholic Church and Zimbabwe, 1879-1979* (Gwelo: Mambo Press, 1979), p. 34

season of 1890/91, first explored Mutoko. He had been told by Selous it had all the ingredients for a mission and he was also motivated by its proximity to where Silveira had given his life more than three centuries earlier. Besides, if the settlers were all fanning out in search of minerals and lands to cultivate why should the Jesuits confine themselves to the environs of Fort Salisbury (Harare)? He went there but he found few people and he caught fever. He returned to Salisbury in time to meet Prestage who had just arrived with the Dominican sisters. Prestage explored a much nearer site close to what became the Cleveland Dam but later rejected it in favour of the Chishawasha valley. They applied for this site to start a mission farm and this was agreed with the British South Africa Company (BSAC). By September 1891 it was marked by beacons.[3] Even in the restricted circumstances described in the last chapter, the Jesuits had tried to develop the missions they founded by planting gardens and keeping some small livestock. Br Vervenne's garden at Pandamatenga had provided a steady supply of fresh vegetables to the Jesuits in the early 1880s.

The Jesuits wanted land where they could grow substantial amounts of crops and rear livestock to supply their own needs and those of the schools they planned to establish. In 1892, in answer to an appeal by Fr Henry Schomberg Kerr, who had taken over as Mission Superior from Daignault, the German Jesuits sent out Frs Francis Richartz and Anthony Boos, together with Brs Joseph Löffler, Augustine Book, William Biermann, Joseph Lindner and Henry Meyer. All were sent to Chishawasha. The brothers were soon developing a farm and gardens in which they reared cattle, sheep and goats and grew wheat, barley, potatoes, oats, maize, tobacco, cotton and coffee, bananas, apples, oranges and a variety of vegetables. They were even making wine and Fr Emil Schmidt made cigars! The whole enterprise would have been impossible without the skilled Jesuit Brothers who came and dedicated their lives to the work. All the older churches and school buildings in the country bear witness to this. The iron gate to the cemetery in Chishawasha, with its decorative designs, still stands as a visible testimony to the trouble they took to go beyond mere function to make things that would last and at the same time be things of beauty.

Chishawasha would not be the only mission farm. As the years passed, the Jesuits became responsible for at least six: besides

---

3 Ibid., p. 47.

Chishawasha there was Empandeni, Driefontein, Gokomere, Makumbe[4] and St George's. The farms prospered when there were brothers to work them as with Br Hugh Bradley at Makumbe. He worked the farms all his life and died at the age of 81 in 1959. 'His particular line was cattle … and for his calves he would steal anything he could get'.[5]

On 31 July 1892, the feast of St Ignatius, Richartz formally founded Chishawasha Mission. Dachs and Rea describe the area as a *res nullius*, a place where no one resided, and one of the first tasks was to attract people to settle.[6] Seemingly, they succeeded as by 1895 there were several villages in the valley. Chief Chinamora visited in November 1892, and in April 1893 eighteen headmen attended a celebration and an ox was killed.[7] When building lime was found they were able to erect a small church which was opened on 5 January 1894. When Fr Edward Biehler arrived in 1895, he started the school and went on to found a brass band which became famous and visited Empandeni Mission with about fifty players on their way to Mafeking to welcome Joseph Chamberlain, the British Colonial Secretary. The young musicians later formed the police band.

The development of Chishawasha drew the attention of many of the colonial stalwarts of the time, including Jameson. Owen Thomas, a professional agriculturalist, wrote, 'I have visited many missions during my travels in South Africa, but I have not seen anything to compare with Chishawasha'. In contrast, Jameson, 'alienated huge tracts of (Matabeleland) to syndicates who were more interested in holding on to them in the hope of their rising in value than in developing (their) agricultural potential'.[8]

But the small Mtenje River, close by the mission, not only gave them water; it also gave them mosquitoes, those old enemies of the Jesuits. Br Augustine Book died of malaria on 6 May 1895 and Br

---

4   I am going to use this spelling of the name throughout for reasons I will explain later.
5   LL&N 1960, Vol 65, p. 109.
6   Op. cit., p. 47, 'There was not a soul on our place before 1892', Richartz, Jesuit Archives, Box 98.
7   Chishawasha Archives, *History of the House*, quoted in Dachs and Rea, p. 47.
8   Dachs and Rea, p. 49. Such an attitude was evident again in the opening years of the twenty-first century among many who were granted land in the 'Land Reform' programme launched by President Mugabe.

Joseph Loeffler on 18 January 1896. Within three years, two more, Boos and Meyer, would die.

I will describe below the Shona rising on 15 June 1896 against the white settlers. When it happened, the Jesuits were advised by the administration in Salisbury to seek refuge in town. They refused, thinking they had built good relations with the people and would not be attacked, and, even if they were, the Jesuits believed they could defend themselves. They were amazed when they were attacked on 22 June but were able to defend the barn to which they, eight lay helpers and eight Jesuits, had retired. They were then ordered to go to Salisbury. When they were able to return, they found only their cattle had been taken. Otherwise they found the mission intact. Rinderpest had struck cattle in the country and the authorities had ordered the slaughter and burning of all infected animals. The mission had isolated their herd and so they were not infected but the people's cattle were slaughtered and they were not allowed to eat the meat. There was resentment at this and, since the mission cattle were untouched, they took them.

Mission farms could also be places of welcome for new Christians who could settle there at some distance from their non-Christian relatives who might otherwise influence them to lapse from the faith. This policy was later to be developed into organised Christian villages as we shall see. Further, the mission farms provided a venue for schools and industrial training. They became centres from which other stations could be founded and often had a hospital or at least a clinic.

Empandeni again

Empandeni, founded, as we saw in Chapter 2, with much labour by Prestage in 1887, could not reopen owing to the on-going hostility of Lobengula towards the settlers. But after his defeat and death in 1893, the mission was restarted in December that year and the Jesuits were welcomed back. One old man came and proudly recited the Our Father. Soon there was an average of 200 attending catechism classes on Sundays. They built eight huts of poles, mud and thatch for £15 each.

During the Ndebele rising against the settlers in 1896, Prestage advised the local *indunas* not to take part. Presumably he knew resistance would be hopeless and he wanted to spare the people the suffering it would cause. But also, he was glad to see the end of Ndebele rule as Lobengula had ruled in an arbitrary way that held people in fear. An example of this was given by Sr Josephine Bullen of the Sisters of Notre Dame (SND)[9] of Empandeni, who tells the story she heard years later: 'A boy of 18 had been on a message for Fr Prestage which had taken about three days. Fr Prestage paid him off and the boy went to his own kraal about a mile and a half away. In less than an hour Lobengula sent out four of his soldiers to kill the boy, his father and all his family and to burn the entire kraal. The unfortunate fellow had been seen taking a handful of mealies as he passed the royal kraal.'[10] Lobengula resisted all missionary attempts to teach and preach and it was only when he saw his position threatened by the 'approaching chameleon', his words, that he allowed Prestage to open Empandeni. Like many of his contemporaries, Prestage believed British rule was good for people – even the Irish![11] His courageous action – in setting out alone and unarmed to meet the *indunas* during the rising – was mentioned in the House of Commons in London. When peace was restored the BSAC wanted the Jesuits to hold Empandeni under their aegis but Prestage refused, saying it was a royal grant from Lobengula. Prestage wrote to Jameson, who was in jail, for confirmation and wrote forcibly about the Company's limitations of power – something on which he accused other Jesuits of not insisting.[12]

Empandeni was the first and most enduring mission of the Jesuits in Zimbabwe. It had both Hartmann and Prestage on the staff and the former would stay there for twenty-eight years. Prestage dropped dead in 1907 while prospecting for a new mission site for Gokomere. In 1899, the new church at Empandeni was burnt down by accident and

---

9 The Sisters of Notre Dame were founded in 1804 in France but moved to Namur, Belgium, in 1809.
10 Josephine Bullen, SND, *Empandeni Interlude 1899-1903, Journal of a woman missionary at the turn of the century in Rhodesia.* Entry for May 24, 1903 (Bulawayo: Cluster Publications, 2008).
11 Prestage wrote in his journal while in Bulawayo on 13 July 1886, 'Much delighted to hear that Gladstone's (Home Rule) bill for Ireland has been thrown out. That so great a mind should favour such an objectionable measure is beyond comprehension.' Quoted in Gelfand, p. 472.
12 'We have absolute ownership from Lobengula's grant. We are not asking the government for a concession but confirmation of the grant,' 18 May 1899, Box 126, folder 2.

in the same year the Sisters of Notre Dame de Namur arrived. 'The transformation they brought about was startling and immediate'.[13] They started a school and in 1901 the average attendance was over a 100.[14] A moment in life on the mission was captured when Sr Josephine described a storm on 26 November 1899, which washed away the roof of the kitchen and saturated everything including the clothes and beds of the children. They saved what they could, including a teapot, 'and in a very short time we were seated merrily over tea and brown cakes.'[15] In 1900, Fr Charles Bick produced an Ndebele Catechism and in 1901, in a sign of the viability of the mission, they sold 235 lbs of butter in Bulawayo for 3/6 a pound! In 1903 a new church was built for 1500 people. 1905 was a dry year with only 270 mm of rain whereas the average in previous years was twice that.

Richartz moved from Chishawasha to Empandeni in 1905 for four years and found the mission was moving out to the people rather than, as in Chishawasha, drawing them in. Embakwe was founded in 1902 and two other outstations were opened between then and 1908 by which year the mission was responsible for five schools. But there was a severe drought between 1912 and 1914 and a threat of starvation. The Jesuits had to beg for money to stave off hunger from the people and themselves. The soil was poor in comparison with Chishawasha and in time the Jesuits adapted by concentrating on cattle grazing. Br Thomas Ashton also developed a poultry farm which was such a success it could almost support the mission on its own.

Embakwe

The publication, *At Kalahari's Brink*, was produced in 1964 to mark the sixtieth year of the founding of Embakwe. Fr Adalbert Balling of the Mariannhill congregation, which took over the Matabeleland missions from the Jesuits in 1931, tells us the mission was built on the site of a battle between Lobengula's soldiers, led by Chief Gambo, and the European pioneers on 2 November 1893. One of Gambo's soldiers, uNjemhlope, became Embakwe's first and best-known catechist. Growing from a single hut near the Umpakwe River, the mission built a secondary school for people of mixed race in 1923, a

---

13 Dachs and Rae, p. 61.
14 Bullen, op .cit., entry for 5 February 1901.
15 Bullen, op. cit, p. 40.

dam a mile and a quarter long and half a mile wide on the Tshankisha River in 1954 and a new church in 1964 in time for their Diamond Jubilee.

Misereor, the German bishops' agency established with the philosophy of promoting self-sufficiency, was founded in 1959 and supported the mission.[16] Soon two more dams were built which enabled a model irrigation scheme to be established as well as a Friesian dairy herd contained with twenty-five miles of fencing. In time, seventy-five acres of crops were under irrigation.

Fr Urban Staudacher, superior of the mission (1932-44), wrote appreciatively of the Jesuits who founded it. 'Their life must have been very difficult and lonely. One priest was there on his own all the time. … the monotonous menu, the shortage of water, the lack of any comfort whatsoever. Fr Charles Bick (Tandabantu, the people's friend) was from Alsace. No one knew when talking to him whether he was serious or pulling your leg!' Fr O'Neil's Sindebele grammar was the standard grammar for the education department. Frs Tilman Esser, Andrew Hartmann, Gerard Pfaehler (an Englishman despite his German name) and Victor Nicot, all served at Embakwe.

At Kalahari's Brink is a model school magazine as it blends informative articles and action photos. Balling ends with comments that reflect his time of writing (1964):

> As missionaries it is not our duty to influence politics directly. However, we certainly must try to put up land marks, sign posts pointing towards a happy and peaceful future. By teaching basic human rights, by preaching the good news, we hope to create an atmosphere that manifests our active participation with God in his work in creation. 'There is a dream dreaming us', say the Bushmen of the Kalahari, a Creator creating us. Who, then, can doubt?

'Embakwe Mission has come a long way from the day when Fr Bick fell from a crudely fashioned stepladder with a pot of paint landing on top of him in 1904, to the day of the solemn opening of

---

16 Misereor deserves far more than a footnote in this account of the Jesuits in Zimbabwe. Their enormous support was continuous and had a quality of trust that was deeply appreciated. Not all the financial support they provided led to successful projects but Misereor continued to support our work believing that we were doing the best we could.

the grand and spacious mission church built in steel and glazed brick and adorned with smooth terrazzo and shining silex plaster in 1964.' Fr Elmar Schmid, provincial, CMM.

The first *Chimurenga*: the Ndebele and the Shona rising, 1896/97

In his revealing study of the Ndebele and Shona resistance to the British conquest of Zimbabwe, Terence Ranger shows how the risings took the whites completely by surprise.[17] Their failure to even try to understand the culture, history and religion of the people whose land they assumed by force, lulled them into a sense that the local people had no culture, history or religion worth understanding. Further, they persuaded themselves that the African people were grateful for the security and order that they, the Europeans, were bringing. They clung to the myths that the Ndebele were glad to be rid of their oppressive rulers and the Shona were happy to be free of Ndebele raids. Ranger shows that the Ndebele were proud of their nation and willing to fight for it even after their king was dead. Further, though the Ndebele regularly raided Shona settlements, they did not penetrate deeply into Mashonaland. A number of Shona paramount chiefs considered themselves to be independent and beholden to no one, and so, when Rhodes used the fudgy language of the Rudd Concession to claim rights over the whole of Mashonaland, they stoutly resisted. The hut tax and enforced labour were two flashpoints that deeply angered the paramount chiefs.

In the 1890s there were three white forces competing not just with the local people but with one another. First the settlers, who were assigned large tracts of land by the BSAC, believed the company did not provide the support they needed. For their part, the company, always with an eye to the shareholders in Britain, tried to keep expenses in check. Finally, the British Colonial Office, while basically supporting Cecil Rhodes,[18] continually tried to clip the wings of his company

---

17   T.O. Ranger, *Revolt in Southern Rhodesia, 1896-97: A study in African resistance* (London: Heinemann, 1967).

18   Cecil John Rhodes (1853-1902) was a British mining magnate and politician in southern Africa who served as Prime Minister of the Cape Colony from 1890 to 1896. An ardent believer in British imperialism, Rhodes and his British South Africa Company founded the southern African territory of Rhodesia (now Zimbabwe and Zambia), which the company named after him in 1895. He also put much effort towards his vision of a Cape to Cairo railway through British territory.

which 'had not received from Lobengula any authority to exercise such sovereign rights as are implied by setting up courts of justice, imposing fines and penalties, declaring what acts shall constitute crimes', and the like. The settlers, believing they were frustrated on every side, took the law into their own hands and Ranger gives the example of a man called Hudson who, on learning of theft from his stores in Mazoe, raided a local headman's kraal, burnt his huts and exacted a fine of five cattle.[19]

Little effort was made to conciliate the local people. The whites appear to have believed they would be invulnerable so long as they managed to instil fear. After the defeat and death of Lobengula in 1893, there was indiscriminate land and cattle grabbing in Matabeleland, facilitated by the company. Jameson gave away the land to 'various white adventurers'.[20] Rhodes' new Administrator, William Milton, found the situation 'sickening' but seemed powerless to control it.

So when the rising happened there was amazement, confusion and anger among the whites. And the missionaries were blamed for the part they were seen to play. W. A. Jarvis, an ally of Rhodes, wrote from Gweru in 1896 when the rising had started and white people, men and women – many of whom had been on good terms with the local people – were being killed, 'I hope the natives will be pretty well exterminated … Poor devils, one can't help being a bit sorry for them for they have of course been imposed upon by those wretched "witch doctors" and the beastly missionaries … teaching the nigger that he is as good as the white man. It won't do. The nigger has to be treated as a nigger the world over. They only become the most brutal scoundrels if you try to turn them into Christians.'[21]

The rising began in March and by April the *indunas* were threatening Bulawayo. There were two reasons for the early success of the rising. Though the king had died, the military and civil structure of the Ndebele nation survived. When the moment arrived, the *indunas* were able to draw on this enduring organisation to call up the regiments and surround the town. Ranger gives great emphasis to the second reason: the influence of the *Mwari* cult which proved to

---

19 Op cit., p. 57.
20 Op cit., p. 104.
21 Op cit.,p. 131.

be a religious and cultural bond not only for the Ndebele nation but for some of the Shona tribes from whom the Ndebele had learnt it. The late Lawrence Vambe, a Shona writer, tells us, 'During the period of (their) conquest (of the Rozwi Shona), the Ndebele learnt with astonishment that the Shona system of government and life generally were centred on a religious conception which accepted God as the maker of all creation ... they were so impressed ... that it became part of their own religious system. They called *Mwari, Mlimo*.'[22] The *Mlimo* priests 'made the rising much more formidable, not so much because they provided additional fighting men for the *impis* (regiments) ringing Bulawayo, but because they forced the whites almost everywhere else in Matabeleland onto the defensive and threatened to disrupt communications between Bulawayo and the outside world'.[23] But not all the Ndebele groups joined the rising – as we saw in our treatment of Empandeni mission where Fr Prestage advised the local chiefs not to join – and they received no support from either Khama of the Tswana (Botswana) or Lewanika of the Lozi (western Zambia). This lack of unity in resisting oppression was to become an enduring weakness during later attempts to resist white control in Rhodesia and it is still there in modern Zimbabwe. Opposition movements seem reluctant to unite.

The Shona also rose in June in the same year, 1896, and also took the whites totally by surprise. 'We had underrated the Mashona ... we were sitting on a smouldering fire and did not know it', wrote 'Wiri' Edwards, Native Commissioner of the Mrewa District.[24] At first the whites blamed the Ndebele for instigating this *Chimurenga*. But it soon became clear this was not true. 'The Shona have shown themselves capable of concerted action', admitted Marshall Hole, Resident Magistrate of Salisbury, in October 1896: '... the rebellion here is of a very different nature than in Matabeleland. Here we have a race who have never been conquered, never even been warred against'.[25]

There was much puzzlement as to how the Shona could achieve 'concerted action'. The paramount chiefs were normally in rivalry with

---

22 Vambe, p. 66.
23 Op. cit., p. 160
24 Op. cit., p. 191.
25 Op. cit., p. 196.

one another and, though they gained great power during the rising, it was hard to see how they achieved the unity they enjoyed for a while. The answer, once again, says Ranger, lay in their religion. While the *Mwari (Mlimo)* cult based on the Matopo shrine contributed to Ndebele cohesion, it had limited influence with the Shonas. What did count with the latter were the *masvikiro* (spirit mediums), of which there were two hierarchies, according to Michael Gelfand: the Chaminuka-Nehanda hierarchy of central and western Mashonaland, and the Mutota-Dzivaguru hierarchy of the north-east and east.[26] Ranger describes the activities of several mediums, of which the best known in Zimbabwean revolutionary memory are Nehanda and Kaguvi, both captured and executed at the end of the rising. These mediums exercised enormous power in co-ordinating action during the rising. Ranger quotes Joseph Chidziwa's *History of the Vashawasha* to show the influence of Kaguvi and also, revealingly, resistance to him. At first, they do not obey him but they later join in the struggle.[27]

Meanwhile in Matabeleland there was stalemate in the Matopos and Rhodes took his famous initiative to go unarmed to meet the *indunas*. For the first time, he listened and understood their complaints and the reasons for the rising. He made concessions, which infuriated the settlers and the local representatives of the imperial government in London. But Rhodes knew that Joseph Chamberlain, the Colonial Secretary, would back him, as Chamberlain was aware, his every move was being scrutinised by a constituency in England that concerned itself with justice for the conquered people of the empire. This group was often called, by friend and foe, after Exeter Hall in London where returning missionaries and left-leaning advocates for understanding subject people, were wont to meet. So the *indunas* would not be prosecuted for rebellion but would be given civic responsibilities and be salaried. As always it is the poor and weak who are the scapegoats and who suffer; individual Ndebeles, who had been urged to kill the whites by the *indunas* were arrested, tried and executed.

There was little Rhodes could do to return land and cattle to the Ndebele, as these had been allocated to the whites and it was beyond his power without huge outlays of money to repurchase them. Nyamanda, Lobengula's son – but not recognised as king

---

26 Ranger, p. 207.
27 NADA, IX, 1 (1964), Ranger, p. 217.

in his place – was prepared to testify in England in favour of continued Company rule in 1896, though Ranger points to the irony that he changed his mind by 1919 when he petitioned the British government to assume direct rule. Clearly the Ndebeles were not happy with what happened in the intervening period. But Matabeleland was devastated by the war; crops were destroyed and there was great hunger.[28]

In Mashonaland the war lasted to the end of 1897. Individual chiefs held out and the mediums kept up the pressure to resist. The Shona even attempted to revive the Rozvi dynasty in early 1897 as a unifying force. The Rozvi had ruled virtually the whole of what is now Zimbabwe from the collapse of the Mwene Mutapa confederacy in the sixteenth century up to the eighteenth century. The claimant to the title of *Mambo* (king) was identified as Mudzinganyama Jiri Muteveri and he was endorsed by Kaguvi and the Ndebele medium Mkwati. But the whites came to hear of the plan and it came to nothing. Yet the incident shows the potential seriousness of the Shona resistance. In the end, the war of attrition against one Shona paramount after another had its effect, and when Nehanda and Kaguvi were captured, the rising fizzled out.

The impact of the risings

After the risings Rhodes at last realised that the people had to be taken into account and Grey too understood what the Shona had been suffering and he grew in respect for a 'strong and daring foe'. He was not the only one to see the force of religion in the rising. After a visit to Chishawasha he was so impressed he wanted to extend widely the educational system he found there, which he could see was such a part of the missionary endeavour.

But if the leaders were more sympathetic, the settlers were more determined than ever to take matters into their own hands and they pressed hard for some say in the government of the colony. It was the whites who were now governed by fear and saw threats of new risings where there were none. Their response was to increase pressure for greater control of their own affairs. This was granted in 1898 when they were allocated four representatives on the new Legislative Council. The Company had five and there was also the Administrator

---

28 Ranger, p. 263.

and the Resident Commissioner. Though a minority at that time, it was clear that settler voices would carry weight and the move towards self-government, granted in 1923, was now set in motion. A French visitor wrote in 1913. 'What dominates all is a pre-occupation with the interests of the whites and the absence of a genuine social policy inspired by the interests of the blacks'.[29] And Fr Richartz wrote of debates in the Legislative Council in 1903, of 'a bitter hatred against natives and their protectors. I am so disgusted by the outburst of rude hatred against the natives that I am considering whether it is becoming of me to have anything further to do with men who are not ashamed to speak as some members did'.[30]

With the re-establishment of peace, or perhaps more accurately, the consolidation of the conquest of the Shona and Ndebele lands, the Jesuits realised there was deep antipathy among the older generation of the local people towards the white settlers and if they were to contribute to the building of a new society it would have to be with the young. They also realised that the BSAC, while running the colony in their own interests, gave the Jesuits the security and the freedom they needed to operate and develop.

While reliance on the colonial presence brought these advantages, it also brought an over-identification with those who made up that presence. This issue has already been discussed in our first chapter and we will have to return to it again. But we have to keep reminding ourselves that many Jesuits slipped easily into the world created by the settlers and took on their world-view. The degree to which this compromised their subsequent mission is impossible to determine. The colonial monolith that developed over the years was difficult to resist as it clawed its way into every aspect of the people's lives, be they white or black. Also the Jesuits were people of their time, as is often said, who were brought up to obey – I am not just thinking of Jesuit obedience – established authority. Mukonori puts it this way,

> Our Jesuit education was very strong in theory but, in the context of colonial Africa, it had one glaring omission. It taught absolute subservience to the authority of the state, not God and people in general … Africans were being trained to be docile and to follow

---

29 H. Rolin, *Les lois et l'administration de la Rhodésie*, quoted by Ranger, p. 337.
30 Quoted in Ranger, p. 343.

without question. I felt the need to counter this …[31]

Many of the Jesuits were not British and had to tread carefully during and after the two world wars when Germans, Austrians and Italians were on the back foot. Finally, this was the time before Vatican II with its 'opening to the world' and its proclamation of Justice with a capital J. Even as late as 1974 there were many Jesuits who felt uncomfortable with, and some who resisted, the teaching of the 32nd General Congregation which had stated clearly: 'The mission of the Society of Jesus today is the service of faith, of which the promotion of justice is an absolute requirement.'[32]

If the overriding consideration in the minds of the early Jesuits in the colonial period was that white rule had brought them the stability they needed to do their work, they did not accept the policies of the administration unquestioningly. Fr Richartz protested in 1901 that thirty-four Chishawasha residents had been taken away and forced to work for the government. The Chief Native Commissioner for Mashonaland responded that they had gone voluntarily but Richartz insisted, saying they had their own work to do.

Richartz further objected to the proposed quadrupling of the African Hut Tax, from 10s to £2. *The Rhodesian Times* of 23 December 1901, declared, 'it was a matter for the statesman not the clergyman to adjust'. It would not be the last time the Church was told to stay out of politics in Rhodesia – or Zimbabwe. Richartz objected in a public letter on 11 January 1902 and followed this up with a letter to W. H. Milton, the Administrator of the colony. Milton replied that he would be willing to make an exception of Chishawasha. Richartz was not satisfied and appealed to the government in London through its local representative, the Resident Commissioner, Sir Marshall James Clarke. The latter knew Chishawasha and supported Richartz in a letter to the High Commissioner in Cape Town. The whites in Rhodesia were furious with Richartz and launched an abusive attack on him in the Rhodesian Legislature. Mgr Richard Sykes, the Apostolic Prefect, told Richartz there was great annoyance at his opposition in the London office of the BSAC. In the end the tax was raised to £1, a partial victory for Richartz.

As we read of Richartz' efforts a hundred years later we remind

---
31 Mukonori, p. 60.
32 GC32, Decree 4, #2.

ourselves there was no African voice to defend African interests. Fr Fidelis Mukonori wrote of one of his earliest experiences in coming to Salisbury to apply to join the Jesuits in the 1960s. He stopped for refreshment at a shop on Second Street Extension and was told abruptly by the white girl serving, 'This is no place for you. You can go round to the back'. A verbal battle ensued with Mukonori growling at her, 'This is not your country'. But it was. They had conquered it and his father had told him so when Mukonori asked him why he had been unable to build the dam he planned: 'It's their country, son. They run the government. They won the war. To the victor go the spoils.'[33]

But the dominance of Chishawasha was passing as other missions grew. Besides, the Great War (1914-18) saw an end to support from Germany and the great drought of 1916 when the crops failed. 1918 was the worst year as Chishawasha was touched by the worldwide influenza epidemic and 151 people died. Fr Rea tells us that 'old men in the early 1960s, speaking of their memories and the stories they had heard from their parents, single out two outstanding events: the *Chimurenga* of 1896/7 and the flu of 1918; in comparison, two world wars left no lasting impression on them'.[34] Richartz is one of the great figures of the early Church in Zimbabwe. He laboured at Chishawasha for twenty-four years and earned the lasting gratitude of the people. Lawrence Vambe, in *An Ill-Fated People,* writes:

> The years between the end of the rebellion and the First World War were those of real partnership and fruitful cooperation between the VaShawasha people and the Jesuits at Chishawasha Mission. The defeat that my people had suffered and the care that they had enjoyed from the missionaries at such a difficult time had obviously much to do with this happy relationship. But from the oral evidence that was given by everybody, including my grandparents, there is no doubt that the one man who made this understanding possible was the Rev Father Richartz. They described him as a unique personality, in fact a saint, if ever there could be one in a white community composed mainly of reckless land-grabbers and spoilers in every sense of these words. He gave the tribe the stamina and the will to rise from the ashes

---

33 Mukonori, pp. 19-20.
34 Dachs and Rea, p. 61.

of defeat and to live in hope once again. By his devotion to their welfare and by his personal integrity, he convinced many of the VaShawasha people that the Church would liberate them from their own darkness and the injustice of white rule.[35]

The railways

It is not difficult to imagine the extraordinary impact of the railways on travel at the turn of the century. The decade that saw the tortuous journeys of the Jesuits in the 1880s was followed by one where efforts were made to improve on the ox-wagons. One quaint initiative was the importation of thirty-four camels from India. They were used in the sandy part of the country between Fort Victoria (Masvingo) and Selukwe (Shurugwi). 'All but one perished a few years later when they drank from a cyanide dam. The surviving camel lived out its final days at Chishawasha Mission.'[36]

The construction of railways in colonial Zimbabwe was due in large part to the work of George Pauling (1854-1919), whose family were associated with railway building for decades. Pauling came out from England in 1870s and by the 1890s was in a position to gain the contract to build great lengths of track in the interior of the sub-continent. The first train arrived in Bulawayo in 1897 and in Umtali (Mutare) from Beira in 1898. Bulawayo was linked to Salisbury in 1902. The link to the Congo was started in 1903, crossed the Victoria Falls in 1905 and was completed in 1909. The age of the ox-wagon was over. One dramatic indicator of the impact of the railway was that in the early 1920s, Fr Gerard Pfaehler, a Jesuit resident in Bulawayo, was able to make the 500 km journey to Hwange, which had about 100 Catholics working at the colliery, every two months. This must be a record distance for any outstation! With these improved methods of travel and of transporting goods, all the Jesuits needed were men and resources. The Jesuit provinces in Europe were ready to help with both.

---

35 Op cit., pp. 168-9.
36 J. Waters, *Urban Evolution Harare: A Photographic History* (Harare: New Zanj Publishing House, 2015), p. 61. Waters does not explain what a 'cyanide dam' is, but presumably some cyanide seeped into the camels' drinking water somehow!

Kutama (1912)

When he returned from Empandeni, Richartz applied the lesson he had learnt there of founding outstations. He responded to the request of some Christians, who had found shelter in Chishawasha during the uprising and later moved back to their homes in Kutama to the west, for a priest in their area. 'I am going there now with Br Puff,' wrote Richartz on 28 May 1912 and he marked out a site. Three outstations were established: besides Kutama, there was Murombedzi and Magaya, and Br Puff built a school at each place. Kutama was to be the birthplace of Robert Mugabe twelve years later.

Fr Jean-Baptiste Loubière was the first resident priest, arriving in 1914. He had already spent fifteen years in Mozambique, at Chipanga on the Lower Zambezi, before the Jesuits were expelled from all Portuguese territories in the revolution of 1910. He immediately applied himself to building the faith though 'industrial training' – a term that covered agricultural techniques, carpentry and building houses and bridges. In this he was warmly supported by the long-term Director of Native Development in Sinoia (Chinhoyi), Mr H. S. Keigwin, convinced 'that the government seriously desires the progress and welfare of the native people'. Keigwin sent Loubière a detailed questionnaire to ask him about what he was doing, seemingly with an eye to persuading the government to encourage his methods more widely. Loubière's exhaustive answers run to eight pages of the *Zambesi Mission Record*.[37] After recording the solid support of the prefect, Msgr Brown, he appeals to Keigwin for fencing to stop cattle destroying the crops. Loubière was a firm believer in 'Christian villages', a subject to be treated in a later chapter. In 1918 he launched this project, which was based on the Paraguayan 'reductions' in the seventeenth century, with twenty houses built of a quality that far exceeded what the people traditionally constructed. Today, the tone of his enthusiasm jars on the ear – 'the missionary has settled and means to live, in the midst of a barbarous people' – until you recall that Patrick used similar words when he came to live among the Irish in the fifth century.[38] Loubière held that 'the native has too much liberty', meaning that

---

37 ZMR, Vol. VI, No 92, pp. 399ff.
38 'I came to the Irish heathens to preach the Good News and put up with insults from unbelievers. I heard my mission abused, I endured many persecutions even to the point of chains...' Patrick, **Confessions**, pp. 34ff.

local people were not showing the same enthusiasm for work that he was showing. Their farming and herding methods were easy-going. They are 'degraded', take easily to drink, etc. Loubière seems to have wanted to compel the people to progress! But 'he managed to bring about a thoroughly Christian atmosphere' and carried on this work until his death in 1930. 'Though he never seemed in a hurry, things moved rapidly and in the right direction so long as he was around … He wanted a miniature Paraguay.'[39]

On 3 September that same year, Msgr Browne wrote a last letter to him in which he said, 'Kutama was the most important part of the Mission.' Fr Jerome (Jerry) O'Hea, who was so respected by the young Mugabe that he named the hospital at Kutama after him sixty years later, succeeded him. In 1921, Msgr Parry bought Rothwell Farm to provide for the needs of Kutama. In 1931 a new church was opened. It was built by Br Mathias Schönbrod and Br Joseph Göll. In 1939, the Marist Brothers arrived and took over the school and the Teacher Training College. There is a picture in the archives of nineteen brothers on the staff there in 1978.

Driefontein

Jan Engelbrecht, the Afrikaans hunter whom Fr Blanca had received into the Catholic Church in Tati in 1880,[40] had settled in the midlands on a farm he called Driefontein and he sold it to the Jesuits 'cheaply' in 1904. A mission was opened there in 1906 but the soil was poor and few people lived in the area. Yet it was to become a thriving mission. It was next door to Chirumanzi, a well-populated area and, following the Empandeni rather than the Chishawasha model, the Jesuits started outstations there in Hama in 1909 and Holy Cross in 1914. These would become missions on their own in due course.

At Driefontein the Jesuits taught the faith to their workers and the first group were baptised in 1908. Among them was Regis Chigwedere whose father had brought him from Wedza (Hwedza) to Chishawasha to be brought up as a Christian. Chigwedere then followed Fr Emil Schmitz to Driefontein where he became a devoted catechist. In time he attracted others to the mission. Chigwedere's son, also called Regis, later became one of the first priests in Zimbabwe and was still working

---

39 ZMR, Vol IX, No 131, p. 141.
40 De Wit to Weld, 14 July 1880, in Gelfand, p. 272.

in New Highfield, Harare, in the 1990s when I used to go there with the juniors[41] for Holy Thursday each year. By 1912, Schmitz and Br Joseph Lindner had built a church and Br Joseph Göll made the benches and did other carpentry work. Göll saw the need for trees and planted extensively at Driefontein. He was one of the first to develop forestry in the country. 'Words are inadequate to express the motive power behind it all, the springs of action. The devotion and zeal which inspire the Jesuit Brothers and Dominican Sisters to such endeavour is beyond all praise, nor is praise sought for or desired.' So wrote the Government Inspector of Schools in December 1924 about Driefontein.[42]

Fr Edward Collingridge took over from Schmitz in 1926 and 're-designed the whole lay-out of the mission; he pulled down buildings and erected others; he introduced electric light and driving power, cleared back the bush and drew up extensive plantations, created a model village which has influenced others in many parts of the territory, reintroduced many crafts and vitalised the training given, co-ordinated religious instruction at the outstations and developed a system of women helpers.'[43] The mission was handed over to the Bethlehem Mission Society in 1947.

Gokomere[44]

A mission was attempted at Mazondo, just north of Fort Victoria, in 1895, but the site was malarial. Three of the four Jesuits sent there died while at the mission or soon after they left. Few people lived in the area. It was closed in 1900. Prestage had suggested an alternative site, at Gokomere, and this was taken up in 1909. Granite was plentiful and the priests' house was built with it (1913) as was the church, completed in 1937. Br Patrick Mellon was the stonemason and, once again, Göll the carpenter. The governor of the colony, Sir Herbert Stanley, flew specially from Salisbury to witness the event. The Bethlehem missionaries took over Gokomere in 1940.

---

41 Young Jesuits who had completed their novitiate and were preparing to go to Kinshasa to study philosophy.
42 Dachs and Rea, p. 87.
43 Harold Jowitt, Director of African Education, quoted in *Letters and Notices*, 1935, 1,64, cf. Dachs and Rea, p. 88.
44 M. O'Reilly, *The Zambezi Mission and the Salisbury Vicariate*, 1939, unpublished MS, JAZ Box 40.

Schools

All denominations started schools. Prestage had tried to start a school when he lived in Tati in the early 1880s and later at Empandeni in 1887. The Jesuits started a school at Chishawasha in 1894, two years after they arrived. They really did not need the instructions from Fr General Martin in Rome but they were encouraging all the same: 'The most important thing of all', he wrote, 'is... education... no residence should be without a school, and if a school is impossible a residence should also be considered impossible'.[45]

In 1899 the government began to take an interest in African education and by 1901 Chishawasha was receiving a grant of 10 shillings per student per year. The school was among the first four 'first class' (a descriptive term, not a value judgement) schools in the country. By 1913 there were more than 130 boys and 146 girls at Chishawasha's schools. By 1928, 43 per cent of all first class schools were Catholic. The Jesuit schools were supported by the Dominican, Precious Blood and Notre Dame de Namur sisters, who contributed greatly to their success. The Jesuits concentrated on first class schools which were boarding and therefore more expensive to run but which gave good results. This was the situation by 1928:

	1st Class	2nd Class	3rd Class
Catholic	16	26	138
Anglican	6	11	213
Methodist (Wesley)	2	3	189
Methodist (American)	6	5	132
Dutch Reformed	7	7	322

Source: 'Southern Rhodesia, Report of Director of Education ...1928', quoted by Dachs and Rae, p. 100.

By the late 1920s the need for systematic training of teachers became urgent not only for the obvious reasons of quality education but because the government was pegging its grants according to teachers' qualifications. Around the turn of the century the Prefect, Msgr Sykes, was cautious about employing catechists as teachers. In a reply to a request for this from Fr Boos, he felt it was asking too much of new converts. So, apart from outstanding individuals like

---

45 Martin to Sykes, 1896, Jesuit Archives, Harare, quoted in Dachs and Rea, p. 95.

Chigwedere, already mentioned, and Umjemhlope in Empandeni who started a school in Embakwe, the recruitment of teachers and catechists was haphazard. Sykes, as he came to the end of his time as prefect in 1919, regretted the lack of progress. 'The success of an out-school depends on the teacher and the catechist even more than on the priest.'[46]

In 1920, at a Jesuit Missionary Conference in Bulawayo, with Msgr Parry, the new prefect, and twenty-one other priests, Fr William Withnell proposed setting up a Teacher/Catechist Training School. This was agreed and in 1921 the school was opened at Driefontein. But few attended and resources were scarce and so the venture ended in failure in 1923. Part of the problem was that students wanted to be teachers but not catechists. At the same time as the Church was failing to provide teacher training the government was determined to improve the level of African education and set up a department with this aim in view. One of its main policies was to eliminate ineffective schools by withholding grants.

One of the likely reasons for inaction on the part of the Catholic Church was the sudden death of the prefect, Edward Parry, in 1922. He had been asked by Fr General in Rome to inquire into the deaths of so many Jesuits in the new Luangwa mission across the Zambezi and he decided to make the difficult journey himself, only to reach Katondwe in a terrible state and die there of the dreaded disease. 'The tragedy caused quite a stir in the Zambezi Mission and was seen as an outstanding, if unwise, devotion to duty and to the wishes of the Jesuit general.'[47]

It was up to his successor, Msgr Robert Brown, to try again to start a school for teacher/catechists, which he did, at Kutama in 1926. He was helped by a visit of the English provincial, Fr William Bodkin, who strongly emphasised the need for well-trained teacher/catechists. By this he meant first of all moral training as well as the subjects they would teach. The notion of giving 'moral training' to people today conjures up a narrow emphasis on rules, especially with regard to a person's sexual life. But 'morality' in earlier times meant the holistic training of a person, covering the whole range of attitudes of a Christian life based on the Beatitudes. English Jesuits born in the

---

46 Quoted in Dachs and Rea, p. 103.
47 Murphy, p. 168.

nineteenth century could not but be influenced by the Victorian ethos best summed up by the priorities of the most renowned headmaster of the century, Thomas Arnold of Rugby, who said, in the rather contorted language of the time, 'He, therefore, who really wishes to improve public education would do well to direct his attention to this point and to consider how there can be infused into a society of boys such elements as, without being too dissimilar to coalesce with the rest, shall yet be so superior as to raise the character of the whole.'[48] Bodkin also recommended that no catechist should be allowed to teach unless he had trained at Kutama. Mission superiors should select – and financially support – students to attend the new Teacher Training School.

A further boost to the prospects of success at Kutama was a letter from Pope Pius XI in 1926, *Rerum Ecclesiae,* which stressed the importance of catechists. His predecessor, Benedict XV, had already called, seven years earlier, for the formation of indigenous clergy in mission lands and this letter of Pius seems to have been a recognition of the need for a preliminary step.

Yet, in spite of this encouragement, Kutama did not flourish and Msgr Brown wrote a strong letter to all the houses of the prefecture insisting that Kutama Training School must be supported. African indifference and opposition must be overcome. There was no question: teacher training was essential. If the Church did not take it seriously, they would soon be squeezed out of education altogether by the government withholding grants. It took this 'severe crisis and grave threat... to rouse the Church from its lethargy'.[49] By 1929 the situation improved and by 1931 there were sixty-nine students. Success was long overdue. The 1930 report of the Director of African Education 'showed that Catholic schools had the smallest percentage of qualified teachers'.[50] In 1930, 25 per cent of the American Methodist teachers were qualified and 52 per cent of the Wesleyans in comparison to just 9 per cent of the Catholics.

Huge emphasis would now be paid to schools and mission reports feature details about teachers, the curricula and salaries,

---

48 S.J. Curtis, *History of Education in Great Britain* (London: University Tutorial Press, 1948), p. 146.
49 Dachs and Rae, p. 106.
50 Op cit., p.106.

student attendance and the state of buildings. Priests who wanted to devote themselves to directly pastoral work among the people, found themselves appointed schools' managers. Fr Joseph Friedrich (Freddy) lamented that, 'for 21 years I had to do a work I did not like; managing out schools, pressing teachers to improve their work and enforcing government regulations'.[51] At this point in Dachs and Rea there is a renewed lament 'that all this went on at the expense of a more profound enquiry on missionary methods, accommodation of African custom or belief, the adoption of a wider pastoral activity or the grave liabilities and responsibilities that attached to so heavily institutionalised missionary activity'.[52]

The thirties became the golden age of mission schools, and Hipler lists the foundations of out schools from Kutama: Murombedzi (1912), Chikambi (1913), Njeri (1918), Karigamombe (1920), Kawandera (1935), Mhandu (1947), Sinoia (1948), Urungwe (1949), Norton (1951), Katsvamutima (1951), Mareverwa (1951), Sipolilo (St Edwards) (1952) and the list continues. Some of these are considerable distances from Kutama. All denominations were doing the same, and it was from these schools that the nationalist leaders and the professionals came. Robert Mugabe, for instance, was a graduate of Kutama Teacher Training School.

---

51 At his Golden Jubilee on 15 September 1976, Friedrich looked back over his years and this was one of his reflections. His personal file in JAZ.

52 Dachs and Rea, p. 107. The present writer allows himself a bit of redaction criticism here. Anthony Dachs, in his preface to their book, gives credit for the lion's share of the task to Fr Rea, claiming only to contribute comments on 'missionary methods, the evolution of pastoral techniques, the raising of the local church and the modern confrontation of the Catholic Church and the Rhodesian state'. Having known Fr Rea a little and been awed by his meticulous historical teaching and writing, I have wondered how he had been able to stand back from the Jesuit enterprise and ask questions about it. The answer is obvious. It is not he but Dachs, a layman, who had the perspective to do this. Cf. p. xii.

4

Growth and Questions

> *The Administrator, Earl Grey, before the whole court told Fr Prestage he was a liar, all missionaries were, it was their trade.*
>
> 'Empandeni Interlude, 1899-1903', *Journal of Sr Josephine Bullen SND, 28* December 1899, p. 46.

For the first sixty years of the Jesuit presence in what was then Southern Rhodesia there was a steady growth in the number of rural mission stations and also in their size and activities. It is neither possible nor necessary to describe all of these efforts but some can be singled out as broadly representative.

Musami (1915)

Fr Patrick (Pat) Lewis, who did so much to build up the order and accessibility of the Jesuit archives in Harare, lists St Paul's Musami mission as starting in 1915. Initial visits did start then but the effective date of the founding of the mission is 1923 when Fr Charles Daignault took up residence and made preparations for building a house, a school and a church. There is a picture in the Zambezi Mission Records[1] of an old church/school building that he found there which was already dilapidated and must have been built some sometime after 1915 when the first contact was made from Chishawasha. Daignault, the nephew of Fr Alphonse Daignault who was the third Superior of the Zambezi

---
1 Vol VII, p. 233.

Mission from 1887-91, wrote in September 1924 of having baked 125,000 bricks. The boys did the digging and the girls the mixing. The following year Br Joseph Linder[2] arrived to supervise the building and soon after Br Anthony Puff[3] came to put on the roof. Br Philip Hogg[4] had a background in engineering and did all the metal work and plumbing at Musami in Daignault's time. He kept the cars and lorries on the road and devised a filtering system for the swimming pool.

By Easter 1924, there were already more than a hundred baptisms and sixteen out schools. But it was hard to persuade parents to allow their sons to go to school and the early missionaries had to give them presents of blankets to attract them. By the end of the 1930s all the out schools, except one, were closed because of lack of funds. In 1941, there was only that one school, Chemhondoro, left. Fr Michael Hannan became superior that year and it is a tribute to him that eighteen out schools were flourishing by 1949. He also opened a homecraft school for girls in 1946. In 1951 the average age in Standard 5 and 6 was 23 years. By 1956 the average had dropped to 17 years. The pressure was on for secondary education and permission was granted for Fr Finnieston to open Form I in 1957. The new dormitories for the secondary school were built by Mr Chinyani and Mr Mukozhiwa and the primary school was for day pupils from then on. In 1959 Hannan started a teacher training course but the ministry tried to back out of the permission granted, which, fortunately, was in writing. So they went ahead.

The Dominican sisters arrived in 1925 to help in the school at the mission and, in time, in the clinic. By 1946, when Sr Kiliana Müller arrived, the sisters were still living in basic quarters. She later wrote:

> I was the first nurse ever sent there. The sisters' house had two big rooms, a bedroom with four beds divided by curtains ... I had a microscope which I kept in my little bedroom cupboard ... I used to go a lot to the villages to visit the sick. I was very thin, but very strong and I had a good bicycle.[5]

---

2   Born in Danschwitz in 1866 and died at St Barbara's in 1945.
3   Born in Moreshausen, Germany in 1861 and died in Chishawasha in 1939.
4   Born in Charlton-on-the Moors near Manchester in 1902 he had to return to the UK when he contracted Parkinson's disease. He had been 29 years in Rhodesia. He died in 1967.
5   Sr Kiliana, August 1990, Box 153/1.

There were only twenty-five beds in the hospital in 1951 but five years later a fifty-bed block was built. In 1960 another eighty-bed block was added and by this time there was a resident doctor.

It is easy to list the progress but it is not difficult to sense the fragility of those years where every step forward had to be fought for and resources were always limited. In 1957 the boy scouts came up with a bob-a-job scheme by which they would dig up a plot to make a swimming pool. It took three years off and on till they reached rock which provided a natural base for the pool and ended up with a 75' by 50' pool for £600. A government engineer's estimate for a pool of similar size was £12,000.

The mission became independent of Chishawasha in 1927. In 1936, four sisters of the newly founded Little Children of Our Blessed Lady (LCBL) congregation arrived to join the mission staff. There were so many boys finishing Standard 6 by 1953 it was decided to start a building and carpentry course. Not only did these students help the expansion of the mission, they went on to find employment in town. The value of this training was felt when the government closed its own industrial schools in 1964.

By 1951 the pressure on the wells to provide enough water was felt but the mission had to wait until 1960 before a two-inch pipe was laid to the river one and a quarter miles away.

The 'Jeep' years

Fr Anthony Davis, otherwise known as 'Jeep', became superior of St Paul's, Musami, in 1952 and stayed there for fifteen years. He earned his name from his practical, rather than his intellectual, abilities. Mark Hackett,[6] who was there at the time, tells us that the new superior decided St Paul's would be the most renowned mission in the country and would achieve this status through football. To attract players of quality to an obscure rural mission he set out to provide them with an education or a livelihood. Chief Mangwende was enthusiastic; it would make his area better known. The chief mobilised the people to provide local bricks and gum trees for expanding the mission and its outstations. Overseas donors were amazed buildings could go up so

---

6   Mark Hackett was born in Bournemouth, England, in 1936, and joined the Society in 1952 when just 16! In his retirement he has written comprehensively about his time at Musami, Makumbe and St George's and I have drawn considerably on his accounts.

cheaply, and Jeep was able to buy a seven-ton lorry with the change from one of their donations.

He set up a building and carpentry school to provide the skills needed under two instructors, the already mentioned Mr Mukozhiwa and Mr Chinyani, who were, of course, also well-known later for their prowess on the football field. Ability to play football became a factor in being accepted for these courses. The Junior Certificate course, the teacher training and the secondary school – all were seen as investments for the soccer team, while also enabling the mission to provide education for the local people beyond primary level. While soccer seemed to infuse every activity, Jeep did not neglect to provide a hospital and domestic science course.

The emphasis on soccer and Jeep's use of mission funds to promote the game did not please everyone. Fr Henry Wardale, who was in charge of the secondary school in the early 1960s, felt that,

> The football at Musami is a standing joke in the mission at large; to me, it is not funny. The yearly expenditure on football is a disgrace. The extravagance that is lavished on the game and those who play it is wildly out of place considering the circumstances of the school and the reserve and the country as a whole. It is interesting that the boys, as far as I can tell, feel no loyalty to the team; they know that it wastes money that should be spent on them …[7]

In the same letter, Henry writes, 'the impression others get is that superiors are afraid to do anything against Fr Davis'. But Terence Corrigan[8] was well aware of what was happening. As early as 1959, when he was fresh to his post as Superior, he had written to Michael Hannan,

> I quite realise that material improvement and success is always attended by the great danger that a reputation for sport or scholastic success, once obtained, can become the be all and end all of our efforts.[9]

Yet it did take time before Jeep was finally moved. In 1967, Fr Edward Callaghan, who succeeded him, told the archbishop, 'The

---

7   Wardale to Corrigan, 7 May 1963, Box 153/2.
8   Mission superior, 1958-64.
9   Corrigan to Hannan, 1 April 1959, Box 153/2.

necessary qualification to be a teacher in this school is ability to play football.'¹⁰ And, underlining Wardale's complaint, he goes on to 'suspect a good deal of the mission money is being directed into the (football) club'. The departure of Jeep led to the halt in the favoured status of football and the game was reduced to a similar level to what it was and is in any other secondary school. A writer in *The Standard* in 2013 lamented the passing of the glory of St Paul's FC: 'The stadium that launched the careers of Nxumalo, Nechironga and George Shaya is now an eyesore', and he accompanied his report with photos of grass taking over what were the tiers of seats and the VIP stand.[11]

But looking back, Mark Hackett felt St Paul's become known throughout the country for its soccer team and this became an important element in the development of the local area.[12] In Rhodesia, there was an annual holiday on the two days of 'Rhodes and Founders' and these were conveniently close to the feast of Saints Peter and Paul. All the schools under the mission came together for sports and competitions – a mini-Olympics – and a special Mass was celebrated with them at the grotto on the Sunday. This event pushed out the name 'Musami' to the margins as it, and the football team of course, became widely known as 'St. Paul's'. The mission became the centre of Mangwende. The team was one of the best and won the national championships in 1964, '66 and '67, drawing widespread support, though, as mentioned, not seemingly at the mission itself. Jeep was 'owner', manager and coach, though his coaching methods would raise eyebrows today. He was not beyond using a sjambok in his passion for results. Jeep hoped he could charge local people to watch their team play and a stadium was built to make this possible![13] He also built a club house to attract people to socialise on the mission. Hackett approached him one day for a donation for the secondary school library. 'No money', Jeep said. The next day a bulldozer arrived to construct the stadium! It was to have a covered stand for the VIPs, changing rooms and a tunnel leading onto the field for the players to make a grand entrance.

But St Paul's was not only football. The pastoral work in the

---

10 Callaghan to Markall, January 1967, Box 153/3.
11 *The Standard*, 25 August 2013.
12 M. Hackett, *Letters and Notices*, 100, p. 501.
13 He later tried to build another stadium on the city boundary when he was at Chishawasha but this was not a success.

outstations, which was combined with running and supervising the out schools, moved ahead. Fr Raymond Kapito, in the years between his ordination in 1956 and his entering the Jesuits, was active and there is a slide show in the Jesuit archives showing his work. He would leave the mission at 5.30 in the morning and visit an outstation such as Rota, which is shown on the slides, where he would hear 40-50 confessions before celebrating the Eucharist. We remind ourselves that this was in the days before the Second Vatican Council when everyone – priests and people – had to be fasting from midnight. He would then spend much of the day going from class to class teaching catechism in the 400-pupil school.[14]

Jeep liked to build big. He built an excessively wide dormitory and a roller for the soccer field that was so big it could hardly be moved. It was eventually buried in a large hole. He built a church so large it could hold the huge crowds that came for the celebration of Peter and Paul. He was developing the mission fast, too fast for the archbishop who had ultimate responsibility and would have to maintain what his maverick pastor was doing. Kutama College, where the Marist brothers had established a fine school, was strict with its pupils and many were expelled. Jeep gave them a home at St Paul's where they often did well and he felt he knew how to run a school. He was upset when the decision was made to start St Ignatius College. The Jesuits should have upgraded St Paul's instead.

Joe O'Neill[15] helped Hannan start the Teacher Training College (TTC) at Musami. Brian Porter joined later. In 1970 Hackett, now a priest, was made principal. The TTC had a good relationship with the people in the district where they did their teaching practice – a relationship the secondary school did not have as many of the students were foreign to the area, coming from urban centres.

On 1 January 1971, the government decided to take over the running of the schools which it was already subsidising with teachers' salaries. This signalled the end Jeep's 'Olympics'. School strikes,

14 JAZ, Box 506. Kapito was the first Zimbabwean Jesuit priest and he had grown up in Mutoko where he was moved by listening to a priest visiting his home. This was probably Fr Charles Shackles (1898-1958). He wanted to attend the school the priest was starting but his father told him to look after the cattle. After some consultation, Kapito herded the cattle in the open spaces in the morning and then took them to school in the afternoon. He sat at the entrance to the classroom with one eye (and ear) on the priest or teacher and the other on the cattle.

15 A scholastic who left the Society in 1963.

obliquely aimed at the white enemy, also occurred at St Paul's. Although missionaries were working for the local people, they were white and therefore associated in part with the government. Mission school students reacted in the only way they could when calls, emanating usually from the university, came to rise up. They rebelled against the only whites available – the missionaries. On one occasion the secondary students put the TTC students' bedding under the showers. The latter were seen to be co-operating with the government as they looked forward to employment under it. Mark Hackett and Gussie Donovan told each student to donate one blanket to the TTC students for the night and the matter ended there.

Fr Desmond (Gussie) Donovan, the mission superior who followed Callaghan, was a prickly character who did not accept fools gladly. In the tense situation beginning to develop his brusqueness could easily be misinterpreted. He was fond of guns and would hunt baboons and shoot the frogs in the pond with a pistol. A perennial problem on Missions was the invasion of pigs, cattle and goats from the villages which would break into the mission gardens and wreak havoc. Compensation was supposed to be made for the damage caused, but in fact never was. The temptation was to take the matter into one's own hands and shoot a pig or send cattle to a pound where they needed to be redeemed. Even the killing of scapegoats, which abounded on the local rocky outcrops, might be viewed adversely. The issue could quickly be seen as one of oppression of the locals by a powerful foreigner which at that time was a particularly explosive matter. Gussie was later moved to Makumbe where he was killed taking communion to a sick person. The reason for his murder is not clear, but it might have been merely that he was in the wrong place at the wrong time and not in any way connected with his use of guns.

In time the mission was connected to the national grid which meant that the pump at the river, which supplied the mission with water, could now be powered from the grid and replace the diesel engine that had been there before.

When the government took over the schools in 1971 the mission had 6,552 students in its out schools, just over half of whom were boys and two thirds of whom were Catholic. There were also 435 in secondary, and it was at this time that Donovan built the science laboratories.

Mark Hackett makes a general comment about those years: 'There was never any money for pastoral work as such in our missions. The salaries we earned, especially as managers of the schools, were supposed to make this work possible. We taught Mondays to Saturdays in the classroom and laboured in the outstations on Sundays. Finnieston used to miss his Monday classes quite often as he was so exhausted when he got back on Sunday night.'

The approach of war

Pastoral work continued during the war years and this meant the missionaries were known to the local people and so to the guerrillas. Fr Christopher Shepherd-Smith was devoted in his rounds of the outstations. But there were incidents. When the students at St Albert's Mission, Mount Darwin, were abducted in 1973 and later escaped, they were sent to other missions to complete their exams and one was Musami. The Jesuits at Musami listened to the German Jesuits who came with them. The latter were less enthusiastic about the direction the liberation struggle was taking. Some of them had first-hand experience of living under Communism, an ideology the guerrillas seemed to espouse.

A further incident was the murder of two School of Social Work students who were doing research near the Nyagui River and came under the suspicion by the guerrillas of being government agents.

The Jesuits became aware of the infiltration of the area (Mangwende) by ZANLA forces and it was inevitable they would reach the mission at some stage. There were stories of *pungwes* where people were compelled to say, 'Down with Christ!' The Marxism avowed by ZANLA and the experience of the German Jesuits led many to expect the worst. Shepherd-Smith, who had experienced the Mau Mau as a boy on a farm in Kenya, began to hear nocturnal noises and Conway and others would talk about what would happen when the guerrillas came. With his familiarity of the times of the 'troubles' in his native Ireland perhaps, Conway expected the worst. 'One day they will come for us just as we are,' he used to say. School inspectors embarrassed the missionaries by arriving armed and expecting hospitality when, to the children on the mission, the ZANLA guerrillas were heroes. Children's art always showed friendly soldiers with AK assault rifles.

6 February 1977

On 6 February, a woman came to the mission and cried, 'I see blood. I see blood. Why do you want to die? You'll all be killed.' But she was ignored.

Mark Hackett, then superior of the mission, was on leave at the time St Paul's became known to the whole world through the news of the massacre of seven missionaries, on 6 February 1977. He returned immediately and found all evidence of the shooting had been removed and the place of the shooting had been cleaned up. Dunstan Myerscough, who had survived the firing squad, and Dennis Adamson, who had been at a teacher's house, were the survivors along with Sr Anna, who had remained in her room saying she was too old. Those who died had been lined up and shot on the main road through the mission. They were Jesuits Martin Thomas, Christopher Shepherd-Smith and John Conway, together with Dominican Srs Magdala Lewandowski, Joseph Wilkinson, Ceslaus Stiegler and Epiphany Schneider. All were white missionaries and killed apparently for that reason.

The passing of time does not seem to have convincingly answered the question of who the killers were. On 15 December 2019, I had a conversation with Fidelis Mukonori who had shown great courage during the war in regularly visiting war zones. He told me,

i. He had been to Musami about two days before the shooting and had discovered that the ZANLA guerrillas had not been to the mission to introduce themselves as they always did when they reached a new area.

ii. The *pungwes* in the district could not have been ZANLA because they did not invite any members of the mission to be present, something ZANLA was in the habit of doing. So, the implication was the *pungwes* were called by Selous Scouts pretending to be ZANLA.

iii. The killers spared Fr Myerscough knowing he did not speak Shona and would be likely, from his background, to conclude the killers were 'terrorists', the Rhodesian name for the guerrillas. This is precisely what Myerscough did.

iv. A 'yellow French car', which had been seen at Bindura where the Selous Scouts were trained, was spotted arriving and leaving a place near Musami that night.

v. It was quite safe to go to Musami after the killings as the Selous Scouts had withdrawn and ZANLA had not yet arrived.

vi. The local people were unwilling to believe the killings were the work of ZANLA. They continued to attend church, something they would not do if a local ZANLA group had been responsible for the killings.

vii. Fr Pascal Slevin, a Franciscan working in the Hwedza area, was told by the ZANLA forces close to the mission that they had sent guerrillas to investigate the issue and found it was not them.

While these points indicate a convergence of probabilities they do not amount to overwhelming proofs.

Henry Wardale, who became Superior of the Salisbury Mission soon after the killings, was told by an army officer that the markings on the cartridges made by the rifles of a group they had killed near Nyamutumbu School matched those found at Musami. Mark Hackett comments that, 'As no use was made of this information for political reasons there are no strong reasons for doubting it.'

So, it seems there is no solid consensus about who was responsible for the murder of the seven missionaries and no one, over the past forty-four years, has come forward to admit responsibility.

For those living on the mission, the events were so painful they were not talked about and it was only much later that any attempt was made to reconstruct and understand what really happened.

The bullet holes in the church roof were initially thought to be part of the incident but probably relate to a later incident when there was a gun battle at the mission.

The funeral of the seven was held at the Dominican convent in Salisbury and Fr Isidore Chikore preached. He placed responsibility for the deaths squarely on the shoulders of government as the inevitable result of their policies. Several white Catholics present got up and walked out at these words.

In this charged atmosphere it is astonishing to read in the house diary for St Paul's of the Catholic Youth Association, run from Silveira House, holding a congress at the mission for 250 young people in June 1977, five months after the killing of the seven missionaries. And the agriculture co-operative movement, also run from Silveira, continued to operate. In July there was even a music course at the mission for sixty people.

ZANLA at Musami

On one of his visits after the killings, Henry Wardale came to the mission when the security forces were there. They said they knew the Jesuits were in contact with the guerrillas and they asked them to persuade the guerrillas to 'come onside' and accept the 'Internal Settlement'.[16] The Jesuits refused. At that time they had not yet been in touch with the guerrillas. And even if they had, they did not believe in the proposed settlement and to try to sell it to the guerrillas would be to invite their own death. Perhaps surprisingly, the officer in command accepted this.

It was soon after this incident with the security forces that Mark had to inform Henry Wardale that ZANLA had indeed been in touch.

> One afternoon I was paying a visit to the hospital when I was approached by a man, well-dressed and with a large wide brimmed hat. 'I am Happy Trigger, the local ZANLA commander. Do you like beer?' I replied that I did and he replied, 'I will have a crate sent around this evening.' And so began a relationship with the freedom fighters in [which] parties and alcohol were to play a large part. ... 'the walls of the Jesuit lounge were lined with AK rifles and rocket launchers, while we and the guerrillas danced to Thomas Mapfumo records and drank beer and brandy long into the night. This easy social relationship with ZANLA helped us to feel less threatened by the situation as we knew we were trusted.

'On only one occasion,' Mark says,

> 'were we invited out to a *pungwe*. These meetings were held at night to encourage confidence in eventual victory. This one was held in Jeep's huge football stadium. Everyone from the surrounding villages seemed to be there and food was being prepared on the spot. We were feted as honoured guests, brought food by the local village girls, and the people were told that these

---

16 This was an agreement between the Rhodesian government and three nationalist leaders inside the country. The proposals did not have the support of the people and met fierce opposition from the guerrillas. While it confused many and may have delayed a final settlement, it could also be argued that it prepared the settler community for eventual majority rule.

varungu (Europeans) were friends of the revolution. It was clearly an attempt to show us that we were not just men in the middle, but committed to the new Zimbabwe. I was once told that, like them, I must be prepared to die for the cause.'

Nigel Johnson SJ[17] was told something similar, but by the security forces, on another occasion. He was told he could be hanged for what he was doing. He was quite shaken by the experience.

Meanwhile the guerrilla visits increased and there were demands for 'shopping'. Nigel wrote in the house diary that Denis Adamson helped enormously.

> He is the greatest asset we have in dealing with (the guerrillas) since his Shona is fluent and he is able to refuse some of their demands while maintaining their friendship. But it is a dangerous business. He was stopped on the road to Marandellas [Marondera] one day by a group of fully armed guerrillas with a lot of bead necklaces on and was told, 'you are a prisoner of the ZANLA forces'. He managed to drop the names of a number of guerrilla comrades saying he was a close friend of theirs 'so I'm in good hands'. The encounter ended with their drinking beer together and the guerrillas putting down their weapons to help push his car which would not start.[18]

Mark recounts other dangerous moments often in a matter-of-fact way.

> School life went on in as normal a way as possible. We were concerned at the beginning of term we might be asked to donate the school fees to the war effort and have to run the school without them. We did not collect the fees the day the students arrived as we usually did, but the next morning and then we dashed into town to bank them. One day I placed all this money in a bag on the saddle of my motorcycle only to find the bag gone while on the way. I made my way back and, just beyond Chemhondoro, was greeted by a woman. After the greetings she asked, '*Ko baba, makarasa begi here?*' (Father, have you lost your bag?) and I was given the unopened bag.

---

17 Born in 1945, Nigel entered the Society of Jesus in 1968 after qualifying as a dentist. He expanded his medical skills during the war to assist many of the emergencies that arrived at St Paul's hospital.

18 Musami House diary, 26 June 1978, JAZ, Box 153.

While Mark was concerned with the school, Nigel was concerned with the hospital. He had spent some time in an Accident and Emergency unit in Glasgow during his training and seen plenty of injuries. When a young man was presented to him with an abdominal wound with an unlikely explanation, Nigel told him that he could see the entry and the exit wounds caused by a bullet. The man admitted to being a guerrilla and had been shot from a helicopter. The wound was full of dirt and Nigel told him he must go to hospital in Harare or he would die. This was out of the question and Nigel had to treat him. The security forces, tipped off by an informer, came to search the mission for him. The nurses at the hospital were warned they were coming and quickly put a *dhuku* (head scarf worn by women) on his head and placed him in the labour ward. He escaped detection.

The end of the war

As the war progressed the strain on the guerrillas and on the people on the mission increased. The likelihood of an accident when drunken guerrillas were handling lethal weapons increased. Nigel warned them about this but it was not taken in good part and may have contributed to the decision to leave the mission. Archbishop Patrick Chakaipa and the Jesuit provincial, Henry Wardale, kept a close watch and decided it would soon be time for the missionaries to withdraw. There had been too many deaths already.

After the Internal Settlement, referred to above, the pro-government auxiliary forces, led by Bishop Abel Muzorewa, complicated the situation by coming to the mission. It was soon clear who were the genuine guerrillas and who were these government-sponsored ones. In April 1979, the 'real' (ZANLA) guerrillas came to the address the students and told them how much the mission was doing to help the cause. On 24 April, Nigel was asked to take a parcel to the city and he replied that if it was war material he could not do so. They did not insist. The next day a bomb went off in Salisbury. Then a landmine exploded in the early morning on the tarmac road the mission used to go to Bhora, the nearest small town where they could buy supplies. Nigel wrote, 'in future we will travel later in the morning'.

On 9 May, a new guerrilla group appeared and held a cocked pistol to Br Adamson's head. The next day a hundred students and staff were abducted from the mission because, it was said, they were in danger of being coerced into joining the auxiliaries of Muzorewa. They did not go very far and many came back to the mission or sought refuge in town. But the confused situation continued, and on 11 May 1979 it was decided to withdraw the European missionaries, sisters and priests as the scope for a fatal misunderstanding was too great.

Fr Chitehwe and Br James Paul, a Jesuit brother, kept the mission going during the months that led up to independence and Fr Gerald (Gerry) McCabe took over as superior soon after. But he was soon needed elsewhere and Fr Nigel Johnson returned to take over responsibility for the mission in August 1980. The issues he had to deal with were very different. They were searching for teachers and accepted a teacher from Canada who turned out to be a fraud with criminal record!

Independence

Fr Michael Chitehwe was transferred by the archbishop to Murewa where a new mission was being opened. Br Joseph Mandaza came to do pastoral work but found the people very different from those he was used to on the commercial farms. They were less pliant and Joe could not get their measure. He had health problems and was weakened by persistent diarrhoea and went into depression. But he gradually picked up and 'started taking life more easily'[19] Another problem was when a certain Mr Chikanga came to sniff out witches. He caused a lot of fear and uncertainty for a time until the new government stepped in and silenced him.

In the post-independence years St Paul's Musami faced the problems that were common to all missions and by the time the Millennium magazine was produced in 2000 it was a well-equipped and well-functioning school. The writers in the magazine reflect confidence and pride in the achievements of the school in the previous seventy-five years. Fr Wolfgang Abeler, a practical man who spent most of his missionary life in the Chinhoyi diocese, built a 'dedicated' water system at the mission. There is now one reservoir for the girls, one for the boys, one for the hospital and so forth. It was a simple but brilliant way of making people conscious of how much water they are using. The girls are often the first to finish their water and have to come begging with buckets to the boys. Need one say more? Fr Stephen

---

19   House diary, 1982.

Silungwe, who was also superior of the mission, adds 'there is one main water plant were water is treated when it is pumped from the Shavanhohwe River. Abeler was also instrumental; installing tanks for the Pedro Arrupe Centre, the high school, primary School, hospital and houses for the workers.'

Musami has received considerable treatment both because, apart from the unusual character of Jeep, it was a 'typical' mission in its growth and development and because of its experience during the war. Yet, it was only one of the missions the Jesuits were committed to.

Mhondoro (1925)

St Michael's Mission, Mhondoro, is sixty miles south-west of Harare. One date for its founding is 1913, meaning Fr Richartz went there from Chishawasha and founded an outstation. The 1914-18 war prevented any German missionaries moving about so it was not until 1916 that Fr Burbridge paid a follow-up visit. Michael Mhishi, of whom more shortly, went as resident teacher and catechist in 1922 and Burbridge kept up his visits once a year until, in 1925, Fr William Withnell took up residence there. This last date is the more generally accepted one for the founding of the mission. Fr Charles Daignault came two years later to replace him.

How often that phrase, 'founding a mission', occurs. It is repeated so frequently in the story of the Jesuits in Zimbabwe, and missionaries everywhere in Africa, that one can pass over what it meant. Often the man and some companions would walk to a new area to which a chief had invited him and he would search for a suitable spot near water and far from the fly. They would put up a pole and mud hut where they would shelter until they could put up something more solid. A school, a church and a residence would follow as soon as possible and gradually the mission would grow. But the beginning must have been hard. The warmth of welcome would have eased the struggle and someone like Michael Mhishi would have been a great help. Fr Pendlebury did a report on the mission in 1937 and found most of the buildings 'primitive and untidy'. 'No account books have been kept ... and there are no title deeds.'[20] The income, from a government grant for the school, was £375 a year and they also made £175 from the mill. There was little

---

20 JAZ, Box 44/2.

production from the land, and bills were irregularly paid.

Mhishi later became Chief Chivero and was interviewed. He spoke of five chiefs who moved from Guru Uswa in the north near the Zambezi River. He came from one of these chiefly families and he knew the names of his ancestors. His great grandfather, Kawodza, was killed by the Ndebele (evidence of how far north the Ndebele raided). Mhishi himself was attracted to the missionaries and went to stay with them at Chishawasha. He accompanied them to Salisbury during the rising and tells how, as we saw in Chapter 2, when they returned they found nothing stolen. 'The spirits of the people told them not to take anything.' Though they did take the cattle as their own were affected by the rinderpest. He recounts how once in a thunderstorm a man was struck by lightning and was 'rubbed with whiskey all over his body' and recovered! He was part of the band that went all the way to Mafeking to entertain the Colonial Secretary. He was later sent to Salisbury to teach catechism for a time and in 1913 accompanied Richartz to Mhondoro, his home area. He had been married in 1899[21] and sixty years later they had Pontifical High Mass at St Michael's for his jubilee. He became chief in 1948 and had to return to Chivero, 30 kms north of St Michael's. Once asked his advice by Prime Minister Whitehead as to what the government should do – possibly on the occasion Whitehead came to the opening of the new church in 1959 – he replied, 'just reduce your farms. ... a black and white ox does not just lick its white spots only.' There was no land for the growing population. Whitehead simply said, 'we will consider it' and there the matter rested. He concluded the interview: 'Our world was a better one then because we knew our traditions and customs.' He was still alive, together with his wife, when Fr Matthew Mhishi brought me to meet them, his grandparents, in 1972.

By 1936, St Michael's had two hostels; one for sixty-eight girls and the other for sixty-six boys. By 1953 there were nineteen out schools run by Frs Tilman Esser and Joseph Kumbirayi, a diocesan priest. But despite the growth, the mission was a poor younger brother of Musami and Makumbe, and the mission superior, Martin Thomas, in the late 1960s and early seventies, who was later shot at Musami, struggled to provide basic necessities. In May 1963, thieves broke in and stole the teachers' wages and the school fees, £1,700 in all. Unrest, stimulated

---

21 He is no 13 in the Baptism register at Chishawasha Mission.

by ZAPU in their frustration at the lack of political progress, spilt over into hostility to the Church. The record tells us that Bridget, sister of Robert Mugabe, was seriously beaten up by ZAPU and Zvinindo church was burnt. It was a year in which Fr James Cogger, the Mission Superior, replied to a Pastoral Enquiry from the Archdiocese saying 'there was a fall off of religious practice'. The young people find religious classes 'boring'. Catholicism just 'came with the whites', implying it was part of the colonial package.

But the mission produced the first local bishop in the entire country, Patrick Chakaipa, who hailed from Guvamombe, one of the thirty-three outstations until the mission was split into two: St Michael's in the south and St Dominic's Mubaira in the north. Chakaipa had been ordained a priest at Gavaza, another of the outstations. St Michael's was handed over to the archdiocese in 1978.

Makumbe

Young people, trained at Chishawasha, aroused curious interest when they returned to their home areas. One of Chief Chinamora's sub-chiefs, Chief Makumbe,[22] noticed this and, in 1918, asked for a teacher for his area. Fr Charles Daignault responded from Chishawasha by opening a school at Chakaoma. Legend or fact, the local kraal head (*sabhuku*) did not approve of Makumbe's invitation and sent two men to either steal or kill Daignault's two donkeys 'as a way of showing him he and his doctrine were not welcome'.[23] But one of the donkeys had a mind of its own, perhaps reminiscent of Ignatius' mule,'[24] and kicked the man trying to untie it and seriously

---

22 For decades the mission was spelt Makumbi, presumably because the European ear felt the way the name was spoken suggested an 'i' rather than an 'e'. I use the new (or restored) form, Makumbe. Another explanation is that Makumbi was adopted to avoid confusion with a mission of the same name in the Chivhu district. Mr Chiuyu. a teacher at Makumbe, says the real owner of the area was Chief Masembure and he gave part of his territory to Makumbe whom he identifies as Chief Chinamora.

23 Nhika, Fr Admire Rufaro, assisted by Mr Chiangwah, long time catechist and Mr Mugamu teacher at Makumbe; manuscript on the history of Makumbi, 2015, in JAZ, Box 604.

24 St Ignatius, in the early days of his conversion, was riding a mule when a Moor he met said something Ignatius considered offensive to Mary, the mother of Jesus. The Moor had gone on ahead while Ignatius pondered whether he should kill him or let him go. Failing to make up his mind by the time he met a fork in the road, he let the mule decide. The mule took the road the Moor had not taken.

injured him. The *sabhuku* let Daignault stay.

But the initiative did not grow roots until Fr Herman Kaibach, who seems to have walked everywhere, arrived in 1924 and founded what is now Makumbe Mission. He was on his way to Chiweshe to start there but stopped at Makumbe's on the Feast of the Visitation and since it was 'hill country'[25] he took it as a sign he should stay there and call the mission after the feast. Mr Sylvester Mugamu,[26] a long-time teacher at Makumbe, says it was the Dominican sisters who gave the name 'Visitation' but it was for the same reason: it was hill country.

The present site is half a mile south of the site he chose. In 1927 Br John Göll[27] baked 70,000 bricks and dug a well, and Br Joseph Linder built the priest's house, the school and a small church. But by 1929 Kaibach reported poor attendance at the school and a fall away in the practice of the Christians. When Ingeborg Neudecker, a research student, visited the mission in 1967 she put down the resistance to education to a failure to link it with life. Until people saw the value of education – reading, writing and speaking English, for example – it would not catch their interest.[28] Neudecker points to this failure to connect as reciprocal. The local people were failing to understand what the Jesuits were trying to do. And Fr Kaibach misread the ritual dance of the people and objected. As a result, relations with Chief Makumbe soured and he moved away. Neudecker concludes, 'It was a great hindrance for any evangelisation that the culture of the Bantu was regarded as far inferior in all its aspects and that Christianity was (seen as) synonymous with western civilisation'. The mission came close to being closed. But they continued, and in 1931 we hear of Br Anthony Puff putting a roof on the boarding school which had opened in 1929 under the care of three Dominican sisters. Thirty girls and twenty-five boys were now housed at the mission, though the boarding was stopped the following year.

---

25 A reference to the visit of Mary to her cousin Elizabeth. Cf. Luke 2:39: 'Mary set out at that time and went as quickly as she could into the hill country to a town in Judah.'

26 Mugamu was excellent at the high jump when at St Ignatius, in my time, in the 1960s.

27 In 1946 John Göll celebrated his Golden Jubilee and it was noted he had helped in building eleven churches in the country, including the Cathedral.

28 I. Neudecker, *History and Influence of Makumbe Mission,* an unpublished thesis for a course at the Teacher Training College, Bulawayo, 1967.

Despite the comment above on Fr Kaibach's reaction to the dance, he was well aware of the tension to which this book constantly returns. He wrote, 'The conquest of Rhodesia was in many ways a boon to the missionaries, yet in other respects it has placed them at a disadvantage. Though the natives soon recognise that the mission estates were being cultivated largely for their and their children's benefit, they could not help identifying the mission with the system which was mainly devised for the enrichment of interloping strangers.'[29]

In 1938 Makumbe had become independent of Chishawasha and there was a decade of progress from 1936 to 1946 under Fr John Kelly and Br Hugh Bradley. The bishop's report of 1938 astonishes the modern eye: among his many recommendations were for three more cows for the mission and hens that could lay an average of 150 eggs a year. These details are listed among an exhortation to fold the vestments properly and teach the students the Mass prayers.

A new church was built in 1942 which could hold 700 and a government clinic was established which could train nurses and midwives. A government TB sanatorium was built in 1945 just outside the mission and there was good co-operation between them and the mission. In 1967, there were twelve out schools and besides the TB Sanatorium with 120 beds there was a mission clinic with about twenty beds built in 1937.

In the midst of all this devoted work there are also hints of failures in understanding and clumsy responses to grievances. In 1953, there was a seasonal fire and Fr Maurice (Bo) Rea, the principal, asked the senior boys to help put it out as it was threatening the mission.[30] The junior boys decided to go too and amused themselves by spreading the fire! Fr Brian Riordan, a teacher in the school, was furious at the seniors' failure to control the juniors and ordered 'no porridge' for breakfast next day. This punishment was seen as unfair and the boys took up stones and started throwing them on the roof of the buildings. Rea tried to control the boys with the help of prefects but the boys jeered and marched off singing 'war songs' to the girls' dormitories. Rea asked a prefect to fetch an old gun and a strong torch from his office. The sight of these frightened the boys and they ran away out of reach. The prefects persuaded Rea not to pursue them but, when it

---

29 *Zambesi Mission Record*, October 1933.
30 His account of what happened is in JAZ, Box 137/1.

became clear they were intending to raid the fowl run, he went for a rifle with real ammunition and fired in the air. The boys then scattered again. Dr Turnbull, from the Sanatorium, hearing the commotion, came with his elephant gun and all suddenly became quiet for a while. Then the singing started again and Turnbull returned and fired his gun in the air and all became quiet for the rest of the night.

The next morning Rea confronted the boys who were now on a hill some way from the mission and told them that all who had not obeyed the night before would be expelled, that the police were coming to enforce this decision. Then he turned away. Some stones were thrown and cries of 'give us our money back' were heard. The boys converged on the kitchen but Rea sat there with his rifle guarding it. Meanwhile Riordan phoned Goromonzi police to come out and help expel the boys identified as leaders of the disturbance. Gradually calm returned but the boarding master was later charged with inciting violence among the students.[31]

Almost seventy years later this incident makes for disturbing reading. About twenty years after this event there were disturbances at St Ignatius College, described in Chapter 9, but the Jesuits understood the students and supported them in confronting the police. In 1953, the Jesuits appeared to have no such understanding and relied on the police to restore calm after they, the Jesuits, had overreacted to the senior boys failing to control the younger ones.

Makumbe's Children Home was founded in 1932 by Sr de Mercedes who began by caring for one orphan. In 1954 there were eighteen orphans, and *The Shield* commented, 'it is hard to provide a real home for orphans'. Fr Henry Wardale, at Makumbe in 1972, came across a birth certificate with the painful details, 'father unknown, mother died in childbirth'.[32] There were few resources and they were 'erratic and spasmodic'. But the priests and sisters felt they were giving the orphans a start in life that many brought up in the rural villages did not have. 'In the 1960s, Social Welfare, became involved and brought orphaned, neglected or abandoned children to the home.'[33] Up to 1993, the children and their carers lived in one big community but in that year Fr Konrad Landsberg built eight separate

---

31 Maurice Rea's report of the incident, 31 October 1953, JAZ, Box 137/1.
32 *The Shield*, September 1972.
33 Nhika, op. cit., p. 5.

houses with twelve children in each, giving the children an experience closer to that of a normal family.

What gave new life to Makumbe in the 1930s was Chichester's decision to open the training course (novitiate) for local girls who were showing a desire to become sisters like the Dominicans. The interest they aroused and the questions their presence raised radically shook up the Mission and considerable attention, friendly and hostile, was generated among the local people. Dominican Sr de Mercedes shepherded through the first group of whom eighteen took their first vows (statements of commitment) in 1934, a year, incidentally, when we begin to hear reports of water shortages at the Mission, an issue that remained unsolved for many decades. Sr de Mercedes continued the work of novice director until 1960 and was buried at Makumbe alongside Fr Kaibach.

In 1934, we read of a visit by Br John Taylor to the out schools and in the following year the government came to inspect them. Lack of teachers and lack of interest among the *vakuru* (the elders) led to closures, transfers, re-openings and further closures. But by 1946 there were ten out schools with an average attendance of sixty students. The presence of seven local sister teachers did much to stabilise the schools. The secondary school for girls opened in 1964 with thirty-two girls and it rose to fifty-seven the following year. In 1971 the school became co-educational with the arrival of forty-one boys.[34] In the 1970s Fr Henry Wardale joined the F2 (technical) school with the now F1 (academic) school to form Visitation High. This decision followed government policy but it was misunderstood. It seemed discriminatory and the new government in 1980 abolished the division into F1 and F2 while retaining the substance of the thinking behind F2.

Gradually the 'technical' students came to appreciate the practical skills they learnt – in carpentry and building – and the sustainability they imparted. In line with this, 1980 saw the introduction of vegetable growing, chicken rearing, pig keeping and dairy cows. In 1988, A-level arts subjects were added to the academic side of the school, followed by science two years later. Sylvester Mugamu was asked in 1990 on ZBC what else he would like to see added to the school curriculum. He replied, 'I wish both male and female students to be taught practical subjects from Form 1.' In 1992 the first female

---

34 Nhika, op. cit., p. 4.

students took up woodwork.[35]

In the mid-1960s, Neudecker was impressed by the amount of lay involvement in the mission. There were catechists and prayer groups (Apostleship of Prayer), and discussion groups on matters of faith and scripture. These groups visited the sick and collected firewood, etc, for the sick and old. There were also Catholic youth groups. She noted that from 1925 to1967, there were 19,531 registered baptisms.

Fr Admire Nyika has recorded an account of the building of St Edmund Mutake Church, one of the outstations of Makumbe, 1971-74. '*Musha Mukadzi*, it is the woman who builds the home.'[36] This was true of Mutake, where the women persevered over three years to complete their church. And it is notable that the women were helped by their friends from other churches – Anglicans, Salvation Army and Methodists. This was long before Fr Husemann came with considerable resources from Germany.

Mark Hackett, whom we met earlier at Musami, was at Makumbe after 1980. He tells us ZANLA never frequented the mission during the war as they did at Musami. Mugamu says the guerrillas 'urged the teachers not to do anything that might cause the school to be closed and the school operated during the war as usual with no disturbances from outside'. Relations with missions depended on who was the local commander and what his understanding was of the missionaries. Some were friendly, others hostile. In Chinamora the attitude was not always friendly. On 15 January 1978, Fr Desmond (Gussie) Donovan disappeared and was presumed dead.[37] It was later learnt that he had been captured while visiting the sick and his motor cycle was found buried near a stream in the valley below the house. He was beaten almost to death and then bayonetted and his body was thrown into the stream. His remains were never found and his coffin in Chishawasha cemetery is empty except for a handful of earth from the place where he was presumed to have been killed. The Govera area, where all this took place, was destroyed in the conflicts of the time where rival groups battled each other. Pastoral work came almost to a standstill.

And the tensions endured even after independence. Teachers, who

---

35 Nhika, op. cit., p. 5.
36 Nhika, History of Mutake Church, JAZ, Box 604.
37 Cf. Chapter 10.

in the past were charged for water, took this as a grievance to ZANLA who remained in the district and sometimes held court at the mission. Mark Hackett, as mission superior, was summoned and when told the water belonged freely to everyone, pointed out it came from a dam and was pumped up to the mission using diesel and was then filtered and chlorinated. ZANLA was convinced but it was an incident indicative of the new dispensation.

Another issue illustrating the fluid transitional situation arose because the mission had allowed young men to live on the mission due to the danger of their being required to act as messengers (*mujibhas*) for ZANLA during the war. They took care of the Tangwena children moved from their home in Nyanga because of the war. When it was over, and the children were going home, it was time for the young men to leave too. They objected that they were being 'wrongfully dismissed' and Mark received a strong message from town that he could not dismiss them. He pointed out they were there because they did not want to be *mujibhas*. This sleight of hand had the desired effect.

Soon after Independence the government announced a huge increase in secondary education. Up to then, the only secondary school in the area had been at the mission and that had been mainly for boarders from town. Now many primary schools were to become secondary schools (Upper Tops) and there was to be a large government school at the show grounds at Parirehwa, half way between the mission and Harare. As pastoral work was still almost impossible, Mark applied to teach at this secondary school. There was 'hot seating' as both secondary and primary were using the same classrooms. He taught in either the morning or the afternoon and so could use the other half of the day to visit Catholic families in the area. In this way he gently coached people to return to the practice of their faith. It also meant he came to know, and be known by, the young people some of whom came from afar.

There was a shortage of teachers to meet this upsurge in education and Makumbe became a pilot scheme for CATORUZI (Catholic Ancillary Teachers of Rural Zimbabwe), volunteers from the developed world. They lived at the missions and their salaries were pooled to cover the expenses of the organisation. They taught at Parirehwa, Nyakudya, Munyawiri, Tsatse and Chiveso and came from

South Africa, Japan, New Zealand, Australia, Belgium, Liechtenstein, Ireland and the UK. Wherever they worked they made an enormous contribution to education in Zimbabwe. When Henry Wardale finished his term as provincial, he taught at Nyakudya and every day the VW beetle set off with two CATORUZIS, Henry and Mark. When Henry began to show signs of Alzheimer's, one of the CATORUZIS gave a lot of time to be with him.

The students' knowledge of English was often rudimentary. One of the classes hardly understood Mark. Sometimes there was no classroom and classes were held under a tree. Often the children had walked for long distances on empty stomachs and were exhausted. Stationery and equipment were in short supply. Discipline could be harsh. At Parirehwa, a boy was publicly and savagely beaten in front of the whole school.[38]

Pastoral work gradually resumed in the mission area. Mark spent Tuesday to Friday each week walking around the villages of Mupandira, Mumurwi, Chiveso and Chifamba in the Musana area. Each day he and his helpers chose a central place to say Mass. It proved to be just what was needed. He writes, 'In one village a lady who had not walked for some time leaped to her feet and danced after having been given the sacrament of the sick. It was symbolic of the general delight in being able to practice their faith again. People appreciated me staying among them in the village and living as they did though I was a little taken aback on one occasion to be invited to share a communal toothbrush.' After a time it was clear the area was ready for normal pastoral work again and they could resume and build on the foundational work begun before the war by Frs Patrick Chakaipa and Cosmas Katuruza.

With independence came an emphasis on decentralisation, and the parish of Makumbe divided into three areas: Masembura, Musana and Chinhamora. Eventually Fr Herman Husemann took over the rural areas. Husemann came with access to a great deal of money from Germany and he built or rebuilt many of the churches, augmenting the efforts of his predecessors. He also discovered an artist who could decorate the churches with paintings, and he built the

---

38 The war accustomed people to violence but this incident sounds particularly severe. Physical punishment of students, especially boys, was accepted as normal all over the world until the twentieth century when a large number of countries outlawed it.

pastoral centre at Manhenga close to the border between Masembura and Musana. At first, neither Archbishop Chakaipa nor the Jesuit provincial, Joseph Hampson, were in favour of Manhenga. It would be one more 'institution' to maintain with resources that were always limited and Mr Chiuyu and five other leading parishioners had the task of 'justifying' it. They were successful and the centre now serves a large area and even the government hires it from time to time for training courses. Young people, as well as men and women, met there regularly in their own groups from all over the district. And there were workshops and all-night prayer vigils which were, to some extent, a Catholic response to the *Vapostori* and the Pentecostals.

By 2015 the mission had thirty-four outstations divided into seven units or sub-parishes. Marriages in church numbered 1,266 from 1993 and baptisms 9,918.[39] Nhika makes the telling point that helping the poor changed from handouts to asking people to work for the help they get. He compares this with the Israelites in the desert. They were given free *manna* because they were helpless but when they got to the promised land, they had to work for themselves.

The Dominican sisters had two convents, one at the mission and one at the government TB hospital. They wanted to leave the mission so that the 'Makumbe sisters', as the LCBLs were often called, had the free run of the mission. This meant, in effect, there would be fewer sisters teaching in the secondary school as the LCBL sisters had insufficient trained secondary school teachers then. For a while the gap was filled by two Canadian Ursuline sisters. The influence of a comparatively young overseas sister on both the CATORUZI teachers and the girls in the secondary school was immediately felt and the convent garden, neglected since the departure of the Dominicans, began to produce fruit again.

The LCBLs contributed a great deal to the mission. They had teachers in the primary school, one teacher in the secondary and provided a 'much-feared' boarding mistress in the girls' hostel. They also had a matron in charge of the children's home and a sister to help with the pastoral work.

Mr Chiuyu, who was also a teacher at the primary school, spoke highly of Mr Kaviya, the head of the primary school where he taught for forty-six years. But, Chiuyu says, success brings its own problems

---

39 Nhika, op. cit., p. 9.

as some children walk 12-13 km to school to get 'quality education'. Further, many of the teachers and the children are non-Catholic and this makes it hard to 'implement the Catholic charism'.

The secondary school was almost entirely for boarders and these children generally came from the urban areas. This had the unfortunate effect of producing an apostolate that was seen as largely irrelevant to the local people. Makumbe had tried to mitigate this, as mentioned above, by changing what had been an all-girls academically oriented school into one where practical subjects, relevant to the rural areas, were also taught: building and carpentry for the boys and fashion and fabrics for the girls. But the main emphasis had been on agriculture. 'Education with production' was in vogue. In addition to market gardening and field crops the school reared poultry and pigs and had a dairy unit – all largely due to one excellent teacher. But the tendency to think these subjects demeaning resurfaced and the school had to revert to being a normal secondary again. The headmaster argued strongly for the relevance of what the school was doing but he was overruled.

Fr Admire Nhika tells us the school had an enrolment of 800 by 2015 of whom 200 were day scholars. 'It is a school in the bracket of catering for lower income earners ... the day scholars come from the neighbouring primary schools ... most of the boarders are from the capital and other towns. It is a school highly favoured by the populace of Zimbabwe due to its closeness to Harare and its reasonable fees.'[40]

An unfortunate development at the school, which later affected the parish, was the arrival of the charismatic movement[41] in an insufficiently supervised form. There was hysteria in the school and one teacher neglected her classes to attend charismatic gatherings in town. In the parish it led to a serious split in one of the outstations, almost bringing things to a standstill and the effects were to last for a long time.

School discipline was quite severe. Canings were not unusual, but a common punishment involved the digging of a deep pit which was

---

40 Ibid. p. 5.

41 The 'charismatic movement' is a catch-all term for Christian churches that emphasise the influence of the Holy Spirit and shows itself, among other ways, in 'speaking in tongues'. Paul's first letter to the Corinthians, in Chapters 12 and 14, speaks about these 'gifts'.

then filled in again. The boys called it 'Heroe's Acre' after the burial ground in Harare for the liberation war fighters. Complaints about the food were common and at one time there was an outbreak of diarrhoea because the students would not accept a reduction in the amount of oil used for cooking vegetables. 'Our parents have paid for it', they said. The manner in which these troubles were handled was vastly improved compred to what what happened in 1953, narrated earlier.

The Children's Home was originally intended to be an orphans' home but during the war it became a home for any children in need. It opened its doors to the Tangwena children, as mentioned above. When they went home it reverted to its original purpose but it was hard to fund. Government support was minimal and the home almost had to close. However, eventually the government raised its subsidy and the danger was averted. It was a happy place, looked after by a succession of devoted sisters: Julian, Diana and Illumina. Fr John Byrne and Mark often spent evenings with the children.

In the late 1990s Fr Roland von Nidda built new science blocks and a big hall. He tried to introduce the Ignatian ethos – an emphasis on seeing education in the whole plan of God for his people – into the schools, especially the secondary school. This involved teaching religion in the framework of Ignatian spirituality in the fifth and sixth forms. He also led workshops and retreats for the teachers and offered a two-month Ignatian retreat in daily life to them, a good number of whom took it up.

At the time of national elections, the mission experienced a war atmosphere rather than a democratic process. During the 2005 elections Makumbe was a polling station and the children were sent home for the occasion. On their return, their buses were stopped at a police block and the drivers were ordered to return to Harare because some children were singing opposition party songs. Roland had to go to the police station and plead with the inspector to allow the buses through. 'Children are children', he argued. The inspector let the buses proceed to the Mission but on the next day, about thirty party officials and youth came, demanding all classes be stopped in both schools and teachers be summoned to the school hall. At the meeting there, the teachers were told that the children on the buses were still singing opposition songs when they got to the Mission. The party held the teachers responsible for this and they were told the youth would go to their houses and throw all their furniture and goods onto the road. 'This is ZANU-PF territory,' they said, 'and no opposition is tolerated.' The teachers were terrified, but the chief intervened saying, 'in Shona culture an accused person must always be given the chance to defend themselves.' When this was agreed, the teachers said they were not even present when the buses came into the Mission. 'We were away at other schools on election duties.' This saved them, but the party officials demanded to talk to the children and gave them a stern warning never to do such a thing again.

The next night, Roland went with the secondary school head and the chief to the house of the party chairman and told him the children, the teachers, the ministry officials, the archbishop and the provincial were angry with what the party people had done and that a report would be made to the highest authorities. The chairman asked them to settle the matter amicably and promised that such action would not be repeated. The promise lasted until the next election.

In Fr Heribert Müller's time as mission superior in the new century, the need for a pastoral centre at the mission was felt to be urgent. Mr Chiangwah, a mission catechist, pressed for a place to welcome all the groups that came to the central mission. A committee was formed and Müller raised funds in Germany to support the building. The centre was opened by Archbishop Robert Ndlovu in 2015 in the time of Fr Admire Nhika who took over from Fr Müller. As with Manhenga, the Makumbe Centre was a venue not only for church activities but also for government training courses.

The Ruvarashe Trust (St Josephine Bakhita) Centre for people living with handicaps was founded in the new century through the efforts of Catarina Savini, a long-time Italian lay missionary in Zimbabwe. She had originally started a self-reliance project for people living with leprosy at Mutemwa (Mutoko, 150 km north-east of Harare). 'The trust aimed at re-integrating into society families of leprosy patients with healthy young children, so as to give them an identity and make them economically self-reliant and socially active, to grow humanly and spiritually and regain their dignity as human beings.'[42] The trust opened the Bakhita Centre at Makumbe in 2010 to extend its activities to any persons living with handicaps. Today,

---

42 Nhika, op. cit., p. 13.

it focuses on shoe-making and sewing. George Kabaya is one of the graduates of the centre. He says, 'Instead of becoming street beggars, the trust provided us with different training skills and we are treated with dignity and made to feel equal to any other person. Disability does not mean inability.'[43]

Makumbe is well equipped with many institutions and, as one would expect, this gives challenges to those who inherit it. Frs Admire Nhika and Peter Paul Musekiwa, the most recent responsible authorities at the mission, have responded by initiating a number of income-generating projects.

-o0o-

Without going into detail, some brief words can be said about other missions founded by the Jesuits and later handed over to other congregations.

Fort Victoria (Masvingo) (Gokomere), Bikita (Silveira), Macheke (Monte Cassino)

When the white settlers came from the south in 1890, they made a detour to the east, skirting the lands of Lobengula, whom they rightly viewed as hostile. The settlers established a 'fort' they called Victoria, close to Great Zimbabwe ruins. Fr Barthelemy built a brick chapel, the first in Zimbabwe, and four Dominican sisters came to nurse the sick in 1892. The town, now Masvingo, was served from Gokomere.

A hundred kilometres further east, Chief Jiri had been asking the fathers to open a mission in Bikita. Silveira, as it came to be called, was founded there in 1931 by Fr Emil Schmitz after Fr John Apel had tried three years previously. It was handed over to the Bethlehem fathers and brothers in 1940.

Monte Cassino had been founded much earlier by the Mariannhill fathers and brothers in 1902 after they had abandoned Triashill at the beginning of the Shona rising in 1896. We will discuss the relations of the Mariannhill congregation and the Jesuits later but for now we can consider briefly the story of Monte Cassino after it was given to the Jesuits in 1929. Br Charles McCann (1903-72) worked on the farm (1932-37). He had a great love of the animals and would care for them as if they were children. Fr John McCann (1911-97,

---

43 Ibid., p .14

no relation to Charles as far as I know) was at the mission (1946-70) and was principal of the secondary school from 1963 'but the sisters did all the work'! Fr Ludger Boeckenhoff (1905-63) was at Triashill (1939-41) teaching 'in his own lively way' and was at Monte Cassino (1941-44 and 1962-63), in charge of the out schools. In 1944 he went to Loreto till 1948 to found that mission with three Dominican sisters. Fr Richard Randolph (1916-2008) was at the mission 1963-68. He had a distinguished war career before joining the Society having been at the evacuation of Dunkirk, the battle of El Alamein and the invasion of Normandy. Before that he had studied branches of agriculture and was sent to Monte Cassino to sort out the finances. By the mid-century all the Jesuit farms were money losers! Randolph stabilised the finances but it was too big a job to make the farms profitable. He built dormitories for the girls and set up a bursary fund for poor students. The Teacher Training School at the mission was started in 1933 but was closed in 1969 for lack of support. Monte Cassino was handed over to the Precious Blood sisters in 1971 though a Jesuit remained as chaplain.

The Precious Blood Sisters (CPS) had been founded around the same time as the Mariannhills and had a similar charism. As mentioned, they remained at Monte Cassino when the priests and brothers were asked to leave in 1929. In July 1970, the Jesuit superior of the then Salisbury Mission wrote to the Jesuit priest, Fr John Eckes, chaplain at Monte Cassino, 'the success of the mission is due to the CPS sisters and we should show them tangible appreciation'. The following year, in January 1971, the Precious Blood Sisters also took over the mission farm which was there to support the secondary and primary schools. There had been some discussion in 1970 of the Franciscans coming in to take over the mission but Sr Theodora CPS, the regional superior, resisted this as she wanted her congregation to be free to make their contribution. The LCBL sisters were also involved on the mission and, it seemed, worked well with the CPS.

In 1995, Benedictine monks from Ampleforth Abbey in England came to start a monastery at Monte Cassino,[44] which, coincidentally, was the name of St Benedict's first foundation in Italy in 529.

---

44 They called their monastery Christ the Word.

Wedza (Hwedza), Gwelo (Gweru), Wankie (Hwange)

A Mariannhill brother, Br Leopold Schimmal, founded an outstation at Wedza in 1924 and stayed there on his own for five years until the Mariannhills withdrew to Matabeleland. A hiatus followed until Fr Ludger Boeckenhoff was sent to found a mission in 1952. Fr John Dove told me he, Boeckenhoff, asked Bishop Chichester for money to found the new mission: 'How much do you want, Boeckenhoff?' '£25 should do, my Lord.' 'I'll give you 20, Boeckenhoff!' So off he went to start Wedza with £20! He was greatly encouraged when the Blue Sisters (the Little Company of Mary) came to start a hospital in 1954. They 'financed everything without a murmur'. Boeckenhoff was well known in the district: he was friends with everyone, full of generosity, hospitality and ebullient humour. But he developed diabetes and Buergher's disease and died comparatively young at 58. In 1961, the Franciscans took over and Wedza became an active theatre during the liberation war.

Being on the railway line, and at the centre of the country, Gweru briefly held ambitions to be the capital city when Bulawayo proved impractical. In 1900, Fr Anthony Stempfel was given two rooms by the Catholic owner of the Metropole Hotel and he used one for a chapel and one for a living room. Fr Isidore Lallemand took over in 1902 and a temporary church was built in 1904. A church in the 'location' (for the local people) was built in 1928 and the main church of the town was completed in 1930.

Three groups of missionaries worked in what is now Hwange Diocese: the Jesuits from 1880 to 1930, the Mariannhill fathers and brothers from 1930 to 1949 and the Spanish Missionary Institute from 1949 to the present. So the Church in Hwange is 141 years old at the time of writing. In 1880, Fr Depelchin, frustrated by Lobengula's refusal to allow the Jesuits to teach or preach, sought to go beyond his territories. One goal was the Zambezi and beyond. They took advantage of the trading post at Pandamatenga on the present border between Botswana and Zimbabwe in what is now Hwange diocese. It was then a month's journey from the Good Hope Mission at Old Tati. They were welcomed there at first and set up a mission which they called St Joseph's. They built a small wooden house and began to till the land. Having established this base they set out for the

Zambezi and the Tonga people but, as we saw in Chapter 2, they were hampered by their failure to understand the rivalries and suspicions between the Ndebele and Lozi with the Tonga caught in the middle. Pandamatenga was abandoned in 1885.

After 1890, and the Jesuits' return to Zimbabwe, Hwange was not a priority. The area was thinly populated in those days in comparison to other parts of the country and for missionaries the climate was hot and there were many languages to learn: Ndebele, Shona, Nambya, Tonga, Nyanja and Bemba. When the Spanish missionaries came, they also had to learn English! Coal was discovered in 1892 and the first workers were Bemba and Senga. We know that in 1915 around fifty Catholics, organised by a Portuguese called Antonio Robo and led by a Bemba catechist, were holding services – mainly saying the rosary and singing hymns – in a mine office.

In 1920 there were around a hundred Catholics at the colliery and Fr Gerard Pfaeler, based in Bulawayo, used to visit them three times a year. In a letter dated 12 April that year he writes in excitement to Msgr Edward Parry, the Prefect Apostolic in Salisbury (Harare), that instead of the usual three or four for Mass he had twenty-four plus eight children. He promised to come every two months from Bulawayo. A year later he rented a site for 1/- a year on which to build a church. By 1923 there were forty catechumens of whom twenty-five were Bemba. That same year, Fr Tilman Esser wrote to Parry to say agreement had been reached about building a school and it would cost about £150 and there would be a priest's room attached to it.

The mine helped to build the school which opened in 1923 with twelve children in attendance. Many of the Catholic children had attended the Methodist school and parents were put under pressure to move them to the Catholic school. In 1934 the school was enlarged and a second teacher added. After 1930, the Mariannhills developed the mission further and when the Spanish missionaries came in 1949, Hwange became the centre of a new prefecture and diocese. In 2013, the first Jesuit from the diocese entered the Lusaka novitiate, Kelvin Munkuli.

-oOo-

Dachs and Rea make the startling observation that the Jesuits, and the Mariannhill priests and brothers who joined the mission, 'were not looking for church leaders but followers… Numbers meant success

... and the missionaries rejoiced in their crowded churches. ... The missionaries were freed from any questioning of the concentration of their effort on erecting schools and institutionalising the church ... they felt little need to examine African religions or to probe the Africa social background...'[45] The authors are referring to the decades after the arrival of the missionaries in 1890. This topic will not go away despite the treatment it received in Chapter 1. For now it is enough to note again the difference between the situation in Zambezia in the early twentieth century and, say, China in the early seventeenth when Mateo Ricci laboured to 'inculturate' the faith in the world view of a people who had long settled in towns and had a written culture and traditions. The conditions in Africa were different. The urgent need was to assist people to settle and develop the security that would be needed if they were to feel confident enough to reflect on their traditions in the light of the new world to which they had been so dramatically and rapidly introduced. 'Width' was the immediate aim. 'Depth' would have to wait. Returning to Pope Francis, referred to in Chapter 1, occupying 'space' was uppermost. Developing processes would come later.

Meanwhile, church structures were developing. We saw that Leo XIII had set up the international Zambezi Mission in 1878. In 1893 the progress of the mission was committed to the care of the English (later, with sensitivity to the Scots and Welsh, British) province of the Society of Jesus. Two years later this was formalised in Church terms as the Prefecture Apostolic of Salisbury and the Jesuit Superior, Richard Sykes, became the first 'Prefect' as well as remaining the Jesuit Superior. For the first eighteen years of the Zambezi Mission the Superior was based at Grahamstown. In 1897, Richard Sykes moved his base to Bulawayo, the railway hub with communications both to Salisbury and across the Zambezi via Victoria Falls. This meant, for example, he had the authority to welcome the Mariannhill priests and brothers.

In 1897, the Nyasa Prefecture was established, cutting off part of the original territory of the Zambezi Mission, a part the Jesuits never reached. A further division was made in 1927 when the Prefecture of Broken Hill (Kabwe, Zambia) was established assigning responsibility for the Jesuit missionary area north of the Zambezi to the Polish

---

45 Dachs and Rae, p. 71.

Fr Henry Delpechin, leader of the Zambezi Mission. (Photo by W. Rausch, Bulawayo).

Fr Augustus Law, Source: *Zambesi Mission Record*, Vol 8, No. 124, p, 389.

Br Francis de Sadeleer c.1920. Source: *Zambesi Mission Record*, Vol. 7 No. 98, p. 145.

Fr Peter Prestage, c.1900 (Photo by McKnaught, Kimberley).

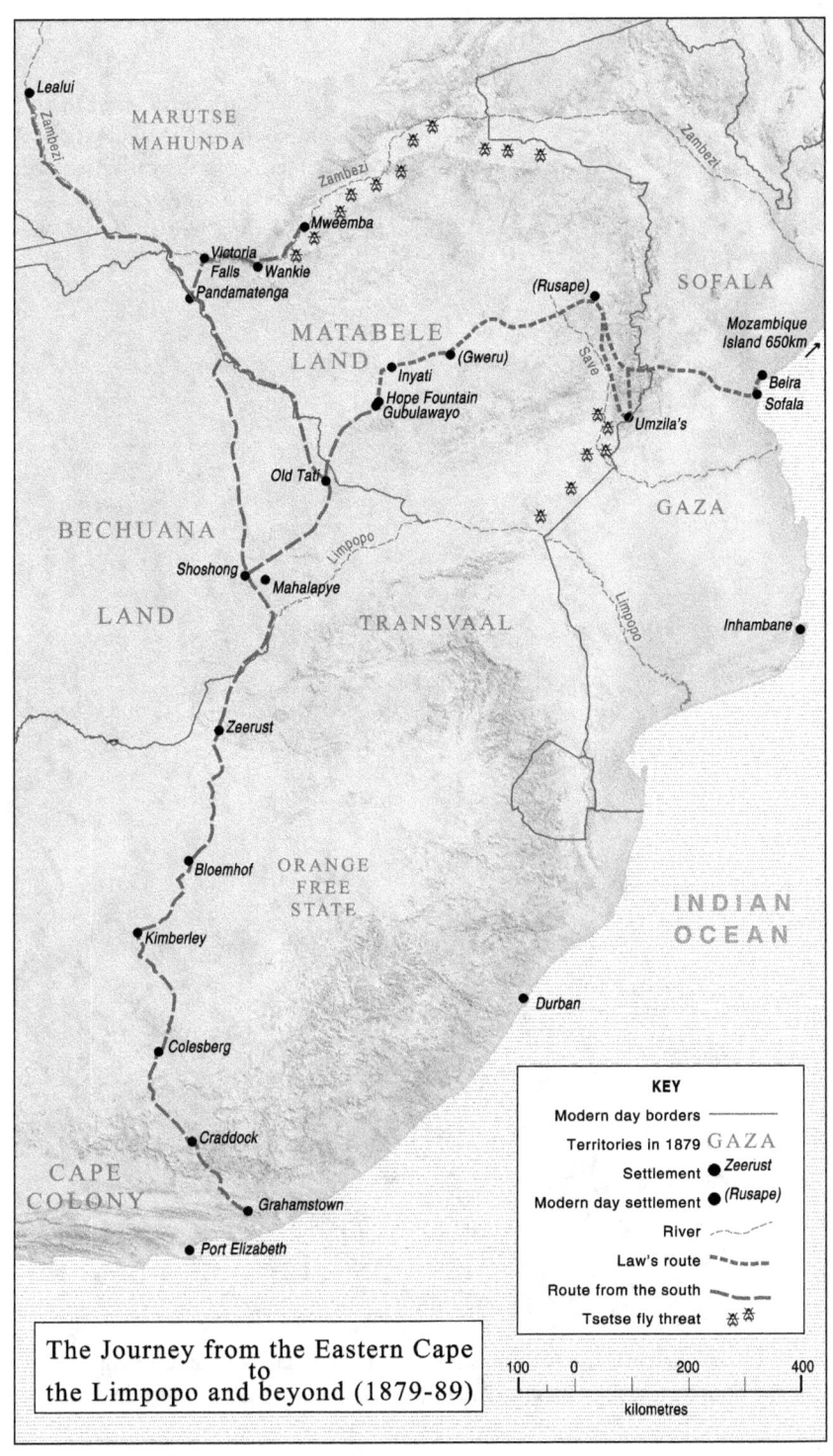

Mother Patrick, leader of the Dominican sisters who worked closely with the Jesuits in the early years and indeed up to the present.
Source: *Zambesi Mission Record*, Vol. 8, No. 124, p. 389.

The first chapel at Empandeni with Fr Charles Bick, c.1898.
Source: *Zambesi Mission Record*, Vol.1, No. 4, 1899. (Photo by Mr Frank Sykes, Bulawayo.)

Building a mission.

Fr Biehler and the Chishawasha band, which he founded, 1905.

Fr Francis Richartz at Chishawasha Mission with catechists and teachers, three of whom helped to found three out-schools, c.1919. Source: *Zambesi Mission Record*, Vol. 6. No. 83, p. 104. (Photo by Rev. C. Daignault, SJ.)

Craft-training for girls, Driefontein, c.1910.

Fr Charles Daignault on a river near Kutama.

Fr Charles Daignault at Kutama, 1918.

Fr Charles Daignault at St Michael's Mhondoro: (r-l) church/school, kitchen, dining room, c.1913.

Charles Daignault crossing the Nyaguwe River near Musami. Source: *Zambesi Mission Record*, Vol. 7, No.107, p. 443.

A general view of Chishawasha Mission, c.1920.

Chishawasha: repairing boots

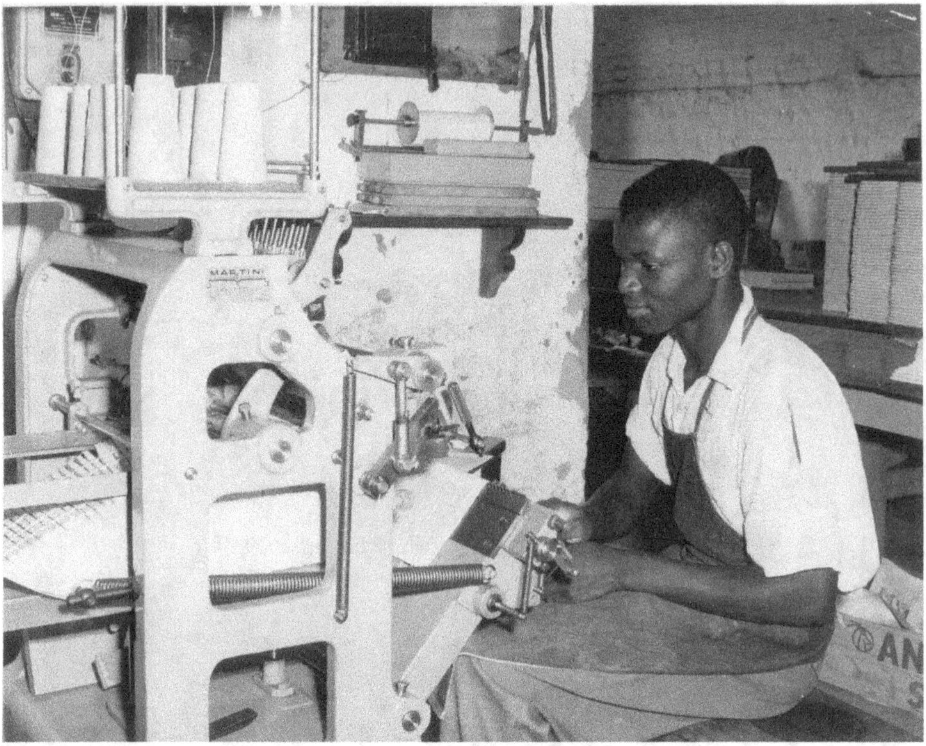

The Chishawasha Press, c.1930.

Brothers retreat at Driefontein in 1932.

Silveira Mission, Bikita. Fr William Withnell at his house, c.1931.

Bishop Aston Chichester teaching at the Regional Seminary in the late 1930s.

Fr Kaibach saying Mass at an outstation near Chishawasha.

Br John Breiten (1869-1955), c.1949.

Sr Kiliana at Marymount Mission with *nganga*, Jacobo, 1961. (Photo by Fr J. Gilick, SJ.)

Sr Michaela at Mhondoro (Photo by Fr. J. Gilick, SJ.)

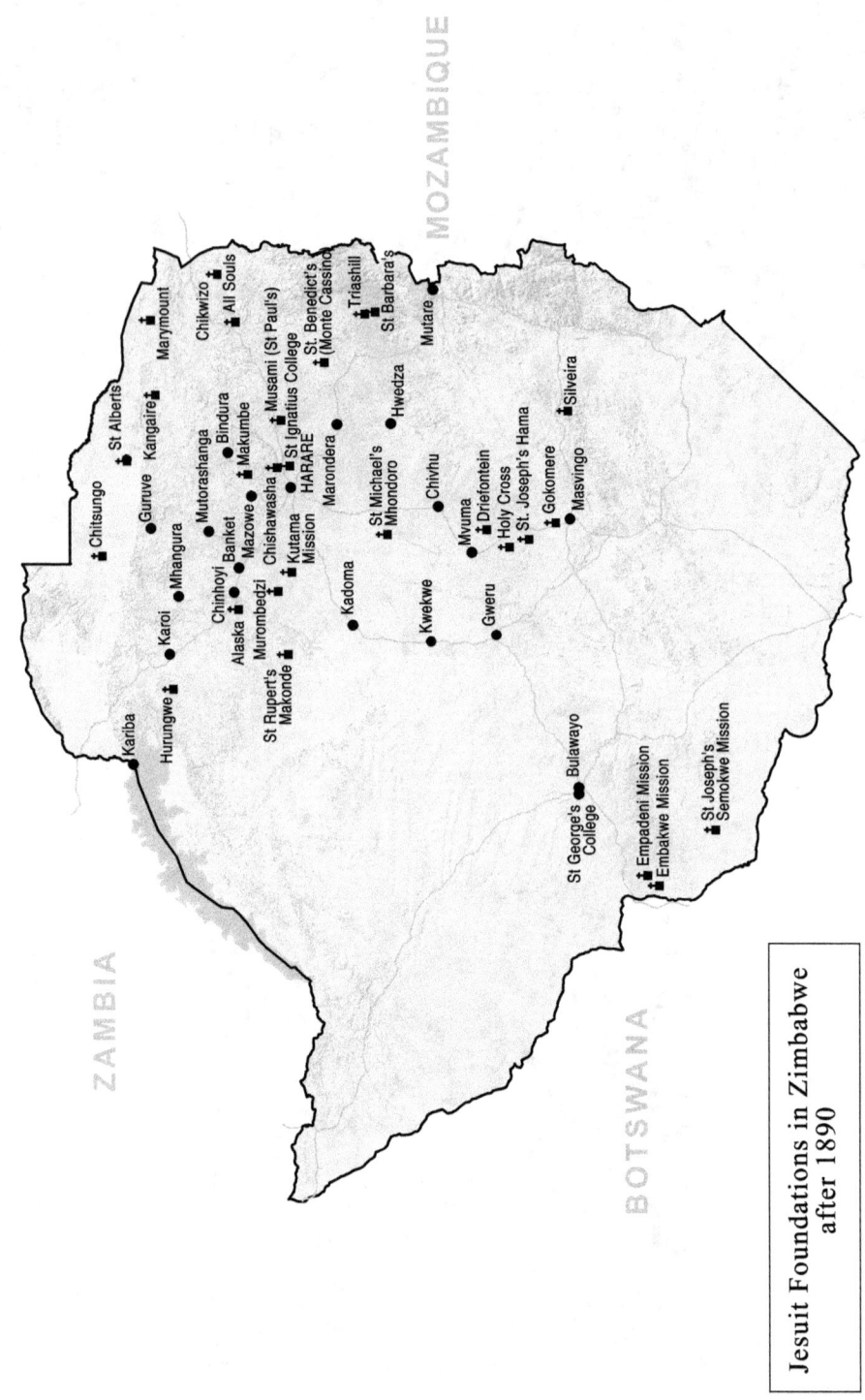

Jesuit Foundations in Zimbabwe after 1890

Ludger Boekenhoff with Frs Isidore Chikore (l.) and Regis Chigwedere at Wedza in 1961.

Reaching for the heights.
Fr Mark Hackett with Scouts at Musami.
(Photo by John Gillick ,SJ.)

Fr 'Jeep' Davis and his Musami 'Olympics', 1961.

Fr Hugh Ross, who taught at St George's for over fifty years with sixth formers, 1965.

Fr Herman Kaibach with a little girl at Makumbe, 1961.

Harvesting sisal. (Photo by John Byrne.)

St Ignatius College students set out to do some outreach work in Chishawasha c.1963/64.

Fr Anthony Watsham examining specimens of micrcoscopic chalcid wasps netted by him in the Chishawasha valley.

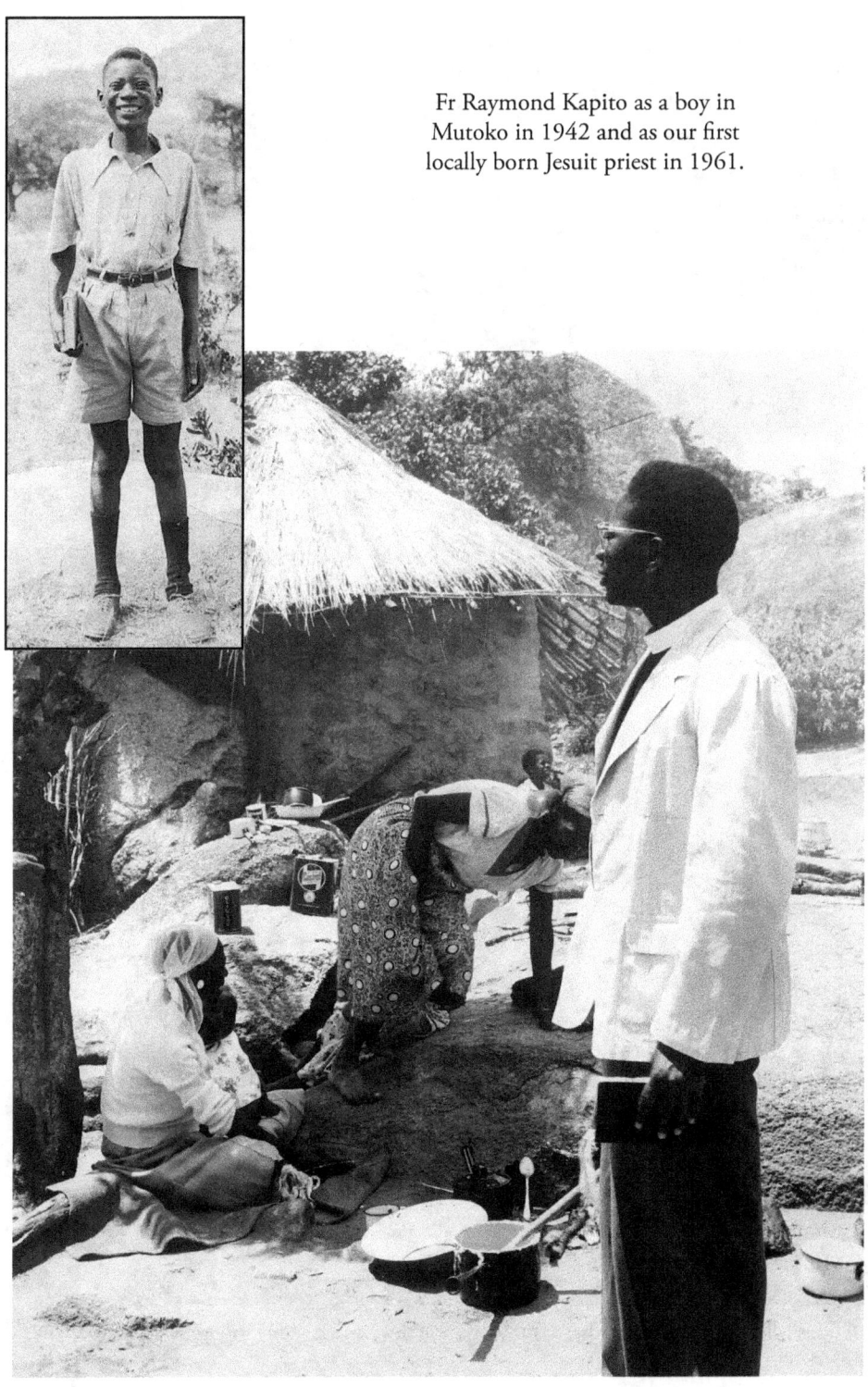

Fr Raymond Kapito as a boy in Mutoko in 1942 and as our first locally born Jesuit priest in 1961.

Church decoration: Driefontein early 1900s.

Church decoration Makumbe: 'The Visitation' by Moses Manyangha, Masvingo, 1989.

Jesuits. Normally, Prefects Apostolic had unlimited terms of office in those days while Jesuit provincials and major superiors have fixed six-year terms. But in this case the term of the prefect seems to have coincided roughly with Jesuit practice as the prefects all served six- or eight-year terms, though Sykes did so twice.

In 1931 the nomenclature altered again and the prefecture became a vicariate, that is, the prefect became a bishop with the added authority and autonomy of that office. Aston Ignatius Chichester stepped out of the classroom at Beaumont College, at the time a well-known English Catholic Boarding school near Windsor, to become the first Catholic bishop in Rhodesia (Zimbabwe). And, to complete the picture, twenty-four years later, the Catholic hierarchy was established with Chichester as Archbishop of Salisbury and Bishops Schmitt, Haene and Lamont of Bulawayo, Gwelo (Gweru) and Umtali (Mutare).[46] The four bishops coming from England, Germany, Switzerland and Ireland represented a healthy cross section of what was a Eurocentric Church at the time.

Christian villages[47]

For those baptised, the question, touched on in the last chapter, arose of how best to preserve their faith when the surrounding culture was, it seemed to many early missionaries, so contrary to Christian belief. One solution was to settle new Christians in special villages on mission land where the atmosphere was permeated with a Christian spirit. The Jesuits in the seventeenth century had developed such villages – or *reductions,* they were in effect towns – in South America precisely for this purpose. Philip Caraman quotes the description of a reduction in Paraguay by a visitor:

> The churches, stone houses, paved streets (of the reductions) were splendid in comparison to Asunción (the Spanish capital of the region); there were tanneries and workshops of different kinds; the store houses were full of grain and the farms of animals. Moreover, in a country where industry scarcely existed the reductions had small thriving factories. There were ten to twenty looms at least in each town.... and highly trained and skilled

---

46 Ibid., p. 187.
47 I am grateful to Fr Wolfgang Thamm for introducing me to the topic of Christian villages.

carpenters, goldsmiths, masons, sculptors, stone-cutters, bell-founders, calligraphers, instrument makers, engravers, copyists and even armourers. Each man had been apprenticed and in turn transmitted his skills to others. This was prosperity rather than wealth.... The Jesuits think happiness preferable to wealth.[48]

The twentieth century Jesuits had no such ambitions, but there was a strong body of opinion that 'social distancing' – I write in the age of Covid-19 – was called for if the new Christians were to persevere in the faith. Chishawasha had six such Christian villages by the beginning of the twentieth century and Empandeni had three.

But this policy was soon questioned by those who believed it was possible to nourish the faith of people where they were. So the contrary view was to develop a series of outstations where there was a school and resident catechist who might also be a teacher. Fr Richartz became keen on this method after his time in Empandeni and travelled extensively to find suitable places. A controversy arose about the two methods. The Christian villages acquired an enthusiastic proponent when Fr Jean-Baptiste Loubière arrived in 1914 after the Jesuits were expelled from Mozambique following the revolution in Portugal in 1910. He had been twelve years on the Lower Zambezi and believed Christian villages were the way forward for new Christians. He immediately introduced them, as we saw above, in Kutama where he was sent and they drew admiration from the government and Jesuit superiors. There was a fervent Christian community with little streets of white-washed huts. The whole presented 'a *little* walled-in garden'.[49] The English Provincial, William Bodkin, on a visit in 1924-25, recommended the villages, and the Apostolic Visitor to the British colonies in Africa, Arthur Hinsley, later Cardinal Archbishop of Westminster, wrote personally to Loubière in support. These villages strengthened the faith of the early Christians and had a strong influence on the missionary success.

Outstations

The strongest proponent of the opposite view was Fr Emil Schmitz,

---

48 Cunningham Graham in P. Caraman, *The Lost Paradise* (London: Sidgwick & Jackson, 1975), p. 129.
49 M. O'Reilly, *The Zambezi Mission and the Salisbury Vicariate*, unpublished, Box 40, p. 101.

who, at Driefontein, could point to two successful outstations in Chilimanzi (Chirimanzu) which developed into the mission stations of Holy Cross and St Joseph's, Hama, as mentioned above. He cited the White Fathers (Missionaries of Africa) in Zambia and Tanganyika who were having great success without Christian villages. At a mission conference in Bulawayo in June 1920 it was a hot topic but no conclusion was reached. Yet the tide was turning against Christian villages. Out schools, at a distance from the mission, were mushrooming and proving to be the way to the heart of the people. We mentioned the unseemly rivalry between the Christian churches in the nineteenth century. This did not die in the twentieth but it took the form of competing for influence with the people by establishing out schools as markers of a particular church. Sometimes there was tension and disappointment, as when Fr Moreau eyed a place for a mission in Chief Monze's area in southern Zambia in 1902 only to find the Seventh Day Adventists had acquired it a few days before he arrived. The government decided on a 'three-mile rule'[50] by which no Christian denomination could build a school closer than three miles from that of another.

With the pressure to open schools it would be impossible to also staff Christian villages. By 1930, the Christian villages had practically come to an end and this coincided with the death of their strongest advocate, Fr Loubière, and the end of the term of office of Msgr Robert Brown, the Prefect Apostolic and another strong supporter. Catechists in out schools now became key in the work of evangelisation and education went hand in hand with it.

Mariannhill leaves Mashonaland

Six years after the Jesuits arrived with the white settlers in 1890 a group of Trappist monks were sent by Abbot Franz Pfanner from Mariannhill, 16 km west of Durban, to join them. They were welcomed by the Jesuits and they began to settle north of Rusape on a farm at Triashill. The first four monks came up from Beira and were just taking over the farm when the Shona rising happened. As newcomers unfamiliar with the country, they felt vulnerable and rushed back to Umtali to

---

50 Fr Eddie Murphy thinks it was more like a twelve-mile rule. This sounds more realistic. I have not been able to find a definitive reference as to what it was, but the intention is clear.

seek protection in the laager, arriving exhausted and sick. For a time they gave up hope of returning but Msgr Sykes pleaded with them to return.

In 1902, they prepared a new beginning, but since by now the railway line was built, they thought of founding their mission nearer to it. They bought a property from the Fairfield Estate, 7 km from Macheke and, as we saw above, called their new foundation Monte Cassino. Br Leopold Schimmel spent six months at Chishawasha learning the language and customs of the country before starting the new mission in April 1902. He was on his own for the first six months before receiving three companions. But then they had disasters. The cattle died, the rains failed, their house burnt down and thieves stole some of their property. A little later the two priests died and the two brothers carried on, on their own They were soon joined by two more priests and when Fr Joseph O'Neil, a Jesuit, visited in 1905 he was amazed at the progress. In 1909 they were joined by the Precious Blood sisters who are still there today. Since the population was small, as at Driefontein, they opened outstations in 1908: St Anthony's forty miles to the south-east and St Peter's, thirty miles more directly south.

Government officials urged them either to re-build the mission at Triashill or forfeit the place altogether. In 1908 they made a second start at Triashill when Fr Robert Duenzenhofer came from Monte Cassino with catechist Robert Tsuro whose son, Simon, became one of the first two priests ordained at the Seminary in 1947. They were soon joined by two brothers who would make Triashill famous: Zachary Riedl and Aegidius Pfister. Rapid expansion followed and outstations developed at St Barbara's in 1909 and St Benedict's in 1914.

But the Mariannhills were Trappists (also called Cistercians) and had problems with their higher Superiors. They are a strict monastic order founded in 1098 by, among others, St Bernard, to live a life of contemplation in total silence. As missionaries they could not observe their rules and so in 1909, they officially left the order and formed their own Congregation of the Missionaries of Mariannhill.[51]

But then a new problem arose. They wanted to have their own Prefecture in the east of Mashonaland. As early as 1924 Bishop

---

51 Michael Cawood Green has written a novel, *For the Sake of Silence* (Cape Town: Umuzi, 2008) about the birth of Mariannhill and the person of Abbot Franz Pfanner. Though written as a novel it is accurate about the facts and makes for astonishing reading.

Fleischer of Mariannhill, who had been Superior at Triashill for many years, had asked Rome for a Prefecture of Mashonaland East. Rome offered them Bechuanaland (Botswana) where they could have a jurisdiction of their own. Fleischer agreed under the condition that they keep the four missions in Mashonaland. In 1924 the Superior of Mariannhill made a formal application in Rome.

But the prefect, Msgr Brown, was against it and there was much correspondence between Rome, the Jesuits and Mariannhill. Msgr Brown argued that a Prefecture Apostolic for Mashonaland East would not work as there were no natural or administrative boundaries, Mashonaland was an entity as a whole. But there is another district, Matabeleland, which is distinct and they should go there. It was nearer South Africa and Ndebele is akin to Zulu, the language spoken where the Mariannhill priests were working. The Jesuit headquarters had moved to Salisbury and Matabeleland is now far from there. The Mariannhill fathers and brothers should take over Empandeni, Embakwe, and Bulawayo and leave their missions in Mashonaland.

The Mariannhills (CMM) argued they had been in Monte Cassino and Triashill for twenty-five years; they have done well there and produced flourishing Catholics. The people were welcoming and easy to work with, whereas in Matabeleland they would have to start again from scratch.

Rome decided to follow Msgr Brown's advice, that they should take over Matabeleland and leave their missions in Mashonaland. In October 1929 Msgr Brown sent Jesuit superiors to all four missions in Mashonaland East. The CMM felt they were being expelled from their own property and were so hurt and disappointed that they did not go to Matabeleland, but withdrew to South Africa. Only in March the following year did they take over what the Jesuits had given them. They found the new area difficult. The Matabele were not as open to Christianity as the Mashona. And some whites in Bulawayo were not pleased by these new 'German' priests, for it was not long after the hostilities of the First World War. The Mariannhill priests remembered what they had left. They spoke of Triashill at Christmas in 1911 when over 200 people were baptised and twenty-five couples were married. And they remembered Easter 1912 with 181 baptisms and thirty-one marriages. They had to leave their thriving missions. It was a sad story and left a bitter taste. The Silver Jubilee of Triashill in

1934 may have helped to soothe the bitter feelings of the two religious orders. The main guest and celebrant was Msgr Arnoz CMM, Prefect Apostolic of Bulawayo, who had been a Superior of Triashill for several years. The Superiors of all the four former CMM missions were present. The irony is that twenty-three years later the Eastern districts of Mashonaland did become a Prefecture Apostolic – under the Carmelites.

All Souls (1930)

All Souls could have been a mission even earlier than Chishawasha if Hartmann's reconnaissance of a site there soon after his arrived in 1890 had proved promising. But it didn't, as we saw earlier. He had been told by Selous, who had been the settlers' guide in 1890, that it was an ideal place to found a mission and had a large, for those days, population of around 2,000. Ashamed to remain in Salisbury when the settlers were prospecting far and wide for mines and farms, he felt he too should move away from the centre.[52] But he found it unsuitable and with a small population so he retraced his steps to Salisbury and accepted Prestage's suggestion of the Chishawasha valley.

Mariannhill Fr Ebner founded the out school that became All Souls in what he later discovered was a malarial site which he aptly called 'Purgatorio'. When the Jesuits took over in 1930 Fr Esser became the first resident priest and moved to a site three miles away and changed the name to a more hopeful 'All Souls'. The new place was freer of mosquitoes but more prone to leopards eyeing the cattle and baboons the maize.[53] It meant that it was hard to draw the children to school when the maize was ripening, though easier after the harvest. In 1940 Fr Charles Shackles took over the mission and the LCBL sisters came in 1951. In 1962, the Jesuits handed over the mission to the archdiocese and Fr Simon Tsuro became superior. He applied for a secondary school in 1966.

A settlement had been established at nearby Mutemwa for people living with leprosy, and in 1958 Bishop Chichester wrote to six religious congregations inviting them to help. None could.[54] The person in charge was negligent and malnutrition brought on by the

---

52 Hartmann to Kerr 21.7.91.
53 *Zambesi Mission Record,* IX, p. 33.
54 JAZ, Box 41.

pilfering of food supplies aggravated the effects of malaria, bilharzia and hookworm – all led to anaemia and gastroenteritis.[55] All Souls took care of the settlement, and relief for the people there came with the appointment of John Bradburne,[56] an English layman, who became warden in 1969. All Souls provided medical care through Dr Luisa Guidotti and Sr Catarina Savini of the Associazione Femminile Medico-Missionaria of Italy.

Chikwizo, St Martin's (1960)

In 1560, Anthony Bex tells us,[57] Gonçalo da Silveira passed near Chikwizo where Langley Lewis, in 1960, offered the first Mass in four hundred years. Chikwizo is near the Mozambican border, 200 miles east of Salisbury but, as Roland Picho, who took over in 1970, wrote, *l'amour abolit les distances*.[58] In 1971, Pichon imagined, and set about building, something new, something to his mind entirely in line with the thinking of the Second Vatican Council which ended in 1965. First, he looked for a *guyo*, a nether grinding stone, for the altar. He found one – in the bed of the Rwenya River. The mission truck and the tractor of the tsetse fly inspector were in-spanned to drag the altar of solid granite to a baobab tree round which was built a *rushanga*, an encompassing of a sacred place.

Soon, other stones were brought and white quartz was used as a gable and a cross. Near the altar was 'the rock of Meribah, where your fathers put me to the test'. (Ps 95), and in an adjoining building, separated from the main church by a red curtain (the Red Sea), the catechumens attended the Mass up to the offertory. The red curtain was then closed each Sunday until Easter, when, after their baptism in a pool designed for the purpose, it was finally opened and they were admitted to 'the Promised land'. Roger Riddell, then a Jesuit student at the university, used to visit Chikwizo and tells us of the precarious water supply and his impressions:

> The mission had no electricity, and water was pumped up from

---

55 D. Rance, *John Bradburne, The Vagabond of God* (London: Darton Longman and Todd, 2017), p. 305.

56 Bradburne was an exceptional person and ended his life by being killed a few days before the Lancaster House Conference, that was to lead to the independence of Zimbabwe, opened in London.

57 JAZ, Box 342.

58 Love abolishes distance.

the Rwenya River, more than a mile away, by an unreliable diesel-engine. Cooking was done using firewood, the one luxury being a paraffin-powered fridge, producing much-needed ice-cold water. During my time there, two young children died after being bitten by a rabid dog. I found an alive button or widow-spider on the curtain of my room, and I almost trod on a crocodile when down at the river with Pichon trying to repair the water pump; fortunately, it scuttled away. Towards the end of my stay, a lion was reported to have been attacking cattle in a nearby village. So – yes – it was remote!

In spite of or because of all this, I loved Chikwizo and as I grew to understand Pichon (as everyone called him) and absorb his theological outlook, I grew increasingly fond of him. He hated humbug, status, colonialism, racism and Ian Smith. He believed the church should first and foremost serve the people and not exist for the glory and privilege of the clergy, and was not afraid to say so. His liturgies were long but beautiful, he preached from the heart, and lived in shorts and a hat, often with a *Gauloise* sticking out of the side of his mouth, his hands often steeped in oil after a morning trying to fix the water pump. He epitomised for me what being a Jesuit priest in Africa ought to be.[59]

Two hundred miles seemed a safe distance from Salisbury and Pichon never told the archbishop of his plans or how he was implementing them, which would have been normal practice. But Archbishop Markall heard rumours and decided to visit Chikwizo. He made the journey and was greeted by a suitably penitent Pichon with a bottle of good French wine. Soothed, the archbishop went on to offer to pay for the roof.

Pichon was demanding, and aspiring Christians were well drilled in the faith. The war put an end to this imaginative evangelisation and the mission was abandoned. Pichon himself had to leave the country because of his strident criticisms of the Rhodesians. On the feast of Martin of Tours, patron of the mission, in 1971, many visitors came to celebrate the mission's patron. 'People of all nations', he later wrote, 'assembled here on November 11, not around the slab that covers the unknown soldier (Armistice Day, 1918), certainly not to celebrate

---

59 R. Riddell, Memoirs (in preparation).

UDI,⁶⁰ but around the altar stone on which the Body and Blood of the well-known Freedom Fighter, who brings victory and peace to all who believe in him,'.⁶¹ Pichon noticed the heavens opened that evening and the people began to plough and sow.

Twenty-five years later he was invited back to teach French at Arrupe and I, assistant (*socius*) to the provincial at the time, offered to take him to Chikwizo. Did I make a mistake? All he saw was the ruins of his work but the church still stood and he met a few people who remembered those days. He was used to disappointments, which is not to say I was right to add one more. He had been expelled from Martinique, Chad and Zambia before coming to Rhodesia for a final expulsion. He ended his days in France highly respected among his companions.⁶²

---

60 Unilateral Declaration of Independence, 11 November 1965, when the Rhodesians declared themselves independent of Britain, a declaration not recognised by any country, not even apartheid South Africa.
61 JM, New Year 1972, p 5.
62 See also Roland Pichon, *Living Stones*, JM, Spring 1971, and *African Martinmas*, JM New Year, 1972.

5

Reaching the Zambezi

We have talked so much about the Zambezi Mission, let us go to the Zambezi.

Fr Joseph Otto SJ

Jesuits from Germany had been part of what became the Zimbabwe Province since 1879 but between the two world wars there grew up a desire to have their own mission area where they could concentrate their minds and resources. The first moves were made in 1935 but progress was interrupted by the Second World War. Fr Joseph Otto was on leave in 1957 and he approached the East German provincial, Fr Karl Wehner, about resuming this project and he found he was pushing on an open door. Wolfgang Thamm explains:

> The East German Province had suffered tremendously by the end of World War II in losing all its Catholic areas in Silesia and East Prussia. Millions of people were displaced from their homes and had to settle in other parts of Germany which were usually Protestant. The priests had to look after them under very harsh conditions, especially because of the communist regime. But by 1958 there were young members of the province who wanted to go to Africa. Among them were Lorenz von Walter and Wolfgang Thamm, both still with us more than 60 years later. There was also Frs Johannes Weisbrich and Johannes Appel, who was also a medical doctor. Their first task was to choose the districts to form the new mission. Sinoia [Chinhoyi] was to be the centre and the

mission would stretch north to the Zambezi, east to Marymount near the Mozambique border and west as far as Chirundu and the borders of the BaTonga. The mission was founded on 8th September 1959 with Fr Otto as the first Superior and Parish Priest at Sinoia. Huge growth now started in the area with centres at Karoi, Banket, Mangula and so on. The main project was St. Albert's Mission, Mount Darwin. It was planned as a hospital and a secondary school from the start.[1]

The two decades after 1959, when the new Sinoia Mission grew and flourished, were also the decisive years in which the country, unable to resolve the confrontation between two world views, drifted into war. The events of the 1960s, when the yearning for freedom clashed with an obdurate isolationism nourished over seventy years, left those who lived through them with an acute sense of impending disaster. It was against this background that the German Jesuits, conscious that the present was charged with uncertainty, used all their imagination, energy and resources to build for the future.

The new jurisdiction was an odd shape. If the country was a bun, it would be the icing on the top. Bishop Dieter Scholz told me if he wanted to travel to some parts of his diocese, he had pass through the Archdiocese of Harare. They inherited Kariba, Kutama, Marymount and Chinhoyi itself but all the other foundations were made in the frenetic sixties and seventies.

In 1962, Otto bought a house in Salisbury, Canisius House, which acted as a base for missionaries coming to town for shopping or rest. Br Franz Gabriel was the much-loved host who welcomed them in peace and in war and attended to their needs beginning with a cup of real coffee.

Kutama (1912)

Though on the fringe of the present diocese of Chinhoyi, Kutama, it could be claimed, is the spiritual hearth *(choto)* of the diocese. Perhaps, in recognition of this, the first bishop of the diocese and most of the priests are buried there. The teacher training college there put out shoots, in the form of its graduates, over much of what became the diocese. When looking at the origins of, for example Sipolilo (Guruve),

---

1 W. Thamm, *A Short History of the Society of Jesus in Zimbabwe* (Jesuit Province of Zimbabwe-Mozambique, 2018).

you find that it was a teacher trained at Kutama that invited Fr Kotzki. We will say more on Kutama later.

President Mugabe initiated the building of Fr Jerome O'Hea Hospital in Kutama and Fr Karl Ferdinand-Schmidt saw the project through to completion in 1991.

Marymount (1949)

Fr Herman Kaibach had a great desire, like Xavier perhaps, to keep moving. He wanted to start a mission in the Chesa area to the north and on 9 October 1923 – the beginning of the rainy season? – he set out for the Mount Darwin area. A school was started at Chaparadza under teacher Johannes Chimusoro.[2] In the event it took twenty-seven years to follow this up with a mission residence. Bishop Chichester endured much pestering from Johannes, who was teaching at Makumbe, which Kaibach had founded in the meantime. Kaibach had written again to the superior in 1928 from Chishawasha, to which he had subsequently moved, to say he was free and 'the people need us. It is urgent.' He recalled that Silveira had died in the area and it was 'matter of justice' we go there.[3] The prefect's consultors urged caution as they feared malaria which, in the 1920s, was still claiming Jesuit lives in the Zambezi valley, especially north of the river.

Kaibach and Fr Michael Hannan surveyed the area in 1941 but the consultors went to see the site they chose and rejected it. Fr Enright, the superior, on the other hand, sided with Hannan, Kaibach and Chimusoro and a site was chosen in 1949. Enright later lost faith in Hannan when he judged he was spending money too freely.[4] Water was a problem and building the school (eight classrooms) was a slow process; the Jesuits lived in temporary cubicles in one of the completed classrooms. At the beginning of 1951 the school was ready. Chaparadza was also rebuilt, and Chakoma and Chiweshe (Fatima) out schools were added. Two catechists had already been teaching in these schools for a few years before they were reopened. Six other out schools were added in 1950. In 1954 a small hospital was built, though it was replaced by a new one by Fr Edmund Wilson in 1958.

---

2   Mission Magazine, Autumn 1950, p 162. See also G. Hipler, The Diocese of Chinhoyi, 2006, p. 14.
3   JAZ, Box 142.
4   Rea, SAA Marymount, Box File B.

Sr Killiana Müller OP worked in the hospital (1956-71) and wrote down accounts of her experiences which give colour to life on the mission at the time.

Hannan was helped by a Canadian mission volunteer, Hughie Heaney, but he was not warmly accepted by other Jesuits. It shocks us today to learn how lay helpers were marginalised in those days. When Hughie stayed a night at Campion House preparing for his fourteen-hour journey back to the mission, the cook was afraid to put meat in his sandwiches out of 'fear of his superiors'.[5] Even the bishop 'does not want lay people on missions. He thinks it is too hard for them'.[6] Hannan felt welcomed by the local people but felt discouraged by the 'strange hostility of ours'.[7] But Br Bernhard Lisson came in the following month and showed 'great enthusiasm about the place, the first Jesuit to do so'. The following April, Hannan reported to Enright that he was 'completely exhausted ... played out'.

Fr Bruno Gasse[8] succeeded Hannan in 1952 and built the church which was opened in 1953. He was succeeded by Fr Georg Muschalek who built 'about 48 new buildings' (Hipler) between 1958 and 1966. Among them were a new boarding hostel for girls, a large dining hall for boys, two new dormitories for boys, a convent for the sisters and he enlarged the hospital. In 1966 there was a tragedy, Br Zochel was killed by an explosion while welding a drum. His loss was deeply felt.

Marymount was right in the war zone during the liberation struggle and Fr Gerry Pieper had been killed at the next mission, Kangaire, in December 1978. In July 1979, seven sisters were abducted with Br Herman Toma and brought to Mozambique. Among the sisters were Pius Katsukunya, Irene Rufaro,[9] de Cora, Dorothy Patini and candidates Gregor Munyaradzi and Bernard. They were jeered at

---

5   Hannan to Enright, JAZ, Box 142.
6   Hannan to Enright, 28 October 1951, JAZ, Box 142.
7   A quaint Jesuit expression for fellow Jesuits. See Hannan to Enright, 17 June 1950, JAZ, Box 142.
8   Gasse later left the Society and married a local woman he met in his pastoral work. Bishop Dieter Scholz remembers Fr Muschalek saying Gasse was highly inculturated. He knew Shona well and stayed with the people for weeks on his pastoral rounds. He was later involved in road-building projects in Zambia.
9   This was her third serious war experience. She had been arrested by the security forces at Wedza (Hwedza) and tortured and had witnessed the deaths of two Jesuits at Magonde (Makondi).

by some of the fighters on the way but when Tongogara, military commander of all ZANLA forces, met them he treated them with great respect. Gregor later wrote a full account of her experiences and explained how she came to understand and respect the guerrillas.

In the early 1990s the bodies of some guerrillas who had been killed during the war and buried in shallow graves, were exposed by the rains. These remains were carefully collected by the mission staff and Dieter Scholz, who was the superior at the time, suggested to the resident minister, James Makamba, that they be re-interred in a local Heroes' Acre. The mission would make half the coffins and the Party agreed to make the other half. On the day assigned for the reburial the mission had the coffins ready but the Party did not provide even one.

Fr Karl Steffens was superior at the mission during the war. After Gerry's death it was decided he should not stay there but he often used to fly in for the day. A landing strip was built despite level ground being hard to find, so the runway sloped down to a river and planes would normally land uphill and take off downhill, unless the wind direction suggested they do the contrary.

Even after independence the troubles of Marymount were not over. RENAMO, the armed opposition in Mozambique, habitually crossed into Zimbabwe and harassed the local people, blaming them for Zimbabwe's support of FRELIMO. During Fr Dieter Scholz's time at Marymount, the mission staff were often involved in the care of refugees from Mozambique, especially at Mazoe Bridge camp where there were 15,000 refugees and Nyamatikiti, near Rushinga, where there were around 6,000.

Though there was a secondary school at the mission run by the Dominican sisters it only went to JC level. After independence, the local Chief, Makuni, and the people wanted a boarding secondary school at the mission that went to Form 6, but the provincial and the bishop were against it. Perhaps they were thinking there was a school just two kilometres away at Nyahuwi. But this school was not for boarding. Nyahuwi was the name of the local spirit medium, a young woman at the time; and she wanted to co-operate with the mission Dieter Scholz welcomed this and it was one of the reasons why he wanted the school. After the Jesuits left in 2006, the school was built by the diocesan clergy.

When Wolfgang Abeler became superior in 1996, he improved the water situation and encouraged 'dry tillage'. Dieter became bishop of the diocese in 2006 and reflected that, while great progress had been made in setting up structures over the years, the faith of the people had not yet put down roots. Many Catholics went over to the Vapostori and when the latter were looking for leaders, they recognised that the former had some formation and they would elect them.

In the 1980s, Fr Edward Hancko developed Rushinga and built a church there.

Kariba (1957)

The Kariba gorge on the Zambezi was chosen as the site of a massive dam by the short-lived Central African Federation (1953-63) to satisfy the increasing demand for electricity in its three territories: the two Rhodesias and Nyasaland, which later became Zambia, Zimbabwe and Malawi. The construction of the dam, started in 1955 and completed in 1959, cost US$480 million and the ensuing lake, with a catchment area of 663,000 square kms, displaced '57,000 Tonga people, making it one of the worst dam-resettlement disasters in African history'.[10]

The building of the dam cost the lives of eighty-six workers, some of whom fell into fast-setting concrete so that their remains are embedded in the dam like the relics of the saints in the altars of our churches. It was this tragedy that inspired the Italian construction company, Impresit, to build a church on the hill above the dam, on the Zimbabwe side, dedicated to their memory. Their names are inscribed on a plaque, though in some cases only the name by which they were known at work is given. It seems the company did not know their family name. The chapel was dedicated to St Barbara, 'patron of miners and underground workers' to quote the citation. It is a round building which respects the heat of the Zambezi valley in being open to the air through filigree decorated wrought-iron bars for half its radius. The other half displays stained-glass windows with the words of the Our Father. In 1962, Cardinal Montini[11] visited and gave a tabernacle to the people for St Barbara's.

---

10 Jacques Leslie, *Deep Water: The Epic Struggle over Dams, Displaced People, and the Environment*, (New York: Farrar., Strauss and Giroux, 2005).
11 Soon to be Pope Paul VI.

Archbishop Francis Markall dedicated this chapel in 1958[12] and Fr de Meulders[13] was the first resident pastor. His parish included the houses built on the heights above the river for the Italian workers which became, in the old Rhodesia, a European area and the houses on the shore of the new lake, Mahombekombe, which were for the local people. De Meulders converted a hall there into a church which became St Augustine's and he started a school. A new priest soon came from Italy for the Italians and Fr Marimanzi was sent to care for the people of the township. The Sisters of Charity from Milan came in 1959 to care for the Italians but soon spread their work to include the local people.

De Meulders was followed by Don Giuseppi Betta and later Don Parenti and gradually *nostra piccolo missioni*, our little mission (Montini) included Chirundu, on the south side of the river, and Siavonga on the north. Don Parenti bought a small house on the lake which became a holiday house for missionaries. Over the years, as the Italians left, the attendance at St Barbara's dwindled while that at St Augustine's increased and it became the vibrant centre of the parish.

In 1973, Rhodesia closed the border with Zambia and the priest at Kariba could no longer visit Chirundu (north side) and Siavonga. Chirundu, with its well-equipped hospital, had to be closed as the sugar estates folded due to the border closure. A new township for the local people developed at Nyamunga, twenty kilometres from Kariba on the road to Salisbury. At the same time the Jesuits assumed responsibility for the parish with Fr Kotski, who built the new church at Nyamunga. He was succeeded briefly by Joseph Friedrich and then Georg Sunder, who served Kariba for eight years.

Mhangura (1958)

Mangula (Mhangura) parish grew out of a request from the operators of its copper mine for the same sisters as ran their hospital in Messina, to staff the hospital at the new mine they were opening at Mangula. The Daughters of Our Lady of the Sacred Heart arrived at the mine in 1958 and Fr George Orr became their chaplain. In 1961 Fr Friedrich replaced him, the chaplaincy became a parish and a church was built

---

12 *The Shield*, 1959, 1, p. 13.
13 He had been 'a great missionary in India' in the view of Fr Hans Belser; Belser to Enright, 15 September 2004, JAZ, Box 1480.

in 1963. In 1977 the parish had 14 outstations and the Jesuits handed it to the newly established diocese in 1987. Norbert Gille, parish priest there 1980-86, found if 'very difficult' as the Malawians on the farms were not interested and the European farmers were resentful that he did not spend time with them.

Chinhoyi (1954)

From 1954, Fr James Wallace, based at the seminary in Chishawasha, used to visit the outstation at Sinoia (Chinhoyi) for Mass once a month. In October 1959, Fr Joseph Otto moved into a house in Sinoia, built by Fr John Caraman the year before, and made it the headquarters of the new Jesuit Sinoia Mission. This is a good place to mention Caraman. Many people on the large commercial farms were left out of the urban/rural mission axis and he filled this gap by constantly visiting the farms where many Malawians worked. He slept in a different bed every night or in his car. Each trip took three months and after a week of rest he began the tour again. He also built chapels in Karoi and in Centenary.[14]

In 1965 the old church in Chinhoyi was demolished and Corpus Christi Cathedral was built by Fr Bernhard Raab. In 1972, Fr Wolf Huwe built St Peter's church in Chikohonono 'township' and in 1985 a second church was built in the township, called Musha weBetania, which was close to the Rural Training Centre set up in 1978 and run by Br Hubert Simon.

Karoi (1963)

Karoi was one of the centres where John Caraman celebrated Mass four times a year, from 1950, in a small church dedicated to St Christopher. When the Sinoia mission was established, Karoi was developed by Fr Wolfgang Thamm, who was well settled at St Albert's, but was asked to move to take over this new parish. He arrived in time to witness a new church hall opened in Chikangwe 'location' on the border of the town on 9 January 1972. The people chose the name St Paul's and danced until 3.00 a.m!derly[15]

Karoi was the centre of a vast area of 252 farms with a population of 1,770 Europeans and around 80,000 of the local people. The number

---

14 Dachs and Rea, p. 171.
15 JAZ, Box 206.

of Catholics in 1972 was put at 1,726 in the town and the twenty-five outstations.[16] This figure rose to 2,233 in 1975 when there were thirty-two outstations and 2,410 a year later. Evaristo Mapuranga made his Jesuit first vows in Karoi on 25 July 1975 and this attracted a great deal of attention. It was another step in the Church becoming rooted in local soil and, interestingly, it was a unique and unrepeated event for the Sinoia mission marking its identity as a Jesuit unit.

In 1976, St Christopher's was dismantled and rebuilt in Chundu, of which more will be said below, and a bigger church was built and dedicated to the Holy Trinity. Unusually, it was jointly owned and jointly blessed by Bishop Burroughs of the Anglican Church and Msgr Helmut Reckter, the Prefect Apostolic. Both communions wanted a church in Karoi at the same time and they decided to share one – a remarkable sign of co-operation perhaps influenced by the Second Vatican Council which had ended only seven years before. The written agreement that the church was indivisible turned out to be prescient in view of the antics of Bishop Norbert Kunonga some decades later. He tried to break away from the Anglican communion and take the Anglican church buildings with him. Lorenz von Walter had to diplomatically acquaint the Kunonga people of this provision in the agreement.

As mentioned, Karoi was a European farming area; Wolfgang enjoyed a good relationship with the farmers and built churches on their farms at Chundu, Kasangarare, Tengwe and Bvuti. The church at Chundu was the reassembled old St Christopher's from Karoi. Fr Lorenz von Walter, who was at Karoi at the time, spent days on the roof carefully numbering the roof sheets so that they could be simply refitted in Chundu. The new church at Shamrock mine was just being completed when the mine was closed and abandoned! When Fr Konrad Landsberg was aiming to build a church in Mutorashanga at '20B', Wolfgang said to him, 'You want a church? I have a spare one. You can have it!' So the church at Shamrock was dismantled and rebuilt at 20B. We are a Church on the move, sometimes physically!

But the European farmers were feeling betrayed by the Church. Thamm would arrive at a church to celebrate Mass and the farmer would greet him with, 'He has done it again!' He referred to yet one

---

16 W. Thamm, *Historia Domus*, JAZ, Box 206.

more speech of Bishop Lamont or the CCJP that had revealed further atrocities committed by the security forces. By 1977, the earlier number of 1,770 Europeans had fallen to 150. By 1978, Thamm reports, the war made it impossible to visit all the centres and the following year refugees began to flood into the town.

Wolfgang told the prefect, Helmut Reckter, he wanted to invite sisters to work in the parish. Wolfgang had trouble with one sister but persevered and, after building a convent for them, witnessed the great work they did running, among other things, sixteen women's clubs. Thamm invited Br Waddelove (Waddy) to start Savings Clubs among the people but when Waddy arrived and found Wolfgang had been lending money to people he exploded: 'You have spoiled them'. Waddy believed that if people were used to getting money easily it would be difficult to teach them the discipline needed for savings clubs.

Thamm also used to gather young people from the farms for one-week courses when he would teach them in the morning and then have soccer in the afternoon and indoor games in the evening. The Rural Council made a site available for them which was called 'Tangwena' – a name often given to any internally displaced people in those days as it referred to the movement of the Tangwena people from their homes in the hills around Inyanga (Nyanga) on the borders of Mozambique. Local and international help poured in to provide them with sanitation, medicine, nutrition, instruction of the infants and some schooling for the children.

In the worst years of the war Mrs Matongo, wife of the medical officer in Wedza, used to gather the internally displaced people and she ran a feeding scheme for them. After the war some zealots among ZANU-PF were hostile to the church and its influence but Mai Matongo used to stand up to them.

Murombedzi (Gangarahwe), St Kizito's (1964)

The early Jesuits were dreamers as well as practical men. Their horizons were way beyond their reach. As far back as 1910, Fr Richartz was not only turning his attention to Kutama, in Zvimba district, but beyond it. He applied for a site at Murombedzi, further west, and got a favourable response from the Native Commissioner. He founded an outstation with a school and fifty-four years later Fr Gilbert Modikayi founded a mission there and inherited nine more outstations. Perhaps uniquely, the mission acquired five names: it was not only called Murombedzi but also Gangarahwe, St Kizito's, Five Miles or simply 'Five'. When Gilbert left in 1966 to enter the Jesuit novitiate, he was succeeded by Fr Regis Chigwedere who built a church there in 1967. A parish hall was built in 1978 by which time there were twenty-three outstations. But it was wartime and the mission was not spared. A former catechist, Edward Chirambaguva, and his son Philip were killed and the priest, by then it was Karl-Ferdinand Schmidt, moved to Chinhoyi. In 1991, Fr Collen Zhuwawo was murdered at the mission. It seems he had surprised some thieves at the chicken run. The mission was handed to the diocese in 1998.

Banket (1964)

The name of this small settlement on the main Harare/Chinhoyi road is because early settlers saw in the rock formation a similarity to the auriferous conglomerate on the South African Rand, called in Dutch, 'banket'. They too hoped for gold but found little. Instead the settlement served the surrounding agricultural district and the mines. One of the farmers, Catholic Colonel Sweetman, gave fifteen acres for a church and a school in 1964. Archbishop Markall hesitated about accepting the grant and so the property is in the name of the Society of Jesus. Fr Sunder had difficulties with the Salvation Army in the beginning as they considered Banket their territory. Banket seems to have been a much 'fought over' place as, at a later date, the ruling party noted that the opposition MDC viewed Banket as 'theirs' and ZANU-PF did all it could to wrest the town from them, with consequences for Thamm.

A church was built in 1965 and St George's Primary School, which Herman Husemann named after Georg Sunder to the latter's discomfort, in 1969. In 1974, Husemann extended the church and new churches were built in 1976 at the outstations in Muriel and Sutton mines. The LCBL sisters came in 1977 and further churches were added at Trelawney and Caesar mines in 1978. In 2000, Wolfgang Thamm, who was at Banket for thirteen years in two shifts, opened the Sacred Heart Secondary School. As it was a farming area there was less scope for building churches in the Mass centres so he used the funds he received from Germany to build this school which had initially eight classrooms and a science laboratory. They developed clubs where religious education and social activities were combined. One girl went back to her home and taught twenty-five other girls. She returned to ask Thamm to open a Mass centre there at Pindipark Farm which was owned by Lance Smith, a former cabinet minister in Ian Smith's government. Wolfgang estimates the population of Banket was far in excess of the official figure of 5,000, and put it as high as 25,000.

It was during the elections in 2002 when the 'Green Bombers'[17] attacked Thamm. As mentioned, ZANU-PF were intent of suppressing the opposition in Banket and the farmers and whites generally were seen to be supporters of the opposition. On his way to the post office one day, Thamm was suddenly accosted by these auxiliaries of the ruling party. A bomber told him, 'You church people are telling the people how to vote', and he hit Thamm in his right eye. Specialists could do nothing to save his sight in that eye.

On another occasion Thamm was asked to go to Trelawney to collect an asthmatic patient and take him to the hospital in Banket. He was accompanied by Sr Josephine Nyikadzino, of the Congregation of Jesus.[18] It was a Sunday around 6.00 p.m. and he had just completed his third Mass. He arrived at Trelawney and had to pass by a barracks. The sister told him a soldier was signalling for him to stop and he did. Two other soldiers arrived and without explanation they dragged him from the car and forced him to sit down in a deep puddle of muddy water. It was the rainy season. They wanted to beat him further but a senior soldier said 'enough'. He was shaken by the experience and was never himself again afterwards. Much later he learnt the reason for the assault. The flag is lowered every night at 6.00 p.m. and all are required to stop for a moment out of respect. Thamm had no idea at

---

17 The National Youth Service (NYS) was a programme of the Zimbabwean government for Zimbabweans of ages ten to thirty. It was introduced in 2000 by the Minister for Gender, Youth and Employment, and the first training camp was established in 2001. Its stated purpose was to 'transform and empower youths for nation building through life skills training and leadership development.' However it was criticised for promoting human rights violations on behalf of the ZANU-PF party. Within Zimbabwe the graduates were known as the 'Green Bombers' after the fatigue uniforms they wore.

18 Formerly called the Mary Ward Sisters after their founder who was born into a recusant family in Yorkshire, England, in the late sixteenth century and started a community for the education of girls around 1610.

the time and had not even seen the flag. In both cases the people who attacked Wolfgang did not know him.

Hurungwe, St Boniface (1968)

Fr Erich Kotzki, based at Kutama in the 1940s, used to visit his former students who were starting out schools. One was at Karareshi in the Hurungwe district west of Karoi begun in 1949. Kotzki ran into opposition with the Salvation Army and appealed to Bishop Chichester to intervene.[19] From the 1950s Catholic Christians had been among those migrating from Mhondoro and Chirumanzu to Hurungwe and so the Catholic population in the district was growing. In 1959, Fr Joseph Otto took up Kotzki's work and the following year Fr Rainer Zinkann joined him. In 1961 they built a church at Chanetsa, another outstation.

The time was ripe for a central mission station and when Fr Dieter Thiel joined Zinkann in the mid-1960s, they planned to open one and call it after the great missionary of the eighth century in Thiel's homeland, St Boniface. Thiel settled there permanently in 1968 and in 1971 the new church was opened. One indicator of progress is given by Fr Friedrich when he was there: the number of church marriages rose from sixteen in 1970 to thirty in 1972. Since water was short no immediate steps were taken to open a school and the emphasis was on pastoral work in the district. There were twenty-two outstations in 1971 and they ran a two-week course at the mission for the catechists and church leaders in scripture and church history. In 1976 the LCBL sisters arrived to help with the pastoral work but two years later the mission staff had to leave as the pressure of the war intensified.

The 1980s was a time of rebuilding and Fr Karl Steffens, who was there for fourteen years (1987-2001), built a carpentry school in 1990 with the help of his *mukuwasha*,[20] Heinrich Lorenz, who helped in many ways to develop the mission. By 2002, there were sixty-three outstations.

Makonde (Magondi), St Rupert's (1964)

The multiplication of the loaves did not end by the Sea of Galilee. The disciples went to Antioch and beyond, even to Makonde on the

---

19 Kotzki to Chichester, 4 June 1949, JAZ, Box 135/4.
20 Brother-in-law.

bank of the Mupfure River. Fr Karl Hermann tells us, in a booklet produced to commemorate the Golden Jubilee of the Mission in 2014, 'it all started with a few families (Kapunza, Zvidzwa, Matienga and Munyanyi) migrating from Zvimba to Makonde'. Fr Otto came from Banket on 9 November 1959 to celebrate Mass. He and Fr Rainer Zinkann continued to come until Fr Rudolph Kensy moved there in 1964 to found the mission with mission helper Walter Müller and Br Johannes Werner. They lived in a classroom at St Cecilia's out school (from Kutama) until they could build a house. At first, they were not given land but Kensy interceded with Fr Rupert Meyer SJ, the 'apostle of Munich') who had died in 1945 shortly after the war ended and was beatified by Pope John Paul II in 1987. The very next day they were given land and so the mission was dedicated to Rupert Meyer even though he was not yet a blessed, let alone a saint. If anyone quibbled, they could mention St Rupert of Salzburg who died in 710.

Fr Joachim von Kersenbrock then arrived with his lorry to carry firewood to burn the bricks needed, and before the year ended they had their own house and a small chapel. Two years later a hospital with twenty-four beds was built and run by three LCBL sisters, Thomas, Rita and Hilaria. Fr Gregor Richert arrived in 1967. He used to write regularly to his family, friends and supporters so that when Fr Karl-Ferdinand Schmidt later wrote his life he had ready material to hand. Soon after arriving Gregor wrote: 'I am surrounded by fallow country. … Out of nothing, other than his tremendous personal commitment, Fr Kensy built an oasis in this stony and sandy reserve.'

He felt the bleakness too of his appeal to the people, until he found a way of reaching them – through the dead. Gregor celebrated the funeral of an old respected man in the community,

> … in a way that was much spoken of, especially among the older people: 'how beautiful and impressive everything had been,' they said, 'and what high respect the Church has concerning the dead.' In Europe. we bury all the dead in one place, away from the living. Here the mounds are visible in the neighbourhood of the homes. With the Africans the dead and the living not only stay close together but they are also much stronger in unity and as a community in their minds. Are there any dead at all? There are only those living on the earth and those in the next world.[21]

---

21 K. Schmidt, in D. Harold-Barry and D. Adamson (eds), *They Stayed On*: *The stories*

Gregor also discovered that celebrating Easter imaginatively opens the eyes of people. On his first Easter he could not find twelve men who were Catholic for the washing of the feet on Holy Thursday and so he invited others to make up the number. The whole community celebrated through the night until dawn.

By 1970 there were 234 Catholic Christians at the mission, the number more than doubling in the following three years to 486. Progress continued with the building by Richert and Br Bernhard Lisson, who arrived in 1973, of a new church and parish hall, both opened in 1976. In that year there were already eleven outstations attached to the mission.

In 1974-75, Roland von Nidda SJ, not yet ordained a priest, did research into 'Shona Moral Beliefs' at Hombwe, thirty kilometres from the mission. He recalls sleeping on,

> a mat *(rukukwe)* together with the boys. A little cupboard behind me contained sugar, and at nights I would hear the rats scampering past my ears, trying to get at the sugar.
>
> Once every few weeks, I would go to St. Rupert's Mission to have a shower and visit Fr Richert and Br. Lisson. He was busy installing electricity in the mission. On one Saturday I asked Fr Richert if I could accompany him to an outstation to say Mass. We set off after breakfast, and travelled as far as the Land Rover could take us. From there we went on foot through a river and over a mountain, to get to the place. We got there at about 1 p.m. and found that the station was a little hut. The congregation consisted of three or four women, and a few little children. After Mass we were kindly offered *sadza* and *muriwo*. It was now getting dark, so we were given a young boy to show us the way back to the car in the darkness. We eventually arrived back at St. Rupert's at about 9 p.m. What touched me was the great sacrifice these men were making for the people. I asked myself: 'could I do that?' They, of course, paid the ultimate price, being shot and killed during the liberation war.
>
> My other recollection was of entering into a completely different world from the one to which I had been accustomed. I used to go to the *mapira* rituals at night, and watch people getting

---

of seven Jesuits martyred in the struggle for Zimbabwe, (Gweru: Mambo Press, 2000), p. 56.

possessed by different spirits *(vadzimu* and *mashave).* It all seemed so 'normal' and real. In my thesis I asked, what is one to make of it? Is this merely psychological, or para-psychological? Or are these really spirits speaking through the people? I thought the spirits would chase me out of the hut, being a *murungu.* They did not allow anything 'modern' into the ceremony, like glasses, watches, etc. Happily, the spirits did not drive me out, and allowed me to watch the proceedings with great fascination.

On another occasion I visited a *n'anga* in the area, who was famous for his healing powers. He performed these through a foreign (Swazi) spirit *(shave),* who gave him healing powers. When possessed by the spirit, he spoke, in a different voice, the Swazi language. The people assured me he had never been to Swaziland and did not know the language. Whilst possessed, people could bring their problems to the spirit. I thought I would give it a try, to see if I could catch him out. I never told anyone that I was a Jesuit. I said I was a university student wanting to learn more about Shona culture. I asked the spirit if I would marry and have a family. The spirit answered that if I remain in my present job, I will not marry. If I leave my job, I will marry.

All this showed me that bringing the Gospel to a culture different from one's own, does not just require one to learn the language. One has to steep oneself in the culture, and ask how best one can present the Good News in a way that is comprehensible, relevant, and acceptable to that culture.

Gregor had been parish priest from 1967 and was active as schools' manager even after the schools were taken over by the government after 1971 as the local council asked him to stay on. He was also active in promoting the economic development of the area and introduced cotton as a cash crop. First, he had to grow it himself to prove it could be done. At first the people were sceptical. 'Why grow what you cannot eat?' But he grew a good crop and six farmers took it up the next year. By 1978, a month before he was killed, Gregor could report, 'Cotton is planted everywhere in the Makonde area.'[22]

As the work flourished the dark clouds gathered. He wrote:

> One time we were mighty proud of our measurable achievements, visible signs, monuments perhaps to our own pride which had

---

22 Ibid., p. 61.

sprung up like mushrooms in the shortest time: schools, hospitals, churches, etc., first and foremost of course for the sake of those entrusted to us. But now, after the closing by force of so many of our buildings, has that all to become desolate, forgotten? ... I think it is now time that after a period of more outward growth the message of Christ takes stronger and deeper root than before. But if this is supposed to be achieved, then the heart of the one who has devoted himself to this task must bleed![23]

These words sank deep into our consciousness in the last years of the war and Lorenz von Walter quoted them with great feeling at the province meeting in 1980.[24]

Just after 4.00 p.m. on 27 June 1978, three armed men entered the mission. They asked Gregor for money and were annoyed he had so little. As they threatened him, Bernhard Lisson, who was close by mending a truck, pleaded with them. They shot Richert and then Lisson.

At their funeral at Chishawasha many words were spoken. We were shocked, numbed, and yet proud of these brothers of ours who 'gave meaning to the ultimate sacrifice which all had to face at the time of the guerrilla war' (Karl-Ferdinand Schmidt). A co-worker spoke of Richert's desire to train leaders 'for the day when no priests would be there any more' and Fr Horst Ulbrich, superior of the Sinoia mission, warned us against becoming bitter.

The sisters left and the mission was closed. The families of Machingura and Chitanda kept on coming to the mission to preserve what could be saved. In 1980, after independence, reconstruction began. From 1981, Fr Wolfgang Abeler and Deacon Makumbe rebuilt the priests' house and renovated the convent and the hospital. Fr Norbert Gille came in 1986 and did further development, building a church at Hombwe outstation where von Nidda had lived for a time. The Sisters of Charity of Milan came to develop and run the hospital. Gradually the mission re-established itself. It was handed over to the diocese in 1999 and Frs Ignatius Chazunguza and Frederik Mabiri came. A secondary school was started in 2000. In 2002 the Jesuits returned with Frs Fabian Masina, Stephen Silungwe and Br Herman Toma. In that same year the Sisters of Charity handed over

---
23 Ibid., p. 63.
24 JN 45, 18 September 1980., Box 469B.

the hospital to the LCBL sisters.

In 2004, Fr Karl Hermann arrived and developed the mission further. Drawing on the connection to Rupert Meyer, he visited his grave when on home leave and prayed for his help. He informed interested people in Germany about the mission and they responded generously. Karl was able to complete the half-done work at the primary and secondary school. He interested the Jesuit St John's Beaumont School, in the UK, and they also helped. Students from Munich came to investigate possibilities of using water, wind or solar power to provide electricity and succeeded in initiating solar power for the hospital, the boarding places and the priests' house. In 2012, the mission organised a sponsored walk to Harare to raise funds for the primary school library. Photos taken of the mission for the Golden Jubilee in 2014 show a huge complex of buildings. Fr Kensy's little oasis by the Mupfure had grown into a thriving centre of learning and development.

Sipolilo, St Edward's (1958); Guruve, St Joseph's (1980)

In 1958, soon after the founding of the Sinoia Mission, Fr Kotzki was introduced by some students at Kutama to their home place at Sipolilo (Guruve), on the edge of the escarpment. In 1952, a local chief gave him a site to start a primary school, which he called St Edward's. No permission was granted to start a mission. He used one of the classrooms for celebrating Mass.[25] Marist Brother Ephrem became manager of the out schools from Kutama, and Sipolilo became one of them. A Catholic European farmer later gave him a site on his farm to build a priest's house and this became St Bernadette's Mission. When eventually a site for the mission was granted near the school, in 1975 St Bernadette's was abandoned.

In 1980, after independence, Georg Hipler decided to move the mission to a new site at Guruve, now called a 'growth point', and renamed it St Joseph's. St Edwards became an outstation and so another large new church had to be built at Guruve. This was completed in 1988, a year after Fr Ignatius Zvaravashe had taken over as parish priest. The Presentation sisters opened a convent there in 1989. Nora Broderick, Eileen Clear and Judith Bingura formed the community and they did pastoral work, dressmaking and running a library. They

---

25 Friedrich to Rea, 15 July 1977, JAZ, Box 208.

also worked with the women and the youth. They handed over to the SOLA[26] sisters in 2016. Georg also introduced Small Christian Communities in the parish and had established around twenty-two by the time he was moved in 1986. The parish was handed to the diocese in 2002.

Chitsungo, St Raphael's (1964)

A hundred kilometres further north from Guruve and in the Zambezi Valley, Fr Kotzki also began Chitsungo mission in 1964. Situated near the confluence of the Dande and the Hunyani (Manyani) rivers, it was said to be so hard to find you needed an archangel to show you the way. Hence, St Raphael's! Fr Friedrich tells us, 'Fr Kotzki was not allowed to build a bridge across the Dande in order to avoid Africans using it as a public road through European farms.' Fr Joachim (Addie) von Kersenbrock started building there in 1964, and in 1970 Fr Rudolf Kensy (at the mission 1968-73) reported there were 184 Catholic Christians. The number grew to 308 in 1971 and 779 in 1973. 'A beautiful round church, thatched with grass, was built with the help of Br Herbert Millahn and Br Günter Gattung in 1975' (Hipler).

By 1977, the boarding place had to be shut down because of the war. The ZIPRA guerrillas made many demands and the Jesuits had to withdraw for a while. In their absence the mission was vandalised and the roof sheets were stolen. In June 1979, Br Evaristo Mapuranga, who had been asked to go to the mission to take care of it as best he could in such a situation, had to leave because the strain on him was becoming too great, even after the ceasefire when a person was shot, though not killed. Georg Hipler was only able to resume his work after independence in 1980. Even then it took more than a year for things to settle down. In 1983, Karl Steffens reopened the newly rethatched church and, in 1988, Gattung and Hipler built a new community house and a large convent for the LCBL sisters. In 1992-23, Hipler saw to the building of a large new modern hospital. The mission was handed to the diocese in 1994 when Fr Ignatius Mhonda became parish priest.

---

26 Sisters of Our Lady of Africa

Kangaire (1970)

Fr Herman Husemann wrote about the founding of Kangaire Mission in 1966.[27] It was an outstation of Marymount Mission from 1962 but when the area, Chesa, became more populated – there were around 600 'Purchase Area'[28] farmers there in 1972 – it was decided to establish a mission there. Husemann was tasked with building the mission. He put up a convent for the LCBL sisters who became teachers in the school, catechists in the parish and one was a nurse. A large workshop was built in 1968 and housed the machinery moved from St Joseph's farm near Alaska when it was closed in 1969. Two highly practical Jesuits, Frs Joachim (Addie) von Kersenbrock and Wolfgang Abeler and a lay helper, Joseph Dold, set up the workshop and trained truck and tractor drivers, instructing them in welding, soldering, equipment servicing, and vehicle and machinery repairs. The mission also assisted the local farmers in ploughing: 100 acres in 1969, 400 in 1970 and 800 (on 107 farms) in 1971.

Later, in Chapter 10, we will record the killing of Fr Gerry Pieper on 26 December 1978, an event that led to the closure of the mission. Unlike other missions closed during the war, Kangaire was never reopened. It is now an outstation of Rushinga.

Mutorashanga (St James) (1979)

Started from Banket in 1979 by Fr Günter Reuter, Mutorashanga became an independent parish. Günter wanted to live in the miner's compound and not in the European area. He was attacked one evening and, although he lived on for a number of years, he never fully recovered. The parish was later developed by Fr Konrad Landsberg who built a parish centre in 1989. The following year it was given to the diocese.

---

27 *The Shield*, November 1972.
28 Part of the hardening of attitudes under the Rhodesian Front government concerned land, which outside the National Parks, was divided in two. One half went to the quarter of a million Europeans while the other went to the five million Africans. The latter lived in either 'Tribal Trust Lands', where traditional land holding custom placed all land in the hands of the chiefs, or in Purchase Areas where individuals could own land according to European law, that is, with title deeds.

Alaska (St John the Evangelist) (1973)

Fr Herman Husemann built a church in this mining settlement in 1972 and in the following year Reuter began to live there. There had been an accident in one of the mines and a Tanzanian, with a family of ten children, died. Reuter decided to hire a Kombi to take the widow and her children home to Tanzania and he drove them there himself. On his way back, I met him by accident at Mbeya on the Tanzanian border with Zambia and, since I was making my way overland from Nairobi after completing my theology studies in England, I joined him for the return trip. I travelled with him for just an hour before the vehicle broke down seriously. The front right wheel simply jammed and would not move. It took us two weeks to sort out the problem and we arrived in Alaska just as Archbishop Markall was blessing the new church. I hitched a lift with the Archbishop to Salisbury for the final leg of my odyssey.

Further churches were built from Alaska at Shackleton mine (Holy Trinity) in 1975 and Lion's Den (Murereka) in 1990, the year when the parish was handed over to the diocese. In 2010, Bishop Dieter Scholz invited the lay community of women and men, the Sisters and Brothers of Jesus of Nazareth, to make a foundation on a hill just outside Alaska. They called their monastery Mariachitubu, Maria of the Well, with reference to the Chinhoyi caves and underground water courses and it is becoming a place for retreats and pilgrimage.

Mount Darwin (Kristo Mambo) (1973)

Fr Norbert Gille worked in the Zambezi valley from St Albert's right through the 1960s. He told me it was 'the happiest time of his life'. The valley was a 'paradise'. He started Mass centres in many places and was 'the first to reach Muzarabani'. During the war he would travel on a bicycle down the middle of the road as the wheel ways were often mined. Before the churches were built, he slept by the roadside while on his rounds. When it came to establishing a base, he first chose Chiutsa but later managed – 'I had to fight for it' – to get a site at Mount Darwin. The white farmers did not want him there but he discovered the tribal land came right up to the border of the small town and he obtained a site from the local *sabhuku*. The whites then 'fenced him in' so that he had no access. Eventually they gave way.

He had been visiting Mount Darwin from 1969 and now, in 1976, he built a priest's house there. Two years later he built a church and a convent. In 1989 it was given to the diocese.

St Joseph's farm (1965)

Fr Georg Sunder followed Otto as superior of the Sinoia Mission and had the idea of having a farm as a source of income for the mission. In 1965, when Fr Lorenz von Walter returned to Rhodesia after ordination, Sunder asked him to run the farm, which they called St Joseph's. It was near Alaska, an active European farming area with the copper mine and smelter in full production. Besides raising funds for the mission the plan was to build a dormitory for students of agriculture. Misereor provided half a million marks (a quarter of a million Euros) for the project. The European farmers had finance, machinery, curing barns and all the know-how to grow prime grade Virginia tobacco and they were not prepared to share their expertise with St Joseph's, where Lorenz had none of these. They made sure St Joseph's did not get the market quota it needed as they were totally against the idea of black students living in what they considered their area of the country at a time when the Smith government was tightening the Land Apportionment Act of 1929 with new legislation. Lorenz had two helpers from Germany, a mechanical engineer and an agriculturalist, but the latter was from Bavaria where farming was very different. Lorenz believed it was an impossible task and he felt emotionally overwhelmed. Sunder suggested other crops, maize, for instance, but though they grew a good crop it was burnt accidentally when a fire jumped a stream which it was thought would have prevented fire. Lorenz engaged a European manager but the project now needed even more finance to make it work and, in that environment, they felt they had no option but to sell the farm.

Fr Zegke was a great help in talking to Cardinal Dössing, head of Misereor, so that they did not have to pay back the huge investment Misereor had made[29] and the funds could be used for establishing St Albert's Mission. Br Günter Gattung told me the machinery was moved to Kangaire and later to St Peter's Kubatana for a while and finally to the Rural Training Centre in Chinhoyi set up by Br Hubert Simon.

---

29 Interview with Fr Lorenz von Walter, 23 May 2021.

St Albert's Mission (1962)

Lorenz was now free, and Wolfgang Thamm was looking for a boarding master and teacher for the new secondary school at St Albert's Mission. Lorenz joined the other eleven Jesuits already there. The late 1960s were a productive time of growth and consolidation at St Albert's and all over the Prefecture. The Jesuits had to work closely with the government on whom they depended and relations were good not only for the school but also for the hospital. When Sr Janice McLaughlin came after the war to interview Lorenz and others at St Albert's she gave the strong impression of being an apologist for the guerrillas and her account[30] and Lorenz's,[31] while agreeing on events, vary on interpretation. Lorenz and the Jesuits at St Albert's had good relations with the local farmers before the war and St Albert's hospital, for instance, which was founded in 1964, the same year as the school, treated European patients as well as the local people. It built a warm opinion of the missionaries just as Sr Patrick and the early Dominicans had done ministering to the sick in Salisbury seventy years before.

All this changed with the outbreak of war. St Albert's is on the escarpment and there were European farms lower down towards the valley, one of which was Altena farm run by a farmer who had a reputation for treating his workers roughly. The ZANLA guerrillas, who were establishing themselves in the valley, attacked this farm on 21 December 1972 and sent a shock wave of rage and fear among the white farmers in the area. They began to see St Albert's as sympathetic to the 'terrorists', as they called the guerrillas, and even a training base for them. 'We are attacked,' they said, 'but St Albert's is unscathed'. They sent a petition with 120 signatures to the government to close the mission or at least the school, which at that time had 197 students, boys and girls. The primary school had 261 children. St Albert's was closed for a while and the students were welcomed at Makumbi, Mount St Mary's Wedza (Hwedza) and St Benedict's.

The military came in February 1973 and for two months established a security camp on the mission with wire fences and lights. They interrogated local people, and the Jesuits protested at the beatings and

---
30 J. McLaughlin, *On the Frontline, Catholic Missions in Zimbabwe's Liberation War* (Harare: Baobab Books, 1996).
31 Interview with Fr Lorenz von Walter, 23 May 2021.

rough methods they used. Janice McLaughlin says the churches were taking notice of the government's actions and began to respond by sending relief, and the Catholic Commission for Justice and Peace (CCJP) started to document the atrocities of the security forces.[32]

Abduction of students

On the cold winter's night of 2 July 1973, after the students had returned to the mission, Lorenz left the community house to go to the classrooms to call the secondary students to retire for the night as usual. As he rounded the corner of a building, he came face to face with seven or eight heavily armed guerrillas. Some seemed drugged, from the strange look in their eyes. The leader introduced himself as 'James Bond' and asked him to lead them to where the students were. Lorenz exploded and started to bellow at them in a loud voice: 'What the hell are you doing? Don't you know we are responsible for these boys?' When I spoke to him nearly fifty years later, he said, 'I let off steam and quickly realised it was the stupidest thing I could do. I could have been shot there and then.' There was a sudden silence and no one seemed to know what to do. Eberhard Fuhge, who was headmaster, tells us what happened next. 'It was teacher Jairosi whose intervention saved our lives. Lorenz had addressed them quite angrily and their commander was about to shoot him, when Mr Jairosi explained to them that the priest had mistaken them for Rhodesian soldiers. Mr Jairosi introduced me to them. I had a brief chat with their leader who assured me that the children would soon return and that in a few months' time ZANU would take over the whole country.'[33]

Although Lorenz had, in fact, not mistaken them for security forces, he could well have done. Fr Clemens Freyer, who was showing a film to students when the guerrillas burst into the room, did think, at first, they were security forces.[34] Jairosi's intervention cleared the air and James Bond explained he wanted to meet the students and tell them about the aims of the *Chimurenga*. Lorenz said he would like to attend and hear what he would say. Thomas Nhari, who had been left in charge of the north-east district of the guerrillas' operations while Rex Nhongo was at a meeting in Lusaka, was present but did

---

32 McLaughlin, p. 87.
33 Fuhge in an email to me in July 2021.
34 McLaughlin, p. 89.

not speak. Lorenz later learnt that Nhari wanted to outsmart Nhongo in recruiting fighters and so advance his own position in ZANLA. 'Jealousy was behind it,' Lorenz thought.

When they went to the classroom there was no one there. It seems the students had got wind of what was happening and hid in the woods. The guerrillas then went to a store belonging to Mr Chibumu; he was away and his wife was forced to hand over the keys. They raided the stores and took away a quantity of food and blankets which they parcelled out among the primary students. Fr Eberhard Fuhge appeared and dissuaded Lorenz from accompanying the students who were about to be led away. There was a noise that sounded like a car and the guerrillas thought it could be the police and they quickly left the mission with the young students and headed north to the valley.

Meanwhile, it was learnt later, Fr Fryer had been accosted with some of the senior students and he accompanied them as they left the mission. He was particularly worried about three boys who were not well and struggled to walk. He eventually got permission from the guerrillas to take those three back to the mission.

As the telephone wires on the mission had been cut, Fuhge and Lorenz made their way to a store some three kilometres distant to raise the alarm about the students being abducted. But the guards there shot in the air and would not allow them to approach until they could explain who they were. Even then, the people at the store could not help as their telephone had also been cut. Fuhge and Lorenz then walked on through the night to a farm where the security forces had set up a base. Arriving around midnight, they approached into the flood lights with their hands up. The commander of the base asked them in which direction the students had been taken.

The guerrillas had captured around 280 students and sisters and teachers and were walking with them down the escarpment – a no-go area and there was a curfew. The CO at the base radioed Concession where there was an army camp and a plane was sent up which dropped flares in the area where the guerrillas and the students were. Lorenz later learnt the army set an ambush for the guerrillas and were on either side of the path as they passed. The commander had the option of picking off the guerrillas but decided there was too much danger of killing the students as well and they held their fire and let them go.

Unused to such a trek, the students grew tired and the guerrillas allowed them to take cover in a *donga* where they would be out of sight and could rest. Meanwhile the army caught up with them and, not seeing the students opened fire on the guerrillas. Lorenz had warned the boys some days before at St Albert's that if ever they were caught in crossfire they should lie perfectly still and not try to run away. They laughed at him then never imagining they would be in such a situation. Now they were and they remembered his words and remained still.

When the guerrillas withdrew the army surrounded the students and gave them food and eventually drove them back to the mission.

Hedrick Mandebvu

While the soldiers and students were waiting for the transport, one of the soldiers took his rifle up either to clean it or to show the students how it worked. Whatever he thought he was doing, he forgot it was loaded and it went off. The bullet went straight through the heart of one student, Hedrick Mandebvu, from Highfield. She was about fourteen and Fr Isidore Chikore later told Lorenz she was an exceptional girl who used to gather her friends and lead them in games and plays and dances. She would also take them into the church and explain the stations of the cross and other images and she would explain the catechism and lead them in prayers. Going down the escarpment that day she took her rosary from her pocket and told her companions, 'We must pray now.'

Lorenz believes her sacrifice saved the mission.

One result of this event was that the white farmers realised the mission was also suffering and they withdrew their hostility. When the parents and the students and members of the surrounding community met to discuss what to do, 67 per cent of them voted to reopen the school. The students celebrated what they considered was their victory.

Closing the school

But by 1975, three years later, there was agitation within the school to take a more active role in supporting the liberation war. The school authorities decided they had to close the school and once again the students had to find alternative schools to continue their education.

As the war escalated it was considered too dangerous for the Jesuits and the Dominicans running the hospital to remain on the mission at night and they withdrew to Concession, only coming to St Albert's during the day. Local people, especially the European farmers, took the opportunity of the abandoned mission to steal roof sheets, doorframes and even washbasins from the mission. After independence St Albert's had to be virtually refounded.

Sometimes easy judgements are made criticising the German Jesuits for not being fully behind the liberation struggle. But they drew on their experience of a Marxist regime, hostile to Christianity, in their own country. Janice McLaughlin, who was so dedicated to the liberation struggle herself, was inclined to make these judgements. She believed Robert Mugabe when he repeatedly said his party viewed Marxism as a purely social and economic system and had nothing against Christianity, and the churches would be free to operate in the new Zimbabwe. But those of us who did not live through the Nazi years (1933-45) and the Communist years (1948-89) have no idea what it was like to live under an atheistic autocratic regime. There was a good deal of anti-Christian rhetoric in the views expressed by the guerrillas towards the end of the war and the Jesuits had three of their German companions – two priests and a brother – killed by the guerrillas. Besides, the abduction of nearly 300 school children, against their will, and their exposure to dangers that could lead to their losing their lives, was viewed by them as a monstrous action. It is not difficult to understand why Jesuits coming from Germany came to be wary of the guerrillas' aims, even if they were in broad agreement with the struggle for freedom.

Chinhoyi Rural Training Centre

In time, they would get a label – Internally Displaced Persons – with an accompanying international status, but towards the end of the liberation war they were simply young people from Zvimba, Makonde, Hurungwe, Sipolilo and Dande who had sought the protection of a population centre and found themselves roaming around Chinhoyi. In response, Fr George Muschalek, tells us,[35] some civic 'bodies' and individuals set up a committee to look into the matter. It consisted of the Sinoia Area Board, the Administration of Chinhoyi location, the

---

35 *Province Newsletter*, 29, 17 January 1980, Box 469B.

Ministers' Fraternal, the Catholic Church, Conex,[36] a businessman and a farmer. The aim was to set up a one-year training course for 150 people, aged between sixteen and twenty-seven, in agriculture and related areas, for example, sheet metal work, welding, maintenance of farm machinery, carpentry and building. A large hall on the outskirts of the town was leased and an acre of land donated by a local farmer. Christian Care and the UN bought the tools and some came from St Albert's Mission, which was temporarily closed. Br Walter Schurtenberger SMB, from Driefontein, was asked to run the course and it began in the last months of 1979. Six Connex instructors were employed and Br Dennis Adamson taught the maintenance course. Mr Ernest Mazhindu taught building and Mr Arwen Mukwata the carpentry. By December 1979 there were seventy-seven students on the course.

In 1980, Br Walter was withdrawn and Br Hubert Simon started with the fifty-seven students who were still attending the training. By 1982 the focus had slightly shifted to engineering, carpentry and motor mechanics. Br Simon wrote: 'They were runaways from relentless harrassment by day and by night in the rural areas caught in the middle between government auxiliary forces and the guerrillas.'[37] Simon tells us he replaced Adamson who only stayed for a year. 'I had learnt British terms for motor-mechanics at Marymount where I replaced Br Gerhard Zochall who was killed in a welding accident.' The tools came originally from St Joseph's farm, a failed project, and had been taken first to St Albert's and then to Kangaire which was vandalised after it was closed towards the end of the war. Simon asked the young trainees what they wanted to learn, 'expecting they would be glad going back home to their farms (but) a great majority opted for work and jobs. So, realising that new opportunities opened up for them after independence, they seized their chance to venture into hitherto white-dominated fields of professional training in motor-mechanics, welding and woodwork. Building, that is, bricklaying was soon dropped because of little or no enthusiasm for it.'

Simon upgraded the course from one year to three and substantial

---

36 The Rhodesian-era Department of Conservation and Extension (CONEX); it developed a bad name as it forced people to adopt European views of sustainable agriculture. This may have been wise in theory but the way in which the ideas were implemented defeated their purpose.

37 Chinhoyi Rural Training Centre, 1979-2008, Hubert Simon SJ, JAZ, Box 466/2.

financial help came from the 'popular street preacher Fr Johannes Leppich SJ in Germany'. It was a long struggle to get recognition for the Training Centre and it only happened in 1996 when Ignatius Chombo, who had presided over the opening of the expanded welding workshop, became Minister of Education. They were now following recognised standards and the 40-50 young people were earning nine O-levels through the training: three in sheet metal work and welding, three in woodwork and three in drafting. Br Evaristo Mapuranga, who was in charge of the motor mechanics, went to America for further training and, Simon tells us, the lay replacement also ran his own store and two grinding mills and so often missed his classes.

After three years the students had a trades test but Br Günter Gattung, who followed the progress of the centre with interest, tells us they were offered jobs in industry even before they graduated and often dropped out to take up 'the bird in the hand'. The centre received orders for roof structures, church benches, tabernacles and other church furniture, tank stands, hammer mills, 'lazy man garage doors', specialised bolts and nuts for the motor industry, window frames and burglar bars. Clearly it had the makings of great project fulfilling a clear need in the new Zimbabwe.

But the deteriorating economy, the growing crime rate (thefts and break-ins), long power cuts, negligence in responsibility and 'ownership' of the centre, failure to maintain tools, carelessness about guarding against injuries – all these things were interlinked and fed on one another, hindering progress. For Hubert Simon it was all 'rather disappointing'.

The Diocese of Chinhoyi (1986)

Starting and developing schools was a large part of the work of the new Sinoia mission and when Fr Weisbrich became superior in 1966, he tried to help the Mary Ward Sisters found a school in Hurungwe but he was unsuccessful. He was greatly loved by the people but died tragically in a car accident in 1969.

Fr Helmut Reckter followed Weisbrich and became prefect apostolic when the mission became a prefecture in 1974. Fr Horst Ulbrich followed him as superior of the Jesuits until Fr General Pedro Arrupe united the two missions in one province in 1978. There was some feeling in the Sinoia Mission that this was done too hurriedly.

Eight years later Reckter became the first bishop of the Diocese of Chinhoyi. One of his main achievements, Wolfgang Thamm tells us,[38] was the 'construction of the spacious pastoral centre which became the venue of all important events in the prefecture and later the diocese'. He also initiated training in Small Christian Communities at a course for 96 church workers at Kutama in 1987 based on the Lumko method. In 2006, two years after the death of Reckter, Fr Dieter Scholz became bishop and was in his turn succeeded by Fr Raymond Mupandasekwa CSsR in 2018.

---

38 Thamm, p. 62.

6

Urban Tensions

My mental frames of reference had to be prised open to see the rural idiom behind the urban evidence in Harare (Mbare).

Tsuneo Yoshikuni

Until the 1930s most people in Southern Rhodesia lived in rural areas. In the 1926 census, of an estimated black population of 834,000, only 173,000 (4 per cent) were employed and of these 117,000 worked on farms or in mines. Only 56,000 lived in towns and some of these had rural homes to which they would retire.[1] This small urban population was about to expand and the missions were, unwittingly, part of the reason. There were 20,177 black employees in Salisbury in 1936 and 32,008 in 1941. That figure rose to 215,810 in 1962 and 336,050 in 1969. The industrial training and living away from their homes accustomed the black population to urban living. When people did move to town they brought their faith with them and so urban parishes began.[2]

Bulawayo

Urban parish ministry in Bulawayo began when Fr Nicot, who combined his work at the new school of St George's with ministry in the prison, started visiting the home of one of the Jesuit workers. This

---
1 Southern Rhodesia, *Report of the Director of Census*, quoted in Dachs and Rea, p. 90.
2 Dachs and Rae, p. 177.

man – the only name recorded is Bob – spoke so well of the Jesuits when he retired to Enketa in 1902 that the people there asked for the priests to visit them and Nicot went. When some of them later moved to town he followed them and so the parish of St Patrick's Makokoba (Mzilikazi) was founded.[3] The 'forts' were becoming towns, workers were needed and 'locations' appeared. Fr Nicot facilitated the building of a church at St Patrick's in 1911 and the Dominican sisters joined him and opened a school.

From 1893 to 1927 Bulawayo was considered the headquarters of the Catholic Church's administration. The Apostolic Prefect lived there where he could more easily communicate with the Jesuits north of the Zambezi as well as in Mashonaland, thanks to the railway. So the main church of the prefecture was built there in 1904 and is now recognised as a basilica,[4] a mark of respect for its venerable position among church buildings in the country. Built in granite in the Gothic style under the supervision of recently arrived Croat masons, it had a capacity of 500. The clerk of works was an American, John Haupt, who later became a Jesuit. Pope John Paul held a gathering of all the clergy of Zimbabwe in the cathedral in 1988.

May I make a small diversion to speak of Br Haupt? There was a Zambian postage stamp, issued in 1990 to mark the fifth centenary of the birth of St Ignatius in 1491, which shows the church in Chikuni built by Br Haupt in 1911. Only the tower remains today. Fr James (Jim) McGloin SJ writes,

> Br John Haupt, S.J. (1858-1921) was born in Wisconsin USA and worked with the Jesuits in the building of Gonzaga College in Spokane. He also worked on Indian missions in the US and tried his vocation as a brother. This did not work out and we next hear of him in Bulawayo building the new church in 1902, where he made a crane to lift the granite blocks. He became an essential part of the Jesuit missionary endeavor and designed and built churches, parish houses, convents and schools throughout

---

3   The Catholic Directory for 2013-2015 gives the founding date as 1902 but Fr Pat Lewis, an intrepid archivist at Garnet House for many years, put the date as 1911.
4   The word has Greek roots and came to denote imposing imperial buildings used for civil administration. When the Roman Empire became Christian the word was adopted by the main churches in Rome and, by extension, to churches throughout the world which have special historical significance or have become places of pilgrimage.

the mission on both sides of the Zambezi. In 1909, at the age of 51, Haupt again asked to enter the Jesuits and his request was granted. The ZMR noted, 'All along he had been a Religious in all but name'. After his vows in 1911, Haupt went back to Chikuni to build the first church and it was there that a young Tonga man who was helping with the work lost his footing and fell from the scaffolding. Haupt grabbed hold of him as he was falling and pulled him back up to the platform. One of the other Tongas said later, 'Haupt was a strong Brother and could eat a whole chicken himself'. Br Haupt worked for another ten years but in 1921, while building a church in Umvuma [Mvuma], a splinter entered his left hand that resulted in blood poisoning. Already a diabetic, John died after a few days. The ZMR concludes he was a 'model of what fellow-workers should be'.

Harari (Mbare) in the early twentieth century

In Salisbury, pastoral work among blacks began in Harari in 1907 when Fr Bernard Lickorish moved from Chishawasha to town. Msgr Ignatius Gartlan SJ, the Mission Prefect, was refused permission when he sought to build a church in the city and they had to move to Harari, where St Peter's was opened on 29 April 1910. The attendance was poor at first because it was so far (four kilometres) from the city, but as more people came to town from rural missions looking for work they settled there and the parish began to flourish.

Fr Alfred Burbridge came to reside at the church in 1913 and active in pushing for improvements in the living conditions of the people. He was especially concerned about those who were married and proposed plots for cultivation and a better water supply. Progress was slow but to some extent the situation improved. In 1914 Burbridge, now a member of the Southern Rhodesia Mission Conference, an ecumenical group of church ministers, lobbied as part of the conference for improved conditions for urban blacks. In 1920, the group, now strengthened by the formidable figure of John White, a renowned Methodist minister, demanded proper accommodation for married people with plots for cultivation and a good water supply. By 1924 there were signs of progress. Burbridge's name was remembered and revered among the people. (In 1972, when I was learning Shona in Mhondoro, an old man recalled Fr Burbridge with fondness.)

Elizabeth Musodzi

One of the women who rallied to Burbridge's ideals was Elizabeth Musodzi.[5] She was intensely active and one of the hidden heroines of the early history of colonialism in Zimbabwe. She was a devoted Catholic, formed in a lived faith in Chishawasha, and was among the first Zimbabweans to make her home in the city. Moving to town in the first decades of the twentieth century was an unprecedented experience for black people. They had no 'relatives in town' to introduce them to this strange new life. Tsuneo Yoshikuni spent years studying the way African men and women adapted to their new environment and wrote,

> I had to constantly remind myself … that I hail from an east Asian country where urbanism has had its place from antiquity, to such an extent that it has now embraced the entire [Japanese] society. My mental frames of reference had to be prised open to see the rural idioms behind the urban evidence in Harare.[6]

In the midst of his study Yoshikuni discovered the life and work of Elizabeth Musodzi and his treatment of her gives us an insight into the township life where the Jesuits laboured. Musodzi lost her parents and other close relatives – including the spirit medium Nehanda – in the 1896/7 rising and its aftermath. This painful experience cast a shadow over her whole life which she turned to good use: 'The magnitude of her sorrow was also the magnitude of her compassion for others in trouble'.[7] She was sent to the newly founded Dominican school in Chishawasha and later married a Lozi policeman, Frank Ayema.[8] Their church wedding was recorded in the St Peter's Marriage Registry in 1917.[9] Yoshikuni discovered that Musodzi was one of the many Shona women with non-indigenous husbands who pioneered

---

5 Born in the Gombe area around 1885 she witnessed the horrors of the first *Chimurenga* when she lost both her parents. Tsuneo Yoshikuni, from Japan, did a study of her and also wrote a major work: *African Urban Experiences in Colonial Zimbabwe: A Social History of Harare before 1925* (Harare: Weaver Press, 2006).

6 T. Yoshikuni, *Elizabeth Musodzi and the Birth of African Feminism in Early Colonial Zimbabwe* (Harare: Weaver Press with Silveira House, 2008), p. vii.

7 Ibid. p. 13.

8 Their son Moses Ayema worked for a number of years at Silveira House when I was there but I never knew this background. Curiosity is a virtue!

9 Yoshikuni, op. cit., p. 9. The marriage of Robert Mugabe and Sally Hayfron was also recorded at St Peter's more than forty years later.

urban life in the city. For different reasons both she and her husband were cut off from their extended families and were free to explore this new reality. Shona men, 'resisting being reduced to proletarians and, struggling to become peasants, were the last to settle in the city with their wives'.[10]

Musodzi was an imaginative woman and after she had reared her five children at Chizhanje (Mabvuku), she gave her time to market gardening and raising cattle. Burbridge gave evidence about her to the Land Commission in 1925:

> She started a plot by paying £3 a year (rent) … five miles from town. It is very rich soil there. The people who are out there are beer brewers, but this woman has come under some christian [sic] influence, and some four years ago she produced one bag of mealies. The following year she produced ten bags, and last year she produced five bags mealies, five bags monkey nuts, five bags of rice, 50 pumpkins and 35 bags of rapoko.[11]

When her husband was assigned to work in town, she moved with him there and rented one of the seventy-one 'posh' cottages built by the municipality as showpiece married quarters in the location of Harari. She combined her life in town with her rural activities at Chizhanje but in 1937 decided to move permanently to town so as to devote her energies to helping women whom she knew were struggling. She was already an active member of St Peter's since its inception in 1907 and became increasingly aware of the problems women faced in town.

Her door was always open and women would come to her complaining their husbands did not give them money and they wanted a divorce. She would tell them about gardens and having an income of their own and not being totally dependent on their husbands. 'Most marriages survived because of this woman.'[12] Musodzi was an early advocate of girls' education and made sacrifices so that her own daughter Lucy would become a State Registered Nurse. 'Sell cattle to educate girls' she would tell the women.

Musodzi's work in Harari came to a head in 1938 when she became the first president of the African Women's Club (AWC), a

---

10 Ibid., p. 1.
11 Ibid., p. 6.
12 Ibid., p. 12.

crystallisation of all the work she and other women had been doing for years. The AWC organised,[13]

- Recreational opportunities for women who were otherwise tied to their homes,
- Classes in sewing, knitting and first aid (Red Cross),
- Encouragement for women to have their marriages registered and thereby secure their accommodation in town,
- Lobbying – successfully - for a maternity clinic and dignity for women, for example, in stopping compulsory examinations of women for STDs. Mai Musodzi went to the Municipal authorities to protest and was arrested but her protest worked;
- Help for the poor and handicapped,
- Outreach services to rural areas,
- Planning a crèche though this was opposed by segregationist Councillor Charles Olley. Musodzi commented, 'the whites are really very hard to understand'.
- Garden competitions.

Charles Mzingeli

Musodzi was not the only one who was a stirrer in Harare in the first half of the twentieth century. I have not come across evidence that Elizabeth Musodzi knew Charles Mzingeli, about whom a study has been made recently by Timothy Scarnecchia.[14] Musodzi and Mzingeli were both residents of Harari location at the same time and pursued the same aims by the same methods. Yet Fr Burbridge, while supporting Musodzi, appears to have been suspicious of Mzingeli and there was a report that he refused him Communion.[15] It seems Burbridge did not take time to understand Mzingeli, who appeared to him as an agitator, though a gentle one, while Musodzi was more discreet. It was a time when revolutions in Russia and Germany were led by people who gave socialism a bleak name and Mzingeli was not afraid to use the word.

---

13 Ibid., p. 17 ff.
14 T. Scarnecchia, *The Urban Roots of Democracy and Political Violence in Zimbabwe: Harare and Highfield 1940-1964* (Rochester, NY: Rochester University Press, 2008).
15 Whether this amounted to formal 'excommunication', an extreme penalty, is not clear.

Charles Mzingeli was the best-known African leader in Salisbury in the 1940s. He died in Mbare in 1980 and, as he grew weaker, Fr Roland von Nidda used to visit him and pray with him. His renown did not reach to every corner of the land but it was there where it mattered – in Highfield and Mbare. It is worth spending a moment following his career.

Mzingeli grew into his role gradually, cutting his political teeth on concrete township issues, the right of women to reside with their husbands, the bus boycott, etc. He was a politician who learnt his trade with specific issues. His vision was to create a common citizenship for all the people. He would refer to 'imperial citizenship' and ask, 'why are Africans denied the right to full citizenship in the empire'? He posed that question repeatedly, chipping away at the oppressive laws governing people at that time. His organisation went by the seemingly unchallenging name of the Reformed Industrial and Commercial Workers' Union. In effect it was an amalgam of a town advisory board, a trade union and a political party. When the Harari Township Advisory Board was set up, he was elected Chairman year after year. He became in effect the mayor-in-waiting of Harare.

Scarnecchia traces the evolution of Zimbabwe politics from its earliest years when it was close to the people and ends where the main political parties, ZANU and ZAPU, were so absorbed in their own internal leadership struggles that they did not hesitate to condone violence in the townships to bolster their positions. The author describes, in contrast, how Mzingeli was a 'bottom up' politician. He drew his strength from his attention to the particular grievances of actual people. He would go to the township authorities and lobby for them. His reputation grew from *within* his constituency. No external force secured his position and, when he was eventually voted out, he went. Scarnecchia describes the role of women in the early struggles and the work of the trade unionist Reuben Jamela and the Southern Rhodesia Trade Union Congress (SRTUC). A feeling emerges of a struggle going somewhere, even if slowly. But I suspect that if most of us were asked to list the genealogy of leaders in Zimbabwe, stretching back from Robert Mugabe via Ndabaningi Sithole and Joshua Nkomo to George Nyandoro and James Chikerema, we would end there. This is no wonder as the next on the list would certainly be Mzingeli, but he represented a quite different politics. If his was from the roots up theirs was from the top down. The politics of the Salisbury City Youth League in the 1950s brushed aside the patient chipping away of Mzingeli and those who shared his approach and demanded instant reforms. The radical nature of the League's politics set markers for every political party that followed.

This became understandable since the white government was showing no willingness to move towards 'imperial citizenship'. But something was lost in the transition from Mzingeli to Chikerema and Nyandoro. For the latter it was now the broad appeal. They felt no need to secure their position by patient listening. They were sure of their position and in fact did all the talking just as their successors did. Anyone who did not agree with them was a 'sell-out', and gradually the support of the people was secured, not by proving one's ability to address their grievances, but by pressure. The final impasse came in 1964 when the Rhodesian government had an easy time in simply locking up all the leaders.

There is little point in speculating what might have happened if Mzingeli's brand of politics had survived. That is all water under the bridge. We have to deal with our situation as it is now more than sixty years after he lost the vote to be chairman of the Harari Advisory Board. But sooner or later, if we are to reach any kind of 'social contract' between the governed and the governing, we will have to learn again the art of listening to people. For too long the ruling party has bent history to their purposes. Terence Ranger called this history 'patriotic' with the echo that every discipline must serve the interests of the state.

Mbare in the late twentieth century

The Jesuits have served St Peter's now for 111 years. After our brief mention of the early years we can look at Fr Anthony Bex's account of the parish in the 1970s just before independence.[16] Bex was writing in the afterglow of the celebration of the life of Fr William (Wim) Smulders SJ, who had died in a car crash on 28 December 1975, aged forty-four. Wim had given his all to the people of Harari and there are countless stories of his identification with them, even to being buried among them. The present writer attended his funeral and there were

---

16 A. Bex, *St Peter's Harare: Portrait of an African town parish* (Gwelo: Mambo Press, Mission-pastoral series No.7, 1976).

thirty-two full-size buses hired that day to carry the people to Warren Hills.

Tony Bex was one of Wim's companions, together with Lawrence Makonora, Augustine Kandawasvika and Fidelis Mukonori. Bex gives a picture of a Rhodesian regime running out of options. They had created a monster of regulations for the urban townships so that they fitted into their overall policy of separating Africans from Europeans. The government spoke a great deal about being part of a southern African bulwark against communism but, in practice, they applied the same command structure used by the Soviets. The local administrators in the township realised the impossibility of combining orders from above with a humane approach to the problems. Bex did not find the town officials heartless: 'The administration and the inhabitants are both victims of an impossible social situation.'[17]

Harari in the 1970s was a hub. It linked town and country and buses came and went from the terminus in the parish. Situated between the heavy and light industrial sites the township was a dormitory for the 25,000 who came to work. They were housed in hostels, well built says Bex, but rabbit warrens with no privacy and endless noise. Men were not allowed to bring their wives as they slept five to a room and the Rhodesians clung to the fiction that Africans only came to town to work, not to live. When they finished their working days they would go back to their rural homes. So the men cooked for themselves in huge kitchens and brought their food to the 'privacy' of their rooms to eat. There were some houses in Harari, such as the one in which Musodzi and her family lived, but there was a twenty-year waiting list. Bex came across people in the 1970s who had put their name down in 1954.

About eighteen beerhalls generated huge sums for the municipality which were ploughed back into multiple social amenities: a huge Beit Hall for dances, receptions and films, a large Community Centre with a reference library much used by students and a weaving centre for hundreds of girls, together with meeting rooms for saving clubs, advisory work and consulting rooms. Nearby were large sports fields for tennis, soccer, athletics, netball and even cricket. There was an Olympic size swimming pool with an entrance fee of three cents! Rufaro Stadium, where Independence was declared, could hold

---

17 Ibid., p. 14 .

30,000 people. There were also care centres for small children and workshops for teaching carpentry and welding and art. A maternity hospital, an infectious diseases hospital and several clinics could also be found in the parish.

Good in themselves, all these amenities eased the pain without solving the problem. People were not free to make their own choices and they were frustrated. The result is they drank too much, quarrelled too much and in general sought relief in ways that only created new problems. Bex describes the plight of 'rightful tenants' who, if they lose their employment, had to move out of their accommodation. Widows had to move back to rural areas, if they had one, where they were often not welcome. And, from the opposite direction, St Peter's had to deal with the rehabilitation of refugees fleeing the war.

The growing number of Catholic Christians to be served stretched the resources of the parish, and Dachs and Rea summarise Bex's description of the efforts of the St Peter's team of priests, brothers and laity to respond the multiple needs of the people:

> Accordingly, the concept of self-ministering Christian communities, already gaining strength in the rural areas, was applied to the urban conditions of Harare. The parish was divided into twenty-four districts, each with its own community, its own registry of members and its own elected leaders who were responsible for arranging prayer services each week. A local community was fostered and representatives of each of these came together in the parish council which collectively assumed responsibility for all the affairs of the parish, including the finances. ... The priest was yielding the initiative to the lay parishioners. From founding and leading the church, the ordained minister was coming to be its servant in providing the sacraments and forming sound Christian opinion and responsibility.[18]

Highfield, Dzivarasekwa and Mabvuku

The population of Harari in 1969 was 57,950 and following close behind was Highfield (52,560).[19] A chapel had been built in Highfield in 1945 and in 1971 a large church supplanted it. Fr Alois Nynate became parish priest.

---
18 Dachs and Rae, p. 178.
19 Ibid. p. 177.

Mass was said in St Stephen's, Dzivarasekwa, by a priest from the Seminary in the government school hall weekly until Fr William Makusha came in 1969 and built a church which was completed in 1974. From 1975, 'Dziva' was a sub-parish of Mabelreign, which the Jesuits handed over to the diocese in 2018. Then the Jesuits remained with Dziva.

The Jesuits were also responsible for St Fidelis, Mabvuku, founded in 1952, from St Peter's Mbare where Henry Swift was parish priest. Swift acquired land for a church in 1955. When Anthony Pathe CSsR visited in 1960, he found there were no windows. 'Windows get broken', Swift told him. Light came in through a perspex section of the roof.[20] St Fidelis became a parish in 1961 and was served first from Chishawasha (John Davies) and then from Silveira House (Peter Kavuma, Raymond Kapito, Gilbert Modikayi) and then from Chishawasha again (Gerry Finneston). Br Francis Fitzsimmons, at Silveira House, ran a vibrant youth club in the parish for seven years which blossomed into the Catholic Youth Association in the seventies with Br (as he was then) Fidelis Mukonori and his team. The parish was handed to the Redemptorists in 1978.

The Cathedral in Salisbury and Campion House

The Jesuit pastoral presence in Salisbury started formerly, that is, in the sense of buildings, when Fr Aloysius Leboeuf built a chapel in 1898. It served the congregation until in 1924 when the cathedral was completed. Catholic Sir Charles Coglan, first Prime Minister of the self-governing colony, used to be seen saying his prayers there in the evening.[21] Leboeuf was the self-taught architect and Brs Mathias Schoenbrod, Patrick Mellon, John Göll and John Conway, the builders and carpenters. Visitors marvelled, and can still marvel, at the hammerbeam[22] roof. The late Fr Brendan Conway researched the provenance of the organ that dominates the back of the cathedral. It

---

20 Enright, B., Mabvuku, 2017, note in JAZ, Box 379/2.
21 O'Reilly, p. 117.
22 Described by the COD as 'Projecting from wall at foot of principal rafter' and by M. Bismanis as 'a decorative, open **timber roof truss** typical of **English Gothic architecture** ... the most spectacular endeavour of the English Medieval carpenter.' (*The medieval English domestic timber roof: a handbook of types,* New York: P. Lang. p. 16).

was made in Canada and shipped all the way to Salisbury in pieces.[23]

In 1927 the Prefect moved to Salisbury and Campion House residence was opened next to the cathedral as the main residence of the Jesuits. The Cathedral became the main parish in the city and Fr Arthur (Pops) Graham, 'one of the ten worst drivers in the world', was the parish priest (1924-57).

Mount Pleasant, Mabelreign, Marlborough, Braeside and Rhodesville

The Jesuit Parish of our Lady of the Way, Mount Pleasant, founded in 1959, was effectively a white parish and accepted as such. It was the parish of renowned figures such as Justice Nicholas McNally who was a firm critic of Ian Smith's policies and was to go on to be a prominent member of the fledgling opposition Centre Party. But the divide in the country in the 1960s was so deeply entrenched that McNally, prominent Catholic that he was, had no way of altering the direction his own Church had taken. The Catholic Commission for Justice and Peace, to be treated elsewhere in this study, found no 'traction' in the 'northern suburbs'.

The white parishes in the cities and large towns of Rhodesia were, in effect, havens which gave their parishioners a sense of security in a surrounding culture which was sensed as 'different' in an undefined but threatening way. Many whites never seemed to seriously consider the future, their future. They lived only for the present and enjoyed their dominant position. Even if the white decision-makers of the 1960s had wanted to think differently, the weight of the history their forefathers had created after the conquest of the country, especially after the risings, made it virtually impossible for them to change.

The Holy Name, Mabelreign, was founded in 1957 and handed to the Archdiocese in 2018. Frs Lewis Clifford and, after him, Pat Kinna ran the parish for thirty years. They were followed by Gilbert Modikayi, Dieter Thiel, Patrick Makaka, George Hipler, Sylvester Kasirori and George Bwanali – all for short periods.

St Peter Canisius parish developed in 1987 from a weekly Mass in Marborough High School opposite Canisius House. In 1996 a site

---

23 Cf. JAZ, Box 175B. Brendan Conway was one of the few white diocesan priests. He worked for close to sixty years in the Archdiocese of Harare. A talented man, he made his own organ in his free time and also went on to build an aeroplane and a boat.

was acquired and Fr Wolf Huwe made strenuous efforts to raise funds. He wrote of receiving letters of regret with 'best' wishes, but 'best wishes don't make good bricks'. In 1998 the church was opened and there was much pride in the congregation at having been involved in the whole process.[24] On 21 July 2012, four Jesuits were ordained at Canisius Church by Bishop Dieter Scholz: Clyde Muropa, Gilbert Banda, Musekiwa Peter and Crispen Matsilele. This was the largest number of Jesuits ordained together in the history of the province.[25] In 2013 the parish was handed over to the local clergy.

St Francis Xavier, Braeside, parish was developed mainly for the 'coloured' people, those of mixed race, in Arcadia from 1958. Fr William (Bill) Thomas ran a devoted apostolate among them. In 1970 there were 1,655 coloured in the parish and 1,673 whites. By 1974 the number of coloureds had risen to 2,848 while the whites had fallen to 1,427. There were never many black people in the parish in those days. It was handed over to the local clergy in 2020.[26]

The parish of the Assumption at Rhodesville started with Fr Bernard Latchford coming from the Seminary to say Mass in a classroom of Admiral Tait school in 1951. A church hall was built in 1953 and Fr John Gough, a *Fidei Donum*[27] priest from Liverpool, moved in as parish priest in 1960. The hall was converted into a church in 1961.[28] When Gough had to leave because of ill health, Gerry McCabe took over in 1979 and the parish went to the Archdiocese in 1985.

Enkeldoorn (Chivhu), Umtali (Mutare) and Gwelo (Gweru)

Fr William Donovan SJ was responsible from 1939 for the whole southern area of the Archdiocese. No missions were founded but he kept moving from place to place. Often he would stay at the hotel in what was then Enkeldoorn for a few nights and then he would be on the move again. 'His wanderings read like those of Moses in the desert' was the comment of a Franciscan successor, but he prepared the way for the friars. Eventually a large church was built by the friars

---

24 *Province Newsletter*, 331, December 1998, JAZ, Box 178.
25 Chiedza Chimhanda in *Province Newsletter*, 493, August 2012.
26 JAZ, Box 175.
27 Literally 'a gift of the faith', meaning a priest of one diocese, in this case in the UK, makes a gift of himself to another diocese in another part of the world.
28 *The Shield*, June 1965, p. 7.

at Enkeldoorn in 1961 with considerable financial help from the Jesuits.

Fr Joseph Ronchi, born in Bologna, Italy, in 1862, arrived in Umtali in 1897 to serve the railway workers and lived in a tin hut as the workers did and used another hut as a chapel. He lived there virtually on his own for many years. The nearest priest was in Chishawasha, 150 miles to the west. He used to go up and down the railway line doing what he could, an Italian among the many Italian workers. A worker on the railways, Portal Hyatt, said he had no love for missionaries, but, 'Fr Ronchi, the old Italian with the little tin church was perfectly fearless and unselfish, the truest servant of his Master I have ever had the privilege of meeting'. In 1916, Adolph Bontemps, born in France in 1858, took his place and three years later Francis Marconnes, also from France, came. He laid the foundation stone for a church in 1923 which was completed in 1926. The Dominican sisters came that year and started a school. Fr Henry Quin followed Marconnes and opened a church dedicated to St Robert in Sakubva township in 1930. Mutare was handed over to the Carmelite friars in 1946 and a new diocese was born.

Fr Anthony Stempfel was in residence in Gweru from 1898 where he had two rooms in a hotel: one for himself and one for a chapel. In 1901 the Dominican sisters joined him and built a school and a convent. In 1929 work was begun on St Teresa's church. It is now the Cathedral. Gweru was handed to the Bethlehem Society in 1953.

Que Que (Kwekwe) (1915, 1953), Gatooma (Kadoma) (1915, 1964) and Umvuma (Mvuma) (1921, 1946)

Stops on the railway often marked the opening of a mine and the Jesuits began what would eventually become parishes at Que Que and Gatooma in 1915 and Umvuma in 1921. These served the settlers as well as the local people and were eventually handed over to the respective dioceses at the later dates written above.

Marandellas (Marondera) (1952)

Fr Bernard Lickorish began to say Mass periodically at Marandellas village on the railway line to Beira in 1910, and Frs Charles Daignault, Ludger Boekenhoff and Francis Markall continued to do so until 1952, when Charles Shackles began to reside there, renting a room and converting a chicken house into a chapel. Fr Patrick (Paddy) Moloney followed him in 1955 and saw to the building of Holy Rosary church in 1960. *The Shield* (December 1960) devoted many pages to the consecration of the altar, in 'a long and complicated ceremony' – the instructions for this runs to 53 pages in the *Rituale Romanum* – the first of its kind in the Archdiocese. Paddy's health was affected by his exertions and he had to withdraw for a while to recover. In 1966 the Franciscan friars took over the parish and Br Juniper built Kuwadzana Hall in the African 'location' (Dombotombo) which Fr Sean Gildea developed into a lively centre. Later, the Kiltegans took over the half the parish centred on Dombotombo, on the north side of the main road, where they built a church, *Mufudzi Wakanaka*, The Good Shepherd, in 1993. The Presentation Sisters came in 1959 and opened Nagle House, a school for girls. Once it became possible to do so, the sisters rapidly went multiracial towards the end of the 1970s.

Bindura (1964)

From 1943, a monthly Mass was said at Bindura mine by a priest from the Seminary. In 1951 this task was assumed by Fr Henry Widlake who stayed at Makumbe and built a church there in 1953. In 1974 four LCBL sisters came to nurse at nearby Trojan mine and teach in the school. The parish was taken over by the Archdiocese in 1978. There is a letter on the files where Widlake complains about the new liturgy in English. 'I joined the Latin rite, not the English rite. ... The language of the Church has been swept aside in one fell swoop.' He found the singing of the Easter Exultet in English 'silly'.[29]

---

29 Widlake to the Superior, 30 April 1965, JAZ, Box 94.

7

Mission and Culture

Inculturation is the incarnation of Christian life and of the Christian message in a particular cultural context, in such a way that this experience not only finds expression through elements proper to the culture in general, but becomes a principle that animates, directs and unifies the culture, transforming it and remaking it so as to bring about a 'new creation'.

Pedro Arrupe[1]

The word is underlined in red on my computer signifying it is not in accepted use, but 'inculturation' expresses the process where one culture meets another and respectfully dialogues with it. In practice it is never simple. People tend to 'cherry pick', choosing those aspects of the culture they meet which appeal to them and leaving aside the rest. Their criteria for choosing can be painstaking and courageous or unreflective and superficial. When the first Jesuits met the people of Africa, they were influenced by missionaries of other churches who went before them who had a default position of the 'dark continent' as full of degradation. We mentioned the evidence that the Jesuits softened this judgement but also went along with it to some degree.

The Jesuits made efforts to learn the language of those they lived among and wrote dictionaries, grammars, catechisms and lectionaries of sacred texts to make their message understood. But they did not

---

1 Letter to the whole Society on Inculturation, *Acta Romana* (1978) p. 230.

go deeply into the traditional religion of the people to uncover the meeting points between that religion and Christianity.

This chapter addresses the Jesuit response to local culture in Zimbabwe. It begins with a brief glance at a perceived understanding of Jesuit attitudes to the dominant culture in Europe, especially in the Society's approach to education, for example, in French schools. This will set the scene for a reflection on what the Jesuits did to reach the hearts and minds of the people in Zimbabwe. Their first step was to find helpers. Paul found Timothy and Titus and the early Jesuits found Regis Chigwedere and Robert Tsuro to help them in teaching the faith. But it became clear the Church would never put down roots until there were African priests.

We begin with a word about the evolving Jesuit thinking about the purpose of education. A rather damning French account of the public perception of Jesuit schools was published in the *Pall Mall Gazette* of 13 March 1880. That this was reprinted in *Letters and Notices*,[2] a Jesuit 'in-house' periodical, that same year shows the Jesuits, since the Suppression, were alert to the reputation they had, justified or not. 'The (French) Republican agitation in favour of the seventh clause in M. Jules Ferry's Education Bill is practically an agitation against the schools managed by Jesuits.' The article notes their success in attracting the children of the wealthy and the aristocracy and their training these boys 'to despise democratic institutions', so much so that the Republicans are desirous to prohibit the Jesuits from teaching altogether. After acknowledging that the Jesuits teach well, pay attention to each individual and 'promote self-esteem in their pupils', the writer of the article says, 'the boys are never left alone for a moment'. Parents feel safer sending their boys to the Jesuits because they are taken care of and compelled to behave themselves, whereas the students in the *lycées* (French government schools) 'delight in breaking rules and seem to glory in contracting bad habits on the sly'. But 'a Jesuit pupil is afraid to do any of these things, because of the spiritual bondage in which he is held by the confessional and the daily, hourly supervision of his masters. ... Here we get one of the worst blots on the Jesuit system. It brings up boys to be nice mannered little formalists or fine scholars but it fails to make manly fellows of them.'

We may wince and write this description off as a caricature but we

---

2   *Letters and Notices* Vol 13, p. 147.

need to remember that James Joyce's description of Jesuit education in *Portrait of the Artist as a Young Man* bore uncomfortable resonances. Both the author of the *Pall Mall* article and Joyce were referring to well-established institutions, not to rural schools in Zimbabwe, but we mention their comments as part of the bigger picture. We had few such institutions in Zimbabwe and certainly the description does not fit the one of which I had experience: St Ignatius College in Chishawasha.

The element of truth the *Pall Mall* article contains is in its pointing to the recognised tension between the Jesuit world-view, one of hierarchy and order where each finds his or her traditional place, and that which evolved from the Enlightenment and the age of Revolution. This latter view questioned the inviolability of established order, cultural or political, and wished to give free range to the human mind to explore the questions posed by science and reason. In this new world, established religion appeared as an obstacle, a drag anchor, and the Jesuits, with their close relationship with the epitomy of this opposition, the papacy, were the vulnerable target of those who saw themselves as champions of free thought.

Enter Aston Chichester, an extraordinary man, steeped in tradition and yet, like Balaam, a man 'with far-seeing eyes'.[3] He could trace his ancestry back to Henry I, who died in 1138. Sir Roger de Chichester fought the French at Poitiers in 1356.[4] But he could also look into the future and could think beyond the perimeters imposed by caution. The British and German provinces were generous with men and with the quality of those it sent out to Southern Rhodesia, men like Prestage, Richartz, Hartmann, Gartlan, Sykes and now Chichester. He had been an outstanding rector of Wimbledon and Beaumont in ways that were long remembered. He once accused a Wimbledon boy of helping himself to the altar wine after Mass. The twelve-year-old was too frightened to defend himself. Towards the end of the morning he was told the Rector wanted to see him and he went in 'fear and trembling', but came away speechless when the Rector said to him, 'I want to apologise, I made a real fool of myself this morning.'

Now, Chichester (Chick) was the first bishop in the growing mission. 'He is the right one to be our bishop', said Simon Taoneyi,

---

3 Numbers, 24:3.
4 F.C. Barr, *Archbishop Aston Chichester, 1879-1962* (Gwelo: Mambo Press, 1978), p .1.

who worked with the Jesuits at Chishawasha for over thirty years.[5] Taoneyi was deeply impressed from the beginning. Once, before he became a bishop, they drove with Fr Henry Seed to Chiweshe and came on a 'gate', of loose bushes across the road. Seed decided to drive through it with the words, 'they'll soon rebuild it', but Chick made him stop and they spent an hour laboriously rebuilding the barrier to make it cattle proof. As far as Taoneyi was concerned Chick's reputation was made that day and I heard him tell the story more than forty years later as if it was yesterday.

Chick never learnt to speak Shona though he gave an address at St Peter's (Mbare) on the day of his consecration. When Taoneyi was asked what people thought of a bishop who couldn't speak the people's language, he replied, 'his tongue won't let him. We saw his work and we loved him for that.'[6]

At Chichester's ordination as bishop in 1931, the Apostolic Delegate Gijlswijk spoke of the 'happy relationship between the Catholic clergy and the civic body'. He was reflecting the sentiment of the time but his words touch a nerve in the modern ear. Even then there were dissenters. Michael O'Reilly SJ, who wrote a brief unpublished history of the church in Zimbabwe up to 1939, seldom gives his own thoughts, but he does here:

> There can be no doubt many of the whites who have used the natives as their servants or workmen in the past have been ignorant people without breeding, culture or religion, and after spoiling and corrupting the native by their own stupidity and bad example have had the affrontery to blame the missionaries for the conditions they themselves have produced. However, white people in this country are now developing a conscience about the native and the more enlightened in the government and among the people at large realise that the natives are not chattels, but have minds and souls to be educated for their own sakes and for the common good.[7]

---

5   Ibid., p. 17.

6   Ibid., p. 85.

7   M. O'Reilly, *History of the Church in Zimbabwe up to 1939* (unpublished), JAZ, p. 126.

Local sisters

As an example of his 'thinking beyond the perimeters', six months after becoming bishop Chick announced he would establish a congregation for local sisters. A number of girls had been desiring to be sisters for some time and Chick opted for Makumbe, an outstation of Chishawasha, which was almost abandoned in 1930 when the people lost interest, as the site of the new novitiate.[8] Dominican Sister de Mercedes was appointed novice mistress and for thirty years was the dominant influence in the formation and spirit of the new foundation. In 1932, nineteen girls began their novitiate in Makumbe. There were few resources and Sr de Mercedes had recourse to a disused cattle dip drum for cooking. It was not properly cleaned and soon there were stomach troubles – and suspicions!

The novices had to build their own novitiate and lay out their own gardens. It was tough and many thought it was bound to fail. 'They will all have gone back home within a year', was the governor's comment.

And there was another problem. Parents saw no sense in the project and would not give their daughters permission to join. Girls were sometimes punished for trying to join and would run away from home. Parents would pursue them to the convent and complain to the Native Commissioner alleging their daughters had been kidnapped by the priest. Chick's response was to require a girl who wished to be a sister to produce a written statement of approval from her father or guardian, signed in the presence of the Native Commissioner. One parent absolutely refused to sign and the NC, in desperation, said, 'Go on, sign it. Your girl will come home again. Whoever heard of a girl not gettting married eventually?' He signed and the girl went off in triumph, joined the sisters and never returned home.

Some families wanted *lobola* from the bishop for taking their daughters and he sometimes complied after the sister was settled and qualified as a nurse or teacher and wanted to reimburse her family for her lost *lobola*. The need for parental consent for girls was, and is, acceptable if the girl is a minor but in customary understanding in those days women were always minors in the sense that they were under the authority of their parents or guardians for life. Chick was not

---

8   Barr, p. 21.

prepared to accept this and believed an adult woman should be free to answer God's call even against the wishes of her parents. The NC, in 1931, urged caution 'at the present stage of advancement' as 'any other course will merely cause dissension in the families concerned, which is bound to be reflected in tribal irritation and unrest'.[9] These final words give an insight into the colonial authorities' anxieties and Chick did not feel the time was ripe to press for a 'general principle' in the matter – a test case, in other words – but he did insist on government backing in actual cases. One might wish that Chick had been less cautious in matters touching on the politics of the colony. If he had pressed for a test case he might have advanced the status of women generally. As it was, although he secured the freedom of women over twenty-one to make up their own minds about religious life, the general question of the status of women remained unresolved.

Chick went to great trouble to draw up constitutions for the congregation but how far he succeeded in embedding them in the culture is a question that remains. The congregation grew, and by 1977 there were 241 professed sisters in 25 convents. Today, in 2021, there are 185 sisters in 45 communities in four dioceses: Harare (27), Chinhoyi (13), Gokwe (4) and Masvingo (1).

Local priests

Chichester saw the need for more priests and looked for help from the East German province. The plan was for them to erect a mission area of their own, as we saw in the previous chapter. In 1935 East German and Lithuanian Jesuits began to arrive[10] but when war broke out in 1939 that source of men dried up – though Fr Eric Kotzki, making use of his passport of the 'Free City of Danzig', managed to come in 1940 via the USA.[11] Chichester fought successfully to ensure that the German missionaries were not interned but this was on the condition

---

9   Quoted in Barr, p. 25
10 I once asked Br Stanislaus Tamkvaitis when was it that he came to Zimbabwe. 'At four o'clock' was his answer and, after a long pause, the date and the year (1938, I think). He was a man of few words interspersed with long pauses.
11 Danzig was a German city though effectively surrounded by Poland. The Second World War, like the first, pitted the Germans against the British and so the same measures had to be taken to try to give German missionaries as much freedom as possible in what was still a British colony.

that they were not made superiors.

Chick also contacted the Bethlehem Missionaries who, in 1950, set up the Vicariate of Fort Victoria (Masvingo).[12] Aloysius Haene became the first prefect and then bishop of what would become the Gweru diocese. Three years later a Prefecture of Umtali (Mutare) was established with the arrival of the Irish Carmelites and Donal Lamont became the prefect and first bishop. In 1958 the Irish Franciscans took over Waterfalls (Harare), Marondera, Hwedza and missions in the Buhera district. There was some talk of this area becoming a diocese but it was decided it was not viable and it remains part of the Archdiocese of Harare to this day. The Carmelites and Franciscans went on to welcome locally born friars to their communities but the Bethlehems saw their mission was to gradually fade out as the local clergy grew.

Chick knew these arrivals from Europe were only a temporary solution to the task of providing priests for the people. A start had to be made in welcoming 'sons of the soil'. Encouragement from Rome had been increasingly strident since Pope Benedict XV had issued his call for local clergy in *Maximum Illud* in 1919, and, for several years, there had been discussions about a local African clergy. Older missionaries were hesitant, as education was still generally only at primary school level. But others questioned how long they could rely on foreign priests and brothers, some of whom, for example, could be interned, as during the war, or expelled at any time? Fr. Schmitz warned that the rising nationalism in Europe might hinder foreign missionaries in their work.

Chichester cut through all the discussion. He decided to go ahead. He went to Uganda to see a seminary there and, on his return, approved of the preparatory seminary founded by Fr. O'Hea in Kutama. On January 1, 1936, a Minor Seminary was opened at Chishawasha at the cost of £1,000. The first buildings were simple huts of unburned bricks for both staff and students and Fr Emil Schmitz was in charge of building. The staff was made up of Fr Thomas Swift (General Science), Sr Cora (Mathematics, Geography) and Sr Benigna (Scripture) (both Dominicans) and Bishop Chichester himself taught Mathematics. The

---

12 The Bethlehem Mission Society (SMB) was founded by Pietro Bondolfi at Immensee, Switzerland in 1921. Their priests and brothers came to Zimbabwe in 1938.

teaching was strict and thorough. Two-thirds of the students dropped out but Chichester expected this. There were misunderstandings and frustrations along the way. In 1939 Chick expected a philosophy teacher would arrive from England but the Jesuit provincial wrote that he could not send one as St George's had urgent needs. Chick exploded:

> you ... treat me of no account. Facts, however, are stubborn things and getting down to tin tacks it comes to this, you are opposing the ecclesiastical authority and the Council of the Vicariate and refusing to cooperate in the work of the Seminary. ... sending five men in the last two years to St George's ... and one (whom I informed you at the time was not up to the job) to the Seminary is turning down the work. I cannot take this sitting down and however disagreeable it is to me personally I must kick ...[13]

Having made his protest, Chick settled down to wait a year rather than risk the failure of the whole project for want of immediate results. In 1940, Chick got his man, Fr Gerard Bussy. He was pleased with him and the war years saw steady progress towards Chick's goal. The Governor of the colony, Sir Herbert Stanley, an Anglican, showed great interest and became friendly with Chick. He later offered a prize for the best essay on philosophy and this was won by Simon Tsuro, one of the first to be ordained a priest. Chick wished to forstall any adverse criticism of his new priests from whites and would sometimes ask them, as they approached ordination, to a European style meal where he would teach them the finer points of European etiquette!

It was six years after the founding of the seminary that philosophy started and at the same time more solid buildings were put up, planned by Fr. John Gröber SMB and built by Italian war-time internees. The feast of Christ the King in 1947 saw the joyful occasion of the first ordinations. Three thousand people, five out of six of them black, witnessed the ordination of Simon Tsuro, son of catechist Robert Tsuro and Isidore Chikore. Stephen Luwisha followed (in Chikuni, Northern Rhodesia (Zambia), four days later) and Alois Nyanhete after a gap of three years.

This event was a moment of extarordinary consolation for Chichester and all those who had worked to establish the Church in

---

13 Barr, p. 40.

Zimbabwe. Sixty years had passed since the first plans for the Zambezi Mission had been drawn up in Rome and Grahamstown and now here was a visible sign that all the efforts were bearing fruit.

Chick hosted a banquet for the newly ordained[14] at the Dominican Convent and among the guests was the Prime Minister, Sir Godfrey Huggins. Huggins later revealed an attitude which he meant with the best intentions but which now sounds quaint and condescending: 'I will not deny that the Africans of any education – and there are still few – have not many points of contact with the European, not culturally. (But) I was at a function the other night and I met two young African priests. No mistaking it, they had a common ground with Europeans.'[15]

In 1947 there were twenty-two minor (junior) and thirteen major (senior) seminarians.

Welcoming communities of Religious

We have seen how the Dominicans arrived in the early days of the colony and the Notre Dame Sisters followed soon after. It was some years before other communities came. The Teacher Training College at Kutama languished in the 1930s and was in danger of being closed by the government because of inadequate staffing. Chick wrote to three congregations of teaching brothers, and the Canadian province of the Marists responded. They worked in Lesotho (Basutoland then) but there were difficulties and they were looking for an alternative field when approached by Chick. Led by Patrick Veilleux they took over Kutama on 1 January 1939 and in the course of a few years transformed it. Any mention of Kutama in those days has to include Robert Mugabe, whose family were part of the Christian village there set up by Fr Loubière. The Marists went on to found a secondary school at Kutama and the college and school flourished in tandem. The brothers also opened schools in Kwekwe, Nyanga and Dett.

There was only one hospital in Salisbury, run by the government, when Chick became bishop in 1931 and he soon wrote to the Mother General of the Little Company of Mary inviting them to open a hospital in the city. In line with the great divide of those days it would have to

---

14 Chick made a practice of hosting dinners for newly ordained priests and was later to write, 'these dinners do more good than my sermons and cost me less effort'. Barr, p. 45.
15 Taylor, D, *Rainbow on the Zambezi*, 1953, 51, quoted in Barr, p. 44

be for whites but Chick wanted the sisters to open further hospitals in the mission stations. St Anne's hospital was opened in 1937 and Fr Ludger Boeckenoff pressed them to open another hospital at Hwedza in 1951. They went on to open two further hospitals: Queen of Peace in Murambinda and one in Chisumbanje in the Mutare diocese.

The Nazareth sisters soon followed when Chick invited them to found a house, for the elderly who needed care, in Salisbury in 1936. An orphanage was soon added and the large chapel the sisters constructed, in 1956, served, then and now, as a parish church.

Nano Nagle (1718-84), founder of the Presentation Sisters, was Chick's great-grand-aunt but that does not mean that it was easy for him to win their agreement to come to his vicariate. In 1948, when Chick was in London, he pursued the Vicar of the congregation – the Mother General being in India at the time – and she told him she was busy, that her train left King's Cross at 2.20 and that if he was there by 2.00, she would see him. By 2.20 the sisters had agreed to come to Rhodesia. The first sisters who came had been working in India for some time and it was from there they came. Chick arranged for them to be met in Mombasa and later in Beira where Fr Francis Ketterer SJ, stationed in Mutare, was there to meet them. They started at Mount Mellary Mission in Nyanga and later acquired land in Borrowdale, Salisbury, where they built St Michael's, as a preparatory school for St George's. It welcomed 33 boys in 1951 and the following year had 250. Later some of the sisters moved to St Kilian's, near Rusape. In 1959, they started Nagle House, a girls' school in Marondera.

Frank Barr, in his memoir of Chick, describes a number of other initiatives. Chick wanted to broaden the minds of Europeans and started a library for them. He wanted a house of prayer to support the work and the Dominican Mother General fell in with the idea, setting up a house for elderly sisters in Borrowdale. But he was grudging in his support for the Precious Blood Sisters in their desire to set up a Teacher Training College for girls at Monte Cassino, near Macheke. Barr comments, 'This was one occasion when the sisters were right and Chick was wrong.'[16]

Fr Charles Ferguson had been living at a mission called Silveira, founded in 1931, and Chick wanted a convent there to teach the girls. A building of wooden poles, cut from the forest, plastered inside

---

16 Barr, p. 65.

and out with clay and covered by a grass roof was the first home of the Dominican sisters who went there but the sisters were happy. Despite this – and the fact that the sisters were established at Musami, Gokomere, All Souls Mutoko and now Silveira – Chick grumbled to Mother General Ignatius that the Dominicans were concentrating too much on white work. This was a reference to their schools for whites in Salisbury, Bulawayo, Gweru and Mutare. Chick was demanding. He had a huge appetite for work himself and expected everyone else to be like him. Barr says he did not seem to understand illness, never having been ill himself, and would visit the sick and discuss work plans with them. Sometimes he would head off to say Mass at isolated farms and once visited eight in eight days.

At a meeting of the bishops of southern Africa the papal delegate proposed that priests should be forbidden to go to watch films, that is, go to the bioscope, presumably because they were seen as dangerous to morals. Some of the bishops meekly acquiesced but Chick objected and said it should be left to the priests to decide what to watch. Encouraged by Chick's revolt the proposal was dropped.

The Second World War brought new challenges to Chick, as German priests were in danger of being interned. In the event Chick prevented this but he had to inform the government when he transferred them from place to place. He tried to help those who were interned or were refugees – Germans, Italians, Poles – by providing care for them and they in their turn contributed their building skills at the seminary and in Masvingo.

Chick also started a study group with Anglican bishop Paget for lay people to discuss social problems in the post-war years. Chick encouraged the Dominicans to open another school in the Midlands for coloured children and Martindale was the result in 1946. This was soon followed by Loreto near Kwekwe which became a school for the deaf.

Every year Chick would visit his missions, staying a few days. Besides the mission superior he would see each of the sisters privately and visit every class in the school and ask questions. He would take an interest in the farm and in the cooking. All this involved a lot of driving and he was a notoriously bad driver!

Chick also took up his pen and edited a magazine he started in 1946 called *The Shield*. He wanted it to be a forum for ideas on politics and social conditions as well as on theology, scripture and prayer. He wrote many of the articles as well as the editorials.

In 1946 he called for a congress in Salisbury for Catholics north and south of the Zambezi with the aim of encouraging them in their faith and playing their role in society. Thousands attended, as well as six bishops or prefects. In 1949 he persuaded Fr Edward Enright, the Jesuit superior of the mission, to release Fr Michael Geoghegan, who had just finished his term as rector of St George's, to be his secretary. Thus began a fruitful seven-year partnership up to the time of his resignation. He needed help because in his final years as bishop he seemed to feel little had been achieved. 'The number of Catholics is not large (under 50,000) and there are few vocations.' Barr tells us he began to lack interest in other people's proposals, founding Marymount, rebuilding the school at St Peter's and other projects.[17] His health began to suffer but he refused to see a doctor. He said he had no trust in them. Geoghegan persuaded him he should at least go and rest in St Anne's. While there he was diagnosed as having pneumonia and was lucky to be alive.

Whatever his pessimism, Rome decided the Church in the country should now become a full province and Chick was to be the first Archbishop. It was a sign of coming of age and a great celebration was held at St George's in April 1955. Eighteen bishops attended and the Governor was there with his wife. Pope Pius XII spoke to the crowd over the radio. In the banquets which followed, the Governor General and the Federal Prime Minister both spoke of the contribution of the Church from the beginning of the country. Archbishop Garner of Pretoria, one of the guests, wrote later to Chick celebrating, a little enviously, the 'happy partnership … and friendship between the Church and the powers, political and civic, in the new ecclesiastical province'.[18] In the light of the subsequent antagonism between church and state, the event seems like a last dance in the ballroom of the *Titanic*.

As soon as the celebrations were over Chick went to visit the people living with leprosy at Mutemwa, near Mutoko. He used to visit them whenever he went to All Souls Mission, also near Mutoko. Fourteen years later Mutemwa was to become the home of John Bradburne,

---

17 Ibid., p. 81.
18 Ibid., p. 83.

an Englishman of great spiritual depth who was to be killed near Mutemwa towards the end of the liberation war.

As he approached retirement, Aston Chichester was persuaded to build a house for his successor. He considered this a 'nuisance' but then threw much energy into it, viewing endless displays of carpets and curtains and insisting on real leather for the chairs. The curtains in the library had to be grey velvet so that they did not 'fight' with the different coloured spines of the books and the rugs. He moved into the new House in August – it, inevitably, became known as 'Aston Villa' – and resigned in December, handing over to Francis Markall, who had been at Kutama at the time Mugabe's father walked out on his mother and left her almost destitute,[19] and was now at Monte Cassino.

Chick felt he must get out of the way and left the country, settling in Preston in NW England as a curate at St Wilfred's. Many tributes were paid to him by government officials, and all those he visited on a final tour of the missions, at the time of his leaving. A year went by and then Markall invited him back and he settled at the 'coloured' school in Martindale where he took an active part in the school. Though the children loved being around him informally they were bored with his classes and he knew it and he stopped teaching. He was delighted to be invited to the Council in Rome by 'Johnny' (Pope John XXIII) and took the opportunity on a day off of visiting Assisi with Fr Bernard Hall (who has just died as I write these lines, nearly sixty years later). On 24 October, as he was mounting the steps to enter St Peter's for the morning session of the Council, he collapsed. He died on the way to hospital.

In this brief account of the life and work of Archbishop Chichester we catch something, perhaps, of the huge impact he had on the development of the Church in Zimbabwe. The founding of the seminary and the congregation for Zimbabwean sisters stand out, but his care for every detail in every corner of the vicariate, later the archdiocese, touched people. Years later the stories still abound. When his remains were eventually transported to Zimbabwe, they were taken to Chishawasha cemetery with an hour's pause on the way at Chichester Convent which was built for elderly and retired

---

19 Markall helped her as best he could with soap and other essentials and Robert never forgot this.

sisters on the edge of the valley. Sr Theresiana Muteme was invited to say some words as the coffin rested in the sisters' chapel and she addressed Chick personally as if he were there. As she listed his many achievements, she grew tired and put her speech on the coffin saying, 'you can read the rest for yourself'.

Welcoming local-born Jesuits

Some twenty years after the founding of the Regional[20] Seminary in Chishawasha, the time was ripe to welcome local people who wished to join the Jesuits. In 1957 a novitiate at Silveira House, also in Chishawasha, opened its doors to welcome the first candidates. In 1961 two diocesan priests joined: Peter Kavuma from Uganda and Raymond Kapito from Mutoko. Seven years later, another diocesan priest, Gilbert Modikayi, entered the society in Edinburgh. But overall the numbers were small and the novitiate was transferred to Mazowe after six years by Terrence Corrigan, the Mission Superior. The novices were eventually sent to Lusaka, where a new novitiate was opened for candidates from all English-speaking countries in Africa in 1969. They began with fourteen novices from seven countries. Fidelis Mukonori remembers: 'Between 1969 and 1972, 120 men went to Mazoe but only 11 made it. We used to work on a farm under difficult conditions but our group made a pact among ourselves that, no matter how hard life was, we would not go back home. We wanted to be Jesuits and would do whatever it took.'[21]

Looking back we can say that the welcome the young men received in the 1960s was more from the head than from the heart. It was clearly fitting and right and much trouble and expense went into the establishment of a purpose-built novitiate at Silveira House. But among the Jesuits on the ground who had been labouring for more than half a century, some almost exclusively among whites, there were those who were not able to accept a new reality where they shared their houses and their table with black people. Many of them had hardly ever sat down to a meal with a black person. Unconsciously perhaps, many Jesuits showed their reservations in their body language or even in their spoken words.

---

20 It was intended to serve Northern Rhodesia (Zambia) and Bechuanaland (Botswana) as well as Southern Rhodesia (Zimbabwe).
21 *Letters and Notices*, p. 445, p. 463 ff.

So, the first generation of those who were welcomed had a hard time. Raymond Kapito[22], whose grandmother once chased a lion from their village in Mutoko, wanted to join the Jesuits at an early age but was told his only option was to be a diocesan priest. Even after his ordination he did not give up his desire. It took some of his grandmother's courage to pursue this particular lion and five years after his ordination he entered the Jesuit novitiate in Edinburgh. It was a great joy to him to make his first vows but he soon found that some of his fellow white Jesuits could not handle this new situation. He often spoke with humour – though also with a trace of bitterness he could not hide – about how he was received. His white brothers did not know what they were doing when they treated him with condescension.

If it was like that for priests, we have to turn up the volume when it comes to brothers. Some of our brothers in those days really wanted to be brothers and they were happy and did great work. Among them were Joseph Mandaza and Canisius Chishiri. But there were others who were told they had to be brothers if they were to be Jesuits. Very few – perhaps none – of those who applied had the basic educational qualifications that were considered essential if one were to manage the studies. So being a brother was the only option. There were some – Denis Adamson and Tobias Tirivanhu among them – who really wanted to become priests. They accepted the decision to become brothers at one level but at another they felt frustrated. I remember Dominic Shoniwa, who entered in 1964 and died in 2018, telling me how encouraged he was when the provincial, Henry Wardale, made him a consultor (provincial's council member) of the province. This was the kind of affirmation that mitigated some of the sense of not quite belonging that some brothers felt. This was an unhealthy situation which marred the early years of locally born Zimbabweans

---

22 Raymond Kapito (1928-2006) was born in Mutoko and joined the Society, despite countless delays, as a priest in 1961. He became Parish Priest of Mabvuku while also giving retreats at Silveira House. In 1980 he became novice master in Waterfalls and later director of the pre-seminary at Mazowe. He was later *socius* (assistant) to the Novice Master in Lusaka. He was renowned for his lively – and lengthy – homilies and used to enjoy telling the story of how the archbishop once interrupted him, saying 'Enough'. His funeral was more of a celebration than a dirge as people told story after story showing his warmth and humour.

joining the Society.

But there was a gleam of light. A Tertianship[23] for the brothers was organised at St Ignatius College in 1976 conducted by Michael Ivens, an English Jesuit renowned for his knowledge of the *Spiritual Exercises* and his empathy with those he guided. This event was crowned by a visit to the combined missions of Salisbury and Sinoia by Fr General, Pedro Arrupe, who received the final vows of the brothers and spoke warmly to the whole gathering of Jesuits about the brothers in the Society.

The second wave, if I may call it that, of vocations to the Society came around the time of independence in 1980. They were not many but they were vocal. They were priests and professed[24] brothers by then and I remember meetings during the 1980s when they spoke out about how they felt in our white-dominated province. I do not remember what they said but I recall the anger with which they said it. The whites listening were confused and hurt in their turn. No one seemed to grasp what was going on. It was, perhaps, a necessary stage we had to go through – like the verbal fights of newly-weds once the honeymoon is over. I am not sure it was well handled and it left a certain residue of bitterness though I think this was gradually integrated into the greater picture of our goals.

At any rate, by the 1990s – and the third wave – the picture was quite different. Numbers were increasing and the new applicants brought none or little of the colonial baggage that had contaminated our earlier efforts to welcome Zimbabweans. They breathed a freer and more open air and soon jostled to make the Society their own. Soon we had our first locally born provincial, Fr Fidelis Mukonori, and subsequent provincials have been born in Zimbabwe. Today they own the province and all its works and the older members among us rejoice at this.

Yet, perhaps inevitably, further questions arise in time. How, for

---

23 The *Tertianship* is Jesuit-speak for a final year of formation when books are laid aside and the person goes back to the *Exercises* a second time and is involved in work among the poor, the sick and the handicapped. It is sometimes called a 'school of the affections', a clumsy translation of a Latin term. Basically the idea is that a person can, as a result of his specialised studies and maybe great success as a teacher or preacher, become removed from 'real' life on the ground 'among the reek of cabbage water' (Ruth Burrows).

24 'Profession' in the language of religious life means the final stage when a person publicly commits herself or himself to the community for life.

instance, are members of smaller groups – Ndebeles, for example – welcomed into the Society? Again we have a dominant group and, probably unconsciously, they see things in their terms. One advantage of the new province emerging in southern Africa could be that questions such as these will simply fall away. But, in the meantime, the question is there on the table. Archbishop Pius Ncube used to talk openly about relations between Shona and Ndebele. He, an Ndebele, recognised that Shona people have a long memory. They still remember the stories handed down to their parents about the ruthless raids of the Ndebeles into Shona territory. Our Jesuits ancestors on their arrival at Gubulawayo in 1879 heard these stories. Augustus Law wrote in his journal on 2 October 1879, 'the King (Lobengula) is about to send out an *impi* (army) to steal cattle to pay for the expenses of (his) marriage. The *impi* has been levied from about 11 kraals & goes (probably) NE (that is to Shona territory) to plunder and murder'. And three days later he wrote, 'Heard some more of these accounts that make one thoroughly sick at heart. When these *impi* go out plundering and murdering (and one starts tomorrow or the next day on that errand) when they arrive at the place, they kill all the men and big boys & load the women with the booty. When they get near their home, they unload these women & and then a man takes an assegai and slaughters the poor creatures like cattle.'[25]

Given this background, if I may stray into politics for a moment, it was a remarkable achievement of Joshua Nkomo to forge an executive for the Southern Rhodesia African National Congress in the late 1950s which represented the whole country and could present a united front to the government. But the unity did not last and the split in the nationalist movement in 1963 brought out the underlying tension between the two dominant groups. This split was never been healed, and was even exacerbated by the disproportionate response of Mugabe to the challenge from Ndebele dissidents in the *Gukurahundi*[26] in the early years of independence. A precise figure of those killed may never be known but a studied estimate based on the research done for *Breaking the Silence* puts it at 20,000 and this has to be seen beside the

---

25 Cf. Gelfand, pp. 116-7.
26 Literally, 'the first rains that sweep away the rubbish (lying around during the dry season)'. The term was used by Mugabe to describe the sweeping away of those Ndebeles who opposed his rule. Cf. D. Coltart, *The Struggle Continues: 50 Years of Tyranny in Zimbabwe* (Auckland Park: Jacana Media, 2016), p. 238.

figure of 60,000[27] for the whole period of the liberation war (1973-79). *Breaking the Silence* was a report commissioned jointly by the Catholic Commission for Justice and Peace and the Legal Resources Foundation to look into the *Gukurahundi* campaign. The Catholic Bishops never approved its publication but the LRF went ahead without them in July 1997. Archbishop Patrick Chakaipa was strongly opposed to publication, presumably because he saw it as divisive. But the victims simply wanted the truth to be told, an apology to be made and communal reparation to be offered.[28] I attended a session in Bulawayo in 2000 which was promoting a programme of reburial of victims' remains. The victims' families spoke movingly about how they gained healing and closure from the programme.

All this is, perhaps, the background to the, perhaps unconscious, attitude of young Ndebeles who might be thinking of joining the Society.

A mischief-maker or a prophet?

Another question centred round people who did not seem to 'fit in'. Pope Francis encourages young people today to 'make trouble', to stir things up! A great idea! But when you actually have someone who stirs things it can be uncomfortable. In Ignatius Zvarevashe, for example, who died in December 2019, we see someone who lived through much of the time I have described. He joined the Society in 1969 and so was a Jesuit for fifty years. He had already been a Jesuit for eleven years at the time of independence and a priest for one year. He was a sensitive person and his Shona novels are highly appreciated. But he found living among whites grated on his spirit and he would lash out at times. There was an article he wrote for AFER[29] which was highly critical of the missionaries and left a scar in his relationship with his own white brothers. Fr Dominic Tomuseni has great admiration for Zvarevashe and helps us understand him better. While doing so he casts a light over white/black relationships

---

27 Again, there is no consensus about the number who died in our liberation war. Estimates vary from 35,000 to 60,000.
28 Coltart, op. cit., p. 240.
29 *African Ecclesiastical Review*, 35(2), p. 115. Zvarevashe had entitled it, 'Racism still lingers in the Church in Zimbabwe', but the editor changed the title to 'Racist Missionaries: an Obstacle to Evangelisation in Africa', a more provocative title which landed Zvarevashe in trouble at the time.

in the Society of Jesus. Dominic has kindly allowed me to use some of his notes on Zvarevashe and I quote them at some length for reasons that I hope will be apparent.

Dominic calls Zvarevashe, 'Mhazi, the lion that refused to be placed in a game park'. But he was a lion that was misunderstood even by as eminent a person as Fr Otene Matungulu, Assistant for Africa to the Jesuit Fr General in Rome. When Dominic asked Matungulu about a writing project, he replied, 'consult Zvarevashe, he writes good Shona books, but that is the only thing he does'. Dominic did not understand this reply but 'sensed some negativity in it'. Later Dominic was in a parish and the people wanted to invite Zvarevashe to give a talk on Mary, but the parish priest was blunt, 'I do not think it is a good idea, he is a loose cannon.'

Zvarevashe often expressed a desire to teach a course at either Arrupe Jesuit University or Hekima University College, but neither was willing to offer him the opportunity. Dominic wonders why. He had first met Zvarevashe through his books when he was in grade 4 and got *Kurauone*, one of his novels, as a prize. This led him to read *Gonawapotera*, which became a set-book for A-level, and he went on to read other books and poems by him. Dominic was deeply inspired and hoped to meet him one day.

Zvarevashe was unsettled. He seemed to see 'karabha' (colour bar) everywhere. He expressed his feelings in the article in AFER, already mentioned, *Racist Missionaries: An Obstacle to Evangelization in Africa*. He told Dominic how he suffered after that article was published. He was summoned and reprimanded by his provincial and had to write an apology in which he said,

> I would like to apologize … I wrote the article in anger, some of the language being almost racist itself, or giving that impression. My intention was not to hurt your feelings, but to challenge us all to the genuine demands of the Gospel, which requires us all to abolish all forms of racism, black or white, so we can truly live as brothers and sisters in Christ. It was AFER that gave my article that title. My title had been, 'Racism Still Lingers in The Church in Zimbabwe'. Thank you for pardoning me.

Zvarevashe felt his protests often hit home and he enjoyed the impact he was making without seeming to realise that he, in his turn, was causing offence. His books had a great impact. It was not just his novels but also his spiritual writings. Dominic once visited an elderly woman in Mbare who was sick. She had a maid who used to read to her every night from Zvarevashe's *Mbiri Nemarwadzo Amambo Wedu Yesu Kristo* (the Glory and Wounds of our Lord Jesus Christ). Dominic comments,

> I started to appreciate Zvarevashe's spiritual and theological books. I realized they had an impact on people, in spite of my reservations. ... I had been critical of his theological texts and felt his strength was in novels. But I have changed my mind and now feel that in order to appreciate Zvarevashe's writing, you must go to his life.
>
> Biography is the key to understanding African thought and theology. If you stay only with what an author has written, you never appreciate fully what he or she was all about. ... In Africa this struggle is about a heritage, which for many decades, has been considered inferior. It is difficult to find that struggle only in the writings of the scholars of the time. It is in the personal stories of these scholars.
>
> Zvarevashe expressed a deep desire for the Church in Africa to be truly African. Because of this desire he suffered greatly. ... He was a man with 'far-seeing eyes', who saw that in Christianity there is more than the European garb in which it was dressed when it came to Africa. ... There is something in Christianity with which Africans in their own way and culture could engage.

Dominic concludes, 'his writings are not the lamentations of a restrained man but the proclamations of a free man'.

Charism and culture

St Ignatius wrote the Constitutions *after* the Society was founded and well established, not before. He wanted to find out 'what we do' before he could write about 'who we are'. As mentioned in the introduction, one of the reasons he insisted on people writing letters describing their activities was that, when circulated, they would explain better to younger Jesuits what the Society was than the rich but abstract 'Formula of the Institute' of the founding fathers in Rome in 1539. Experience precedes insight. When the Jesuits came to Africa – or Asia or South America – they came with their 'way of proceeding' based on their *charism*. This is a word, like 'icon' or 'subsidiarity', which began as 'church-speak' and has recently moved into the secular sphere. It means 'grace', which itself has the connotation of 'gift', even an unconditional gift – something without any definable (logical) cause. Our 'way of proceeding' is a gift. It is not just a logical, worked-out code of work and living, though, hopefully, it is also that.

Our *charism* attempts to hold together imagination, initiative and flexibility with a focused, shared vision, discerned and lived in a community where the members are bound to one another and give their obedience to one of their number. Fr General is, ultimately, that person and he is elected for the task by delegates from all over the world where the Society is working. He directs the different works in line with this *charism*. The genius of Ignatius was in providing a way of holding in a creative tension the imagination and drive of the individual and the overall vision and mission of the whole.

We touch here on the question: how does this *charism*, conceived in Europe, operate in Africa? This is a complex subject, as it opens up a discussion on universal, as opposed to culturally conditioned, values. The understanding of people who join the Jesuit Society is: there are fundamentals which we all share and subscribe to but there are differences, from place to place, as to how these are lived. We can take a trivial example. Sixty years ago, everybody was Fr A and Br B (his surname). Then in the sixties, probably under the influence of the Americans, whom we can blame for most things, revered figures were suddenly reduced to their first names, often abbreviated. Fr. John Diamond, one-time rector of the large college of theology and philosophy in the Oxfordshire woods and an 'establishment' figure in the British province of the Jesuits, became simply 'Jack'. But this kind of irreverence was not acceptable everywhere. When I was responsible for the 'Juniorate' in Harare in the early 1990s, we had two Korean scholastics studying English with us. They were roughly the same age but one was 'senior' to the other and I discovered the junior never addressed his companion by his first name.

Perhaps such a minor matter alerts us to more serious differences. Again in the sixties, Pedro Arrupe, the Fr. General at the time, addressed a group of Irish Jesuits, among whom were some who had held a succession of high positions in the Irish province. In his usual ebullient manner, Arrupe was speaking about the need for wide consultation in the Society. 'We must listen to the novices', he said. After the meeting one elderly priest was overheard to say to another, Fr John Hyde, 'What was he talking about? Listening to the novices!' To which Hyde replied, 'Well now, that goes to show it's the end of the likes of you.'

The cultural shifts in the sixties were hard to take even within cultures. What happens when two very different cultures meet? Individuals have the task of adjusting to an alien culture with which they are now to be intimately connected. What happens when this feeling of alienation touches decision making about work? We will see, when we come to discuss the School of Social Work, how the school was discerning its way in the late 1960s. In the context of Rhodesia, the staff discovered they had to part company with the mainstream emphasis of standard social work which relies on case work, that is, the 'problems of an individual such as poverty, housing, relationships, marriage, substance addiction, medical needs' and the like. Instead, in consideration of the strength of the extended family among African people, the board felt their emphasis should be on group or community work.

There were some who weathered the breakers[30] with patience and humour. Canisius Chishiri wanted to work among street children and later started a 'half-way house' (Zambuko) for them before they could be reintegrated into society. He cheerfully worked his way through the permissions, paper work and the laborious business of raising funds.

Chishiri's task was not on the scale some Zimbabwean Jesuits find themselves called to do today. They are asked to run and develop large projects started by others in more favourable times and find themselves daunted and anxious. They are disturbed by the sense they may fail. They are aware they are the first generation of Zimbabwean Jesuits and history will expect them to make a distinctive mark which expresses a Zimbabwean as well as a Jesuit identity for the work. But they may feel alone and unsupported in the individualistic Jesuit culture they have inherited. The Society of Jesus both rewards and frowns on individual 'lone rangers'. Fr. John Dove felt the cold air blowing from St George's College in the 1960s when he was struggling to set up a

---

30 Perhaps, in a landlocked country, an explanation of this apt expression is needed. When you walk into the sea you have to make your way through the waves roughly breaking on the shore. You have to get through these if you want to enter the sea proper.

centre for 'leadership training and development'. His fellow Jesuits at the college, without any evidence, saw him as pandering to extreme nationalism and even communism. He felt lonely, and only a few Jesuits, fortunately among them the provincial, Terrence Corrigan, and the general, Pedro Arrupe, supported him. But he was working with, mostly, English people like himself. He could understand them and level with them. He could even have furious rows with them. In this sense he had an advantage over Chishiri. If he had had to face confrontations, which he didn't as far as I know, he might have felt highly frustrated.

Aware of the need to tread warily when speaking of the culture of others, it may still be worthwhile observing characteristics which have, to the outsider, seemingly good and not so good elements. When I was the delegate (coordinator) of a community of scholastics, one of them, in a moment of anger towards another, poured boiling water on him causing him pain and some minor temporary damage. I called the group together that evening to reflect on the incident and found that all those who came from Kenya and the countries south of Kenya took one view, while those from Sudan and Nigeria took another. It could have been just coincidence but I did not think so then. I had a distinct feeling of some people not wanting to give their own view but to follow the view of others. This could be good news in the sense that people work towards consensus among themselves. But it could also be bad news if someone is not ready to state their own view.

But the real issue is not with people of another culture but with the way the *charism* of the Society is interpreted and lived in any culture. Today we celebrate the achievements of, for example, those I called 'lone rangers', but can we say what they did was 'province policy' at the time? The province, and maybe the whole Society, is not always able to draw up policies and pursue them. The general or provincial cannot, like Napoleon, give orders and expect them to be obeyed all the way down the line. He has to govern 'according to times and circumstances' as our constitutions repeatedly remind us. In the end, what actually happens is dependent on the initiative and courage of people on the ground who act within the general parameters of the Society's mission.

As the Shona proverb goes, 'To climb the mountain you have to go round it rather than straight up'. Where are we on this particular mountain of culture and *charism?* In our case, it seems, *charism* will transform culture and, in turn, will be transformed by it. Zimbabwean Jesuits, like Jesuits everywhere, are being transformed by the *charism* they have embraced and are, in their turn, also contributing to the universal *charism* of the Society in a way we can perhaps not perceive clearly now. In the actual daily life in our communities, we find it hard to hold on to the deeper implications.

Resourcement

In the run-up to the Second Vatican Council one of the catchwords was *resourcement,* a word that needs a whole sentence to translate. It means going back to the original documents of the Church (Scripture, the Fathers) and, in our case, of the Society. It was something like the Renaissance which had such astonishing results in the Europe of the late Middle Ages. The Spiritual Exercises of St Ignatius took on a new lease of life when they came under this lens. In my younger years 'spiritual direction' was, I exaggerate, reduced to, 'How are you? Do you sleep okay? Do you eat enough?' And the Exercises were a series of talks, which often seriously invaded the time allotted for prayer, with optional visits to the retreat giver. *Resourcement* changed all that and we now have a far greater understanding of, for example, what Ignatius meant when he wrote:

> When the one who is giving the Exercises perceives that the one making them is not affected by any spiritual experiences, such as consolations or desolations, and that he is not troubled by different spirits, he ought to ply him with questions.[31]

Such questioning is an example of the deeper implications of the *charism* left by Ignatius. The reserved English are not alone in fighting shy of speaking about their personal feelings and experiences. It is something most people avoid: either they do not have the language to express what they feel or they do not have the confidence to say it even in the specially set up environment where such sharing is encouraged. *Resourcement* did not end with Vatican II. It is a guiding star that is still with us, and the most recent General Congregation (GC36) of the Jesuits in Rome (2016), attempting to face the complex situation we find ourselves in today, 'returned to the roots' of the Society when

---
31 Ignatius of Loyola, *Spiritual Exercises*, VI.

they recalled the experience of the first companions in Venice. They had to 'confront the frustration of their plans to go to the Holy Land'.[32] They were driven to a 'deeper discernment of the Lord's call' by setting aside time to be together and listen to what the Lord was saying to each of them in their own hearts. They set aside their own 'thoughts' and 'reasons' and attempted a naked listening to the Spirit which they then shared. Gradually they came to a firm and united decision to pursue their goal in Rome, convinced that it was to be within the structure of the Church, flawed as they all knew it was in the sixteenth century and as it still is today.

The key message of GC36 is that we Jesuits should face the frustration we often feel in our time in the same spirit. The GC called for conversation among Jesuits but not just ordinary conversation. The GC did not invent but re-burnished the phrase 'spiritual conversation', which does not mean conversation about spiritual things but conversation about practical things spiritually, that is, while listening to what the Spirit says about them. This is not easy. It takes conviction that this is the way forward and patience to listen to others at a deep level – and not just superficially noting the words the other utters.

In 2021, rhe Jesuits in Zimbabwe joined other jurisdictions in southern Africa to form a new province from Kitwe to the Cape. There are concerns about many aspects of this enlarged entity, especially how individual Jesuits will find their place in it. The impasse at Venice and the new horizons that emerged from it can guide us to trust that we too will find new life in this new structure. And, since the new province is being proposed in the same decades that foreign-born Jesuits have definitively handed over responsibility to locally born Jesuits, the opportunity arises to resolve all gnawing fears through the method bequeathed to us by our founding fathers.

---

32 GC 36, 1 December 2016, #6.

8

A 'Dual Mission'?

> *If it would be possible to have at least* SOME *of them at St George's, it might iron out the tendency to have the mission falling into two halves ... What is wrong with St George's? Perhaps this very isolation from its total environment. Its absorption in the European scene.*
>
> Peter McIlhenny SJ, Secretary to Fr General Jean-Baptiste Janssens' English Assistant, writing to Fr Terrence Corrigan, Superior of the Salisbury Mission, 8 December 1959.[1]

On the second page of Dachs' and Rea's *The Catholic Church and Zimbabwe* there is the fateful sentence; 'Thus, a dual mission to serve both white and black was inaugurated'. The authors are faithfully reflecting the thinking and practice of the time when the Catholic Church, bowing to practical necessity resulting from the political culture, pursued not one integrated mission but two parallel ones: a mission to the whites and a mission to the blacks, with little interrelation between them. There were priests, like Nicot, Götz and Nesser in Bulawayo, who combined teaching whites in the classroom with working in the prison or the black township. But, looking back over the 130 years since the Jesuits and Dominicans arrived in the wake of the Pioneers, it is hard to escape the basic inconsistency imbedded in the pursuit of a double mission even though there are reasons for accepting that this was the only way it could have been at the time.

---

1   JAZ, Box 26B/4.

What is harder to understand is how we allowed the thought patterns and practices of the whites to seep into our own way of life when we were under no pressure to do so. When Fidelis Mukonori, a future Jesuit, arrived at Chishawasha as a schoolboy in 1959, he noticed a silver plate was handed to each white person before they received Communion. When it came to the turn of the blacks, the plate was withdrawn. Fidelis comments, 'you pass something a thousand times before your notice it'.[2] The practice appears to have been seamlessly adopted without anyone being aware of what it implied.

It may sound naïve and disingenuous to insist the Church has only one mission and that the Jesuits failed to develop an imaginative and creative attitude towards race relations from the beginning. As already mentioned, given the circumstances in which they found themselves, we can find reasons for their adopting practices which resonated with the world-view of those who had conquered the country. Among these was the gap in literacy and numeracy between black and white children, which the settlers saw, in those early days, as unbridgeable. This gap, we now realise, was used by the whites to award themselves with a sense of entitlement to the best land, exclusive suburbs and opportunities for education and employment which they felt were their due. Arriving in the country in 1966 and trying to understand the fury of the Rhodesian Front government at what they considered Britain's, and particularly Prime Minister Harold Wilson's, betrayal of their interests, I often heard the refrain, 'the blacks are nowhere near ready for self-governement'. Yet, it was clear the convenient 'gap' was being rapidly bridged and, if the door was opened to them, the blacks would quickly learn all the skills needed to run a modern state. The tragedy is the door was not opened and so when independence came and the new rulers had no preparation for their new responsibilities, they lapsed into the only model available and imitated the Rhodesisn policy of ignoring the gap – this time between black rulers and black ruled.

The missionaries, Jesuits and Protestants, did achieve 'a degree of fluency in the local languages which enabled them to provide such early training either directly, or through a new generation of African teachers (and) ensure a development in African education way beyond what was intended by the government, even though initially only for

---

2   Mukonori, p. 14.

a small percentage of the indigenous population.'[3]

A conclusion this study repeatedly finds it impossible to avoid is that the great achievements in founding the Church in Zimbabwe, which this book describes, were tarnished by an on-going failure to challenge the whites, who designed a policy of separate development, interacting with blacks only when, for example, they needed labour. The whites and, because their fortunes were so interlinked, the blacks were both the ultimate losers. The persistent avoidance of facing up to 'the native problem', as the whites called it, meant that an explosion, which in the event would cost many lives, became inevitable. My generation of young Jesuits, arriving in the 1960s, could see immediately the contradictions imbedded in the country and in the Church and we wondered why the latter were doing so little about it. The missionaries of all churches co-operated with the positive aspects of the colonial legislation while resigning themselves to what they viewed as the practical necessity of living with the negative results. Some missionaries – Arthur Shearley Cripps from the Anglican Church and John White from the Methodists were outstanding in the 1930s – did oppose the creeping separation of the races but they made little impact. The churches never came together to challenge the direction the country was taking. In fact, looking back over the past century, it seems they bent over backwards to put a good interpretation on some aspects of it:

> It appears that the missionaries approve all the avowed initial intentions of the (Land Apportionment) Act (of 1930) to separate and guarantee areas for exclusive African occupation in order to protect Africans from European exploitation and to keep out undesirable Europeans from African areas.[4]

How easy it is to justify pragmatic choices! We find reasons for accepting a policy 'for now' but forget how difficult it is to do anything about it later once we see the unfortunate consequences.

So we developed two missions. When the decision came through that I was to go to Rhodesia in 1966, I knew I would be sent to teach. But where? At St George's, still a virtually whites only school, or St Ignatius', a virtually blacks only one? I remember thinking I would

---

3   John McCarthy, personal communication. I am grateful to him for his detailed and enlightening comments on my draft on St George's College.
4   Dachs and Rea, p. 122.

prefer to go to St George's as, to my raw mind, it would be a gentle introduction to Africa – rather than being thrown immediately into a black school whose students, I feared, would not welcome me, a white, less than a year after UDI. In other words, I was succumbing even before I set foot in the country to a mind-set that wanted to avoid, at least at first, the challenges that engaging with blacks would involve. Fortunately, I did not get the soft option I wanted and for me St Ignatius College was the best possible introduction to the country.

Cities and towns in Zimbabwe often had two churches, reflecting the division of the races. This was a practical necessity, as no whites lived in black areas and no blacks, except domestic servants, in white ones. Again, despite the difficulties, there might have been ways in which links could have been built between the communities. Peter Bunnett, a devout and generous Catholic who enjoyed the unofficial title of being lay Catholic no. 1 (!), never seems to have got beyond greetings in the local language and even these were given in an excruciating colonial way, of which he seemed quite unaware. Twin churches were built in small settlements like Que Que (Kwekwe), where the Bunnetts lived, and Sinoia (Chinhoyi), as well as the larger centres of population like Salisbury (Harare), Bulawayo and Gwelo. In Salisbury we were, and still are, responsible for Our Lady of the Wayside parish, where the main Sunday Masses were for the whites, though some blacks from the multiracial University College of Rhodesia and Nyasaland, founded in 1957, attended. An afternoon Mass was celebrated for black domestic servants who would have finished their duties by then. In the Cathedral, blacks were not even permitted in the body of the church until 1959, though they were allowed in the side aisles.[5]

St George's College

St George's was the epitome of this well-intentioned but ultimately deeply flawed aspect of our mission. Despite the fact that we were all Jesuits there were divisions among us. We managed to be tolerant and polite to each other but found it hard to achieve 'union of hearts and minds'. There were Jesuits on the missions who could not bring themselves to set foot in St George's and there were Jesuits at St George's who, for example, thought Silveira House was a breeding

---

5 P. Hackett, SJ, *Catholic Cathedral, Harare, 1925-2000* (Harare: Catholic Cathedral, n.d.) p. 26.

ground for revolutionaries!

St George's was founded in Bulawayo in 1896 and generations of Jesuits have devoted their lives to the school which is now a renowned centre of all-round education. At the time of writing, John McCarthy, the college archivist, estimates 10,000 plus students have passed through its doors. A number became Jesuits and one became provincial. To return to the theme already referred to above, the college was exclusively for whites until 1964. The Jesuits in the 1930s were pushing ahead with preparing blacks to become priests but they do not seem to have pushed equally hard against the current and admitted blacks to the college. It might have meant some parents withdrawing their sons from the school at a time when enrolment was still low and so constantly presenting challenges of viability. McCarthy tells us there were less than 150 students at the time the school moved from Bulawayo to Salisbury in 1927 and it 'lived a fairly hand to mouth existence ... until the late 1950s'. He cautions that the school would have even risked closure as white sentiment, before the Second World War, would have been instantly hostile.

Yet I want to stay with this issue a little longer even if it seems anachronistic all these years later. St George's was a major commitment of the Society of Jesus to the new country emerging in central Africa. The white settlers worked hard to develop Southern Rhodesia. When I arrived, in 1966, I was struck by the economic health visible everywhere: on the farms, in the mines, the infrastructure, the tourist attractions. We did not know what a power cut was in those days nor could a pothole have a life expectancy of more than a day or two. The trains ran on time and, despite real sanctions affecting every aspect of the economy, there were few shortages that the ingenuity of people could not address. The natural beauty of the country was augmented by the imaginative use of flowering shrubs and colourful trees that lined the avenues of the cities and towns. It was astonishing coming from drab England.

But there was one thing glaringly missing. Black people, the indigenous inhabitants, were excluded from sharing in a substantial way in the headlong development. True, there were black teachers and nurses, businessmen and some lawyers and other professionals. Teachers could afford cars, something rare today more than fifty years later. But black progress was progress with the brake on. It was orchestrated in such a way that it never challenged white hegemony. The point here is that these attitudes went virtually unchallenged by the Church and, in the first half of the last century, that meant the Jesuits. Clearly, it would have been a risk, a huge risk, for St George's – and the Church generally – to challenge the direction the country was going. But the consequences of the failure to do so are still with us in the third decade of the twenty first century. The country is still being run for the benefit of the few. The wielders of power are different but the system is the same, though not so well managed. One is reminded of Yeats's poem, 'The Great Day':

> Hurrah for revolution and more cannon-shot!
>
> A beggar upon horseback lashes a beggar on foot.
>
> Hurrah for revolution and cannon come again!
>
> The beggars have changed places, but the lash goes on.

The roots of our present malaise go back to the 1920s and 1930s, just when the college was getting on its feet in Salisbury. Doris Lessing, in her novel *The Grass is Singing*, and even more so in her autobiography, *Under my Skin*, paints a raw picture of white fear and prejudice with regard to the 'native problem'. She records the words of an old black man which 'got to me'. The old man noticed her embarrassment at yet another insulting racial incident they both witnessed, and said to her, 'You see, I am very old and you are very young.' Lessing writes, 'I had been given the mildest of snubs, with a smile that forgave ... Nothing was said but everything was said… It was lodged in my mind as a paradigm.'[6] Lessing later wrote, 'the only black man we were continuously in contact with (in the 1940s) was Charles Mzingele who for years had been the old Left Book Club's "token" African. There, in those meetings, he had gently and humorously repeated that Britain, because of the entrenched clause in the Constitution that gave the colony independence, was responsible for the bad treatment of the natives, yet no one ever reminded her of this dereliction of duty. With us he did the same. For him, this was the nub of the situation. If Britain could be aware, she would tell the Southern Rhodesian government to behave.'[7]

---

6 D. Lessing, *Under My Skin: Volume One of my Autobiography, to 1949* (London: HarperCollins, 1994), p. 159.

7 Ibid., p. 304.

The British government didn't. It knew it had lost control when it handed it over to the whites when granting self-government in 1924. At the time of the Pearce Commission (1972) which tried to reach a settlement that would avert the looming war, Lord Goodman, working with Sir Alec Douglas Home, defended what was proposed. 'The terms of settlement were not a sell-out. The African had been sold-out long before ... during the long years of British colonial administration, which, notwithstanding our reserved powers, accepted discriminatory legislation. ... it is against this background of constant moral capitulation ... that the terms we negotiated – have to be set.'[8]

The Jesuits at St George's, it seems, did not spend time agonising over these questions. They got on with the job. Far from challenging the authorities, they went out of their way to prove their loyalty. They devoted their energy and imagination to the task. The buildings, the grounds, the playing fields, the classrooms and science labs became magnificent in terms of the standards in the country. I suspect that so much energy and resources were devoted to the college to prove that the Catholic Church had arrived and was claiming to be recognised and respected as an equal by the establishment, in England, at the time. The Church had only recently emerged from centuries of hot and cold persecution[9] and it was within the lifetime of the parents of the founders of the college that the British government, at the time of the restoration of the hierarchy in England and Wales, had sought to outlaw the titles of 'bishop' and 'archbishop' for Catholics.

So it was natural for the Jesuits to want to prove their loyalty, and the name, St George's, could not be more English. The architecture evokes Windsor Castle and the college crest includes the flag of St George, the national flag of England and two roses, the Greek word

---

8   Quoted in M. Meredith (1980), *The Past is Another Country: Rhodesia, UDI to Zimbabwe* (London: Pan, 1980), p. 84.
9   The Catholic Church has a long memory. Her unity was shattered in the sixteenth century by Luther and his followers in what became known as the Reformation. Martyrs appeared on both sides of the ensuing divide. While struggling with the effects of this schism, she was hit in the following century by what became known as the Enlightenment, the age of science and reason. This seemed to strike at the very heart of the Church: her faith. She was quite unable to respond creatively to this challenge until well into the twentieth century. Finally, the eighteenth century closed with the French Revolution whose ripples flowed out into the nineteenth and twentieth centuries. Only in recent years, especially since the Second Vatican Council (1962-65) has the Church come fully to terms with these movements and integrated them into her own world-view.

for which is *rhodon*, a word that deliberately evokes the name of Rhodes. The motto, until the early 1920s was, 'for merry England'![10]

The school was founded with six boys in a corrugated iron shed in Bulawayo in January 1896 by Fr Marc Barthelemy, a French Jesuit who had done some of his studies in Ireland. New buildings were put up 1898 and again in 1907. The still standing much expanded building, in Bulawayo, was completed in 1912. The following year Fr Barthelemy died and was given, for those days, an enormous funeral with 80 vehicles which 'took 27 minutes to pass a given point'. The Great War of 1914-18 took 26 lives from the fledgling school and some other casualties too. Fr Nesser, a German national and a devoted teacher at the college, was arrested, imprisoned and eventually exiled. He was never allowed to return even after the war.

We can note, in passing, the excitement generated by the arrival of the first plane in the country in 1920. The school closed and the whole town took the day off to witness it landing on the racecourse. Its take off two days later was less spectacular – or perhaps more – for it crashed into a tree and had to be written off. The pilots escaped with minor bruises and one of them, Quinton Brand, a Catholic educated at the Christian Brothers' school in Kimberley, visited the school the next day to talk about his experiences. Later, in the 1950s, he sent his own son to the school for his A-levels.

The 1920s were dominated by plans for, and the execution of, the move to Salisbury. The discernment that led to the move seemed to be fuelled mainly by the need for more space to expand and the fact that the Jesuits still owned a 'rather isolated property three miles from the town centre' outside Salisbury. It was an ideal place to move to. An indication of its isolation can be gained from the experience of Fr Aloysius Leboeuf who lived there for a while and one day met a lion while he was cycling back from town.

A picture of life at St George's Bulawayo is given by Fr Fran Jones on his arrival in 1926:

> My expectations of finding the college the leading school in Southern Rhodesia received a decided setback. It had an auspicious beginning in that it was the first school ever in the colony and so received all the flattering notice of 'the great' and

---

10 T. McCarthy, *Men for Others: St George's College, 1896-1996* (Harare: Old Georgians Association, 1996), p. 71.

> the patronage. The college did pass through a certain stage of celebrity in its earlier years, but by the time I arrived there it was all *Ichabod*.[11] The community was dreadfully clothed ... The food was worse and the cheapest. If that was so for the community, you may guess what the boys' fare was like. When I first took over the refectory the plates were of enamelware, cracked and chipped and broken. ... One of the usual suppers consisted of a stained jug full of molten fat which each boy poured over a piece of bread. ... I think there was one large round sponge bath ... The boys went into the water one after another, just like sheep in a sheep dip.[12]

This bleak description was confirmed by Fr Austin Whiteside who later wrote, 'The transfer to Salisbury was a release as from prison'. When I was in our novitiate in London years later Br Edward Toon told me he was part of the team who packed up in Bulawayo and moved to Salisbury over the Christmas days of 1926. I had no context in those days to question him much about it.[13]

It was the same Aloysius Leboeuf, who met the lion, who also designed and oversaw the building of the new college. He had taught himself architecture and had already constructed the Dominican Convent, the Gothic style chapel at St Aidan's in Grahamstown, the cathedral in Salisbury in the same style and now St George's. In the *Zambesi Mission Record*, we read of the view from the tower in those days;

> In front of the school stretches 50 acres of land that provide ample space for cricket and football grounds. On either side unfolds a splendid panorama of open country, sometimes interrupted by blue hills or patches of woodland. Away to the right, the white buildings of Prince Edward School are especially prominent. The back of the schoolrooms opens onto Alexander (sic) Park, a beautiful solitude, rarely visited by any save our boys.[14]

---

11 A quaint phrase, probably current at the time, referring to the name the daughter-in-law of Phinehas gave her child, meaning 'the glory has departed' (1 Sam. 4:21), that is, the ark had been captured and her father-in-law and her husband were dead.

12 McCarthy, p. 55.

13 Edward Toon, who somehow acquired the nickname Tessie, was one of those oft-found brothers who were pillars in the old Manresa, solid and eccentric. He was in charge of the refectory and one day I saw a cake in the pantry and asked him if we were to put it out for tea. 'No, brother', was his reply, 'if you do, they will eat it.'

14 McCarthy, p. 63.

The contribution of the Jesuit Brothers here, as elsewhere in the early days of the mission, is noted in McCarthy's book. Matthias Schönbrod was the site foreman and principle ironworker. His lasting memorial is the intricately wrought iron gate to the swimming pool. John Göll, John Conway and James McGuigan were the carpenters and Patrick Mellon the stonemason. The usual forms of punishment were replaced, at the time of settling in, by work, clearing the builders rubble and laying out the sports fields. Because of the hard ground in Bulawayo, Barthelemy had insisted on soccer, but with the move to Salisbury it became possible to lay out fields that were suitable for rugby. The game receives fifteen pages in Terence McCarthy's book and the first time the college beat Prince Edward, in 1935, is vividly described by one who was there. It was a proud moment of arrival and a reward too for Fr Fran Jones who coached the team with a whistle in one hand and a rule book in the other.

St George's has perhaps an unfair reputation for its emphasis on sport. Michael O'Halloran, rector in the late 1970s and early 80s, teasingly described the school as a 'sports club with a few classrooms'. It is true they offer a wide variety of games. Beside rugby there is cricket (nine pages in McCarthy), boxing (banned in 1956), athletics, basketball, golf, hockey, shooting, soccer, squash, swimming and diving (for a time), water-polo, rowing, tennis, volleyball, judo, karate, cross-country and archery.

Prefect of Studies, Fr Gavan Duffy, in the first academy held at the new site, criticised the Rhodesian school boy of 1927 as a 'non-worker with regard to his capacity for school work and said that study did not come easily to him.' He went on to say the matriculation exam should be seen as a step not as an end. His speech caused a stir and was objected to by the Director of Education. But he was vindicated later when the Cambridge Higher Certificate and A-level were introduced.

Fifty-eight former students of the college gave their lives in the Second World War. A Memorial Chapel was created to record their names and remember their sacrifice together with those who went before them in the First World War and those who came after them in the war of liberation.

Black enrolment in the school eventually began in 1964. Titus Munyaradzi was the young brave who ventured into 'enemy' territory.

'I had no idea what to expect', he wrote, 'society was rigidly divided into black and white and having few close friends I had no one to discuss this with.' Nicholas McNally, a renowned lawyer of Irish descent, prepared him for the move and eventually brought him to the school.

> We entered the college at exactly 10.00 am. Nicholas McNally looked at his watch to make sure. Some students were on the sports field but most lined the road to the school to get a glimpse of the oddity arriving. A few boys climbed up trees and others perched on rocks; everyone was quiet as if great sadness had befallen them. I was not shocked but amazed. I did not know what to make of this new environment. ... The atmosphere was tense. Most students, like their parents, believed integration was not possible – it had taken whites generations to be 'civilised' so how could blacks do it in less than that? A few boys wanted to be friendly but they were unable to stand the peer pressure. One night everyone watched as I got into my bed which someone had filled with water. They all gazed at me and the culprit hoping I would start a fight, but the school prefect came to diffuse the situation. A few boys, like Philip Alcock, came to me privately to say they were sorry.
>
> The annual school dance, however, destroyed every chance I had of feeling at home. ... I was not to attend. Our school prefect explained I would not find a (Convent) girl to dance with and the boys would not like me dancing with white girls. They feared a riot and it was agreed that I should not go. I was hurt not because of the dance but because I was excluded from a school event. This was reversing the decision to integrate and the incident has always remained on my mind.[15]

Maybe there were reasons I have not discovered but it seems an odd decision to admit just one boy and let him carry all the weight of white teenage incomprehension. Efforts were made to identify black students who could enter 'seamlessly' into the college, that is, they had the right academic and sporting abilities. They would 'fit in'. James Mushore was younger than Munyaradzi and started the St George's journey at St Michael's, the preparatory school in those days for the college. He and his sister had been destined for the local school in

---

15 McCarthy, p. 227.

Highfield until one day the Archbishop came to breakfast. He told James's father he was trying to promote multiracial education and asked him if he could use his children as Trojan horses to enter the forbidden citadel. Mushore senior was delighted and so it came about that his daughter went to Nagle House and James to St Michael's, the foot of the ladder that would eventually lead to the college and greater things thereafter. James was only six and so, I suppose, more fragile than Titus as he faced the ordeal of adjusting in an alien environment away from the comfort and security of home. On top of the usual skirmishes of going to school he had the added challenge of boarding. Sr Enda lives in his memory as a caring mother to whom he could always turn. 'She did not mind getting blood and tears on the spotless habit nuns wore in those days.' But there was another nun who was the opposite; the boys had to line up for baths as there were not enough to go round. The water was only changed after several had washed themselves. This nun would ask James to stand aside while all the white boys bathed first. She did not have the imagination of Enda and one can almost enter her mind; she had an unconsciuously ingrained racial attitude.

Archbishop Francis Markall was pushing at the colour bar but the Catholic Church was not significantly denting the consciousness of the Rhodesians. There was considerable 'pushback' from the whites, and when the Rhodesians eventually agreed to a quota system the Church went along with this, presumably thinking they had their foot in the door and it would soon open wider. But it didn't. With hindsight, we might wish, once more, that the Church had fought a more vigorous battle in the classroom, and other areas of civic life, which would create turmoil at the time but might have prevented the far worse turmoil of the seven years' war.

There was a bursary fund set up by the independent schools in 1963 to make multiracialism work and most black students benefited from this. In time, Munyaradzi was joined by others and Fr Edward Ennis, as rector, pushed ahead with integration despite the highly charged atmosphere surrounding UDI in 1965. John McCarthy tells us there are boxes of correspondence in the St George's archives on the integration question that show 'the college came under considerable sustained pressure from the RF government. But the college refused to budge, even threatening to close and was supported in this by other schools such as the Convent, Arundel and Chisipite.'

Ennis was encouraged by Fr Gordon George, who was sent as 'visitor' by Fr General at that very time to the British province and all its overseas works. A Jesuit visitor in those days had full powers from the Superior General to look into matters and take necessary measures. The British Jesuits were responsible for Guyana and South Africa as well as Rhodesia. Gordon George was a man many Jesuits at the time loved to hate. His good recommendations, which I mention elsewhere, were put in the shade by his decision to close two colleges – one in England and one in South Africa. Despite efforts to consult parents, teachers and Jesuits, and despite good reasons for his decisions, the abiding impression was of a clumsy operation which hurt many people.[16] I do not think St George's felt they were under threat. George praised the steps they had already made towards racial integration though he wanted them speeded up. 'As long as there exists a fundamental curtailment of equal opportunity because of colour or race,' he wrote in his report, 'there exists a fundamental injustice against God-given rights.'[17]

I was in the country in 1968 but I was not aware it was a year in which Fr Brogan, as the new rector, put up a stout resistance to the government's policy on integrated sport. 'The government attempted to force the College to field white only teams by introducing regulations whereby, if any government school parent objected to their child playing against a multiracial College side, then, either the game was cancelled or the black players had to be withdrawn.' (McCarthy).

Brogan reacted with vigour;

> This directive on which we were not consulted and of which we had no direct official notification, is quite unacceptable to us. ... for several years now we have been striving to run a multi-racial school ... we are quite unwilling to put the whole enterprise at hazard by re-introducing a principle of discrimination ... we Jesuits have a reputation for being masters in the art of equivocation – or to use the modern term 'double talk' – but I submit that we are apprentices in the craft in compared with the recent standards of

---

16 I had an uncle who had been head boy at Beaumont, the college Gordon George closed in England. Every time I saw him subsequently, he berated me on the closure. It was a subject I had to wade through, like the breakers of the sea, before settling down to an enjoyable evening with him and his family.

17 *Letters and Notices*, 455, p. 200.

performance set by the Ministry of Education. ...

He gave an example where the ministry,

> insists heads of government schools consult their advisory councils or PTAs before continuing with multiracial fixtures. Then, when these bodies, in many cases, failed to come up with the right answers from the ministry's point of view, we had all the rigmarole of official-secret oral directives and confidential non-communicable decisions – which I submit are intolerable methods for a government department to use towards the teaching profession in a democratic society. [18]

By the time the liberation war was at its hottest, in the late 1970s, St George's was witnessing the deaths of twenty-nine of its former students who had been called up by the government and compelled to fight. Those called up, John McCarthy tells us from personal experience, had four options: to join up, to leave the country, to prove you had a medical condition preventing you from serving or to go to prison. Other Jesuits schools and institutions in the country were having a similar experience but with the sacrifice of lives on the guerrilla freedom fighter side, though it seems there was at least one St George's boy who joined the guerrillas. It is quite unfair on my part, but difficult to resist, pointing out that Terrence McCarthy only mentions the war in terms of the inconvenience it caused to games fixtures! They felt 'its impact on the playing of matches against schools outside the city limits. Matches had to be arranged to end early enough to allow teams to return home before dark'. Actually, McCarthy had two sons in the bush and his mother 'spent a lot of time on her knees'. John Conway, one of those killed at Musami in 1977, was a first cousin and as children the McCarthy boys used to visit him at Hwedza and Musami.

Fr Jim Berry became rector of St George's in 1984. It seems probable that he was chosen because of his extraordinary experiences at St Ignatius during the war years and just after independence. There was no better man to guide the college into the unfamiliar ground inaugurated by the new dispensation. But when Jim died in 2012, his obituarist wrote,

---

18 McCarthy, p. 100.

His period at St George's had been frustrating for him, because the staff, both lay and religious, resisted the Africanisation that the changing times in the country required and that his time at St Ignatius during the liberation war had made him aware of. At St Ignatius he had been able to use his talents as an efficient administrator who could convey a real empathy with the staff and students to great effect. St George's was still in partial denial of the realities of the situation and subsequently was unable to appreciate his attempt to guide the school through difficult times.

Fr Mark Hackett followed Jim as rector. Like Jim Berry, he was an awkward adjustment to the college in the eyes of many of the staff. They had both been in African schools and one staff member greeted Mark, 'you must find it very different here from your previous appointment'. The provincial gave him clear policies to follow: continue to make the college mainly a day school, one in which Africans would feel at home; hand over the headship to an African layperson; move the community out of the college buildings into a separate house. This last instruction was in line with recently evolved Jesuit policy to separate working space from living space. Mark also had his own agenda: he wanted to establish a 'service project' for students awaiting entry into Form 5.

Mark Hacket made changes in how the college was run. The existing structure favoured a boarding school. The rector was the headmaster and was assisted by a prefect of studies and of discipline. Under them were the dormitory masters who knew the pupils best and could counsel them. Class masters had less influence. Mark made the prefect of studies, Kevin Brennan, vice-rector as a step to his becoming headmaster. He then appointed two deputy heads: Brendan Tiernan for the senior school and David Pasipanodya for the junior. Under them, line masters dealt with the out of class activities of the students and discipline, while class masters watched over their studies. These officials knew the pupils best and were able to help and guide them.

Mark felt, 'St. George's was an outstanding educational facility producing academic and sporting success way beyond what its numbers would have expected, both of which were important in local opinion. It also was exceptional in fine arts under Dawn Bannister, music with Paul Coleman, and drama, led by Elaine

Gillespie. Boys were proud to have been there and rightly so. But all this was achieved at a cost.' Jesuit teachers, who worked for low salaries, were becoming fewer. High standards could only be maintained with quality staff who expected attractive employment conditions. But the government's determination to keep school fees down, at a level the college considered unsustainable, meant there was unending conflict.

Rugby remained a dominant measure of a school's success even in the new Zimbabwe and attendance at 1st XV games was compulsory. This was partly a relic of the dominance of boarding, but had become a feature of inter-school games where the vociferous support raised the atmosphere and even led at times to fights between parents when things were not to their liking. In the face of considerable opposition, Mark reduced this compulsory attendance to a couple of games. It was crazy to demand attendance for students who relied on public transport.

Mark wanted St. George's not only to shine in academics, sports and the arts but also to form 'men for others', a specific Jesuit goal emphasised by our superior general, Pedro Arrupe. A 'service project' seemed to be the answer. The college was fortunate to have Fr Vernon Heinz who had been involved in one in the USA and was able to give us a blueprint on how to proceed. There were three weeks available at the beginning of the school year before the A-level classes started and the college decided to make entrance to A-levels dependant on participating in the service project. The Ministry of Education made no objection. Vincent Haddad, who was in charge of the seniors, was enthusiastic and identified where the boys could go and undertook most of the organising. Some parents objected but they were persuaded to give it a try. The results were amazing. Boys, initially resistant, came back enthusiastic, but shocked by what they had seen in parts of Harare which they had never visited. Parents were happily amazed at the change they saw in their sons and enthusiasm replaced their doubts. Another result was that the Lenten campaign was now led by the boys who wanted to support projects they knew at first hand. St. George's welcomes students of all religions and none and they all found a common purpose in the project. They tried to build on this success with retreats in daily life but with limited success.

Another initiative was the introduction of prayer services leading up to the celebration of the sacrament of Reconciliation. Vincent Haddad saw to the impressive decoration of the chapel and many teachers were involved. The teaching of Religious Education in a multi-faith school remained a problem not really solved. But the RE room, run by Vincent, was an important resource where much valuable counselling and religious education took place.

1996 was the centenary of the founding of the college and projects to raise funds for its development were made and celebrations planned. The celebrations were notable but the fundraising was not, though some teachers' houses were built. Mark suggested one of the houses should be allocated to the community to allow it to return to a site on the college grounds.

Part of the celebrations was the identification of the grave of the founder, Fr Marc Barthelemy in Bulawayo. There was also a bicycle ride from the old site in that city, which is 500 kms south-west of the present site and Lorenz von Walter rode with the boys. A centenary book was written by Terence McCarthy and proved to be a valuable resource for this writer. The most spectacular event was the Passion Play performed on the college forecourt which involved two live camels. The college is now co-educational and offers bursaries to ten students from poor backgrounds. A visitor to St George's today will be struck by the beauty of the place. The architecture, the grounds, the shrubs, trees and flowers – all give a creative and enticing environment for striving in study, sport and the many other activities that make the day of a student – boy and girl, black, brown and white, Catholic and other faiths. The facilities at the college too are constantly being improved – science labs, computer rooms and the like. There are few Jesuits on staff now but the lay teachers and support staff who run the college keep up the best of the tradition they inherited and have quietly dropped the worst. There are also fewer white students now. White parents seem to prefer to send their sons – and daughters (from this year 2021) – to St John's, Peterhouse or Hellenic Academy. James Mushore has often heard the comment, 'St George's has gone rural' – meaning, I suppose, it has gone so far in welcoming black students that whites no longer feel at ease there. Further, it is alleged by some prospective parents to be so identified with the ruling elite as to be unquestioning about the source of the fees it receives.

Recently the present writer spent some years in Zambia and had occasion to descend to the Boiling Pot below the Victoria Falls and remember it was the spot where James Chaning Pearce, a Jesuit friend who spent some years at St George's used to offer rafts, constructed at the college, to the mercies of the Zambezi. The boys who went on these 'outings' never forgot them. They were stretched to their limits and more than one tumbled into the frothing river going over the rapids. James prepared everything to the minutest detail and there were no serious accidents. I believe I am right in saying that it was these expeditions that started what became a tourism 'must'.

What did the boys who passed through the college over the years think of it? Besides the reminiscences McCarthy mentions, a brochure was produced in 2013 by the 'class of 1963'. Many of the entries speak warmly of the school though they mention the multiplicity of rules and frequent use of the cane.[19] There is an appreciative undertone in the joking comment of Brendan Tiernan, boy, teacher and headmaster at St George's, who describes the Jesuits as a 'group of eccentric English bachelors in Holy Orders'.[20]

Mike Auret, one of seven Aurets at the college, who at the time of writing has recently died in Ireland, went on to be chairman of the Catholic Bishops' Justice and Peace Commission after independence and later a member of Parliament for the opposition Movement for Democratic Change. His chatty two-page contribution to McCarthy's book begins with the words: 'I loved the college with a deep and lasting love.'[21]

---

19 The cane featured at St George's from the earliest times, with some Jesuits earning reputations for their use of it. The archives tell us, for example, that 1,049 'cuts' were administered in 1961. Peter Acton, a boy at St George's in the 1960s, was caned 55 times in a term of 83 days!

20 McCarthy, p. 6.

21 Two other OGs were in the Justice and Peace Commission during the war — Michael Leslie Leach and Tim McLoughlin.

9

Education for Development

When it is impossible to carry on the immediate task of evangelisation and your educational work, neglect your churches in order to perfect your schools.

Arthur Hinsley, Rome's Apostolic Visitor to east, central and west Africa, later Cardinal Archbishop of Westminster, to a gathering of bishops in Dar es Salaam in 1928.

By the 1960s it was clear that education had to go beyond the academic if it was to respond to the current needs of people. The Jesuits responded in three ways and, as in the early days when men with leadership qualities arose – Richartz, Hartmann, Barthelemy, Prestage – to lead the way, so in this new time four names in particular come to mind: Terrence Corrigan, Edward (Ted) Rogers, John Dove and Francis Waddelove. Corrigan was the Salisbury Mission Superior and the enabler of all that followed.[1] Rogers led the way in establishing the School of Social Work, John Dove in founding Silveira House as a development education centre and Francis Waddelove was among the pioneers of the Savings Clubs and Credit Unions movement.

We can discern a progress from the 'known to the unknown'. We knew about schools, so the first step was to start one which would provide for blacks what St George's provided for whites. So, we started

---

[1] At the moment of writing I have just received a letter from Kpanie Addy, a Jesuit involved in setting up the Arrupe Jesuit Institute in Accra, Ghana. Speaking of his interest in the history of the Society of Jesus, he says, 'For me, just reading the biography of Terrence Corrigan in *Letters and Notices* was deeply inspiring'.

St Ignatius College. It was to be on a par with St George's and so aimed at the 'upwardly mobile'. But we also started St Peter's Kubatana which was for more disadvantaged students. We then moved into Social Work – a new field in which the founder was only a page ahead of the students! A similar comment could be made for Silveira House, except that the founder would have said he was a page behind them. And then there was, as mentioned, the movement to promote Credit Unions and Savings Clubs.

St Ignatius College

Missions and parishes focused on primary education up to 1939 when the Anglican Church opened the first secondary school for Africans at St Augustine's, Penalonga, near Mutare. The Marist Brothers in Kutama followed in 1945. The government then opened Goromonzi, near Harare, in 1946 and Fletcher in Gweru a little later. St Paul's, Musami, began in 1957. But these efforts, significant as they each were, resulted in there being only nine African students eligible for university entrance in 1960. The need to respond to the thirst for higher education had exercised the minds of Jesuits for some time in the late 1950s. There had even been a suggestion of sending African students to Jesuit schools in England. Fr Peter McIlhenny, secretary to the English Assistant in Rome, mentions this in a letter in December 1959 to Fr Corrigan in which he continues, '(but) I tend to agree with you that present conditions and stages of development would be helped more by a direct enlargement of their educated experience within their own setting'.[2]

So the pressure was on among the Jesuits to provide a significant witness to answer the deep-felt need of African parents for an education for their children that would help them compete with Europeans who controlled every aspect of the economy. McIlhenny's letter shows how seriously the question was taken in Rome and the Jesuits there found in Fr Terrence Corrigan the right man to see words put into action. I remember Corrigan, newly appointed Mission Superior, visiting us in the novitiate in London in 1959 and being dazzled by his vision of the emerging urban-based awakened mind of African people. He was determined to help.

Looking back, we can see the early sixties provided a last 'window

---

2   Fr P McIlhenny to Corrigan, 8 December 1959, JAZ, Box 26B/4.

of opportunity' to start a school like St Ignatius before the Rhodesian Front curtain came down. In 1962, the Jesuits were able to make representations to the Federal and Southern Rhodesia governments leading to 'enabling acts' allowing private schools to integrate.[3] Corrigan wanted a first-class school similar to St George's. Not everyone among the Jesuits were happy. Some felt the amount spent on St Ignatius could have built four less ambitious schools in the rural areas and educated far more people. But Corrigan was out to set standards and it was reasonable to expect that, once set, other denominations and groups – even the government in time – would follow suit. The Federal government at the time was geared to 'partnership', even if it interpreted it one-sidedly. St Ignatius was built just in time. It was the first Catholic school to offer A-level for black boys and, later, girls.

A site was chosen on a hill in the west of Chishawasha estate and building began in July 1961. The estimated cost was £250,000 and the British South Africa Company, Barclays Bank, Standard Bank, Anglo-American, and the Beit and Dulverton Trusts – all with a shrewd eye to the future – contributed, as did the British province of the Society of Jesus. Fr Desmond Ford, who finished his term as rector of St George's in 1960, was entrusted with the project which envisaged a parallel two-stream boarding school with a full academic course leading to the Cambridge School Certificate at Form IV and Higher Certificate at Form VI. The other founding Jesuits were Frs James Cogger and James Fitzsimmons as well as Brian Porter, still a 'regent' at that time.[4] The school was to be multiracial, though when the present writer arrived there in 1966 the few European boys who had been welcomed in the early days had left. Simon Rous was one of them and he wrote in the Jubilee magazine fifty years later, 'my parents hoped racial tensions might be overcome if the next generation grew accustomed to each other in the class room and the playing field. It was expected that a flood of whites would follow us! In the event, with UDI, I was sent back to St George's.'[5] In 1966 I found there were

---

3   *The Shield*, a Salisbury Archdiocesan magazine, February 1965.
4   This is a quaint sample of Jesuit speak, referring to the period of training between the first and second round of studies when a Jesuit student does some practical work. The only other use of the word that I know is when a king is too old or too young or too mad to govern and a relative takes over responsibility, as in the film, *The Madness of King George*.
5   Jesuit Archives, Harare, Box 586.

around six Afro-Europeans and the rest were African.

A bursary scheme was created by a multi-denominational group in the English town of Malvern which adopted three students each for four years and the idea spread: four Oxford colleges each adopted one and five Catholic schools adopted a total of eight. Fees were £30 and £10 for uniform and books. The government gave £7 per student and the Jesuits ploughed back their salaries to try to cover the rest. In the 1960s the staff were virtually all Jesuits or volunteers from English Jesuit schools, though Patrick Chakaipa, future Archbishop of Harare, taught Shona while still at the seminary. Today the staff is virtually all lay.

The early years were filled with both managing the day-to-day teaching and sporting activities and building for the future. This meant finding an unending supply of finance. For example, in 1969 Fr Jim Hughes, the rector, asked the government for an interest-free loan of £20,000 to expand the school and take the two streams to Forms III and IV. Fortunately, schools don't start with all forms in place on day one and each phase of expansion could be faced in two yearly intervals. The big challenge, they all knew, was how to obtain permission for A-levels (Forms V and VI). By 1965 the Rhodesian Front was in power and were in no mood to grant the necessary permission. The Jesuit authorities searched for a way round the refusal. Should they bus the boys in each day to St George's? Should they create room at St George's and simply transfer them there?[6] In the end the government gave way when they foresaw the rumpus that would occur should any method of using St George's be attempted.

At the same time the demands of the students at St Ignatius grew. The Jesuits had concentrated on academic quality education but had no time or resources to develop other activities and parents were beginning to complain. Slowly sport came into focus and on my arrival in 1966 the large swimming pool was in its last stage of completion. I was immediately put in charge of swimming, even though I can hardly swim myself and twice came close to drowning. Fortunately, more competent people were soon found and the college went on to achieve stardom in swimming competitions, especially in the time of Fr Brian Enright in the 1970s. In the Africa Inter-Schools Swimming Gala in 1975, St Ignatius was victorious over St Paul's Musami, the

---

6   St Ignatius House Consultation, 12 July 1965, JAZ, Box 586.

Marist Brothers' schools of Inyanga (Nyanga) and Kutama and four other schools. Other 'extra-mural' activities followed: debating and public speaking, music (*marimba* and *mbira*[7]), chess and choir. Fr Brian Porter used to take a group yachting on a local dam and he also developed a photographic society. A scout group was started by a Marist brother who was at the school for a while. I 'directed' a play in my last year, *Garandichauya* (Wait, I am coming) by Patrick Chakaipa. It was in Shona, a language I did not understand at the time. Fortunately, the play directed itself, the students enjoyed it and drama gradually found its way into school activities.

In the light of the permission eventually granted to go ahead with A-levels we were all on a tight rein to show results. Some produced them. Others didn't. But we gradually improved and the college went on to excel in its academic work. In 1974, 79 per cent of those taking GCE passed with a division 1, 16 per cent with division 2 and the remaining 5 per cent with division 3. But Brian Enright wrote in his regular letter to his friends in May 1971 of the bitterness of former students of St Ignatius. One wrote to him, 'I have desperately tried to get a job for the last four months, applying for one hundred and nineteen jobs, but to no avail. Not even one employer has called me for an interview.' When Brian showed this letter to another student he got the response, 'Obviously he has been brainwashed by propaganda that advancement is on merit, whereas he should have been realistic and faced the fact that the colour of the skin is the major qualification.'

In 1997 there was a report in *The Herald:* 'St Ignatius gets highest pass rate in the country'. '(Lay) headmaster Ignatius Mabveni said 67,6 per cent of the students who sat for the O-levels examinations passed with five As or better. The average country pass rate was 20,7 per cent.' At the time of the Jubilee (2012), the reputation of the college was such that hundreds applied for places in form I. Only seventy-two could be accepted, which was less than 10 per cent of those who applied. The pass rate had jumped to an average of 98 per cent and students were going on to do medicine, pharmacy, law, engineering, veterinary science and following other professions. Among the appreciations of Fr Anthony Watsham at the time of his

---

7 *Marimba* is a local version of a xylophone. **Mbira dzavadzimu,** voice of the ancestors, is a 'piano in a gourd', where different lengths of crafted steel keys are fixed in a frame and plucked.

death in 2019 was a list of thirty doctors and five pharmacists who passed through his hands.

The house diary for 1966 carries the brief words, '19 September, Fr Norman Dennis died'. It was high drama. Norman was fifty-four and had worked for years in England, most recently at Ipswich. He had kept up an interest in biology and was asked to go to boost the teaching staff at St Ignatius as we tried to strengthen our A-level teaching team. I was almost thirty years younger than him but we were both due to start our teaching that Monday in September. We both lived in the Senior House[8] and I had woken the students and turned on the showers as usual. Soon a student, Richard Aisam, came racing up the stairs, 'sir, there is someone in the showers'. The tone rather than the content of what he said told me something critical had happened and I, in turn, raced down the stairs to find Norman stretched out, dead and already purple, on the floor. I had five classes that first morning and I do not know how I got through them, but Jim Hughes, our rector, put on a special supper for us all to lessen the strain of the day. After Christmas, Fr Anthony (Seamus) Watsham came to take Norman's place and teach biology and he stayed for decades.

The school progressed and all seemed to be going well but politics was never far away. In 1968, there is a laconic note in the school diary for May 16: 'Boys return (after the holidays) less the seventeen expelled in March.' I looked in the archives for some details about this, as I was not fully in the picture at the time, but could not find anything. There had been a school strike for what seems to have been two reasons.

A brave but unsuccessful attack near Sinoia (Chinoyi) on 28 April 1966 startled the country. It was the first serious armed response to UDI in November 1965. Seven ZANU guerrillas faced forty BSA police backed by four helicopter gunships and they were all killed. But the 'Battle of Sinoia' had the mystique of the failed Irish Easter Rising of 1916, which drew from Yeats, 'a terrible beauty is born'. Although this engagement was a disaster for the guerrillas it came to be seen as the first act of the second *Chimurenga* which would eventually lead to the freedom of Zimbabwe. Edgar Tekere wrote in his memoirs that

---
8   The two boarding houses we had then were called after our early Jesuit missionary pioneers, Law and Richartz, but the names did not catch on, and when a third house was later added the school followed the pedestrian style of Senior, Middle and Junior.

when news of the battle reached nationalists detained in Salisbury Maximum Security Prison, they 'went wild with joy'.[9] In the follow-up to the operation other guerrillas were caught, tried and – despite a pardon from the Queen – executed. A number of schools, including our own, protested in the only way they could. They went on strike. They came to meals but they either did not go to class or they went and sat there passively. Teaching was impossible.

The second reason was to do with our school. There were complaints about food and there were complaints about one or two of us. The rector, Fr Jim Hughes, called in Mr Luciano Gutsa, our builder and a man of wide experience (he had fought in the British army in North Africa during the war and, legend or fact, had rescued a British general in a sticky position on the back of his motor cycle) and asked him to listen to the students to try to find out what was behind the strike. I do not recall Gutsa succeeding. Strikes and demonstrations were to be a feature of our life up to independence in 1980 and, to some extent, even after.

1968 was a particularly tense year, locally and internationally. Bobby Kennedy and Martin Luther King were assassinated and French students took to the streets of Paris in protests of their own. Locally there was a second of two failed attempts by the British Labour government to negotiate a settlement with the Rhodesians. One incident at the school showed the underlying tension. When Paul Edwards, a scholastic regent at St George's, brought out some of his boys on 21 June to visit St Ignatius, it was extremely difficult to get any of the latter's students to show them round.

But when the next major brush with politics came, the school was much better prepared. It was three years later and Fr Jim Berry was headmaster. On 28 June 1971, the CID (police investigation branch) arrived unannounced and, after searching their lockers in the presence of Jim Berry, took two students away 'for questioning'. Brian Enright recalls that the incident was sparked by a visit of some of the boys to Wedza where they had met a teacher who was encouraging students to cross the border and join the fight for freedom. Word had reached the CID and they came to investigate, since they had even been given names by their informant, though they never explained the purpose of their sudden visit to St Ignatius.

---

9   E.Z. Tekere, *A Lifetime of Struggle* (Harare: SAPES Books, 2007).

On their arrival word quickly spread and a large group of students surrounded their vehicle. The police arrested some of the students for further questioning but the students surrounding them, tried to prevent them from leaving. A white officer produced a revolver and waved it in the air threateningly and the students fell back and allowed the jeep to proceed, but they pursued and stoned it. They followed the vehicle and began to walk to Salisbury. Jim Berry decided to go with them and try to keep them from harm's way. They expressed sympathy for him as they knew it would mean he would miss his lunch!

The police stopped the students at Chisipite, halfway to the city, and warned them they would be breaking the law if they proceeded. After discussions, it was agreed they would send a delegation to the Provincial Education Officer the next day. The school then sent the lorry to collect the students, who declined being carried in the police trucks which were offered. The school authorities then arranged food and held meetings with the students so that everything was aired.

It might have ended there but the police could not stay away. They came again next morning. Jim Berry asked them to park at a distance as their presence was like 'a red rag to a bull'. They did so but said they wanted to take away more students for questioning and they wanted the boys who had stoned the police vehicle the day before. Jim Berry wanted this left for later. One policeman was heard to say, 'These bloody priests know who the ring leaders are but they won't tell us.' While the discussions were going on, the students overturned the police vehicle. The police called up reinforcements and a riot squad drove through the students and was stoned by them. Eventually the police managed to round up 150 students on the football field where they were guarded by police with dogs. Sr Hildegardis from Mary Ward Convent said the boys were shouted at 'as if they were dogs'.

The college staff came with bread, fish and water for the students. The police selected nineteen boys and took them away. An exasperated policeman was heard to say, 'that's what education does for them'.[10]

---

10 It was only eleven years since the appearance of Doris Lessing's *The Grass is Singing*, in which she writes of Dick, the embattled white farmer, saying Moses was 'a mission boy. The only decent one I've ever had.' Like most South Africans, Dick did not like mission boys, they 'knew too much'. And in any case, they should not be taught to read and write; they should be taught the dignity of labour and general usefulness to the white man. D. Lessing, *The Grass is Singing* (London: Flamingo, 1994), p. 155.

Jim Berry informed the parents of the boys detained and the rector obtained a solicitor to defend the boys. Attempts to visit them in detention were only partially successful. There was going to be a court appearance for the boys but it was eventually postponed and the boys were collected by the college and returned. The school kept changing meal times and rising times over the days to accommodate the students and put on films. Gradually classes resumed. A Parents' Day had long been planned for 4 July and this was an opportunity to brief the parents about what happened.

Thames, an independent British TV network, interviewed some of the St Ignatius boys at the time and one of them said, '(Prime Minister) Smith will not listen to reason, so obviously we have to resort to violence.' When asked if he was not afraid, he said, 'I don't care. I am prepared to suffer for this country.' And another boy, who had some contact with white boys of his age, said, 'there is a tendency among them to realise what the African is suffering. They can't do much about it: there is a growing gap between them and their parents but some of them are trying their best to understand.'

In August 1976 Jim Berry had to inform the parents again that their sons had demonstrated and walked to town. They were turned back by police. The school was closed and the students told to reapply. Fr Brian Enright, reflecting on the demonstrations at that time, wrote,

> Great play is usually made that the troubles affect mission schools more than government schools. ... part of a campaign to discredit the missions ... (but)

i. Four out of five African secondary schools are run by the churches,

ii. With two exceptions, all government schools are day schools in urban areas whereas mission schools are boarding in rural areas,

iii. Students at mission schools feel freer to express themselves, and

iv. Trouble in government schools is played down or suppressed.[11]

Although the Rhodesian CID were never far away, towards the end of the seventies it was the turn of the guerrillas to visit the college. They would ask Jim Berry for clothes and medicines. On one occasion, confusing his name with mine, the CID visited me on the other side of the valley at Silveira House to inquire about my assisting

---

11 Friends of Fr Brian Enright, November 1976.

the guerrillas. It took me some time to realise their confusion, and when they left I was able to phone Jim to warn him of their coming. He took it calmly as though he was quite used to these visits. If they asked him, he would simply say 'yes' he was helping them and then see what they would do. By that stage of the war the Rhodesians were running out of options and in the event did nothing.

Although St Ignatius started as a boys' school there was a plan to welcome girls from the earliest days. The Mary Ward sisters (now called the Congregation of Jesus (CJ)) had planned to start a school in Urungwe, at St Boniface Mission, but the plan was changed and they came to St Ignatius in 1967 with a twin plan of providing sixth form accommodation for girls and running a domestic science programme. They built a large hostel for these purposes and soon the girls joined the boys in the classroom for A-level. The demand for places for A-level outstripped the demand for domestic science and after some years the latter was dropped. The Mary Ward contribution to St Ignatius is perhaps an unsung one but at the funeral of Sr Stephana, who served the college for longer than anyone, in 2019, Roland von Nidda celebrated her contribution and that of so many sisters who had taught at the college. Stephana was the driving force behind annual retreats for the students in attractive surroundings away from the college. During the war she was fearless and gave the visiting freedom fighters stern lectures on keeping away from the girls' hostel.

The boys had been welcomed at the bottom and the school grew with them. The girls came in at the top and there were plans to extend 'downwards', as it were, to make it totally co-educational. A design for a new hostel was even drawn but, in the end, it was decided to put the plans on hold.

In 1983 Fr Jim Berry moved to St George's and Fr Anthony (Tony) Berridge became headmaster at St Ignatius. Jim had provided a steady hand during an uncertain period. The school was still growing – it was little more than twenty years old when Tony took over. He had all the academic demands of administering an expanding school. There were constant building projects during and after his time: a magnificent library, an imaginatively designed chapel, a science block, a gym and staff houses. It was always a struggle to find the funding and, even when it was found, building progress lagged behind growth in the student numbers. Brian Enright tells us there was a time when boys were 'lodged in the swimming pool', presumably the changing room, while their hostel was being built.

Brian also tells us of the 'auction' in his May 1987 letter. This is the Sixth Form Selection committee made up of the heads of the eighty schools who offered A-level studies at the time. A ministry official reads out the name of each student and the school of his first preference. Heads have had a few days to study the list and 'bid' for each student. Since 'a large number of the most capable students put down St Ignatius as their first preference' the other heads watched the proceedings with some frustration and would occasionally cry 'foul'! But there was little they could do. The reputation of the college was such that it got the best students.

At the same time the security situation created tension among the students and staff. The students were not always cooperative and in December 1980, that is, after independence, while Jim Berry was still headmaster, he wrote a letter to parents describing some of their children's behaviour. They damaged school property, breaking windows and furniture. They stole books from the library and there were those who 'broke bounds' and went to the villages where they could find beer and dagga (cannabis). And there were constant complaints about food. In the fifteen years since I first arrived the menu changed from porridge for breakfast to a quarter of a loaf of bread per student with margarine, tea and sugar for breakfast; vegetables and beans most days of the week for lunch and supper, changed to meat, twice a day most days, and chicken on Sunday.

But the overall picture of St Ignatius in the last two decades of the century was one of steady consolidation and progress. Brian Enright reported in 1982 that 'the school has settled down to a smoother routine.'[12] The 'Annual letters' for 1984 report 'another peaceful and successful year'. In April that year a lorry and two cars carried food donated by the students for the Mozambique refugees in the Mazowe Bridge Camp near Marymount Mission in the Mount Darwin district north-east of Harare. In August there was a meeting of the bishops of southern Africa at the college which was opened by the prime minister, Robert Mugabe.

1985 was described in the same terms as 'peaceful and successful' and in April that year the college held a celebration for the 400th

---

12 Letter to his friends, November 1982.

anniversary of the birth of Mary Ward whose sisters were now well established as part of St Ignatius. There is a list in the archives of the many Jesuits who served at St Ignatius from 1962 to the time of the Golden Jubilee. It is impressive in length but there were some who stood out for the striking quality of their presence. I have mentioned Jim Berry who guided the college through the most turbulent decade of the 1970s. Jim was compassionate, focused, decisive and calm – just the right combination of qualities needed at the time. Fathers Gregory (Greg) Croft and Anthony Watsham were there almost simultaneously for quarter of a century; Croft from 1965 to 1991 and Watsham from 1967 to 1994. Others who gave long devoted service were Fr Brian Porter, Fr Brian Enright and Br Benedict Ngawaseke. Allow me to focus on just two of these.

Greg Croft was self-taught in every area of his work at St Ignatius – from the laboratory to the gardens and grounds. He arrived just as the United Nations imposed far-reaching economic sanctions on the country (1965) and his remit was to set up the physics programme as the Rhodesian government had (reluctantly) agreed to allow A-level at the school. He was a genius at making sophisticated equipment out of 'rubbish' material which he picked up wherever he could find it. John Gambanga, writing in *The Herald*[13] at the time of Greg's retirement from St Ignatius in 1991, quoted Greg as saying, 'no good teacher actually teaches, he simply starts the learning process'. Greg's gift was his enthusiasm for his subject which he shared with his students and they simply picked it up and did the work. He was not successful at first as his enthusiasm spilled over the restricted channels set by the syllabus. He was disconsolate with the first A-level physics results but he steadied himself and learnt to focus and his results steadily improved. He became so successful that he was invited on to the Joint Matriculation Board setting up a new physics course at Witwatersrand and Rhodes universities in South Africa. In 1978, new laboratories for chemistry, physics and biology, paid for by the German Catholic development agency, Misereor, were completed.

Greg also developed a large vegetable and fruit garden behind the laboratories and studded the campus with flowering shrubs and flowers. My first memory of St Ignatius in August 1966 was of walking to the Senior House on a path bounded on both sides by

---

13 5 December 1991.

multi-coloured petunias. The path remains but the petunias are long gone. As if these activities were not enough Greg also took over the grading of the gravel road to the bridge at the foot of our hill. The rains lacerated this stretch of the road but Greg was quickly out on the tractor to manicure it back into shape.

Anthony (Tony or Seamus) Watsham shared much of the inventiveness of Greg but he took it to new heights. An only child, he probably learnt to invent his own life at an early age. His experience during the war years in India was in making three-dimensional reconstructions of enemy positions from aerial photographs. Later, as a Jesuit, he was asked to teach machine drawing and metalwork which meant he had to study at night so as to teach the next day. Destined for colonial Zimbabwe, he was diverted to St Aidan's, the Jesuit college in Grahamstown, after the sudden death of a Jesuit teacher there. Asked to teach geography he had, again, to first learn it himself. Another sudden death and another moved brought him to St Ignatius where he was to teach biology, yet again a subject he had to first teach himself. Broadening his interests and drawing many students with him, he began to focus on insects in general and microscopic parasitic wasps in particular. He collected many hitherto unclassified specimens in the Chishawasha valley and had a genus and a species named after him. He became a member of the Royal Entomological Society in 1970 which gave him new contacts, and eventually a coffee-table book of his drawings of Chalcids was published in 1995.

There were many other men and women who devoted their imagination and energies to build up St Ignatius on the foundations laid in the 1960s. Mention has been made of the Jubilee celebrated in 2012. It marked, perhaps, the end of the early period and an important decision was made in the years that followed. Fr Lawrence Daka, rector at the time of writing, presided over, in his words, 'a major development in January 2020 when the school (parents, teachers, former students and Jesuits), frustrated by the government interference in the school that went with being a grant-aided school, decided to become independent'. A little over a year later, Lawrence says the decision 'seems to be bearing good results'. The school was now free from the excessive government interference and they are able to choose the teachers they want and the students they want. The government had also controlled the fees so that 'the school had been unable to keep up with the maintenance of our aging infrastructure'. The consequence of all these influences was declining examination results and parents turning elsewhere for the education of their children.

It was a brave decision entered into fully conscious of the possible results. Would it mean a momentous shift in direction by the college? Fr Antony Berridge, headmaster in the 1980s, used to hold as an ideal that the student intake should be one third from the rural areas, one third from the high-density suburbs and one third from the low-density ones. Such an ideal was not easily reached in those years and with an inevitable rise in fees will be even harder to reach under this new dispensation. The college seems to be one more victim of the economic collapse we have seen unfolding in the country over the past two decades. While there was wide consultation before the decision was made, and one can clearly understand why it was made, it still remains an open question whether, in the long run, it might not have been better to struggle on bearing in mind the undoubted limitations the present circumstances Zimbabwe impose on all of us, and wait for better days. Unless there is considerable progress in building up the bursary fund, which accompanied the opening of the college in the early 1960s, it is hard to avoid the view that St Ignatius will be even further from the reach of the poorer income families than it has been all along.

From my own time in the college in the 1960s I know that there is always a tension between striving for the best results in studies and games and nurturing growth in the spirit among the students. Brian Enright reflected on this in his 1997 May letter in the following terms:

> St Ignatius is probably the most Catholic school in the country in terms of the percentage of Catholic students and teachers. And it goes a good deal deeper than that: every class in the school, Form 1 to Form 6, has four periods of religious education a week and a class Mass in addition to the Sunday Mass for the whole school. There are several religious groups active, some with a social justice dimension.

Yet Brian asked the question – in 1997 – is it still a Jesuit school? It is a question every rector is likely to ask. When we look at The

Characteristics of Jesuit Education,[14] the question seems daunting. But a year later Brian says he soon discovered that he did not have to do everything himself: 'all I had to do was encourage'. It sounds so simple and yet it can often be neglected. A word of appreciation can make a huge difference.

At the time of the Golden Jubilee in 2012, it was estimated that 5,000 students had passed through the college since its founding. Fr Corrigan and the founding fathers would be happy.

St Peter's Kubatana

In the early 1960s, just when the colony of Southern Rhodesia was beginning to implode under the pressure from the nationalist movement for freedom, the two missions – Salisbury and Sinoia – that would soon make up one province developed new initiatives to respond to the evolving situation. Terrence Corrigan, newly appointed superior of the Salisbury Mission, visited us novices, as mentioned above, in London in 1959, and told us the new frontier would be the cities. Up to then the emphasis had been on rural missions. But change normally comes from the cities. Paris, in 1789, was the birthplace of a revolution that inaugurated the modern age.

Corrigan began by calling Edward (Ted) Rogers in from St Paul's Musami to take up 'social work' in Salisbury and it is Ted's account of the founding of the school in his *Memoir* that is the basis of what follows.[15] Neither Corrigan nor Ted had much idea what this would involve but that is not unusual for Jesuits. Exactly the same was later to happen with Silveira House, as we shall see. Ted writes, 'large numbers of young people were "walking the streets" after primary school. There was only one government school for blacks but fourteen for whites.'[16] Callisto Kamera was one of those frustrated youth who came to Salisbury after his primary education at Regina Mundi, Gwai. He wanted to become a priest but in the meantime became involved with Ted in starting a community secondary school. It was 1963 and 250 applied for places of whom eighty were chosen. They used the primary school premises in St Peter's, Harari (Mbare), in the afternoon when

---

14 *The Characteristics of Jesuit Education* (Rome: International Commission on the Apostolate of Jesuit Education, 1986).
15 Ted Rogers, *A Memoir* (Pietermaritzburg: Cluster Publications, 2012), pp. 85ff.
16 Ibid., pp. 87ff.

the younger children had gone home.

This was the beginning of St Peter's Kubatana. They relied on volunteers, Paddy Brett, one-time Inspector of Education, and Fay Chung, Minister of Education after independence, were among them. Nicholas Weeks, who was later to join the Jesuits for a while, came out from England in 1963 to help. In 1964 there were 400 applicants for places and again eighty were accepted. So the school now had 160 students. In 1964 it moved to share the premises of the School of Social Services (later 'Work') at the former premises of Morgan High School.

In 1965 the school was recognised by the Ministry of Education and so students could take the same exams as other schools. But the hardline Rhodesian Front government told them they were on European designated land and would have to move and they were given a wing of a new school in Kambazuma, near the industrial area. The school now had its own premises and Fr John Byrne became headmaster, although his poor health[17] curtailed his stay after a few years. The school expanded from 200 students in 1966 to 785 in 1970. But the Ministry started demanding a hefty (in those days) rent of £40/month and Ted went to the ministry to complain. The Minister was Mark Partridge, an Old St George's boy and a Catholic. Negotiations dragged on with a certain amount of bluff on both sides and in the end Ted got the whole school building for a rent of 'a few pounds'.

The school gradually moved from reliance on volunteers to locally trained and paid black teachers. About 1971 the school acquired the present site between Highfield and Glen Norah and Fr Anthony 'Jeep' Davis, a practical man who had added many new buildings to St Paul's Musami during his seventeen years there, joined the school and taught building by doing, constructing the school with students at the newly started technical wing. Jeep also had musical talent and encouraged the young people to make and play the *marimba*. 'Each separate wooden key had to be tuned by shaving off parts of it by

---

17 David Hoy, rector of the old Heythrop in the woods, once gave a 'domestic exhortation' which included a saying they had in the army: 'If it moves, salute it; if it doesn't move, pick it up, and if you can't pick it up, paint it.' Some wit was heard to tell JB as he left the chapel, 'if you don't get a move on, John, we'll paint you.' John and I were in St Anne's hospital at the same time in 1987. I came out, he didn't.

hand. Jeep spent long hours making these keys and then he trained the young people how to play'. The St Peter's Marimba Band soon became well-known, playing both traditional and classical pieces.

When the school still relied on volunteers, Martin Prendergast was one such and he later recalled arriving in 1967 as,

> a spotty, callow, 18-year-old never having been confronted before by a mass of forty expectant faces, some of whose owners were older than me, and having no idea how to teach anything whatsoever, my first lessons were truly daunting. However I had known for several months that these moments would have to be faced and, somehow, I managed, perhaps not least because of my pupils' extreme forbearance and politeness. Gradually things improved and within a few months entering the classroom and engaging the interest of the pupils became a pleasure.[18]

In 1971 St Peter's got a new name, 'Kubatana', literally 'to hold together', to unite and help each other, a concept made universal by the Poles when they formed their trade union in the Gdansk shipyards and called it 'Solidarity'. In that same year, the school was handed over to a Board of Governors which included Jesuit representation. In 1978, Jeep was joined by two Jesuit brothers, Dominic Shoniwa and Tobias Tirivanhu, to strengthen the team in the technical school. Dominic became head of the technical school. St Peter's Kubabana (SPK) was now one school with two wings – academic and technical. Jeep kept putting up new buildings but their quality was not lasting. When Misereor became involved, the school was provided with an 'imposing new purpose-built high school and technical school'. During the war, SPK was able to give temporary accommodation to some rural schools who could not safely operate where they were: Monte Cassino, St Paul's Musami and Kutama.

Chris Crompton[19], from the UK, was headmaster from 1968-70 and tells us of the struggle to attain academic recognition. He started with a general comment about racial segregation. It 'was more subtle than in South Africa. A restaurant in Salisbury might have a sign over the door, "Right of Admission Reserved" whereas in Durban it would say "Whites Only" but it meant the same thing'. He then went on,

---

18 Rogers, p. 100.
19 At the time of writing (2021) Chris died, after a long battle with cancer.

> Up to my time St Peter's operated only up to Form 2 ... we sought to extend this by preparing pupils for College of Preceptors[20] examinations but the Government would have none of it; the last thing they wanted was measuring white and black ability by the same yardstick. There was nothing to stop us from entering pupils for external London CSE examinations so we settled for that, introducing Form 3 in 1969.

And Tim David, the headmaster who followed Crompton wrote,

> One important strand in St Peter's School history was the rapid growth in enrolment ... Over the years St Peter's made an enormous contribution to African education despite the ambivalence bordering on hostility that the Smith government evinced towards it and other community schools. It was acceptable that we should take otherwise troublesome young people off the streets, but unacceptable that we should seek to provide them with a serious education.

Finance was a problem as the school tried to be self-supporting. Students paid $5 a term and extra for books. Stephen Silungwe, a former student and now a Jesuit priest, tells us many poor students were helped with fees though some were sent home to look for them. On one occasion Chris Crompton was stunned when 'called to a house in Mufakose where a girl I had sent home had tried to commit suicide. I was shown the noose and the chair. Luckily a neighbour had spotted through a window what was going on and intervened.'

After independence the technical wing, now called the Industrial Training College,[21] was registered as a properly constituted technical institution by the Ministry of Manpower Planning and Development, teaching building, carpentry, fitting and turning, motor mechanics and auto electrics.

Among the former teachers and students at SPK were Tom Zawaira, who later became the Mayor of Masvingo, George Charambarara who became head of the school, Chad Gandiya who became Anglican bishop of Mashonaland and Stephen Silungwe who, as mentioned,

---

20 The College of Preceptors dates back to 1846 and is the oldest surviving teaching association in the United Kingdom. Its founding principle was to certify teachers, thus assuring a common standard of education.

21 This represents recognition by the Ministry of Higher and Tertiary Education.

became a Jesuit priest. Bishop Gandiya was the guest of honour at the Golden Jubilee celebration in 2014 and was asked to concelebrate at the Eucharist. He was invited to be at the altar with those of us who concelebrated and joined us in spirit if not in theological exactitude. Br Dominic Shoniwa, on his retirement in 2010 said, among former students were 'lawyers, doctors, nurses, graduate school teachers, accountants and reputable bankers'. One might notice the adjective attached to bankers!

After independence the school lost many of its influential board members as, presumably, they found greener pastures. A new principal, Mr Makawa, was appointed but, in Ted Rogers' view, he was unable to maintain the vision of St Peter's. The new government built many new secondary schools and St Peter's lost its unique status. Enrolment dropped and it became more difficult to attract overseas funding. The school started to struggle financially and ran into a spiral of difficulties. There was pressure from parents and others for the Jesuits to take back responsibility. After a year of discussions and negotiations with the Board of Governors and government ministries, it was handed back to the Jesuits in 2005 and Dominic Shoniwa became the director of the whole complex.

Shoniwa was followed by Fr Paul Mayeresa in 2008 who writes:

> The High School has become popular in terms of academic achievement. One of its students, Sandra Maponga, finished A level in 2011 as head girl and went on to join Midlands State University to do a Law degree. She became the first women in Southern Africa to get a first class with 24 distinctions and she scooped all the prizes that were available in that Faculty of Law. She was an orphan who benefitted from one of the scholarships provided by St. Peter's Kubatana. The enrolment at the school is now 1000+ and at the Technical School it is 400+.

Fr Roland von Nidda followed Mayeresa in 2012 and he refurbished the science block, built a multi-purpose hall and a school chapel for class masses. State of the art equipment for the motor mechanics department in the Technology Centre followed. Other shorter courses were also introduced to promote self-reliance. One in cosmetology was very successful. Students started their own cosmetics businesses – hair, nails, skin. Plumbing and waste management, especially for plastics, were also popular.

Fr Anesu Manyere took over in 2015 and Fr Admire Nhika, the present director, in 2020.

The School of Social Work

Fortunately we have Ted Rogers' own account where a whole chapter of his autobiography is devoted to the School of Social Work, a training and research centre for social workers.[22] As mentioned above, in 1962 he was teaching at St Paul's Musami, an hour's drive north-east of Salisbury, and was asked to move to the city 'to do social work'. It was a vague term in those days but the Jesuit superior, Terrence Corrigan, knew that Ted would fill in the gaps in what was a response not only to Pope John's encouragement to listen to the 'the signs of the times'[23] but also to the evolving new Jesuit orientation that would emerge in their 31st and 32nd General Congregations (1965/6 and 1974/5).

An indication that he was still thinking along traditional lines appeared when his first initiative was to start a normal school for the poor which was to become St Peter's Kubatana, treated above. Ted soon realised he could not do social work on his own and if he was to work with others they – and he – would need training. He invited an impressive group of professionals to help him design a programme, including Clyde Mitchell and A.M. Jenkins from the university, William Clifford from the Lusaka Oppenheimer School of Social Service, members of the City Council and leaders from industry. The course would be open to mature students who had passed Form II and it would run for a year, beginning in 1964. This was the final year of Federation and the little group of Ted and his volunteers were able to use the auspices of the Federal Ministry of Education to obtain the former Morgan High School premises. 'In spite of being in a rather busy area, near the Kopje, the original centre of Salisbury', Ted tells us 'it was fairly quiet and during the early summer months clouds of birds used to nest in the trees'.

The course was to be practical so that graduates could be employed by local authorities, churches or businesses. It was recognised by the government from the beginning and was given an opening grant of

---

22 Rogers, *op. cit.*
23 John XXIII wrote two powerful letters on the subject to the whole Catholic Church; *Mater et Magistra, New Light on Social Problems* (1961) and *Pacem in Terris, Peace on Earth* (1963).

£500. The Dulverton Trust in the UK also donated £5,000 for staff salaries. The School of Social Services, as it was called then, opened with eighteen students, seven of whom were female, in February 1964 and the full-time staff were helped by many volunteers. Sixteen passed and were employed mainly by the municipalities of Salisbury, Bulawayo and Gwelo. The first graduation ceremony was a joyful event and the Advisory Committee sat down to plan the future with confidence. They were helped by a professional social worker from Ireland, Margaret Horne, a cousin of Fr John Dove. The result was to set up a 'full professional course in social work'. A Board of Governors now took the place of the Advisory Board and it included representatives from the Ministries of Education, and Labour and Social Welfare and a syllabus committee was established. The full professional course was to begin in 1966.

Ted writes that, despite the gathering clouds caused by Rhodesia's unilateral break with Britain in 1965, there was much goodwill and hope in the air and he remembered the late 1960s as 'the happiest years I can remember'. The staff built up a bond nourished by vacations to the mountains (Nyanga) and the sea (Beira).

The next challenge was to find common accommodation for students from outside of Salisbury in a divided society. Donors helped them buy a property in Westwood, 'a residential area for all races', but – one problem solved led to another on the horizon – they had to look for a bus to transport the students each day. They found a 1948 Leyland 44-seater which still had life in it.

As the School of Social Service became better known, consideration was given to linking it with the university. Professor Desmond Reader, of the Sociology department, facilitated the approach which led to a broadening of the range of studies to include, for example, psychology and sociology, and a change of name to School of Social Work. This may seem a small change to most of us but it marks a ratcheting up of the professional status of the school.

All the time, the school was discerning its way and in the late 1960s the staff discovered they had to part company with the mainstream emphasis of standard social work which relies on case work, that is, the 'problems of an individual such as poverty, housing, relationships, marriage, substance addiction, medical needs' and the like. Instead, in consideration of the strength of the extended family among

African people, the board felt their emphasis should be on group or community work. In this way the school upgraded its diploma and in 1969 became an associate college of the University of Rhodesia, where some of its students had already been attending courses.

But Ted himself needed upgrading! He had no qualifications and he could hardly be a teacher at the university without something to his name. Fortunately, there was a one-year programme for mature students available at the University of Wales, in Cardiff, and Ted took advantage of that. While there he made many contacts with people who would later help at the school or provide funding for it. To mention just one, he met an American Jesuit of Norwegian descent in Helsinki, Finland. This was Al Jolson and Al came to Rhodesia to work at the School even before Ted had returned from Cardiff. He was to be a great asset and, in Al's words, 'we worked together without any disagreement for six years'. But tragedy struck while Ted was still away and it was a blessing that Al was on the spot. Fr Jim Wallace ran the school in Ted's absence and was overburdened with the work. He went for a break to Inyanga with some of the volunteers but on the way back the driver, Nick Unsworth, a volunteer from Stonyhurst, a Jesuit school in the north of England, was blinded by the evening sun as he rounded a bend and lost control of the car. Jim was killed and two of the volunteers were injured. Ted felt he should drop his studies and return but Al told him to finish them and he would hold things together in the meanwhile.[24]

On his return, Ted faced the next challenge which was to find a permanent site where they could put up buildings commensurate with their new status as part of the university. Many sites were looked at but they met with objections from local residents. These were couched in language which said one thing and meant another. The racial issue was not mentioned but was the real reason. Eventually Mark Partridge, whom we have met before, a member of the Rhodesian Front government and a former St George's boy, found a way of awarding them the present site near the kopje. This had many advantages – perhaps the main one being that it was at a distance from the university and so its autonomy had a physical as well as a formal foundation.

---

24 Al went on to become Bishop of Reykjavik, Iceland, and died of a heart attack, aged 64.

By 1976 there was a need for a higher qualification in social work and the academic board of the school proposed a Bachelor in Social Work degree to the university. This was accepted. After independence, Minister of Health Herbert Ushewokunze further proposed a degree in psychiatric social work and this too was accepted, though it did not last. And this was followed by a Master's degree course for social workers who could train others and so guarantee the continuity of the school as well as contributing to the development of social work in the whole Southern Africa region.

As the school developed its competence it looked to the critical need to train people to deal with the immediate challenge of rehabilitation after the war. A one-year certificate, echoing the first efforts of the school in its founding years, was established in 1979 in Rehabilitation, Resettlement and Community work with an enrolment of twenty-five students. The International Labour Organisation, based in Geneva, heard of the school's efforts and offered to fund, and supply a staff member for a certificate in Social Work (Rehabilitation). It began in 1984 and ran for three years and then became a degree programme.

The research work of the school flowered into the founding of a *Journal of Social Development in Africa* by Fr Joseph (Joe) Hampson. The first editor was the late Bridget Wilmore. Joe also made a study of the effects of the rapidly evolving Zimbabwean society on the aged and wrote a book on this subject. Joe took over running the school when Ted retired in 1985. The late Edwell Kaseke, a long-time member of the staff, took over when Joe became provincial of the Zimbabwe province of the Jesuits in 1988. Kaseke also did research into women's organisations and social security. Nigel Hall, a lecturer at the school and a social worker, researched burial societies. Others, researchers, lecturers and social workers, were Professor Rodreck Mupedziswa, whose focus was refugees, Helen Jackson on HIV and AIDS, and the late Professor Andrew Nyanguru.

The school was, in the mid-1980s, firmly established as a national and regional centre for training in professional social work. Government recognition came in the form of half salaries for lecturers which later became full salaries and included some help for students. In 1998, ninety-five students graduated:

- Certificate in Social Work   21

Fr Anthony 'Jeep' Davis with the Marimba band that he began c.1970 at St Peter's Kubatana.

Staff of the School of Social Work in 1988. Fr Joe Hampson (far right).

The translation team for the Shona Dictionary, the New Testament and parts of the Old, with Fr Michael Hannan.

Fr Clemence Freyer and a Rhodesian Air Force pilot help an injured man back to St Albert's Mission. Source: *Jesuit Missions 1922-1976*. Vol. XIX. No. 156, p. 14.

Bernhard Lisson on right with Konrad Landsberg on left facing camera, c.1968, killed at Makonde on 27 June 1978.

Gerhard Pieper teaching science at St Albert's Mission, 1972, killed at Kangaire, 26 December 1978.

Martin Thomas at St Michael's Mhondoro c 1970, killed at St Paul's Musami, 6 February 1977.

Gussie Donovan, standing, with (l-r) Edward Ennis, Patrick MacNamara and Brian Porter c 1969, killed 15 January 1978 near Makumbe Mission.

Christopher Shepherd Smith with his mother c.1973, killed at St Paul's Musami, 6 February 1977.

St Raphael's Church, Chitsungo, damaged during the war.

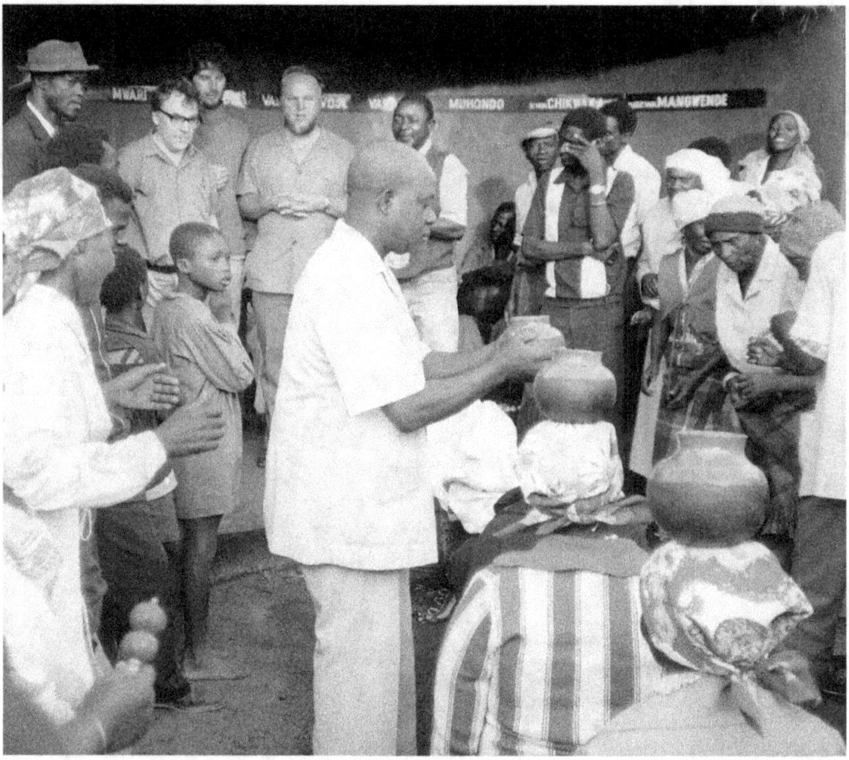

Br James Paul of St Paul's Musami at the ceremony in 1982 inaugurating the memorial to the seven sisters, two priests and a brother killed on 6 February 1977.

Jesuits from Germany gather for Fr Carl Brosig's Golden Jubilee in Chinhoyi in 1978. (Gerry Pieper, kneeling (on far left), was shot dead in Kangaire in December of that year.)

Prime Minister Robert Mugabe at Silveira House in 1983. Fr John Dove (hidden), Archbishop Chakaipa, Edward Muchenge, Provincial Henry Wardale and in foreground, Agnes Mapfumo.

Fr Brian MacGarry, at inauguration of bio-gas plant at Chishawasha working on a methane gas digester at Mr Zenda's home c.1984.

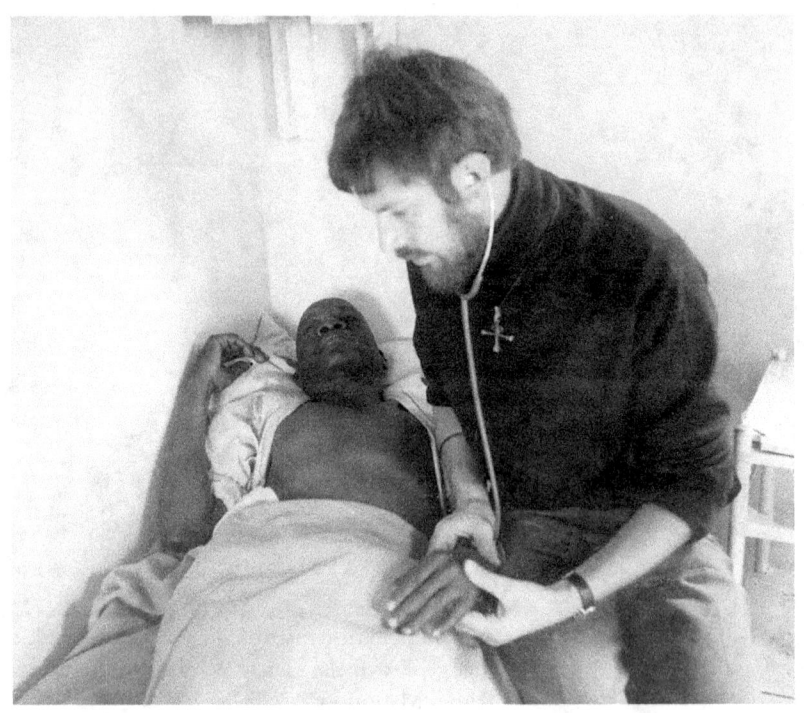

Fr Nigel Johnson, SJ at the hospital in Musami in 1980.

Three fellow novices celebrate their Silver Jubilee, 1994. (l-r) Fr Ignatius Zvaravashe, Bishop Paul Lungu, Br Augustine Kandawasvika.

Fr Karl Steffens, c.2008.   Fr Clemens Freyer, 2012.

Ashton Mugochi teaching at Emerald Hill School for the Deaf c.2014.
(Photo: Arrupe Jesuit Media Centre)

Lovemore Mashiri and Norbert Rwodzi at Arrupe Jesuit University. 2021. (Photo: Arrupe Jesuit Media Centre)

Nobert Rwodzi, Talent Rungano, Elphas Ndlovu, Kudakwashe Zinhumwe and Roland von Nidda at Arrupe in 2021. (Photo: Arrupe Jesuit Media Centre)

Chiedza Chimhanda, in the 'clean-up' project at Mbare in c. 2016. (Photo: Arrupe Jesuit Media Centre)

Fr Chiedza Chimhanda, the final provincial of what was the Zimbabwe-Mozambique Province.
(Photo: Arrupe Jesuit Media Centre)

A clutch of veterans at Jesuit Missions, London in 2008. L-R: Brian Porter, a teacher, mainly St Ignatius College, where he was also administrator, as well as being province treasurer for many years; Paul Edwards, also a teacher, but at St George's College, where he was first rector, then university chaplain and later pastor at Our Lady of the *Wayside*; David Harold Barry; Tom Jackson who spent his whole life 'in the bush' as a pastoral priest with an interest in economic development; and Anthony Bex, also a pastoral man but at St Peter's Mbare, later librarian at the Seminary and finally province archivis

- Diploma in Social Work   43
- Bachelor of Social Work   24
- Honours in Social Work   6
- Master's in Social Work   1

I have focused in this brief account of the School of Social Work on the founding and development of the school. It was a unique work. But Ted would be the first to acknowledge that he relied on many people to move the project along. There is no doubt that his was the imagination, initiative and energy that led the way but there were many devoted Jesuits, other religious (Sr Veronica Brand RSHM) and lay people who contributed. Edwell Kaseke's term lasted more than twenty years (1988-2009). In 2010 Mrs Petronella Dadirayi Motsi was acting principal until the late Professor Andrew Nyanguru came for a year in 2011. Professor Kefas Nyikahadzi was the last principal of the School, 2012 to 2016, while it was still on the Kopje.

In the first decade of the new century the Jesuit presence was confined to representation on the Board of Governors. Finally, in 2016, because of difficulties with the university and lack of finance, the school was absorbed into the university as a Department of Social Work and the premises were leased out to Midlands State University from January 2017.

Ted Rogers, by then retired[25] to Boscombe in the south of England, sent a message to those gathered at the Golden Jubilee celebrations in 2014 in which he said the School set out to address the long-term needs of Zimbabwe and beyond. Perhaps to make his point, he contrasted these with Silveira House, which he saw as addressing 'short-term' goals – something those who laboured at Silveira House would dispute! Both centres had the same purpose: to set in motion what Pope Francis calls processes which, in time, would contribute towards transforming society. But, of course, their emphases were quite different as we will see when treating of Silveira. Ted reminded his hearers that 'training had to be down to earth – not an academic discipline, but practical, with supervised fieldwork'.

---

25 Roger Riddell writes in a private communication: 'I don't think Ted would like to read that he was sent to Boscombe to retire. He went because of his health (he needed to be at sea level), but he spent the first few years at Boscombe working ferociously hard writing. Tim David and I had a rote to go and see him, always with a large bottle of whiskey which kept him going!'

Silveira House[26]

It all began with discussion groups in Highfields in the early sixties. Fr John Dove was the archbishop's secretary and was alert to what was happening. Highfield was a suburb for blacks in segregated Rhodesia. Frustration, both with the government and among their own leaders, was growing among the emerging nationalists at the time. An insight into this was given by Nathan Shamuyarira, one of the leaders, in a letter to Terrence Ranger, a lecturer at the University who had been deported for his support for the nationalist movement:

> The nationalist movement has never been split so sharply in known SR history ... generally opinion among the educated ... is behind [Ndabaningi] Sithole [leader of the splinter group ZANU] and the mass opinion is behind Joshua [Nkomo, long-time leader of ZAPU] ... In Salisbury, Highfield and Mabvuku are behind us [ZANU]. Harare [now Mbare] and Mufakose are totally against... At the University the students ... are solidly behind us but the staff and waiters are with Nkomo.[27]

The division fed into the white prejudice that blacks could not be trusted to rule and white politics began to harden in opposition to African sentiments. The way forward seemed blocked. Gradually, among Jesuits and people we worked with, the idea evolved of having a place away from the charged atmosphere of the township where people could meet and discuss and explore ways forward out of the political impasse. Silveira owes its beginning to this desire; to provide a forum where discussions on the situation in the country could be held freely and be animated by the developing social teachings of the Church. These teachings had evolved from the conditions of the working classes in the nineteenth century when the Church, in the person of Leo XIII, spoke up on their behalf in 1891. A further boost was given in the time of Pius XI, forty years later, as he observed the emergence of the totalitarian systems of Fascism and Communism. Nazism was soon to follow.[28]

---

26 Silveira House has changed its title and its logo several times 'according to the circumstances of persons, times and places' – a phrase often found in the Jesuits' constitutions, for example, #238. The current title is 'Social Justice and Development Centre'.

27 T.O. Ranger, *Writing Revolt* (Harare: Weaver Press, 2013), p. 158.

28 Pius XI drew attention to the concept of 'subsidiarity' as a 'fundamental

At first they tried Mazowe, recently donated to the Society by the Acton family, but then the novitiate was moved there. This, in turn, freed Silveira House and it was Terrence Corrigan, the mission superior, who took the courageous decision to replace a traditional work of the Society (the novitiate) in its custom-built premises, with what must have appeared then to many as a vague project with no plan, staff or money.

John Thurston Dove had no formal education beyond his secondary school at Shrewsbury in England but his years in the army during the Second World War gave him much experience in planning and administration. Besides, he had great gifts of imagination, compassion and charm. And he was determined. This potent mixture led him to explore how he could become engaged in the struggle of the time. At the Silver Jubilee celebrations in 1989 he was asked to speak about those early days. He began by referring to someone who said Jesus got it wrong in the parable of the Good Samaritan:

> 'He should have attended to the masses not to an individual'. But if everyone looked after his neighbour the masses would be cared for. Mother Teresa started with one dying man in the gutters of Calcutta. I would like to think there was something of this spirit in the beginnings of Silveira House. We had no solutions and nothing material to give people at the time. I had initially wanted to focus on retreats and give spiritual nourishment to people in their civic struggles but I found I had to begin with the burning need for practical knowledge and training. Besides, donors would assist in such programmes – not in retreats.[29]

Yet Dove was still quite taken aback when, to use his expression, 'there was a knock on the door' and he was asked, 'Father, can you help us start a trade union?'

> I soon realised my task was to organise expert help. We were soon

---

social principle' in his encyclical, **Quadragesimo Anno**, #79. It has since been taken up in a big way by the European Union. The principle states: 'Just as it is gravely wrong to take from individuals what they can accomplish by their own initiative and industry and give it to the community, so also it is an injustice and at the same time a grave evil and disturbance of right order to assign to a greater and higher association what lesser and subordinate organizations can do.'

29 D. Harold-Barry, *Knocks on the Door, Silveira House: the First Forty Years, 1964-2004* (Harare: Silveira House, 2004), p. 3.

running courses – civics, trade unions, youth – with the help of the team Fr Paul Crane had trained at Claver House in London: Tom Zawaira, Augustine Mutyambizi, Edward Muchenje, Chris Kabasa and others. They worked for a pittance ($20 per month) and had no transport facilities.

The heart of Silveira House manifested itself in the warm reception of students by the staff: Srs Bonaventura (in the kitchen) and Angelina (secretary), Evangelista Chakaipa, Agnes Mapfumo and Chicago Marijani (driver)... and they attracted the students to come to daily Mass and courses ended with old-fashioned Benediction where tough nationalist and trade union leaders sang *Ngatirumbidzei Mwari* (Blessed be God) with gusto.

The CID (now CIO) came all the time in the 1960s wanting to know what was going on. They were at the Wonder Shopping centre when we picked up students and at the airport when students were going to Claver House. John Bradburne was our guest master and, since he did not know what was really going on, he warded them off, charming them into believing that whatever it was we were doing it was harmless.

John Dove continues:

Finance was a huge problem in the early days. We had some lean years and strange helpers. Then, in 1968, I met Herr Steber of Misereor, the German Catholic develolpment agency for aid to Africa. Misereor became our oldest, greatest and most enduring partner. They also financed major building in 1974. (They are still with Silveira House today, 2021, in a partnership which has lasted 53 years). Cebemo, the Dutch Catholic Church foundation, joined us in 1978 and over the years we had 32 funding partners.

I had only one disagreement with them. They wanted us to work through missions and parishes but our experience was that superiors of these structures had different ideas: one was in favour of development but another was more interested in church guilds. The only way to prevent people suffering from the whims of local superiors was to encourage their leaders – nationalist and traditional – to ask for projects they wanted themselves.

Silveira House could never have started without the warm support of Terrence Corrigan, the far-sighted Regional Superior at the time. There were a number of Jesuits who were against the plans of Corrigan and Dove, seeing it as some sort of subversive anti-establishment centre – which it was! When, in his old age, with his mind going, John Dove was interviewed by Fr Francis Gibson Munyoro, this was the one thing he remembered clearly and he kept refering to it in the short interview. It hurt him and in some way isolated him from his fellow Jesuits.

The political discussions hosted at the centre were called, said Dove, 'for the benefit of the CID', civics, an anaemic title. Later, after independence, the Civics programme moved into research, gender issues, peace building, national dialogues and advocacy – especially for indigenous languages. Chris Kabasa, Sr Janice McLaughlin and Ronah Mugadza were active in this work over the years.

In responding to the request to 'help us form a Trade Union' Dove searched for someone who had the experience and Edward Muchenje came and stayed for about fifteen years building up a formidable training programme from which even Morgan Tsvangirai[30] benefited. At one point we had nine Industrial Relations trainers in the field throughout the country. But the new government after 1980 was also wary of too much freedom for trade unions and made it practically impossible for the workers to organise on their own. Our annual report for 1982 says the proposed legislation 'so restricts the right to strike as to make the workers' most powerful weapon of little use'.

The farmers were the next to knock on the door as they had tasted the possibility of new farming methods through the Catholic Association (CA), a mass movement of Catholics founded by Fr Michael Hannan under the banner: 'Better hearts, better harvests, better homes'. The CA only created awareness. It did not show how the new farming techniques were to be applied and so the way was open to Silveira to respond. But the staff at Silveira did not know how to do so. At the jubilee celebrations in 2014 Chris Kabasa explained what happened. Fr Dove asked him to go and start a co-operative group in Rota, Mangwende. Chris protested that he was not a farmer and knew nothing of farming, let alone co-operatives, to which he got the answer; 'Chris, you go; you will discover what to do when you get there.'

With advice from seasoned people and the engagement of a trained

---

30 Founder of the most effective post-independence opposition party, the Movement for Democratic Change.

government agriculture extension officer, Richard Mukonyora, the scheme aimed to combine the advantages of group involvement with individual initiative. When I arrived in 1973 there were six *mushandirapamwe* (co-operative) groups and two years later there were twenty-eight. The next year there were 109. The 1976 Annual Report listed '77courses, seminars and retreats, plus field days, congresses and above all education in the field'. As the war intensified it became more difficult to accompany these groups and it was stressful for our staff when thirty farmers died in 'crossfire' incidents.

There was nothing the centre could do directly to effect change in the country and I remember being shocked by Ian Linden, director of the Catholic Institute of International Relations from 1986 to 2001, stating the obvious:

> Otherwise the Church, eschewing violence within the State to bring about its overthrow, was virtually powerless to achieve the ends of social justice. Beyond the important but not immediately threatening work of Silveira House, where annually 1,500 Zimbabweans were given training in development and leadership, preparing them for independence and that of the Catholic Commission on Social Service and Development, the state was able to parry the more direct threats to its hegemony by the Justice and Peace Commission.[31]

After independence many of our groups registered with the government through the Agriculture Finance Corporation and we thought this meant they were now safely weaned from us. This was not so and it is worth giving some space to this issue as it is a key to development generally and the challenge was not solved then and is still with us now. John Reid, a former student at a Jesuit School in the UK while John Dove was teaching there in the 1950s, came out to give expert advice on questions of financial management and other areas of administration of the agriculture programme. He wrote in the 1982 annual report and I quote him at some length:

> In addition to the great expansion in credit availability after independence a basic change in the character of the credit arrangements also took place. In our (Silveira House) scheme,

---

31 I. Linden, *The Catholic Church and the Struggle for Zimbabwe* (London: Longman, 1980), p .212.

although credit is restricted to farmers who are part of the group, the loan is still made and accounted for on an individual basis. Thus when it comes to repayment, although group pressure can be brought to bear by threatening to withhold future credit from the group if the loans are not repaid, responsibility for repayment remains tied to the individual. If he or she doesn't repay, funds belonging to others in the group are not withheld.

However, in the new AFC-funded scheme credit responsibility and repayment are now tied to the group. All members are expected to market through the one group Grain Marketing Board number. A stop order would then divert the necessary funds to the AFC to repay totals loaned to the group. If a member of the group failed to market enough to cover his part of the group, the difference was automatically made up from surplus marketing by other members of the group. The result was that much of the risk in loan repayment was shifted off the shoulders of the AFC and on to those of the group.

Significantly, at the same time that the AFC was happily granting large loans to the Silveira House groups on a collective liability basis, they were promoting an individual loan scheme based on loosely knit groups such as the Agritex organised GDAs (Group Development Areas). Despite a study on agricultural credit conducted by the Whitsun Foundation with government and AFC participation, which came out in favour of group credit, by far the bulk of AFC's small farmer credit has been devoted to development and support of the individual credit model rather than the group credit approach adopted by SH groups. This attitude is hard to understand in view of the obvious advantages that group credit offers the AFC in terms of lower loan recovery risks and loan administrative costs, quite apart from the obvious benefits it could offer toward the development of strong co-operatives – a prominent part of government policy and a socially desirable objective.

I wrote at that time, 'the Titanic is heading for an iceberg', and indeed the scheme collapsed. Twenty years later when I met Bernard Darare of Munamba near Musami he was palpably in mourning for the collapse of the great scheme.

The next knock on the door came from the youth, and Br (now Fr) Fidelis Mukonori worked feverishly in the 1970s to develop the Catholic Youth Association, which had five aims: recreational, economic, social, educational and religious. By 1976 there were 194 groups in the archdiocese involving 2,500 young people. And each year they had a huge congress at a different mission centre. This was a gigantic affair spread over three days. The young people had to be alert as the security forces suspected anyone young of being in sympathy with the guerrillas and the freedom fighters themselves would often question the young people about their allegiance. I used to encourage out trainers to write monthly reports and I remember Exavier Makwengura once writing 'there is some danger of my disappearing'. I remind him of it still when we meet; 'You have not disappeared yet?'

During the war years Fidelis was delicately combining his youth work and his work with the Catholic Commission for Justice and Peace. Not only did he travel abroad to meet people who could influence the situation – Andrew Young, US President Jimmy Carter's representative at the UN and David Owen, the British Foreign Secretary under Prime Minister James Callaghan – but he also crossed the lines between the Rhodesian soldiers and the guerrillas. It was a knife-edge balance but he was just the man to do it.

The work with youth also involved crafts, tool making, and poultry and piggery projects. In the 1990s the youth work virtually ended for a number of reasons. Youth trainers moved into other work, the guiding hand of Fidelis was no longer there and the Archbishop was unhappy at the autonomy the association enjoyed. Also, it has to be said, some youth trainers moved from inspiring the young people to scandalising them by their behaviour. Funding was becoming harder to secure. Yet I would meet young people later who were grateful for the start in life they received from the CYA.

Appropriate Technology research and implementation was initiated by Fr Brian MacGarry and his assistants, Elfigio Chivhanga and Herbert Kazingizi. Their remit was wide:

- Domestic fuel: Lorena stoves, solar cookers, bio-gas, charcoal cookers, *tsotso* stoves.
- Water: 40 litre carts, solar pumps, hand pumps, Vanek pumps, borehole drilling rigs.
- Sanitation: ventilated pit latrines.
- Food processing and storage: solar vegetable dryers and baking

ovens.
- Tools: handmade maize shellers, Haydock planters, sorghum dehullers, maize weighing scales, wire mesh fencing.
- Building: sisal cement roof sheets

Allied to this initiative was a Technical Apprenticeship Programme, enthusiastically promoted by Aaron Mareya, which taught people across the country skills in building, ironwork, carpentry, bicycle repairs, even hairdressing. I once visited one of Mareya's projects in Guruve which employed eleven people.

Br Ladislaus Bvukumbgwe SJ taught building at Silveira House and in the field. Though he learnt his trade in Scotland, he was impatient with technical colleges, accusing them of wasting people's money. He believed in learning on the spot and if someone later wanted a trade certificate well and good. But first learn on the job.

Bvukumbgwe had a second string to his bow that made his name known throughout the land wherever Shona songs were sung. He was a composer, and his songs are preserved on discs. He died on 1 August 2000 and I heard his funeral at Silveira House was the biggest for any Jesuit ever. Whether this is strictly accurate or not it is an expression of his wide reputation and the warmth with which he was remembered. He was one of those to whom I refer in another chapter where I speak of sons of the soil joining a Society dominated by whites with their unconscious eurocentrism. He suffered from much insensitivity but always with a smile. He was bigger than the slights he received.

From the earliest days, Silveira ran a dressmaking school with Adrienne Blackie, wife of Judge Fergus Blackie, Evangelista Nyawata and Mai Chakaipa. Many such schools sprang up later, and the aim was always to provide an income for mothers of families. Sabina Mugabe, sister of Robert, took this one stage further and developed a nutrition, health and hygiene programme for rural women in 1978. Despite the war they operated in eight districts, from Mount Darwin to Mhondoro. Anne Hope, in her 1983 evaluation, praised the programme, which now had 36 promoters in the field for its 'excellent balance of reflection and action'. Sabina worked with two former guerrillas, George Mukonde and Gibbs Mlamba, as well as the women. When Sabina retired, Thokozani Mugwetsi continued the programme and extended it to the workers and families on the commercial farms. One farmer commented, 'the programme benefits us indirectly as we now have a healthy work force and the kids are no longer disturbing their mothers during working hours'.

The project soon found itself deep in the crisis of HIV/AIDS in the 1990s and Thoko wrote, 'we aimed to intensify awareness-raising about how the disease is spread and how the same people who spread it could also prevent it'. She and her team trained home-based carers. One of them told Mukonde, [32]

> There are three very sick people just in this village. The situation forces me to go there four or five times a day to help them stay clean. We have no painkillers or any sort of drugs and I do not have any protective clothing. I am now worried about my health and that of my children. Sometimes I feel useless. The families' problems are too much. Sick parents, hungry children in tattered clothes, no schooling and no work.

In the early days John Dove also started a Commercial School which gave training in secretarial work, typing and book-keeping. Mary Hayes from Scotland started this programme and handed over to Sr Angelina Katsukunya who ran it for many years. A number of young people obtained employment as a result of the training.

In the 1990s a research department was started under the driving force of Fr Peter Balleis who initiated the publication of more than twenty studies on the social and economic life of the people entitled SILVEIRA HOUSE SOCIAL SERIES. The impulse came from the pressure the global financial institutions were exerting on developing countries like Zimbabwe to cut government subsidies on essential goods and services. These policies formed part of what was termed an Economic Structural Adjustment Programme, which resulted in the erosion of the living standards of the poor. Balleis, assisted by Brian MacGarry and others, traced these effects and painted a dire picture in the booklets. which included: *ESAP and Theology* (Balleis), *Land for which People?* (MacGarry), *ESAP Empowerment or Repression* (Rodreck Mupedziwa), *People of the Great River,* (Michael Tremmel) and *ESAP and Education for the Poor* (Anthony Berridge and Ronah Mugadza).

Retreats were John Dove's original idea when he first came to Silveira,

---

[32] Harold-Barry, p. 38.

as mentioned above, but though he dropped it then it remained in his mind, and when Fr Raymond Kapito became free in the mid 1970s, retreat work began in earnest. Misereor paid for our new buildings on the condition they be used for training in development, but they allowed us to house retreatants in one hostel. Kapito was enthusiastic to have the chance to develop this work, and when Fr General Pedro Arrupe visited Rhodesia in 1976 he, Kapito, asked for a dedicated retreat centre. The general was hardly in a position to answer on the spot but he encouraged the work, and retreats were always part of our work at Silveira. In 2002, Fr Konrad Landsberg gathered funds to construct the St Peter Faber (Pierre Favre) Centre a little away from the main cluster of buildings. Fr Anesu Manyere now runs this centre. There are ideas of integrating the retreat work with the other work of the centre but so far they have not been decided.

Sr Janice McLaughlin MM joined Silveira House in 1998. She had known the centre since the late 1970s when she first arrived in the country and quickly became involved in the struggle for freedom and was arrested, jailed and deported. She wrote then,

> Silveira House impressed me as a safe space where people could speak openly about the liberation war and their hopes and dreams for the future. It offered programs that prepared youth, women and trade unionists to shape a future non-racial society. [33]

Then, at the turn of the new century, she arrived just when the centre was faced with downsizing. She wrote in the booklet to celebrate the Golden Jubilee of the centre in 2014, 'Donor funding was starting to dry up, Misereor in particular could no longer provide the bulk of the funding that kept most of the programs afloat. It was necessary to re-examine the changing needs of society and find a new direction for the centre.' Janice further explained that, 'where possible, programs were relocated as with the dressmaking and commercial schools which were taken over by Young Africa in Chitungwiza. The youth and labour relations programs simply ended and the skills/crafts department became semi-autonomous.'[34]

---

33 J. McLaughlin, *'The Color of the Skin doesn't Matter': A Missioner's Tale of Faith and Politics* (Harare: Weaver Press, 2021), Chapter 24.

34 Janice died in March 2021 after a long struggle with a lung condition that refused to respond to medication. In her striking memoir, she was too ill to write the chapter on Silveira House where she was for ten years. The present writer and

Meanwhile, she continued, the need for new programmes to meet the changing situation of the volatile politics of the new century emerged. A peace-building project was set up offering short courses in conflict resolution and mediation. National dialogues were started in an effort to get people with different political viewpoints to listen to one another, and an effective programme in advocacy and lobbying was started. In Binga, in the Zambezi valley, the local Justice and Peace Commission asked us to design a programme to promote their own (Tonga) language. We shelved our own expectations of what we thought they would want and used every means available to meet their request. The result was a bill in Parliament facilitating minority languages – not only Tonga, but also Venda, Sotho, Kalanga and Shangaan. Teachers were trained and books written to implement this decision. The preservation of indigenous cultures and languages was enshrined in the new constitution of 2013.

But the first decade of this century saw the country slide into destitution, mostly as a direct result of government policy. The steps the government took to preserve its grip on power still baffle us today. They ruined flourishing commercial agriculture by reforming it in a way that 'threw out the baby with the bathwater'. Reform was needed. Land hunger had never been effectively addressed since independence. But the method used destroyed most of the commercial farms and the industry that depended on them. Meanwhile 900,000 of the poorest people – commercial farm workers and their families – suddenly had their livelihoods taken from them.

Halfway through the decade a new onslaught was made on the poorest of the urban dwellers. While claiming to clean up the informal settlements and unapproved housing in the cities, the government, in an unbelievable act of cruelty, unimaginable even in the worst days of the Rhodesians, moved in with bulldozers and destroyed the homes of the poor without any meaningful work being done to relocate them elsewhere. And all this happened in the midst of winter.

Folly followed folly and by 2008 the rate of inflation had reached unrecordable levels and the country was on its knees. But the government still insisted on remaining in power and only reluctantly allowed mediation from South Africa to bring in the opposition in a coalition. This arrangement brought some improvement, but when

---

Arkmore Kori did it for her.

the time for new elections came round the government made sure there was no way their supremacy would be challenged.

This is the background against which Silveira House tried to continue its presence and its contribution. Donors were sympathetic, but funded the work at a reduced rate. Silveira feels the pinch and any visitor to the centre will notice the decaying structures, now almost impossible to maintain.

Our present director is Fr Anold Moyo, who wrote recently about the centre:

> There is no way of measuring the appreciation in the hearts of those that Silveira House has touched and brought some change in their lives ... my hope is sustained by listening to their stories, particularly in the challenging economic and political context we have to operate in. A mother who can now afford school fees for her kids from the money she earned through her livestock project, a father who was able to build a small house for his family using the skills he was taught, a community that is able to articulate boldly its demands to local authorities who, in their turn, constantly invite us to offer them training in leadership. These stories serve to remind us that what we are doing is worth doing.[35]

Moyo goes on to confront the challenge of financial sustainability:

> Dependence on donor money has at times proved detrimental to the realisation of our mission. This dynamic of aid dependence sheds light on a contradiction that exists within development work today. We work towards empowering people but often end up making ourselves and the poor we serve charity-dependent instead. This flawed model, in addition to the ever intensifying donor fatigue, undermines the power of the gospel and impedes the authentic liberation of those trapped in poverty.

In the most recent annual report for Silveira House (2019), Moyo reaffirms the long-cherished dream of the centre: to help people here and now out of their poverty and give them the means to sustain their improvement in the future:

> We, at Silveira House, are working to assist the less privileged of our nation by doing the little that we can with the little that we

---

35 Jesuit Year Book, 2020, p. 53.

have. And by so doing, (we hope) that you may be inspired to partner with us, in whatever way, even in your own community, to kick poverty out of our country and help bring about real transformation that will augur well and bode good tidings for the future generations of our great nation.

Moyo reminds us of the often-told story of the young man on the beach rescuing star fish stranded by the high tide and throwing them one by one back into the ocean. An older man watches him for a time and eventually feels constrained to tell him he is wasting his time as there are just too many stranded fish. The young man throws one more into the sea with the remark, 'that fish doesn't think so'. This parable echoes the Good Samaritan used by John Dove at the Silver Jubilee celebrations in 1989, mentioned earlier. Isaac Mumpande, a senior staff member at Silveira, developed this theme in the same report showing how:

> The older generation has not only been conservative but also expected the younger generation to be equally conservative. Yet the younger generation, exposed to western education and imbued with mantras of democracy, is liberal in nature and willing to explore … Creating a long-lasting bridge between the generations was both challenging and fascinating. … Both camps were prepared to listen to an outsider. This was an opportunity every development agent would exploit. My greatest testimony in 2019 has been to manage to build bridges on this almost impossible generational gap through mind-set change. It was refreshing to see the generational gap slowly closing and community members appreciating their differences of opinions for development. This was revolutionary! Especially in that the inclusion of young people into the communities' governance structures to ensure that development plans from the village to ward and then the district are all-inclusive in nature. With the young as part of the community governance structures, the transitional process is guaranteed to succeed. 2019 will go down as an eventful year in which many people had personal paradigm shifts in their mentality and have been left all the better off for it. The year also changed my perception of community dynamics. I am now a development agent who is not only patient with development processes but also values small changes and steps towards the right direction in the

development of the communities.

The paring down of donor financial support for Silveira House is in the minds of all who work there. It is obvious that this process will continue even when the world economy recovers in the coming years. The centre now concentrates on the essentials: paying its staff and maintaining the skeleton support services needed to fulfil its reduced programmes. It has never, as far as I know, received financial help from the province.[36] Now that international donors are no longer able to help as in the past the desire to receive some help from the province increases. But, as Moyo points out, if we are teaching self-reliance to others, we need to bite the tough bullet of self-reliance ourselves. It is a tough call. When the centre just manages to take care of the essentials, there is no spare money for the refurbishment of the centre and those who live there witness the rust and decay advancing by the day. When I returned last year after an absence of seven years the description that sprang to my mind was from Charles Dickens: a bleak house! Even the water tower, the distinguishing feature of the complex, has lost its tank and its high cross. And the weather vane, so meticulously adjusted to point exactly north by Arthur Law, a relative, John Dove believed, of Augustus Law who died at Umzila's 140 years ago, lies abandoned on the roof.

Yet, despite the atmosphere of decay, it could well be that Silveira is more attuned to its real mission today than it has ever been. The staff may be a 'remnant' and the plant a 'shadow' but it could well be that in these lean years the centre is building on its past to discover a new 'depth' in its response to these charged times.

Rural credit

Sometimes someone, searching in English, asks us to 'borrow' them some money. The concept of lending and borrowing seem to blend into one another. At its best, credit is a sign of trust between people and a way of building relationships. It also builds wealth. We have come to surround the idea of credit with written guarantees and penalties for defaulting because a person's word is only reliable in closely knit communities where defaulting would have immediate social consequences. Credit, or the investment of other people's

---

36 There were some loans at times but they had to be repaid.

money in a person's business, has been the motor driving progress and development for centuries. Large banks and investment companies have set rules but people have struggled to find suitable practices to govern the lending of a few hundred dollars to give the required initial boost for launching a small enterprise.

Francis Waddelove (Waddy) was a Jesuit Brother who came to Rhodesia in 1937. He spent many of his early years in Chishawasha and soon became aware of the constant inability of the people to break free from the cycle of poverty in which they seemed trapped. He received great support from Terrence Corrigan to search for a solution. He heard of the Credit Unions and Savings Clubs Movement which was being fostered in Nova Scotia, Canada, in the 1940s and '50s and it struck him: Chishawasha in the 1960s was not unlike Nova Scotia in the 1930's. In Canada, it was industrialisation which edged out the small person while in Rhodesia it was the large commercial farmers. As in Nova Scotia, young people of ability, the very people who, given the chance, could turn the situation around, left to look for brighter prospects elsewhere.

In 1962, Fr Paul Crane, an English Jesuit, encouraged Waddy to meet Paddy Bailey from Trinidad, who was having great success in promoting the Credit Union movement in the United States. Crane persuaded Bailey to visit Rhodesia and explain what he was doing to Waddy, with whom he left some literature. Waddy adapted the material to his needs. His overriding aim was to build the community, and particularly the women. He knew the administration of funds would call upon people's integrity. If the movement were a success, many purposes would be served, as the people would improve their own lives and grow in confidence in their own ability.

Savings would be the first step and it became officially known as the Savings Development Movement (SDM). In a letter to Fr Edward Ennis, his Jesuit Superior in 1968, Waddy expressed his intense belief that despite the growth of the movement in other places, which 'almost surprised me', it had to succeed in Chishawasha. He had no desire to travel to Antigonish, Nova Scotia, which had transformed its experience into an academic study. It had to be homegrown, based on knowledge of the people and with a 'proving ground' in Chishawasha. The only qualification for joining was 'spontaneous interest'. He had little taste for the exhortations of salaried officials. A year earlier, in 1967, Waddy had organised a meeting at St Ignatius College of all those interested in the movement. A thorough exposition of the work of the SDM was given and an evaluation of progress so far made. Attitudes of jealousy and mistrust were already evident among members as was a failure to follow simple procedures. But on the whole the picture was positive and the movement grew. People came from Mabvuku, a nearby high-density suburb, to learn about the movement and soon other townships followed.

Fr Tom Jackson gives us a picture of the Savings Clubs, including the written guarantees and penalties for defaulting, in action in Seke in 1973.[37] Four women are seated at a table under a tree. Mai Thomas is receiving money from the members. Mai Gideon is tearing off the stamps, each representing a saving of 5 cents and Mai Mudye sticks them on the member's card, which Mai Mudimu then stamps with the date. Chris Howse, the OXFAM representative at the time, noted how it was a shared task and, since all the members took turns to do the work, in effect they checked up on each other and mistakes were virtually impossible to make. In those days each club collected about R$30 (Rhodesian dollars) from the members each week. The money was saved so that it was available when needed for agricultural inputs: seeds, fertilizers, and insecticides – and school fees. Economies of scale were achieved allowing services to reach people who otherwise could not afford them. Besides the financial aspects the group received instruction from government trainers in methods of ploughing and planting, storing grain and making compost, in home economics and cooking, in baby care, and there was a library, which held reading classes.

The clubs fulfilled Waddy's dream. He had started in 1963 in Chishawasha and this is the date given for the commencement of the savings movement in this country though, as pointed out in a study by Raftopoulos and Lacoste,[38] burial societies had existed since the early days of the European occupation. Waddelove insisted that saving

---

37 *Jesuit Missions*, Summer, 1973.
38 Brian Raftopoulos and Jean-Paul Lacoste, 'From Savings Mobilisation to Micro-Finance: A Historical Perspective on the Zimbabwe Savings Development Movement', paper presented at the International Conference on *Livelihood, Savings and Debts in a Changing World: Developing Sociological and Anthropological Perspectives,* 14-16 May 2001, Wageningen, The Netherlands. (A copy is in JAZ, Box 386).

money was simply a means. The aim was to do something about the 'moral and social degradation' he found in the Chishawasha people after seventy years of Jesuit presence in the valley. Waddy was from Lancashire in the UK where people spoke their minds bluntly!

By 1972, there were 210 Savings Clubs and 10 Credit Unions with 7,200 members and savings of R$125,000. By 1998 these figures jumped to 7,000 clubs with 100,000 members. Two Jesuit General Superiors in Rome – Fr Baptiste Janssens and later Fr Pedro Arrupe – wrote warmly commending the work. A Newsletter, *The Depositor*, was launched in October 1969. Francis Waddelove and the Self-Help Development Foundation, as the movement had become after independence, were short-listed for the King Baudouin African Development Prize in 1982. The prize eventually went to the Sarvodaya [awakening] Shramadana [sharing energies] movement in Sri Lanka – also a rural movement of co-operation among the poor.

But expansion brought problems. Waddy wanted it to remain small until it was well proven. But the pressures to grow were great. Misuse of funds and jealousy have already been mentioned. There were cases of chickens, owned by members, stolen at night. The Credit Union in Highfield managed to set up sewing classes for the women: twenty in the morning and twenty in the afternoon. The women gradually produced items which – when sold – made a noticeable difference to their family finances. It was at this point that the men became jealous of the success of their women for 'making too much money' and tried to take over the project. The result was collapse. There were a number of other similar failures – all of which persuaded Waddy he had pushed out the boat too far. It would be better to build up more gradually. Together with his colleagues, notably Mr Pat Arnold, he worked on strengthening the Savings Clubs. In future people would only be able to use money they had saved. The concept of credit was put on hold.

In order to have a clean start Waddy moved his operations to Seke, where Tom Jackson's account above comes from. Jackson was the parish priest and worked closely with Waddy. Perhaps it helped that they both came from the north of England – Waddy was born in Leigh, Lancashire, in 1915, and Tom in Castleford, Yorkshire, nine years later – and were shaped in the same 'no nonsense' mould! They were known for their frank assessment of situations and people, superiors included![39]

Soon, Savings Clubs were started in neighbouring Mhondoro and then Makumbe, Chikwaka, Mutoko, Rusape and further afield in Matabeleland. George Smith, of the Adult Education Department of the then University of Rhodesia, was a great support to Waddy as was Pat Arnold, a chartered accountant.

Although these clubs started in the Catholic Church, they soon spread to the Salvation Army in the Mazowe area and to the Methodists who proved more reliable than the Catholics in the administration of the movement. The Savings Clubs were never associated with any one church. There was often good cooperation with the government extension officers – a notable case being in Mutare where the officer, Mr Sithole, worked with forty-two clubs for over thirty years.

The war years of the late 1970s put a brake on activities but with the coming of independence in 1980 the SDM, as it still was then, regained its momentum. By 1985 the government wanted to control what was by now a very successful predominantly women's organisation. They even feared that it might turn into a political party! In practice this meant removing the existing leadership, which was mainly white, with government appointees. A false accusation was made that Z$170,000 of the organisation's funds could not be unaccounted for and this gave an excuse for the suspension of the management committee. A successful case for defamation of character was subsequently heard in the High Court and damages and costs were awarded against the government official concerned. In the meantime, the suspension had been quietly lifted but damage had been done to the reputation of the movement. And the government brought in their own appointees anyway together with the new name, as already mentioned: the Self–Help Development Foundation [SHDF]. There was no alternative but to work within the new structure if the original aims were to be pursued, and things gradually settled down.

Raftopoulos and Lacoste say that extending credit has to be combined with mobilising savings. In the 1980s the government was more interested in the former, which was politically attractive. The Agricultural Finance Corporation followed precisely this policy,

---

39 I once met Waddy shortly after I arrived at Silveira House. It was around 1975. He was devastatingly critical of what we were doing, particularly in industrial relations training. He felt it was all hot air with no substance.

as we saw in describing the work of Silveira House, but it soon led to widespread indebtedness among small farmers. The government's reaction was to throw further money at the problem but this did nothing to deal with the fundamental constraints the small farmer faced. The repayment rates for credit were unsustainable and the introduction of the Economic Structural Adjustment Programme in the 1990s made the situation much worse. Interest rates jumped from 10 per cent in the 1980s to 50 per cent in the late 1990s. The business of banks is not the alleviation of poverty but of making money.

The SHDF responded to this hostile climate by again retreating to savings only, but by 1996 some international organisations, notably the Konrad Adenauer Foundation and ADRAI – a Belgian foundation for development – encouraged them to look at credit again. It is borrowers, not savers, who drive the economy. It was noticeable in the clubs how borrowers dressed better! Savers were quieter. Yet there was considerable reluctance to move again in the direction of credit as the economy had not recovered from the battering it had under ESAP. Cautious moves were made and they met with success. The big names in international banking were beginning to realise that financial viability often conflicts with the aim of alleviating poverty. Urban businesses are more attractive to bankers than remote rural villages. Yet small steps began to be made to make banks more small-person friendly. The SHDF was encouraged to revisit its mission statement and to articulate more precisely what had been obvious up to then. Banking and training emerged as the twin aims of the movement.

In the year 2000 the SHDF had eighty-eight full-time staff serving all the major centres of the country. Various tensions continue to challenge the foundation. 'Credit delivery continues to be more important than savings mobilisation'. 'Qualified credit staff sometimes clash with long term training staff though field credit officers promoted internally [are] more effective than highly qualified newcomers'.[40] SHDF staff found it hard to accept that 36 per cent of their salaries come from people poorer than themselves and that the aim is that it be 100 per cent.

The challenge to make banking and credit more small-person friendly continued. Accountancy practices create confidence if backed by annual audits by recognised firms. But the fees of such firms would

---

40 Raftopoulos, op. cit.

swallow up the hard-earned savings of small financial associations. How can this impasse be resolved?

A more fundamental question is the attitude of government. The majority rule ushered in with such fanfare in 1980 was just as controlling of the small person as its colonial predecessor. It would not allow people to develop their own structures and practices, despite what is said loud and clear in its 1980 election manifesto:

> ZANU believes that the common interests of the people are paramount in all efforts to exploit the country's resources, that the productive processes must involve them as full participants, in the decision making, management and control of those resources.

This high-minded statement of subsidiarity could have come straight out of Pius XI's encyclical, *Quadragesimo Anno* of 1931. Alas, they were just words. Those involved in the SHDF had to constantly look over their shoulders to see if they were transgressing this or that regulation. A hen gathers its chicks under its wing but it also allows them to wander where they will, so long as she can see what they are up to. The same suspicions that caused the downfall of the Highfield Credit Union in the 1960s fuelled the attitude of those in government to this highly successful – mainly women's – movement in the 1980s. It was all but choked by legislation.

Towards the end of his life[41] Waddy felt the essential element of building the community was lost sight of. The SHDF became all about the administration of money. Yet the movement continued into the present century, achieving results and a sign of this was the continued substantial backing of donors who paid for a large training centre in Bulawayo and a smaller one in Harare. The FAO funded an unofficial visit of interested people from Mozambique to study the movement in Zimbabwe and the movement also took off in Zambia.

Fr Gerry McCabe spoke at Waddy's funeral:

> To see Waddy engaged with old *ambuyas*, grandmothers, teaching them how to read and keep the simple accounts the savings club needed, was a revelation. It was done with humour and patience and he built relationships which lasted for years. Waddy was one of the best speakers of Shona among the Europeans in the province. One of my earliest recollections was of Waddy, when he

---

41 He died in 2007.

was at St Michael's Mhondoro, coming out of the dining-room after supper and remarking he would be spending an hour with Fortune's Grammar[42] before bed. He said this after a full day building the new church.

The Self-Help Development Foundation, with its headquarters in Hatfield, Harare, has a website that suggests a flourishing movement where women's dignity and rights are promoted. Waddy would be pleased. He spent fifty years trying to make it so. He died in 2007 at the age of ninety-two, seventy of which were spent serving the people of Zimbabwe.

---

42 G. Fortune, *An Analytical Grammar of Shona* (Cape Town: Longman, 1955).

10

Justice and War

> *'The mission of the Society of Jesus today is the service of faith, of which the promotion of justice is an absolute requirement. For reconciliation with God demands the reconciliation of people with one another.'*
>
> General Congregation 32, Decree 4, #2, (1974/5)

A General Congregation (GC) of the Society of Jesus is a representative body of the whole Society scattered through the world. It is also the highest authority and it delegates this authority to a general superior who in turn delegates it to provincial superiors. Of all statements, and they were many, of the ten GCs that met in the twentieth century the one quoted above had the most far-reaching effects. It expressed the conviction of Jesuits, especially those living in developing countries. The Vatican Council, which ran for four years in the early 1960s, called the Church to 'open the window' and look out at the world with rinsed eyes. The result was a shift in perspective from a narrow concentration on the interior life of individuals – nourished by scripture and the sacraments – to a broader awareness of the structures on which we build our societies. Latin America was bedevilled by dictatorships and Africa was emerging from the colonial era and entering another form of oppression as new elites took power and retained it, often through corruption, but usually to the detriment of the poor majority.

Promoting justice was not a new idea. The Church had always combined some form of development with its preaching. French Fr

Joseph Moreau, the first Jesuit to open an enduring mission in what is now Zambia, was criticised by his fellow Jesuits for being 'little more than a farmer'. He had settled among the Tonga with a bible – and a plough. He answered simply, *'Ventre affamé n'a point d'oreilles.'*[1] A hungry stomach has no ears. If you want to preach the good news you have to hear the needs of people first.

For the first six decades of the twentieth century, Catholic church-state relations in Zimbabwe were co-operative, even friendly. Both worked together to establish mission stations, provide schools, clinics and other services – even an observatory. The government knew that the missions provided services that it could not provide. The much loved Bishop Chichester, whose imagination and drive had given powerful impetus to the Catholic Church's missionary work in the 1930s and 1940s, kept away from politics. At the time of the Land Apportionment Act (1929), when land was divided up between whites and blacks, Anglican Fr Arthur Shearley Cripps looked for Jesuit support in his campaign to defend black people. Stephen Buckland tells us Cripps went to a meeting of the English Jesuit provincial and his advisors in Driefontein in 1931 to ask their support; they 'were very kind to me and charming but (they) do not commend themselves to me altogether as furthering Africa's horizons'.[2]

The eruption of African nationalism in the 1960s was the catalyst that spurred the Catholic Church to seriously rethink her attitude. The English Jesuit province had been sending out to Rhodesia some of its best men since the beginning. We saw this when we considered the early years of the century and the work of Sykes and Gartlan. In the sixties the province sent out Terrence Corrigan, as superior, and other men of imagination like Edward (Ted) Rogers and John Dove. These were men who could see immediately what was wrong and each in their way sought to change things. Corrigan was no sooner off the plane than he noticed the segregation in the Cathedral: Europeans in the nave, Africans in the side aisles. He put a stop to that at the first opportunity.[3]

We saw earlier how it was under Corrigan's watch that St Ignatius

---

1 Murphy, p. 150.
2 *Crossroads*, the Zimbabwe Catholic Bishops' Conference Newsletter, April 1994.
3 There is a rather innocuous note in the Jubilee publication of the *Catholic Cathedral, 1925-2000*, which states: '1959, Africans, hitherto usually domestic workers, now worship alongside their employers', p 17.

College was founded, Silveira House was turned from a novitiate into a Social Justice and Development Centre and St Peter's Kubatana Technical and Secondary school was started. All these initiatives and others, like Francis Waddelove's Credit Unions and Savings Clubs, were established before the end of the Vatican Council and ten years before the 32nd General Congregation formulated Jesuit policy as stated at the head of this chapter. So there was a growing body of people among the Jesuits in Rhodesia who understood the aspirations of black people and their subsequent frustration with the intransigence of the whites who ruled the country. The Catholic Church became more sharply aware of her mission at the very time the settler government was becoming more uncompromising towards African advancement. In Rhodesia, a black middle class was emerging and whites felt threatened by the black majority with whom they had never built a relationship of respect. Politically, it became vividly obvious through UDI in 1965.

The liberation war started in earnest in 1972. Unrest occured periodically even in Catholic institutions, as we saw in earlier chapters. Even in the Regional Seminary, in 1976, John Berrell had to step down as rector due to a strike by the seminarians, unhappy with his administration. Infiltration of freedom fighters, *vakomana*, started especially in the north-east of the country.

But we were divided. A number of us taught at St George's College or in the predominantly white parishes of Mount Pleasant, Mabelreign and Rhodesville (for a time) as well as the Cathedral. Working in such places meant inevitably breathing the air of hard line 'not in a thousand years' segregationists at worst or 'yes, but not yet' gradualists at best. The allure of the white lifestyle was enticing and I remember feeling its draw on my arrival in the mid-1960s. The roads of the city were lined with blue jacaranda and red flamboyant trees and the gardens were rich in varied shades of bougainvillea. And the life was lived in a world of servants, swimming-pools and sundowners.

In the late 1970s, when seven Jesuits were killed in or near rural missions, the division among us became clear. Stephen Buckland felt 'a deeper uncertainty and ambiguity within the Jesuit consciousness was exposed'.[4] Despite this vacuum of policy, which black Jesuit Fidelis Mukonori called 'a coherent policy of having no policy', there

---

4 *Crossroads*, op. cit.

were two series of events that showed where the Jesuits stood officially. One was their commitment to and participation in the robust stance of the Catholic Commission for Justice and Peace (CCJP) – even to the extent of imprisonment and deportation – and the other was the killing, already referred to, of seven Jesuits.

The Catholic Commission for Justice and Peace

Dieter Scholz[5] was one of the lead persons in the CCJP during the war (1972-79) and in the Zimbabwe Project (ZP) and the Jesuit Refugee Service (JRS) shortly after it. He has shared with me the text of a presentation he gave on all three at Arrupe University on 17 May 2021. They are related and indeed flowed one from the other. The Second Vatican Council taught us 'peace is never attained once and for all but must be built up ceaselessly' and encouraged us to work for justice so as to achieve peace.[6] Following the council, Justice and Peace Commissions were set up in countries around the world and Rhodesia was one of them. It came into its own almost immediately because of the developing struggle in the country. It was later to define its purpose as the 'reconciliation of the warring parties and in endeavours to assist and promote initiatives for peace'.[7]

To this effect, it published a number of major documents which had to be clandestinely secreted out of the country so as to be published:

- *The Man in the Middle* (1975)
- *Civil War in Rhodesia* (1976)
- *Rhodesia - The Propaganda War* (1977)

Scholz tells us that 'in 1975, I was asked, as deputy chair of the Commission, to take the first report *(The Man in the Middle)* to the UK for publication by the Catholic Institute of International Relations (CIIR). However, when I arrived in London, I discovered that the documents had been stolen from my suitcase. There was only one

---

5 Dieter Scholz was born in Germany in 1938 and entered the Society of Jesus in 1958. At first, he was due to go to Japan but it was later changed to Southern Rhodesia. Ordained priest in 1969 he was heavily engaged in the 1970s in the struggle for justice in Rhodesia. Imprisoned and then deported, he worked with the Zimbabwe Project from London and throughout the 1980s in setting up the Jesuit Refugee Service. In the 1990s he was parish priest in Marymount and later director of Silveira House before being ordained Bishop of Chinhoyi in 2006.
6 *Gaudium et Spes, The Church Today*, #78.
7 CCJP, Chairman's report for the year ending 31 December 1978.

spare copy and that was in the drawer by the bed of Bishop Lamont, in St Anne's Hospital, where he was recovering from a car accident in Chimanimani.'

'The third report *(Rhodesia – the Propaganda War)*', Dieter tells us, 'angered the Rhodesian authorities most. They claimed the war was an onslaught by foreign communist terrorists on a peaceful, Christian and civilised little country, while our report proved it was our own sons and daughters, students and parishioners who went to Zambia and Mozambique to join the struggle and fight for the liberation of Zimbabwe from racist oppression and injustice. At the core of the struggle was the demand for land.'

By 1978, the CCJP had had little success in 'reconciling the warring parties' and, if anything, the situation had grown far worse. It reported that 1,088 primary schools had been closed since 1973 affecting 268,000 pupils and 3,900 teachers.[8] Hospitals and clinics also had to close as well as mission stations. Regular cattle dipping had ceased and tsetse fly control had lapsed with the resulting death of 500,000 animals. In total, 13,700 whites left the country, a figure 60 per cent higher than the previous exodus record, just after the collapse of Federation in 1963. Indirectly, by declaring martial law, the government admitted it had lost control of 90 per cent of the country. Far from reconciliation, Rhodesia was more polarised than it had ever been.

The CCJP saw its main task as revealing the truth of what was going on in the rural areas away from the eyes of the media and contrary to the propaganda of the government. Together with the CIIR, the CCJP prepared a series of booklets called *From Rhodesia to Zimbabwe*. Roger Riddell, a former Jesuit, was deeply involved in this project. He writes:

> Its focus was on the future – when the country had gained its independence – discussing what policies would need to be adopted if the incoming government were committed to seriously addressing the problems of underdevelopment and poverty, as the series assumed it would be. My job was to raise funds for the whole initiative, to write and commission further booklets in the series, which would look in more detail at specific problems the country faced and to ensure the booklets were read by those who

---

8 Op. cit.

needed to, inside Rhodesia and outside the country…

Those completed covered the central issues of land, unemployment, skilled labour, the informal sector, community development/rural administration, health, food security and education.[9] The series was published by CIIR in collaboration with the CCJP in Salisbury with copies printed in Rhodesia by Mambo Press.[10] As the purpose was to stimulate debate and discussion among a wide readership – ordinary Zimbabweans as well as policy-makers – about Zimbabwe's development future, we aimed to produce booklets based on in-depth research and academic rigour, but written in as non-technical language as possible. The whole initiative was framed – ambitiously - within the best historical traditions of pamphleteering.[11] …

But what was just as important for us was that the booklets were read by Rhodesians. Within the country they were bought up in their hundreds and, through the work of the CCJP, were discussed in small citizens' groups and by the business community. But they were also distributed and used as study tools in the refugee camps in Zambia and Mozambique where thousands of young Rhodesians had fled, including (we were told) would-be fighters in the guerrilla training camps. …

In those days, numerous exiled Rhodesians passed through our offices, many attracted by CIIR's up-to-date documentation on contemporary Rhodesian affairs which they were eager to read. Regular visitors included officials from both parts of the Patriotic

---

9   #2 Roger Riddell, *The Land Question*;
    #3 Duncan Clarke, *The Unemployment Crisis*;
    #4 Colin Stoneman, *Skilled Labour and Future Needs*;
    #5 Rob Davies, *The Informal Sector: A solution to Unemployment?*
    #6 Michael Bratton, *Beyond Community Development;*
    #7 John Gilmurray, David Sanders and Roger Riddell, *The Struggle for Health*;
    #8 Vincent Tickner, *The Food Problem*; and
    #9 Roger Riddell, *Education for Employment*.

10 At the time, Mambo Press was run by Father Albert Plangger, with whom we worked closely. He took over as Managing Director from Father Michael Traber who ran the Press from the early 1960s and started a weekly newspaper called Moto (meaning fire) which grew in popularity as it started to report, comment on and publish studies covering social, economic and political as well as religious issues. Michael Traber was deported from the country in 1970 (and died in 2006). Albert Plangger died in 2019 aged 94.

11 Thomas Paine, John Milton, John Calvin, George Orwell and The Fabians were all influential pamphleteers. The CIIR was never shy of aiming to be ambitious!

Front – the Zimbabwe African National Union (ZANU), led by Robert Mugabe and the Zimbabwe African People's Union (ZAPU) led by Joshua Nkomo.[12] Although we didn't know it at the time, these included a number of future ministers of independent Zimbabwe;[13] through them we first learned that the booklets were being read by the top leadership of both parties as they came out, and were being used to stimulate debate and discussion at party headquarters.[14]

The CCJP also acted as a forum where representatives of the major parties could meet, though substantial progress was impossible without the two guerrilla groups, ZAPU and ZANU, having high-ranking representatives present. The commission also engaged the British and American governments in the process of searching for a way forward. Fidelis Mukonori and John Deary travelled to London and Washington as well as Lusaka and Maputo to meet all those concerned so as to brief them of the situation and keep all lines of communication open. It would only be when all parties involved finally gathered at Lancaster House in London on 10 September 1979 that progress could be made.

The Rhodesian government saw the activity of the CCJP as reaching out to the enemy and they took every opportunity to thwart the commission. 'In July 1977,' Dieter Scholz continues, 'their Special Branch raided the offices of John Deary, Chairman of CCJP, Marist Brother Arthur Dupuis, Secretary, Maryknoll Sister Janice McLaughlin, and myself. All four of us were arrested and charged

---

12 The Patriotic Front was formed in 1976 when the military wings of ZANU and ZAPU – the Zimbabwe National Liberation Army (ZANLA) and the Zimbabwe People's Revolutionary Army (ZIPRA) – came together, not to to create a unified command structure, but rather to establish a loose alliance. The two parties formed one negotiating team, the Patriotic Front, at the 1979 Lancaster House Conference, but fought the independence elections separately. Seven years after Independence, in 1987, the two parties merged under the name ZANU-PF, to the dismay of many ZAPU supporters.

13 They included ZAPU's London representative Arthur Chadzingwa, and ZANU representatives Frederick Shava, Simba Makoni and Didymus Mutasa. Dzingai Mutumbuka, later to become Zimbabwe's first Minister of Education, and Fay Chung, who succeeded him, also spent a good deal of time around the CIIR office during this period. Witness Mangwende, a student at LSE, who later became Minister of Foreign Affairs, had a part-time job in the office cutting and filing stories from the Rhodesian newspapers.

14 From the forthcoming memoirs of Roger Riddell.

under the Emergency Powers Regulations. Sister Janice and I were refused bail and taken to prison, she to Chikurubi and I to Salisbury Central. I was charged additionally with 162 offences under the Official Secrets Act, arising out of the contents of the three books the CCJP had published.'

Dieter Scholz was released on bail and, 'For a full year,' he tells us, 'we worked on our defence. Our lead lawyer was Mr Israel (Issy) Aaron Maisels from South Africa. Maisels was a Judge of the High Court of Rhodesia and the Judge President of Botswana, Lesotho and Swaziland (Eswatini). He practised law in South Africa during the apartheid era, was widely regarded as pre-eminent among his generation of advocates and one of South Africa's most formidable legal minds. In addition to his legal practice, he is best remembered for his defence of those prosecuted for their political beliefs. He was a man whose life and interests reflected a deep concern for human rights and civil liberty. He led the defence team in the South African Treason Trial of 1956 to 1961, in which the accused, including Nelson Mandela, were all acquitted.'

'The enormous legal costs of our defence were paid for by the British Defence and Aid fund. At the request of the CCJP, our Superior of the Sinoia (Chinhoyi) Mission at the time, Fr Horst Ulbrich, who was very supportive, freed me from all other commitments so I could work on our defence documents. The general charges, excluding those under the Official Secrets Act which concerned only me, alleged that our three reports, and many other publications of the CCJP, were causing alarm and despondency among the Rhodesian people. Our defence would argue that what we had published in our reports on abductions, torture, killings, communal punishments – like the burning of entire villages and the deliberate infection and poisoning of cattle with anthrax – may indeed have caused alarm and despondency, especially among the whites, but it was actually happening in much of the country and especially in remote areas which we knew well: we were working there in our missions, schools and hospitals. We would be able to show the true nature of the war, which the government was denying. We wanted to aim at the young white men sent out into the bush to fight their fellow countrymen, young black men, of their age.'

There is evidence that the message got through. David Coltart, who was a strong supporter of Ian Smith in his school days until his eyes were 'subtly' opened by the Christian Brothers in Bulawayo, became aware of *The Man in the Middle* which Dieter Scholz had managed to publish on behalf of the CCJP despite the copy he had carried to London being confiscated at Salisbury airport, as mentioned above.[15]

Dieter continues, '[O]ur defence strategy was, to prove that what we had published was true, for every incident described in our reports to be supported by three more examples of the same kind of atrocity. The prosecution's main witness, a police officer, Daniel D. Stannard, himself a victim of Mr Ian Smith's propaganda machine, was given a helicopter to fly around the country and visit the places and people mentioned in our reports, order to check the facts.

'By August 1978, a year after we began, I had completed the defence document and it (1,300 pages) was typed out professionally by Patricia Deary, wife of our chairperson, John Deary, and sent to Issy Maisels in South Africa. He studied it and then flew up to Salisbury to give it to the Attorney General here. Three days later, the four of us, who were still under arrest, were called to court and told that the state was withdrawing all charges. Brother Arthur and I were declared prohibited immigrants and ordered to leave Rhodesia within 24 hours and so we followed Sister Janice who had been deported a year before. After visiting our families,[16] we regrouped in London to see how we could continue to support the struggle in another way from there.'

The Zimbabwe Project

'Welcomed in London by the CIIR, which had been warm and active in their support and was headed by Mildred Neville and Tim Sheehy, we set up the Zimbabwe Project (ZP). Brother Arthur was again our Secretary and Sr Janice McLaughlin was our reference person for Zimbabwean refugees in Mozambique. I was appointed Director of the Project and we were joined by Judith (Judy) Todd, daughter of the former Southern Rhodesian Prime Minister, Garfield Todd. Judy was jailed by the Rhodesian authorities for her active opposition to the Rhodesian Front and had excellent contacts with ZAPU and ZIPRA and had the full trust and friendship of Joshua Nkomo. She became

---

15 D. Coltart, *The Struggle Continues, 50 Years of Tyranny in Zimbabwe* (Auckland Park: Jacana Media, 2016), p .52.

16 I went to visit my elderly mother who was anxiously awaiting to see me in Berlin. She had followed the German radio accounts of the fight between the Rhodesian Government and the CCJP.

our reference person for Zimbabwean refugees in Zambia. We were also joined by Dr John Conradie, whom I had met in prison back in Salisbury. A highly respected lecturer at the university, he had hidden hand grenades and other weapons for the comrades in his garden in Mount Pleasant and been given a lengthy prison sentence, but was released early because of a terminal illness. John was an excellent administrator.

'Our main concern was to offer a personal and pastoral presence to Zimbabweans in refugee camps in Mozambique and Zambia. Sr Janice went to live in a camp in Mozambique.[17] Fr Nigel Johnson did his tertianship[18] experiment living in a small tent at the Jason Moyo camp in Solwezi in NW Zambia and found 8,000 boys living in other overcrowded tents there. When he had to leave, he was replaced by Jesuit Patrick (Paddy) Moloney for a short while. During a visit to Lusaka, Joshua Nkomo asked me to send sisters to the Freedom camp in southern Zambia, a camp entirely for girls and women. A congregation which initially showed a keen interest in this work, later withdrew their offer.

'So the basic intention of the ZP was to be *with* refugees, rather than, as we have learnt, doing things *for* them. And this intention was what Fr Pedro Arrupe wanted for the Jesuit Refugee Service (JRS). Yet, you cannot be with refugees, sharing their life without trying to help. So we did try, mostly in small ways, by sending medicines, food and clothes to the camps. Perhaps the most important service we were able to provide through our London office, was to establish contact between the young people in the camps in Zambia and Mozambique, and their families back home in Zimbabwe. Viewed from Rhodesia, Zambia and Mozambique were enemy territories from which terrorists launched their raids into Rhodesia. Any communication across the border was closely watched by the Rhodesian forces. Young men caught trying to cross the border to join the struggle, were invariably arrested, sentenced to death (if the State could prove that they had reached the age of 18) and hanged in Salisbury Central prison. The death sentence was mandatory. So, young Zimbabweans in the camps

---

17 McLaughlin, pp. 87ff.

18 This is a reference by Dieter Scholz to the final year of a Jesuit's training, 'a school of the affections', where he tries to integrate the different aspects of his life – intellectual, spiritual and emotional – through a varied programme of reflection, prayer and insertion into 'real' life.

had no way of communicating directly with their families back home. But they could post their letters to the ZP in London and we would arrange for the letters to be taken to Rhodesia and delivered to their families.

'Although we tried to keep a low profile, our work attracted the attention of white security officials in Rhodesia and our funding partners in Europe. A Rhodesian paper described the staff of the ZP as the seven most dedicated enemies of Mr Ian Smith. Even the rector of St George's College wrote a passionately bitter letter of complaint to Bruce Kent, an influential monsignor of the Archdiocese of Westminster, demanding the ZP be closed down. And a leading Catholic funding agency in Europe had the ZP blacklisted with CIDSE.[19] They circulated a so-called "black letter" claiming that any grants or donations given to the ZP office in London would be used to purchase guns for the communist terrorists in Mozambique and Zambia, who would go back to Rhodesia and kill white missionaries there. The staff at the ZP, the letter continued, were all well-known communists, sharing the ideology of the terrorists to destroy Christianity and civilisation in Rhodesia. The diocesan newspaper in my hometown, Berlin, ran hostile articles suggesting I was unnecessarily criticising the government in Christian Rhodesia.

'In contrast, we had the unflinching support and trust of the Jesuit Provincial back here in Rhodesia, Fr Henry Wardale, who knew what we were doing and approved and supported our work. The majority of bishops in Rhodesia, unfortunately, did not. Among our Catholic funding partners, CAFOD in England and *Trocaire* in Ireland ignored the black letter and continued to support our work as much as they could. Also, several Protestant funding agencies, who understood the nature of the struggle perhaps better than many Catholics, supported the refugees in the camps, through the ZP. CIIR was our closest friend during those difficult months. They knew many leaders in the struggle personally, and also had strong and trusted contacts in the British Government.

'The life-span of the ZP was short. It dated from our expulsion in August 1978 to Independence in April 1980. After much discernment and soul searching, the staff decided not to dissolve the ZP but to bring it back home to assist with the reintegration, education and

---

19 Coopération Internationale pour le Dévelopment et la Solidarité.

vocational training of the former refugees and of those former guerrilla fighters who wanted to join civilian life, rather than the newly formed Zimbabwe National Army. Since the ZP project was a Catholic organisation, I informed the ZCBC[20] in Harare of our plans and asked for their approval to bring the ZP home. The bishops objected very strongly. They did not want to see what was still considered by many whites as a terrorist organisation led by a Catholic priest, in their jurisdiction and therefore under their ultimate responsibility. So, after yet more discernment and soul-searching, we decided that I would resign as director and return to the Zimbabwe Jesuit Province to receive an assignment from the Provincial, and Judith Acton, who was not a Catholic, would be appointed the new director and take the Project back to Zimbabwe, as a non-Catholic organisation – although Sr Janice McLaughlin was deeply involved – to do exactly what we had decided earlier.'

Jesuit Refugee Service

'As I was packing to fly back to Harare, I received a letter from Fr General Pedro Arrupe asking me to come to Rome for a consultation. Fr Arrupe was deeply moved by the tragedy of the Vietnamese boat people and by the suffering of refugees in Africa's Sahel region who were perishing from hunger after several consecutive years of drought. He invited about a dozen Jesuits engaged in refugee work in different ways and in different parts of the world to meet and he asked each of us to describe our work with refugees and the organisation we were attached to. He then asked us to leave the room so he could speak alone with his consultors. The following day, I was called back to meet him and his advisors. He told me he liked the model and way of proceeding of the ZP and asked me if I could stay on in Rome for a few months to help get a Jesuit Refugee Service (JRS) off the ground.

In October 1980, Fr General wrote a letter to the whole Society announcing that he was launching the JRS, and was appealing for volunteers to work in the camps in Thailand and in southern Ethiopia. Former missionaries from Congo and from India volunteered and were joined by Jesuits from America, France, Australia and other parts of Asia. The work of JRS grew rapidly. Fr Arrupe wanted the office in Rome to be a kind of switchboard. He saw the refugee issue as a

---

20 Zimbabwe Catholic Bishops' Conference.

short-term temporary phenomenon. As Chairman of the Conference of Superiors General in Rome, he motivated other orders and Congregations, women and men to help. Many welcomed Ethiopian refugees into their houses, and helped them to reach the United States and Canada.

'But with the growth of JRS went the growth of problems! In 1981, 10 months after he launched the JRS, Fr Arrupe visited several provinces in East Asia. The last stop of his exhausting journey was Bangkok, Thailand, where serious conflicts had broken out between the local Church, the JRS workers in the camps and the Spanish Jesuit missionaries working in Thailand. Fr Arrupe first met Cardinal Michai, then the Spanish Jesuits, and then the JRS men. Later that evening, before he went to the airport to fly back to Rome, he met all Jesuits together. Towards the end of his speech, he said something remarkable and very moving. Perhaps he had a premonition of what would happen a few hours later, back in Rome.'

> I will say one more thing, and please don't forget it. Pray. Pray much. Problems such as these are not solved by human efforts. I am telling you things I want to emphasize, a message – perhaps my swan song for the Society. We pray at the beginning and the end – we are good Christians! But in our three-day meetings, if we spent half a day in prayer about the conclusions we expect to come to, or about our points of view we will have very different 'lights'. And we will come to very different syntheses – ones we could never find in books nor arrive at through discussion.
>
> Right here we have a classic case: if we are indeed in the frontline of a new apostolate in the Society, we have to be enlightened by the Holy Spirit. These are not the pious words of a novice master. What I am saying is 100 per cent from St Ignatius. When I decided to come to Thailand, they said I would visit refugee camps. I have been to camps before. What we have done here is much more important. I am so happy, and I think it is providential that I came here.[21]

On arrival in Rome he had a stroke and Dieter stayed with him that night. Arrupe lived for another ten years and Dieter took visiting JRS workers to see him in his room.

---

21 Jesuit Refugee Service. *Everybody's Challenge: Essential Documents of JRS*, 1980-2000, pp. 33-7.

Dieter returned to Zimbabwe at the end of 1989, after almost ten years with JRS and was sent to Marymount where there were camps for Mozambican refugees fleeing the civil strife in their country in the 1990s. Two were near the mission – at Mazowe Bridge, where there were 35,000 refugees, and Nyamatikiti with 3,000. Dieter Scholz and Fidelis Mukonori provided pastoral care. In the villages of Mount Darwin there were many traumatised people. Fr Norbert Gille helped them to come to terms with their grief by organising all-night meetings to lament and cry over their killed relatives and so get the pain out of their system.

The reader will notice that I have relied heavily of Bishop Dieter Scholz's own words for this treatment of the CCJP, ZP and JRS as he was deeply involved in all three. At the end of Chairman John Deary's 1978 Annual Report for the CCJP he speaks of the 'high quality of Dieter's work, his dedication, sound judgement and commitment'.[22] Deary also acknowledged the 'dedication and courage' of Canadian Marist Brother Arthur Dupuis and he ends his appreciative comments about his colleagues by mentioning his wife, Pat, who was almost killed when a grenade was thrown into their home while John was away in the US. Not only was his family in physical danger but his children had to endure the taunts of their schoolmates. 'They bore the brunt of the antipathy shown by many towards the commission.'

'Healing wounds, healing a nation'

Mention has been made of the trauma people suffered as a result of having their family members brutally killed during the war and of the efforts of some, for example, Fr Norbert Gille, to bring healing. We will also see in the next chapter the efforts of Br Canisius Chishiri to bring healing through 'crying retreats'. This task was not lost sight of in the following decades, but there was opposition. When new atrocities were committed in the *Gukurahundi*, the campaign ostensibly against dissidents in Matabeleland in the 1980s, the Legal Resources Foundation (LRF) and the CCJP prepared a report, *Breaking the Silence, Building True Peace* which recounted the horrifying details of what happened. The publication of the report was intended to be a step towards healing the wounds. There had been a news blackout and most people did not know what was going on. Brian Enright was

---

22 CCJP Chairman's report for the year ending 31 December 1978, p 12.

representative of many of us when he wrote in his newsletter to his friends in May 1985, 'in the south of the country ... there is a certain amount of dissident activity'. There was frustration among many of the Ndebele people at the outcome of the independence struggle and small numbers of 'dissidents' did take up arms but, seemingly, with no clear goal.

The response of the government was to send in a brigade of soldiers trained by North Korea. In their operation against the dissidents they killed a large number of innocent people. There seems to have been a revengeful tone as up to 20,000 people were killed. A powerful, because understated, account of how it affected families in the region is given by Christopher Mlalazi in *Running with Mother*.[23] The people in the story have no idea what is going on and constantly say, 'if the prime minister (Mugabe) knew what was happening he would stop it'. Mugabe knew exactly what was going on. He ordered it.

The Catholic Bishops were split on what to do; three were in favour of issuing the report investigating the atrocities while three were against.[24] This meant, in effect, the bishops would block the issue of the report. They probably shared the view of President Mugabe that its publication would be divisive and open old wounds. Mugabe was fiercely opposed and blasted 'the likes of ... the Aurets and Coltarts (Mike Auret was Chairman of the Justice and Peace Commission and David Coltart was a lawyer active in justice issues) of our society who seem bent on ruining the national unity and loyalty of our people'.[25] He wanted Gukurahundi swept under the carpet and forgotten.[26] In the end the LRF issued the report on their own. Inevitably, its impact would have been stronger if it had also been broadcast though the Catholic church.

Zimbabwe is still in need of healing. We have had no equivalent to the Truth and Reconciliation Commission which took place in South Africa in the 1990s.

---

23 C' Mlalazi, *Running with Mother* (Harare: Weaver Press, 2012).
24 Coltart, p. 241.
25 Coltart, p. 244.
26 I write this on the day (15 July 2021) when the British government has announced plans to issue an amnesty for all atrocities committed over thirty years in Northern Ireland (1968-98). There is outrage on all sides, with the Irish Prime Minister saying in Parliament, 'how can you offer an amnesty for murder?'

The violent deaths of seven Jesuits

In 1979, while the war was still hot, the Catholic Church in Rhodesia[27] celebrated its centenary. It was a consoling event which could lighten, for a moment, the sufferings the people were enduring. Numbers were, inevitably, mentioned as signs of growth. They are the only tangible indicator available. So, from the eleven original missionaries who made their way up by ox-wagon from Grahamstown and crossed the Limpopo in 1879, there were now among black Catholic Christians, three bishops, sixty-three priests, twenty-one brothers and five hundred and thirty-four sisters. The bishops' letter for the occasion played down the war, simply referring to 'the present difficulties'.[28] They were conscious they were bishops for white people as well as blacks and had no wish to come down on one side rather than the other.[29] The rural people 'in the middle' bore the full impact of the war. One woman, in the Musami area, lost her husband who was shot for breaking the curfew by the Rhodesian soldiers and her brother was shot by the guerrillas for failing to give them food.[30]

It was a coincidence, but still a reason to reflect, that the years surrounding the centenary were marked by the deaths of seven Jesuits who in many ways echoed their forbears of 1879. Like them they were from different countries – Germany, England and Ireland – and like them they were priests (five) and brothers (two), and finally like them they were mostly in their thirties and forties. If I tell their stories[31] briefly here my aim is to show how ordinary they were. They were just

---

27 It was actually at the time called 'Zimbabwe Rhodesia' – a desperate last-minute attempt to please everyone, but which only reinforced the apprehension that things were about to change. The name lasted for one year.

28 The letter is dated 8 April 1979 and is signed by Patrick Chakaipa (Harare), Henry Karlen (Bulawayo), Tobias Chiginya (Gweru), Ignatius Prieto (Wankie) and Helmut Reckter (Sinoia).

29 At the funeral of Archbishop Francis Markall in 1992 President Mugabe mentioned Markall's support of the liberation struggle, but he also mentioned his direct words to him: 'But remember, Robert, no violence!' That advice must have been given in the 1960s because by the time Mugabe came out of prison in 1974 violence was in full swing in the north-east of the country. Markall would have been on first-name terms with Mugabe as he knew him at Kutama in the 1930s and helped his mother when his father left her and went off to Bulawayo and married another woman.

30 D. Harold-Barry (ed.), *They Stayed On, The Stories of the Seven Jesuits Martyred in the Struggle for Zimbabwe* (Gweru: Mambo Press, 2000), p. 13. See next footnote.

31 I have done this at more length in *They Stayed On*.

like us. Yet their deaths set a seal on the century of Jesuit presence in the country.

The seven died in four different incidents during the closing years of Zimbabwe's protracted war. Three were German, three British and one Irish. They were all serving in rural missions, easy targets for guerrillas who interpreted in their own way the general instructions they received from their distant commanders. It was never the policy of the liberation movements to target missions but there were some guerrillas with private agendas.

The opening and most dramatic event occurred on 6 February 1977, when a group of armed men arrived by night at St Paul's, Musami, 80 km east of Harare.[32] They lined up four Jesuits and four Dominican sisters, all European, and shot and killed three of the Jesuits and all the sisters. The Jesuit and Dominican Superiors, Patrick McNamara and Sr de Pace, drove out next day consoling each other as they went but cautioning that, 'some of our best people will falter and we may have to cope with reactions that are not to be misunderstood … Fear will grip many … Is it us next?'

Although we had vague expectations that we might be caught up in the war, when it actually happened we entered a state of shock. The British, for instance, knew all about their martyrs under Elizabeth I, but that was four hundred years ago. They did not expect something similar in the time of Elizabeth II. We were numbed into a belief that our support for the aims of the liberation struggle, though not some of its methods, would be our protection. Superiors knew they were risking our companions' lives by leaving them in rural missions when they could have withdrawn them to the safety of the towns. But they discerned that our witness to the gospel called us to this risk. The seven Jesuits who died could have asked to leave but they didn't.

In all of Africa only six counties – Algeria, Angola, Guinea Bissau, Mozambique, Namibia and Zimbabwe – had such drawn out and bitter wars of independence. South Africa too had a long struggle but it was less of a rural guerrilla struggle than a political confrontation in the cities. We have seen how European settlers arrived in Zimbabwe in 1890 intending to stay permanently. They claimed the country was never a colony. Over the decades they took step after step to ensure that African advancement would be measured and would never be

---

32 This has also been treated in Chapter 4 above.

able to compete with European control. Smouldering resentment among Africans, which had first erupted in war in the 1890s and been crushed, showed itself again in the 1950s and twenty years later it flared up into a costly but successful uprising.

Unlike the situation in El Salvador, in the 1980s the Jesuits in Zimbabwe were on both sides of the conflict, as has been mentioned above: they served the Europeans and the African communities. The 'official' position of the bishops and the religious communities was to support the aims of the struggle. But there were weighty dissenting voices. Europeans were never more than 5 per cent of the population but they carried disproportionately strong influence even in church circles. And Jesuits who served among them were not untainted by the propaganda that poured forth daily from the *Rhodesian Herald* and the Rhodesian TV. Besides, some of our Jesuits who served in remote rural areas and who came from East Germany where they had had first-hand experience of Communism in action, were wary of the propaganda coming from the other side of the border in Mozambique.

The result, in the words, referred to above[33] of Stephen Buckland, a locally born white Jesuit, was 'a deep uncertainty and ambiguity within the Jesuit consciousness'. And he went on, 'the Jesuits were apparently unable as a body to produce a coherent policy even on such practical matters as how to react to the presence of guerrillas at missions, let alone more theoretical questions about the church's attitude to the political aspirations of the people'. On the other hand, in a typically generous and healing comment, Fidelis Mukonori, a locally born black Jesuit, said, 'the Jesuits had a coherent policy of having no policy, because some worked among the blacks, some among the whites'.

We cannot leave it there and I would like to quote more of Stephen Buckland's thoughtful words in the 1994 *Crossroads* article referred to above:

> There is a deeper uncertainty and ambiguity within the Jesuit consciousness which was exposed particularly painfully at the time of the deaths. That agents of the Rhodesian Security Forces may have perpetrated the murders (at Musami) was, for many, an idea which had dangerous implications. And there were others for whom the idea that the guerrillas were responsible was equally

---
33 Cf fn 4.

unsettling. Why were these Jesuits, whose lives spoke of simplicity and dedication, the targets of such brutal attacks? None of them was actively involved in any kind of politics which could have conceivably been considered subversive…

We need to respond to this in two ways: firstly, to find the courage responsibly and creatively to re-examine and if necessary to re-assess our own Jesuit contribution to the history of Zimbabwe. The question here is: has our Jesuit presence over the past 100 years been of such a nature that it has truly spoken of the gospel witness to justice and peace – not just in abstract principles but in practice? This is not to imply that the personal discipline, sacrifice and commitment of earlier and even present generations of Jesuits must count for nothing. The question is larger than that of personal presence. The loss of seven men was more than merely personal: it raised quite fundamental questions about the role of the Jesuits, of the Church, and even of the gospel in Zimbabwe. There are aspects of our own history which, without losing sight of the genuine and acknowledged achievements, we need to interrogate: we need to orient those achievements for future generations of Jesuits. And, secondly, we need both to renew our commitment to theological reflection on our continuing role in Zimbabwean society, and to widen and deepen the sources which feed into that reflection. Here the question is: what are the sources of our renewed reflection on our presence?

Buckland goes on to mention the work of Ian Linden, whose 1980 book, *The Catholic Church and the Struggle for Zimbabwe*, is quite critical of the Jesuits. Linden's interpretation comes down to the concept of 'two churches', an idea that echoes an earlier treatment in this book about a 'dual mission'. First, there is the institutional teaching church which is largely white, and then there is the 'church of the people', largely black and poor.

Linden argues that the institutional church, influenced predominantly by the Jesuits… was so involved with the colonial project that it failed to confront the settler state on the central questions of justice[34] … and took refuge in the building and

---

34 Roger Riddell, while still a Jesuit in the early 1970s, did confront the regime with other students at the University of Rhodesia. They were arrested and, 'In the late afternoon, we were filed into the Salisbury magistrate's court

protection of institutions and, concerning social justice, in the teaching of theoretical abstractions rather than practical action ... (When the church did confront the regime) it was not on issues principally concerned with the realities of injustice facing ordinary Zimbabweans ... but those concerned with rights of Church institutions vis-à-vis the state.

Dieter Scholz had written something similar much earlier; When 'the churches attempted to bring about a change in attitudes and behaviour of white and black... the bishops recognised the basic weakness of their arguments: the fact that legally institutionalised injustices had for far too long been allowed to exist without protest and as if they were inevitable.[35] I believe that it is this dilemma which gives rise to the Church's sustained attempt to retain racial segregation as a matter of convenience, while at the same time affirming non-racialism as a matter of practice ... The Catholic Church in Rhodesia can no longer efficiently operate on these two conflicting levels.'[36]

According to Linden, the Church went through a conversion in the late 1970s when 'brought face to face with violent realities of the nation's situation. ... It was only through this slow and painful process ... that the Catholic Church learned to "listen" to the voices from below rather than "teach" from on top. ... The initiative in the church passed from the hierarchy... to a smaller, younger, more aware group of laity and clergy spearheaded by the Catholic Justice and Peace Commission...'

Buckland observes that Linden's 'sharp critical tool' was not popular with Jesuits who saw him as 'anachronistic', 'pushing back into the past questions which are themselves modern'. But there is no escaping the truth of a 'great division ... between the institutional church and the church of the people. We were a racially divided Church.'

---

in batches of 10 to 15, where we were formally charged under the Special Emergency Regulations of the Law and Order Maintenance Act with having taken part in an illegal procession. We were then released on $20 bail and ordered to appear in court again in two weeks' time. Somehow, I made my way back to Prestage House (the Jesuits residence near the university) where I explained what had happened and - distressingly - was almost universally condemned not just for being arrested but even for demonstrating.'

35 Plangger, p. 62.
36 Scholz, pp. 199, 209.

In conclusion, Buckland writes,

> It would have been easier to assimilate these deaths if we could see them within the context of a Jesuit struggle for justice. But, as it is, they defy any simplistic interpretation and require us to continue to interrogate our own experience in the light of the gospel for which they were prepared to die. We cannot afford to let their memory die; but we must face courageously the questions that their lives and deaths pose for us. This may be their most important legacy. ... To what extent are we able to acknowledge a popular African Christianity...? To what extent are we able and ready to encourage it to grow? To what extent are we able to draw strength from it ourselves?

It is amazing to think how relevant these questions are today, forty years after Linden wrote and more than twenty-five years since Stephen gave us his analysis. The institutional Church throughout the world has been shown to have a terrible record in facing its own responsibility for the abuse of vulnerable people in its schools and homes. Bishops, the visible centres of authority in the Church, have been numbed and confused by the assault. The 'church of the people' has observed all this with a mixture of sadness and excitement. This church feels for its bishops, knowing they largely inherited a situation for which they, personally, are not responsible. But this church is also excited at the prospect of a seed dying and bearing much fruit. In 1980, a year after the euphoria of the visit of Pope John Paul to Ireland, Frank Duff, founder of the Catholic lay movement, the Legion of Mary, gave a talk just months before his death in which he reflected on the Church in Ireland as being 'in the grips of winter'. His hearers were astonished but he ended, 'one day, spring will come'. That kind of hope is there, solidly, in the 'church of the people' even though they are now much reduced in number. They go about their business only half-interested in the anxieties of their bishops. They know there is a springtime coming.

Fyodor Dostoevsky wrote in *The Brothers Karamazov*, 'Salvation will come from the people, from their faith and their meekness. Fathers and teachers, watch over the people's faith and this will not be a dream. I've been struck all my life in our great people by their dignity, their true and seemly dignity.' And signs of the 'people's church' are with us everywhere. There was a time when the missionaries were in charge. The war changed that. The people knew better than the missionaries what was happening in the district, and the lives of the priests, sisters and brothers were now the responsibility of the people who advised them what to do. That has not changed since the war. Although there are priests who would like to be in charge, they find, or they will find if they have not already, they can do nothing unless they are prepared to be servants.

-oOo-

Many other religious and countless laity died in our bitter war. The deaths of so many Christians – clergy, religious and lay – together with the stirring work of the Catholic Commission for Justice and Peace, meant that the churches came out of the war well respected. And as regards the four incidents where Jesuits died, memorials were erected to remember them. The shrine at Musami, which was unveiled by Vice President Simon Muzenda, sees a commemoration service each year on 6 February.

So who were these seven? Were they Miguel Pros playing cat and mouse with the Mexican revolutionaries or Edmund Campions 'bragging' to the English government that 'the price is reckoned'? No. None of them stood out as particularly brilliant or noticeably saintly. At least two of them were difficult to live with.

Martin Thomas (1932-77)

Martin Thomas was quintessentially English. At St Michael's Mhondoro, in the middle of the African bush, I was entertained by Martin to afternoon tea with trimmed cucumber sandwiches in the large thatched hut that was the community room. It was as though in order to give himself fully to Africa, he had to keep a hold of his own roots. He grew up in Wimbledon, a suburb of London, where there was a Jesuit church and college. His father was an officer in the Boer war and fudged a report on a young man who fell asleep while on sentry duty, an offence for which the mandatory sentence was execution. The man was spared. Martin must have learnt that discerning kindness at home for he was well known for it. He wore his watch upside down to enable little boys at Hodder primary school (in the UK) where he taught for a while to read the time and he never changed þack when he left the school. Never a high flyer in academic matters he was gifted in practical details and saw to the drilling of two boreholes at St Michael's which gave adequate water to the growing mission. School fees at £4 a year were beyond the reach of many parents and Martin introduced a flexible system whereby they could pay in buckets of maize or bags of vegetables.

In 1974 Martin moved to St Paul's Musami. He was no longer in charge and so was free from the heavy responsibility he had carried at St Michael's. He taught in the school and each weekend would take off on his motorbike for the outstations to celebrate Mass and visit the people. In 1975 his parents died and he went home for a month's leave. It was a happy time with his family but with hindsight his sister, Dr Elizabeth Clubb, recalled a more sombre note. Martin gave her a book[37] which had a poem (*The White Horse,* about the death of St Columba) containing the lines:

> …my departure is nighing.
> Dying's but awaiting, my end is tomorrow.

Martin made his final commitment as a Jesuit on 2 February 1977 at Chishawasha, and the next day returned to Musami. Fr Dunstan Myerscough, who survived the shooting, later reported that on 6 February 1977, intruders with guns came to the mission at night and gathered the missionaries they could find on the road by the convent. There were four Jesuits – three priests and one brother - and four Dominican sisters. Realising what was about to happen they asked absolution[38] of the priests. There was a burst of gunfire and the sound of running feet and then all was quiet. Myerscough had instinctively fallen with the others but was untouched by the bullets. He picked himself up and went to each to see if there was any sign of life in any of them. There was none. He later reported one of the gunmen as saying to him beforehand, 'We are not going to shoot you, we just want to show you something.' In view of the lack of clear consensus about who the gunmen were at Musami, these words simply muddy the waters. If this gunman were a guerrilla, why would he say this? If he was a Selous Scout and wanted to incriminate the guerrillas in the eyes of the missionaries, as one theory proposed, why would be give

---

37 P.H. Gosse, Philip, *The Romance of Natural History* (London: J. Nisbet, 1860).
38 Absolution is the word used to denote the forgiveness the Church gives to people who try to turn from sin. In John's gospel, when Jesus rose from the dead, he gave power to his disciples to forgive sins, John 20:23.

himself and his comrades away, as he would do with these words?

For many years after the terrible events at Musami opinions as to who was responsible oscillated this way and that. Fidelis Mukonori, a Jesuit who was deeply involved in the CCJP at the time, showed courage and steady resolve in researching this and many other incidents during the war. When I discussed the event yet again with him forty years later his verdict was clear and direct: it was the Selous Scouts. And he gave five reasons in support, mentioned in Chapter 4.[39]

When Jesuit Superior, Patrick McNamara, and the Dominican Mother General, Sr de Pace Pauler, came out next day and saw the disfigured bodies, De Pace remembered the prayer they used to say at home in Germany when the bombs fell, 'Hilf Maria, es ist Zeit'. Mary help, this is it. They 'rang the bell for Mass for the dead and all the silent Mission stirred as hundreds of students filed into the church'. Later, 'buses of pressmen arrived, some mocking and jeering, "now you have it, you bullet-proof missionaries"'.

Martin, the most gentle of people, died a violent death. His charm and kindness hid a steely determination. I noticed a change in his last years. It was as if everything – his Englishness, his family, his Jesuit vocation – all came together into a final 'no fuss' giving of his life for others.

John Conway (1920-77)

There were two other Jesuits among the seven killed on that terrible night at Musami. One was Br John Conway from Tralee, Ireland. His first application to join the Jesuits was lost and he waited a year before applying again. In Rhodesia, his official job was to care for the boreholes, pumps and vehicles on the missions where he worked, but he soon developed his special gift with children. Everywhere he went he told them stories – true or made up on the spot – and revealed the gospel to them in a way that held them. There was so much noise in his room that his fellow Jesuits 'banished' him in Musami to a hut of

---

39   Personal conversation with Fr Fidelis Mukonori SJ at Chishawasha Mission, 15 December 2019. The Selous Scouts were a 'fifth column', an organised military group working with, but not under the direct command of, the Rhodesian government. In *Selous Scouts: Top Secret War* (Alberton: Galago, 1982), Lt. Col. Ron Reid-Daly denies any involvement in the Musami massacres though the author mentions the mission in the context of the disinformation that accused the Scouts of being behind it. He says the police investigated but found no evidence of it. Pp 468-470.

his own a little way from the main house, which became known as 'Conway Castle'. I once asked him how he liked his life in Africa. 'One long holiday', was his reply and yet beneath all the fun and banter, which sometimes drove his more staid English companions crazy, was what his companions called 'a hidden core'. 'One day they will come for us just as we are' he told them and, of course, they shared his sense of impending crisis. Yet his sense of fun was undimmed and he told Gerry Finnieston of his plans to escape disguised as a nun. I visited his relatives in Tralee a year or two after his death and they showed me a plaque in memory of him in a corner of a square in the town. There is also a stained glass window devoted to him in the Jesuit college in Sydney, Australia.

Christopher Shepherd-Smith (1943-77)

The third Jesuit who died that night was Christopher Shepherd-Smith (Sheppy). He was born in Kenya and the family moved to Geita mine in Tanganyika where, in his mother's words, 'it was the old story of drink and debt and I had to leave'. She got a job as matron in Loreto Convent School in Nairobi, and Chris and his brother and sister grew up near the precincts of the convent. As a child Chris would wander into the nuns' quarters while they were having a silent breakfast and cause hilarious havoc. He joined the Jesuits in England and made his way back to Africa in 1965 where he studied Shona, missiology and social science. Sr Dr Aquina Weinrich OP found him sensitive and an excellent analyst. After his ordination in 1974 Chris went to Musami where he single-mindedly applied himself to work on the outstations. But it was here that a trait which had been observed all along showed itself. In his uncomplicated way he did not understand why others did not see things as he did. His companions found him narrow and more papal than the pope. For Chris everything was clear. There were no grey areas. Mark Hackett, his superior at Musami, found him 'impossible'. Years later when I was putting together my book on the seven, I asked Mark if he would like to revise his judgement. He just added an adjective: 'He was absolutely impossible'.

If I labour what John McCann, another Jesuit who worked with Chris at Musami, calls 'Chris's wave-length, and with the best will in the world it was difficult to tune into him', I do so, knowing that at the deepest level Chris *did* fit in.[40] One who knew him, but whom I have been unable to identify, wrote, 'a month before his death Chris told me, that the missionaries' sufferings were nothing compared to the people's. All of us, he said, had to be prepared for the worst – even death. All this was said most calmly, peacefully'.

Such, briefly, are the stories of the three Jesuits who died on that night of 6 February 1977. There were also four Dominicans shot at the same place on the same occasion. It was almost ninety years since the Jesuits travelled up to what became Fort Salisbury (Harare) and were followed some months later by the Dominican sisters. They had shared so much over the years on different mission stations; it was somehow fitting that they stood together facing those bullets on that dark night.

There were three other incidents in which four more Jesuits were killed: one at Makumbi, two at Makonde and one at Kangaire.

Desmond 'Gussie' Donovan (1927-78)

'Gussie' – I never remember him being called Desmond – was killed while visiting an outstation of Makumbe Mission on 15 January 1978. But this date was not known with any certainty for four years. His motorbike was later found but not his body.

Gus was born in Leeds in England in 1927. His father, a teacher, died when he was three and his mother struggled – the 1930s were the years of the depression – to care for him and his sister. A Jesuit family friend, Fr Augustine Ganley, suggested Gus go to St Aidan's in South Africa and it was there that he completed his schooling. He joined the Jesuits in 1947 and spent four of his student years teaching in St Ignatius, London. His contemporaries remember him as a man with a short fuse and in one exasperated moment he poured a pot of marmalade over the head of Michael Campbell-Johnson, later the English Jesuit provincial. After ordination Gus returned to South Africa and St Aidan's. Fr Gregory Croft[41] tells us he had a genius for caring for 'bad' boys and gave them his time. And Gus could be tough with those in his care, one of whom was Michael Lewis SJ, who had cause to remember. Gus was a perfectionist with himself and with everyone else. In 1967 he came to the then Rhodesia and

---

40 Harold-Barry, p. 26.
41 Croft, a close friend of Gus Donovan, wrote the account of him in ***They Stayed On***.

applied himself to learn the language with awesome thoroughness. He was first posted to Musami, where Fr Mark Hackett remembers his exhaustive attention to all the details of running a large mission. But his perfectionism could cloud his judgement, as when during wartime he shot some pigs that, despite repeated warnings to the owners, strayed into the mission vegetable garden. Mike Lewis was to say later, 'he was a warm and affectionate man who never learnt to deal with his emotions'.[42]

His last posting was Makumbe Mission, where he threw himself into the pastoral work in the outstations seemingly oblivious that the war was all round the mission. He was warned several times by the people[43] to stay away but he took no notice. On the fateful day he was captured by ZANLA[44] forces when visiting a sick person at his second outstation. He was beaten and bayoneted and his body thrown into river. Mark Hackett considered Gus 'a great man. He lost his patience a lot, but always made up. I can't think of any other Jesuit whom I would rather have with me in a difficult situation.'[45]

Gregor Richert (1930-78)[46]

Two German Jesuits, Fr Gregor Richert and Br Bernhard Lisson, were shot by ZIPRA[47] guerrillas at St Rupert Mayer Mission, in Magonde (Makondi) 200 km west of Harare on 27 June 1978.

Richert was a good correspondent and his letters were published ten years after his death.[48] He was born in 1930 in Danzig (Gdansk, then part of Germany and now in Poland) and his family had to flee west at the end of the war. He joined the Jesuits in 1948 and came to Rhodesia in 1961. He worked in Marymount, Guruve, Chitsungo and St Albert's, Mount Darwin, before arriving in Makonde in 1968. All of these places were in their foundation stages and he built his own missionary approach in tandem with the physical building of

---

42 *They Stayed On*, p. 47.
43 Personal conversation with Fr Fidelis Mukonori SJ at Chishawasha Mission, 15 December 2019.
44 The guerrilla movement headed by Robert Mugabe.
45 *They Stayed On*, p. 49.
46 Fr Karl-Ferdinand Schmidt wrote the account of Richert's life in *They Stayed On*.
47 Zimbabwe People's Revolutionary Army, a guerrilla movement headed by Joshua Nkomo.
48 *Euer Busch-Pater von Umpfuli* (Leipzig: St Benno-Verlag, 1989).

the missions. This was evident when he came to Makonde, 'a fallow country... (where) Fr Rudolf Kensy had built an oasis in this otherwise stony and sandy reserve'.[49] Sometime later he wrote:

> (Easter) was really celebrated at Magondi.[50] On Palm Sunday we went in a solemn procession through the villages waving proper palms. On Maundy Thursday some ... were most impressed by the foot-washing ... I (hadn't) got twelve (Catholic) men ... so I invited twelve influential men of the neighbourhood, all of them non-Christians. It was a sweeping success ...

But Gregor saw the dependence of the people on maize, and in a bad year there would be hunger. He proposed cotton as a cash crop and after a faltering start it took off in the area. He was also deeply involved as 'schools' manager' even after the government took over the schools. He loved the work but it was exhausting. In the early seventies, Makonde had been spared experience of the war but towards the end of that decade, people talked of the war drawing closer. In late March, 1977, Gregor wrote, 'It really can't be denied any longer that the whole situation is becoming more tense every week.' I quote again the words we first saw in Chapter 5:

> One time we were mighty proud of our measurable achievements ... but now has that all to become desolate, forgotten? ... [I]t is now time after a period of more outward growth for the message of Christ to take stronger and deeper root than before. But if this is to be achieved, then the heart of the one who has devoted himself to this task must bleed. ... We are not spared the fear and distress of the heat caused by the terror all around us through which we also, like Him, must live. This is part of our self-sacrifice. But what this world considers mad, senseless, futile and foolish wastefulness is – if we really take God's word at least once seriously – the fulfilment of all our longing, the final arrival at our destination, for which we were created, to win everything.[51]

Around 4.00 p.m. on 27 June 1978 three armed men entered the mission and one of them asked to see Gregor alone. He offered them tea and the discussion was of money. It appears there was little in the

---

49   Richert in *They Stayed On*, p. 55.
50   The mission was still known by this name in his time.
51   See Chapter 5, fn 21.

mission at the time and the three became angry and shot Gregor and also Br Lisson who was repairing a truck at the time.

Bernhard Lisson (1909-78)

Like Gregor, Br Bernhard Lisson grew up in a part of East Germany which is now Poland, where he qualified as a blacksmith. A powerful man with what Wolfgang Thamm calls 'a frightening physique',[52] he was more used to a hammer than a pen. But he did write of himself that as a boy he wondered, 'How long did the little boy Jesus have to wait in the shed of Bethlehem until he was allowed out! Then the light dawned on me. He and the Holy Family needed help.' He joined the Jesuits in 1931 and in the novitiate he 'began to develop his talent for invention and improvisation, converting a rusty old locomotive into a potato steamer with which to process wagon loads of potatoes for cattle feed' (Thamm). In 1935, he said farewell to his family at home in Bowallno and there is no record he ever returned there. He was one of the four Jesuits who founded the new mission of the East German province, formalised in 1959. Bernhard worked at Triashill for thirteen years before moving to Musami, where he was badly burnt when he helped fix a car that had broken down on the way to Salisbury. It took Sr Kiliana OP months to cure his dreadful burns. In 1959, he went to Marymount, from which St Albert's was founded. Br Lisson was the driving power behind the building of the new mission, 200 km north of Harare. Fr Norbert Gille SJ remembers the day when all the priests and brothers and mission helpers were summoned to 'lift the trusses with nothing but a long rope and the booming voice of Br Lisson shouting, "Pull! Pull!" We did. The walls vibrated; the gable wobbled but with the genius of Br Lisson we succeeded.' Lisson trained the people he worked with so that when he was away everything continued to work well. And he was ever available for the endless requests for fixing cooking pots, bicycles, scotch carts and so forth.

In 1972, now over sixty and beginning to feel his age and the effects of a back injury he sustained at Musami when he fell into a well, he moved to a smaller place where he would be in semi-retirement: Makonde.

---

52 W. Thamm, in *They Stayed on*, p. 66.

Gerhard Pieper (1940-78)

Gerry's room at the old German philosophate in Pullach, Oscar Wermter tells us, was a virtual tavern! Gerry's hospitality stretched to filtered coffee, cigarettes and cognac. From his novitiate, when the second years demanded the first years' strict observance of all 656 rules and Gerry branded it 'fanaticism', to the day he died, Gerry was an advocate of humanity and common sense. He had a vivid imagination which he used to develop his pastoral work and was organised and deeply committed to the people.

He left St Albert's after it was closed for the duration of the war in 1975 and went for his tertianship to Australia. His tertian master, Frank Wallace,[53] later reflected on Gerry's life and quoted from T.S. Eliot's *Murder in the Cathedral,* 'Martyrdom is always the design of God, for his love of men, to bring them back to his ways. It's never the design of man; for the true martyr is he who has become the instrument of God, who has lost his will in the will of God, and who no longer desires anything for himself, not even the glory of being a martyr.'

He was shot on St Stephen's day 1978, at Kangaire Mission, some 250 km north-east of Harare. He had been warned, but wrote in his final Christmas letter to his relatives and friends, 'Many of you will perhaps ask, "Is it worthwhile? Would it not be better to leave these people to their own fate? Why try to help when everything is going up in flames anyhow? Why invest money and one's life's work if the people show no gratitude?" Believe me, if we were to leave now, we would be like the shepherd who leaves his flock because he is only a hireling.' He stayed and was riddled with bullets outside his house.

Oscar Wermter SJ, who was assistant (socius) to Provincial Henry Wardale at the time, wrote that Henry was deeply shocked by the death of Gerry Pieper, the last of the seven to die. 'For the rest of the war he was absolutely determined not to let another Jesuit die. It is no exaggeration to say that for the whole of 1979, the last year of the war, Fr Wardale did not allow himself to be distracted for one minute from

---

53 Born in Melbourne in 1914, Frank Wallace joined the Jesuits in 1934 and was ordained in 1948. He was tertian director for about five years but was also head of a school and a major source of Ignatian spirituality for last fifteen years of his life. He published two books, and for a while edited the magazine, *The Messenger of the Sacred Heart*. He died in 1993.

watching his men and concerning himself with their safety. Literally day and night he was weighing up against each other the need to let his men stay with the people, ensuring at least minimal pastoral and medical care, and his firm resolve not to put another Jesuit life at risk. Maybe this ruined his health and brought about his own early death.'

Jesuit General Superior Pedro Arrupe called these seven, 'average, obscure, unrecognised ... people who never took part in broad national controversies. ... Why did the Lord choose them? I believe it was precisely because of their evangelical life ... There can be no slightest doubt about the unaffected simplicity of their lives.'

11

'And there was much else ...'

As we move towards the end of this account, I take a cue from John,[1] by pointing to the many other initiatives taken up by the Jesuits in Zimbabwe over the past fourteen decades. There is no particular common chord running through the following nineteen projects other than their origins in the one mission, but they deserve mention as indicators of the variety of initiatives that arose out of, and contributed to, the different works the Jesuits were engaged in.

Small Christian communities

Comunidades Cristãs de Base (CCB) – 'base communities' – was a catchphrase in the 1970s when the South American model of pastoral effectiveness centred on the small group where evangelisation could take place in depth in contrast to the large mission or urban parish where the individual could be lost. Africa took note and produced a variety of her own versions of the central idea that 'small is beautiful' in terms of pastoral care. In Zimbabwe, there were different emphases. Bishop (later Archbishop Chakaipa) initiated a Christian Community Programme (CCP) involving the training of ten leadership promoters who would train lay pastoral workers people in the archdiocese. The aim was to hasten the growth of a 'self reliant Church'.[2] The Jesuit archives index in Harare has a CCP Box 368 card but it bears the ominous message 'missing'. Memory and luck had to fill the gap. The bishop drew up a programme with the priests for a training programme

---
1   John 21:25.
2   Annual Report of the CCP 1981, p. 4. Box 391 A.

at Silveira House for seven lay leaders, two Jesuit brothers (Chishiri and Mandaza) and Sr Gemma Chifamba LCBL. It was a four-month course in scripture, the sacraments and pastoral care and it included elements of development work for the farmers and the youth. Frs Chikore, Mavudzi, Ribeiro, Modikayi SJ and Kapito SJ rooted the themes in the local culture and practice. The Silveira House staff were involved in teaching finance and accountancy. It was remarked at the time how the trainees, all from such different backgrounds, formed one community. At the conclusion of the course the promoters each went to a different area – three urban and seven rural – and began their work. They soon encountered the limitations of transport, communications and war, but a start was made.[3] Canisius Chishiri wrote in 1979,

> At least one feels the first part of the programme has been achieved which was to give people courses and bring about a general awareness of the changes in the Catholic Church and the call for lay people to be involved in the life of the parish. People are more aware of their duties in the parish. They may do things wrongly or badly but the fact remains they now know the running of the parish is their duty. We should allow room for mistakes; it is in that way people will grow.[4]

The Annual Report of the CCP for 1981 shows how the programme depended largely on the promoters, the trainees and the priest working together. If any of these did not 'buy into' the programme it failed. Joseph Mandaza, the other Jesuit in the scheme, wrote,

> I involve the people as much as possible in workshops, discussions and sharing groups. In some places it is hard to find people interested in Christianity. Usually women are more interested than men. To win these people, I visit them and discuss with them in a friendly way and try to see their point of view. … our Zimbabweans today are conscious of their dignity, their culture and their beliefs. The challenge is to help people integrate Christian teaching with their very life and customs so that they can live out Christianity in a way which is meaningful to them.

---

3 *Jesuit Missions*, Autumn 1975, p. 19.
4 Jesuit Province Newsletter, No 29, 17.1.80.

> ... In general the key is to be with people and among them.[5]

And Chishiri again,

> After independence people often think that the political party should do everything for them. I try to get across to my people that they cannot just sit back but have to take the initiative and accept responsibility.[6]

Reading the reports, I have the impression the CCP focused on supporting people during the war and consoling them afterwards. There is much emphasis on teaching while at the same time trying to understand the concerns of people. It does not appear that there was a focus on building small self-reliant communities where the members felt bound to one another and addressed social concerns in concert.

In Chinhoyi diocese, Bishop Helmut Reckter also promoted small Christian communities and called his pastoral workers to a course at St Peter's Training Centre for this purpose. There were ninety-six participants, priests, sisters, and catechists under the guidance of Fr Oskar Hirmer from the Lumko centre.

Looking back, one can see these as first steps towards a more participative church. The default position in the Catholic Church is top-down, meaning the people are told what to believe and do from above. But this no longer works and young people are voting with their feet, as the saying goes, leaving the Church and joining Pentecostal groups where everyone is involved. There they find a sense of belonging many of our Catholics do not experience in our church.

Francis has prepared the ground since the begining of his time as pope for a 'synodal' church and has now (late 2021) started a process with a set timetable. 'Synod' means 'walking together' and indicates a way in which the whole church moves forward as one.

University chaplain

Students at universities and other tertiary colleges do not easily fit into parish structures and they deserve special attention. Nobert Rwodzi SJ wrote,[7] 'One thing that drew me to desire to know better about the

---

5 Annual Report of the CCP 1981, p. 4. Box 391 A.
6 Jesuit Province Newsletter, op. cit.
7 In a private memo.

Jesuits was the simple fact that they had delegated someone to take care of us young people in universities.' From its inception, as the University of Rhodesia and Nyasaland in 1956, the national university had Jesuits[8] who were involved in the pastoral care of the staff and students. If there is truth in the assertion that Jesuits are at home in the academic world it was shown by their enduring involvement in tertiary institutes. Rwodzi believed the university chaplaincy played a huge role in his vocation and 'most importantly in guiding me and others in finding God in my studies. … When students are at university temptations are many, peer pressure is at its peak and it is time to make life decisions.' Without some guidance a person can make decisions they later regret. 'Simple Ignatian workshops, church gatherings, and conferences were instrumental in aiding us to make good decisions which many of us are proud of. … I regard this apostolate as very important and it should be strengthened.' Rwodzi points out there is only one Jesuit in Harare in this work and he is also the National Chaplain and cannot effectively visit all the third level institutions which fall within his responsibility. He would like to see at least one other scholastic given to chaplaincy work. The province could also invest more in student accommodation to help young people with a place of stay and worship. This would be in line with our chosen preference: 'to journey with young people in building a hope-filled future'.

Elphas Ndlovu also speaks of the impact of the university chaplain on his joining the Jesuits. 'The notion of loving and serving particularly struck me. Coming from a country where there is much injustice and corruption and little is done to curb them, the Jesuit mission of announcing a faith that does justice gave me a sense of belonging and a desire to offer myself for this mission.'

Fr Nigel Johnson was chaplain from 1990 to 2000 and saw the task as helping the students to apply their faith to the reality they faced in the country. It was a decade when the love affair with ZANU-PF gradually faded. In 1990 the government was still paying the students' grants and living expenses. These were generous enough for them to be able to pay some of their siblings' school fees and buy the latest

---

8 Ian Falconer, Paul Edwards, James Chaning Pearce, Nigel Johnson, Heribert Müller, Mpumelelo Moyo, Eugene Phiri, Dominic Tomuseni, Clyde Muropa, Tinashe Mhaka, Gilbert Banda, Isaac Fernandes and now Ashton Mugozhi.

fashions in clothing! What was more, the students had secure jobs waiting for them when they graduated. And they enjoyed the freedom of being able to make their voices heard without being harassed. Nigel had occasion to go to an international student chaplains' meeting in Hong Kong during those years and he was shocked to discover the pressure some students in other countries were under. They had neither the time nor the energy to raise their voices and many did not have the freedom.

All this was about to change. The government after 2000 was feeling the pressure of international displeasure and economic retraction. Pay-outs to students were one of the casualties. It was not government strategy to keep the students poor and hungry so as to keep them quiet, but in the new century over the years, this is what happened. The students' appetite for protests and raising their voices evaporated so that today all is quiet on the campus. Regular closures of the university and banning of individuals, due to disturbances, had an impact on their studies and survival, and obtaining a degree became uppermost in their minds. Two students who were banned found refuge at Silveira House and the late Sr Janice McLaughlin, who was there at the time, suggested they write about their experiences. The result was a well-researched small book which, unfortunately, contained one paragraph which the person referred to considered defamatory and he threatened legal action. The book[9] had to be withdrawn and unsold copies publicly burnt in a twenty-first century version of an *auto-da-fé*. Janice, before she died, proposed we reprint the book after removing the offending passage. This was seriously considered but, for a variety of reasons, was not followed through.

The head chaplain at UZ in Nigel's time was Sebastian Bakare, one of whose first observations to Nigel was, 'When there are problems at the university the chaplains are never there.' Nigel decided that would not happen on his watch and he was careful to keep a close eye on developments on campus so that he was there when there was trouble. If students were arrested, he would visit them in prison, bring them food, find a lawyer and inform their parents. He would appear in a Roman collar to make it clear he was there in a purely pastoral role

---

9   C. Chibango and G. Kajau, *Voice of the Voiceless: Student Activism in Zimbabwe* (Harare: Silveira House, 2010). Although the book was not reprinted, a copy is being made available on the internet 'open access' with the passage that was objected to removed.

and not encouraging the students to riot, as the authorities thought he was. In fact, he was urging the students *and* the police to be non-violent. As minister of higher education, Ignatius Chombo was frustrated by Nigel's presence and tried to have him deported, only to discover Nigel was a citizen.

As chaplain, Nigel helped the students to analyse their grievances and their demonstrations from a Church and wider perspective. He was fond of quoting the saying of Bobby Kennedy that 'Politics is an honourable profession' which echoed the Second Vatican Council[10] and the perhaps equally potent aspiration, 'when you are elected to a position you are there not just to work for those who voted for you but for everyone, that is, including those who voted against you,' a saying that echoes Edmund Burke's address to the citizens of Bristol.[11] A chaplain can encourage students to think about such issues as well as the pastoral concerns of nourishing their faith directly through liturgy.

Prisoners

Inmates of our prisons are another group that can be overlooked. Jesuits, down the decades, have tried to find time for them in the midst of their other tasks. Two names stand out in the story of prison ministry: Frs Victor Nicot (1858-1935) and Henry Swift (1900-73). Nicot was teaching at the fledgling St George's College in Bulawayo when captives from the Ndebele rising were in prison awaiting execution. He visited them, consoled them, instructed them in the faith and stood by them in their last moments. He wrote: 'to walk

---

10 *Gaudium et Spes*, *The Church Today*, #75.
11 'Certainly, gentlemen, it ought to be the happiness and glory of a representative to live in the strictest union, the closest correspondence, and the most unreserved communication with his constituents. Their wishes ought to have great weight with him; their opinion, high respect; their business, unremitted attention. It is his duty to sacrifice his repose, his pleasures, his satisfactions, to theirs; and above all, ever, and in all cases, to prefer their interest to his own. But his unbiased opinion, his mature judgment, his enlightened conscience, he ought not to sacrifice to you, to any man, or to any set of men living. These he does not derive from your pleasure; no, nor from the law and the constitution. They are a trust from Providence, for the abuse of which he is deeply answerable. Your representative owes you, not his industry only, but his judgment; and he betrays, instead of serving you, if he sacrifices it to your opinion.' 3 November 1774. In our age of gender consciousness, the relentless hammering of the male pronoun in this passage irritated one reader so much he felt it blunted the impact of the quotation. But that is the quotation and it was the eighteenth century.

with the prisoner to the scaffold and stand a yard or two from it as the man is jerked into eternity is consoling to one's faith but nerve-racking to flesh and blood.'[12] Years later in the 1930s, when Nicot was retired at St John's, Avondale, Fr Charles Bert, who also worked in the prison in Salisbury for a time, went to visit him and was distressed to see a picture of the patron of the school with a noose hanging over his head.[13] Nicot's work with prisoners seems to have led to his breakdown in 1917. He went to England in the 1920s to recover and was a 'missioner' at Richmond in Yorkshire for some years in the 1920s before returning Southern Rhodesia where he died in 1935, aged 77.

That same year Henry Swift began his prison work when he was posted to St Peter's in Harari (Mbare). He gradually taught himself what the work involved and he too stood by the scaffold of around a hundred condemned men,[14] over the years, as they left this world. Fr Michael Geoghegan wrote of him: 'He was indefatigable. For many years before the prison service was reorganised, he was practically the only minister of religion who visited the prison regularly. He would say Mass for the Catholic prisoners at least once a week; hold instruction classes for any who chose to attend and generally see to their welfare. For many years he assisted at every execution in the main Salisbury prison and whoever died, died Catholic. When a man was condemned to death, no matter who he was or what he had done, Henry would visit him in his cell and, when necessary as it so often was, would give him basic instruction in the Church's teaching. He would visit him every day and, so gentle and calm was he, the prison authorities always welcomed him. On the evening before an execution Swift would baptise the prisoner who had entered the prison as a pagan; on the morning of the execution, he would say Mass in the condemned cell, give the prisoner his First Holy Communion and within an hour or so afterwards the man would be dead. A trying apostolate indeed ....[15]

---

12 *Letters and Notices*, Vol. 25, p. 44.
13 St John of Gorkum was a Dominican priest, one of nineteen religious hanged in 1572 by militant Calvinists in Holland for defending Catholic teaching.
14 Fr John McCann wrote to Corrigan, in a PS to a letter, that Fr Esser was upset at Swift claiming that he 'reintroduced' the practice of standing by the scaffold of people when they were executed. 'Esser maintains that he, Nicot and Phaeler all accompanied the condemned to their death.' 4 December 1960, JAZ, Box 144/1.
15 *Letters and Notices*, Vol. 78, p. 240.

Henry himself describes his activities in 1960 in some detail: 'I tell those "Awaiting trial" how to get in touch with relatives and employers who do not know where they are.'

> With my long and regular prison work I am permitted to go anywhere in the prison ... It may take two months for the murder case to go through the Magistrate's court and the High Court, between which, the police will have to go long distances to verify statements ... The relays of guards are very considerate towards the condemned ...With Catholics, the faith helps them to die well. ... After Holy Communion ... I tell him that later his hands must be strapped behind him so that he cannot hurt himself – saying nothing about the fall – that his eyes will probably be covered, that he will hear my voice on his right and that he will have time to say the name 'Jesus' about three times before the rope is made quite tight, at which moment he will die and should be thinking of going to God. ... as he is being strapped, I tell him the executioner will do everything without hurting him...[16]

When Tony Bex was archivist, he listed the names of Jesuits who served in the prisons of Bulawayo, Salisbury (Harare), Sinoia (Chinhoyi) and Karoi for long or short periods; besides Nicot, Bert and Swift, there were also Joseph Moreau, Fidelis Mukonori, Clemens Freyer, Anthony Bex, Hermann Husemann, Konrad Landsberg and the present writer. The Jesuits gave special attention to this work in the Missionary Conference in 1924 which proposed changes in the treatment of prisoners to the authorities. It was probably in Swift's time that a large chapel was built in the Central Prison which was surprisingly decorated. There was a filigree communion rail installed and an old-time pulpit high above the heads of the inmates. I used the chapel often when I was visiting the prison in the first decade of the present century. Henry Swift was replaced by Fr Emmanuel Ribeiro who has just died at the time of writing (June 2021). He was a renowned composer and a particular inspiration to me in his prison work, the hardest period being during the war. He too attended executions at Chikurubi and he would come out to us at Silveira traumatised by the experience. He did not want to speak to anyone but just walk in the Chikurubi

---

16 *Letters and Notices*, Vol. 65, pp. 33ff.

woods, to regain peace in his sore and boiling heart.

Freyer sought and received considerable help from Germany to provide blankets, medical supplies and supplementary food. A delegation of officers and inmates attended his funeral as a sign of how much he was appreciated. Fr Joe Arimoso has tried to continue this work with the help of the St George's students. Caswell Machivenyika and two other scholastics from Arrupe College, who later left the Society, used to come with me to the prison and Tafadzwa Mandimutsa SJ, there at present, would like to see this work restored once Covid is conquered.

My own involvement began in 2004 when Jean Vanier, on his final visit to Zimbabwe, asked to visit one of our prisons. I took him to Central and after he had addressed close to a thousand inmates sitting in the courtyard in the blazing sun, one of them stood up and asked why Catholic priests were no longer visiting. On my visits I was always touched by their singing and suggested to Nigel Johnson, at that time trying to set up a Catholic Radio station in Bulawayo, that he come with his team and record them. The prison authorities were enthusiastic and four prisons came to Central – Khami, Whawha, Chikurubi and Central – and recorded the CD, *Ndaive Mbavha* (I was once a thief), *Songs from Prison*, in 2008.

In 2012, I was able to give more time to prison work but was there less than a year before I was suddenly and unceremoniously barred. No reason was given but a letter was sent 'greatly appreciating the religious services you have offered'. I later surmised that it was something I wrote in my weekly column in *The Zimbabwean* that caused offence. Later, on moving to Zambia, I was able to join the team, which included Charlie Searson SJ and successive novices, in visiting the five prisons in and around Lusaka.

In 2012, there were forty prisons in Zimbabwe, with a total population exceeding 40,000. Conditions have improved since the time Paradzai Zimondi, the Prisons Commissioner, likened every prisoner in the country to a man on death row; 'One prison,' he wrote, 'accounted for 127 deaths in one year.'[17]

People living with HIV/AIDS

Zimbabwe had one of the highest HIV prevalences in sub-Saharan

---
17 Report to the President, 2008.

Africa at 12.8 per cent, with 1.4 million people living with HIV in 2019. For forty years this plague has wounded our society and is only now coming under control. Many Jesuits worked with so many others to try to bring awareness of the disease to people through their work in parishes and schools, and among them two names stand out: Br Kizito Makora[18] and Fr Edward (Ted) Rogers. Courage Bakasa, in his obituary of Makora, describes him as, 'perhaps the most recognisable Jesuit in many of the poorer suburbs of Harare. His work with Mashambanzou Counselling and Care Centre took him to the heart of the city and into the hearts of many people living with HIV/AIDS and of orphans and their families.'[19] Makora was available to counsel and help people get their medicine and the necessary food at any time and those who lived with him would often see him begin to cook his own meal at 9.30 at night. Orphaned children treated him as a father, and even in the UK, where he did a few years of study, he was in touch with Eritrean refugee orphans who would run to him. Bakasa describes him as a man who lived Pope Francis's call that we be people who know the 'smell of the sheep'.

If Makora was the hands-on man available round the clock, Ted Rogers was the great organiser. On learning of the gravity of the epidemic, he proposed that the bishops organise a seminar to develop a national response. He set up the AIDS Counselling Trust in 1987 and later the Jesuit Aids Project. Ted organised 'peer' workshops where young people educated those of their own age about the dangers of the sickness. When Ted became director of IMBISA, the regional grouping of bishops of Southern Africa, he used his position to persuade the bishops to take a more active role in combating the AIDS epidemic.[20] Some years later, in 1996, Ted tells us he was 'given away' to the Jesuit Superiors of Africa and Madagascar by his own provincial, Fr Konrad Landsberg, to research the situation of HIV/

---

18 Kizito Makora (1952-2014) was born in Triashill and, Fr Fidelis Mukonori tells us, was one of 120 who became candidates for the Society of Jesus at Mazowe between 1969 and 1972. Of the eight who joined the novitiate in Lusaka in 1971 only two remained two years later: Kizito and Fidelis. Makora became a kindly boarding master at St Ignatius in the 1980s and spent some time in the UK in the early 1990s before returning to take up his second great work at Mashambanzou. He was troubled in later life by diabetes and kidney problems and had a stroke in 2010.
19 *Letters and Notices*, Vol. 101, p. 463.
20 *Letters and Notices*, Vol. 103, p. 350.

AIDS in the various countries where Jesuits were working. He did a tour of their countries and came up with conclusions that gradually fed into the foundation of AJAN (Africa Jesuit AIDS network), based in Nairobi, which was set up by Fr (now Cardinal) Michael Czerny and currently co-ordinated by Fr Elphège Quenum.

In 2020, JCAM, the new acronym for JESAM,[21] issued a statement for AIDS day, 1 December, celebrating progress in the fight against the disease:

> Since the start of the epidemic of HIV/AIDS, 75.7 million people [worldwide] have become infected while we have lost 32.7 million people to AIDS-related illnesses (UNAIDS, 2020), while millions bear the impact of the disease on their families. On the positive side, we look back and acknowledge the tremendous achievements in the fight against the epidemic – thanks to the generosity, resilience, and tireless efforts of governments, international organisations, civil societies, religious organisations and communities. It is encouraging that a united global initiative has recorded gains in HIV testing and treatment with the result that 81% of people living with HIV know their status, and an estimated 25.4 million of the 38.0 million people living with HIV had access to antiretroviral therapy by the end of 2019, thus averting 12.1 million AIDS-related deaths since 2010 (UNAIDS, 2020).

Young people on the streets

Zambuko House, in Hatfield, Harare, was the last of a number of initiatives of Br Canisius Chishiri. In the mid-nineties, Chishiri conceived a plan of going beyond visiting young people who found themselves on the streets for a variety of reasons. He wanted to give them a home, a temporary anchorage, where they could regain their bearings and perhaps be reunited with their families. Zambuko (a ford, a place where one can cross a river) House, in Chishiri's eyes, was to be a Jesuit work with a Jesuit ethos. It was to help a person find the tools they never had to 'have a life'. He raised the money with appeals to people near and far and would send out regular informative newsletters – and further appeals! Chishiri wanted to give the young

---

[21] Jesuit Conference of Africa and Madagascar and Jesuits of Africa and Madagascar, respectively.

people skills in metalwork, gardening and the like and sometimes formal education. 1,500 young men have passed through Zambuko since it was founded in the mid-1990s. Two other homes were founded in Mbare for street children by Fr Wolf Schmidt.

Shingirirayi

Shingirirayi (be patient and courageous) is a project to reach out to many young people. Fr Norbert Gille explains that he began this initiative by providing entertainment (football) and organising youth into 'streets' with a street captain. Then they move into moral formation through publications he writes, taking tips from the internet about how to compose short stories in attractive booklets. Funding from Germany goes into building 'lodges' which generate income for the activities. 'The project is self-sufficient for the next eighty years', Gille told me.

People living with disabilities

Chishiri also founded a home for what he called 'wobblies', a lighthearted and affectionate term in context, for people living with physical disabilities. He was responding to a need he discovered while at Musami in the 1980s and he called the centre after Pedro Arrupe, our Fr General, then retired. In so far as it was possible, the aim of the centre was to provide therapy, training in self-reliant skills and a community of mutual support.

During tertianship in Toronto in 1976, I was introduced to Daybreak, a l'Arche community where people with mental disabilities (residents) were living with 'normal' people (assistants) in a community. I expected to see 'patients' and 'staff' with separate living spaces but everything was shared. The residents did everything they could – shopping, cooking, gardening – and the assistants helped them where needed. That was what happened at the basic level but I soon discovered there was something deeper happening. The residents, experiencing acceptance, started to exercise their new-found confidence and challenged the assistants! The latter had come all starry-eyed with good intentions, only to discover their discomfort when the residents spoke and acted without the usual social inhibitions society imposes on 'normal' people. Residents, discovering that expressing their anger was 'allowed', did so when they felt the need. The assistants, discomforted at first, soon discovered it was liberating for them, too, to absorb and respond constructively to the anger. I remember an occasion in a l'Arche community in Ireland when Richard, a resident with Down's syndrome, got annoyed and chased an assistant round and round the table. It was hilarious and left all of us, including Richard, weak with laughter.

Daybreak was one of around 150 such communities worldwide which followed the lead of Jean Vanier[22], who started the first community in 1964 in Trosly, France, which he called l'Arche after the ark of Noah – a place of security and hope. I was so struck by this example of the weak healing the 'strong' that I decided we should try to have such a community in Zimbabwe. Provincial Henry Wardale was encouraging when I returned from tertianship, but it took twenty years of to-ing and fro-ing before we were able to begin in 1997, in Waterfalls, a southern suburb of Harare. Today, almost twenty-five years later, the community is well established and visitors, for short or long periods, who allow themselves to enter deeply into the community, pick up that same astonishment and joyful recognition.

A mutual relationship has grown up over the years between l'Arche and the Jesuits, many of whom have spent time in l'Arche.[23] In its turn, l'Arche has drawn on Jesuit spirituality for its own way of proceeding. Elphas Ndlovu, a scholastic at Arrupe, calls his month at l'Arche

> a life changing experience. I got to recognise the other person in me which I had never done before. I was exposed to an experience

---

[22] Jean Vanier (1929-2019) was a French Canadian who joined the navy young (14) and later did a doctorate in philosophy (Aristotle) before discovering people living with disabilities. He dropped out of his teaching (in Toronto) to devote his life to them and, with his inquiring mind as well as his warm heart, discovered much wisdom which he shared in his talks and writings. After his death, evidence was discovered that seemed to point to some form of sexual exploitation on his part of six young women – not people with disabilities – and an investigation supported these allegations. The thousands of people who knew and revered Jean were deeply hurt and many institutions which had adopted his name, promptly changed it. Jean, we knew, was drawn to the most wounded and vulnerable people and was undoubtedly, as he repeatedly acknowledged, wounded himself. The precise nature of the wound that enabled him to write and speak so movingly of humanity's vulnerability remains unclear. It is now (July 2021) eighteen months since these allegations were made and to date no properly obtained evidence of sexual misconduct has been publicly produced. Although it is too early for clarity to emerge it would seem that an alternative assessment is at least possible.

[23] *Letters and Notices*, Vol. 102.

that led me to value a human person. I went on an eight day retreat to meditate on what I had gone through ... I felt God speaking to me in an intimate way ... What is it I should do? ... In no time I found myself in the vocation promoter's office!

Abandoned babies

The liberation war succeeded in establishing Zimbabwe, but there were devastating social ruptures. One was the surge in unwanted pregnancies. The phrase 'baby-dumping' appeared in our newspapers frequently. Penalties were imposed but no sustained solution was proposed. Fr Ted Rogers' name once more appears, as it often did with regard to social issues. He was the chairman of a group that included Professor Timothy McLoughlin and Dr Felicity Zawaira which set up Shelter Trust to give temporary secure accommodation, in a home they called *Mwana Anokosha* (A Child is Precious), to young pregnant women who had been abandoned by their families and the father of their child. In giving a 'supportive healthy atmosphere while they awaited the birth of their child', the trust also provided skills for the women so that, when they left the home, they would be able to support themselves and their child. The trust also tried to provide an 'outreach programme' to provide support for desperate women residing with a member of their extended family. Finally, it aimed to educate the public and create awareness of the issue.

Meteorology, astronomy, entomology, apiculture and archaeology

When Fr General Peter-Hans Kolvenbach officially opened Arrupe College, as it then was, in 1998, he encouraged the students to have 'hobbies' outside the mainline of their studies. He wanted them to be curious and follow up any path that caught their imagination. Many of our ancestors on the Zimbabwe Mission had followed this advice.

As soon as he was settled in Bulawayo, Fr Victor Nicot proposed that meteorological observations should be made to learn about the possible link between climate and fever, and he published his findings in the *Zimbabwe Mission Record*. In 1896 Fr Alphonse Daignault suggested an observatory be established, in the tradition of Clavius,[24]

---

24 Christopher Clavius (1538-1612), a Jesuit, was a member of the late sixteenth century commission to reform the calendar, which was then out of sync with

Ricci[25] and Schall[26]. The prefect, Richard Sykes, agreed with the idea and selected Fr Edmund Götz for the task and sent him to Paris and the United States to learn the craft. In 1901, the observatory was established in Bulawayo with Götz as director. He contributed valuable advice on rainfall and droughts and other matters over the years and they are documented in the *Proceedings of the Rhodesian Scientific Association*. The observatory later moved, with St George's College, to Harare.

Another branch of science that drew the interest of Jesuits was entomology. Fr Joseph O'Neil studied insects, snakes, wasps and moths as early as 1898 in Empandeni. He contributed twenty-three articles to the *Zimbabwe Mission Record* and was elected a member of the Royal Entomological Society. Fr Anthony (Seamus) Watsham collected Chalcid wasps in the later decades of the twentieth century while teaching at St Ignatius College in Chishawasha. Some species of these microscopic creatures are named after him. He attended entomological congresses in South Africa and Canada and, being an artist as well, made drawings, accurate to the scale of 1:20. They are now available on the internet as well as on the walls of some of our houses where you will find Fr General on one wall and Watsham's wasps on another.

Fr Joseph Kendall was reputed to be a pioneer in Rhodesian apiculture[27] but I cannot find evidence in the archives of more than

---

science. His proposal that Wednesday, 4 October 1582 should be followed by Thursday, 15 October, was accepted by Pope Gregory XIII. The Gregorian Calendar was gradually adopted although the Russians held out until 1917. Clavius further proposed an ingenious device that would prevent 'slippage' in the future.

25 Mateo Ricci (1552-1610) was an Italian Jesuit who, between 1583 and 1610, made a slow journey to the capital of the Chinese empire. He was continually frustrated, tracing and retracing his steps. Eventually he reached his goal and his knowledge of mathematics, astronomy and other branches of science won the favour of the authorities in what was then Peking. He also mastered the language and wrote books on scientific and religious topics and opened the way for generations of Jesuits to work in China until the time of the Suppression of the Jesuits in 1773. So sympathetic was he to Chinese culture that he developed a 'Chinese rite' that was accepted by the Vatican throughout the seventeenth century only to be suppressed by 'hard-liners' in the beginning of the eighteenth.

26 Johann Adam Schall von Bell (1591-1666) was a German Jesuit and astronomer who continued the work of Ricci in China. He worked on the reform of the Chinese calendar from 1630 with Xu Guangqi and compiled the Chongzhen calendar which provided more accurate predictions of eclipses of the sun and the moon.

27 Dachs and Rae, p. 127.

a fondness of keeping bees, both while he was studying theology at St Beuno's in Wales and while in St George's in Rhodesia. Frs Philip Gardner and Philip Stapleton, on the other hand, do seem to have done some ground-breaking work (literally and academically) in archaeology near Bulawyo and at Gokomere.[28] The Rev Neville Jones wrote, in an article about Gardner's work in *The Herald*, 6 June 1931, 'For the past thirty years, Fr Gardner has been assiduously working towards the solutions of the problems of our country's pre-history ... His attention was first drawn to the large rock shelter on the south side of the hill (next to Gokomere Mission). ... Fr Gardner has amassed a wonderful collection of minute tools of extreme delicacy and beauty.'[29]

Retreats

Accompanying people in the Spiritual Exercises is the number one priority for Jesuits and has now been formalised as our first 'apostolic preference' by our present Fr General, Arturo Sosa. There are Jesuits who seldom, if ever, give retreats but they would say that the dynamics of the exercises informs all their work. That is, hopefully, true. But today, when lay people are responsible for many of the works we have done for generations, there is an opportunity for us to give renewed focus to this task. Provinces in the 'developed' world have, or had, dedicated retreat houses where people could come for weekends or longer for 'preached' retreats, or — much more common now — for individually guided retreats. In the provinces in Europe, in those 'damp off-shore islands' I know best, there are two such houses: Manresa in Dublin and St Beuno's in Wales. There one can go for a weekend, a week, a month or three months' exposure to the exercises.

But in Africa, retreat houses are still low down on the list of priorities. When Pedro Arrupe[30] visited us in 1976 Fr Raymond Kapito gave an impassioned plea for a retreat house in Zimbabwe. I cannot remember Fr General's response but one of the hostels at Silveira House which we were building at the time ('green doors')

---

28 Dachs and Rae, p .128 and references to the journal of the *Rhodesian Scientific Association*, Vol. VII (1907).
29 Boxes of his findings are in the museum at St George's College, all labelled.
30 Jesuit Superior General 1965-83.

was, with the approval of the donors, designated as a part-time retreat house. Kapito ran many retreats at Silveira House and found his métier in this work. When Konrad Landsberg came to Silveira, in the opening years of the new century after his time as provincial, he set about building a dedicated retreat centre a short distance from the main complex and separated from it by a small wooded area which gave privacy to the retreatants. It was named after St Pierre Favre (Peter Faber), the first companion of St Ignatius, and had seven self-contained units with two beds in each and a central area with a unique (two in one) chapel, conference and dining area. This has proved popular especially for individually guided retreats though it is also used for small groups and even large ones (school groups) who just come for a day.

Nobert Rwodzi speaks for many young Jesuits in hoping to see the link between Silveira House and Peter Faber developed. 'We have a treasure that we must give to people, showing the way to God through the Spiritual Exercises and the practice of discernment. … We really need to invest in this project …'[31]

There is a great variety in the way in which the Exercises can be used and Canisius Chishiri developed an imaginative way to use them to respond to the trauma many suffered at the end of the war.[32] 'The idea first came to me last year when I was working with the refugees,' he told a *Herald* reporter. 'I realised there were those who were affected materially and those affected mentally. The latter desperately needed someone to listen to them. I used to go home at night feeling frustrated and depressed because I did not have the time to listen to them.' He devised a plan. 'When I hold these courses at weekends I must have no sense of time; if I am impatient or in a hurry it will add to the wounds these people already have.' He selected ten women to help him, who, he said, 'must be trustworthy first and foremost, they must be able to keep secrets and they must be dedicated.'

There were three stages to Chishiri's 'rehabilitation retreats'. The first is 'very emotional. We have a time of silence when they bring the atrocities they witnessed to the forefront of their minds. Many of them had to watch their relatives being hacked to death with a threat to their own lives if they made a sound. Consequently they have

---

31   Personal submission.
32   *Jesuit Missions*, Vol. 24, No. 183, Summer 1980.

become totally wrapped up in themselves without the ability to bring their emotions out.' So, in this first part there is no talking but a lot of screaming, crying and mournful singing. 'We try to make them be themselves once more with the help of the scriptures.'

The second stage is when fear is conquered. They share their experiences and how they feel. 'Talking is the best healing agent for the disturbed. It creates a togetherness and their burden becomes much lighter. Every one becomes more at ease.' The third stage involves two things: there can be something too painful to talk about in the group. 'We give them a chance to discuss this with a counsellor who listens and gives advice' Finally the counsellors are ready to strengthen the people for the future. Anger, bitterness and fear are overcome. With the help of the scriptures they are able to face life again. 'We tell them the war is over, and they have children, and we ask them what they plan to do. Then we help them to form a plan and give them hope. They still have to live despite their husbands and relatives being dead.' One women was brought back from the point of suicide when 'life had lost its purpose and she was ready to take her own life.' And she was not alone in this despair.

There is enthusiasm among younger Jesuits for this type of work. Lovemore Mashiri puts it this way:

> I feel that we should be setting up a powerful Retreat Centre. I mean powerful in the proper sense of the word. It should be big enough to accommodate more than 80 people. We need something which represents our spiritual seriousness and something we can hand over to the next generation. The Southern Africa province will make use of it for province retreats, Arrupe University will make use of it, the youths, collaborators and many others. This dream scares me, but that's what we want to see in Zimbabwe as young Jesuits. Maybe, I am being too ambitious, but I am pretty sure that this is the mindset of my fellow Arrupeans as we all try to look at our apostolates in the country.

Education co-ordination

Schools are among the most traditional of institutions. There is often little push from below to reflect on long established procedures and students seldom have the confidence to seriously question how they are being educated. Sometimes they are even more wedded to 'tradition' than their elders. So, normally, renewal has to come from above. It is not easy for busy heads and staff to stand back and review how their school is running beyond the ever present pressure of 'results' in the classroom and on the sports field. Sometimes it helps if outsiders cast a sharp eye on what the school is doing and school boards have multiplied to fulfil this useful function.

The Jesuits, along with artisans of education everywhere, have taken this cue and set up boards for their schools and, speaking as one of them, we feel we have a particular ethos we wish to share with our staff and students. Fr Joseph Arimoso, province delegate for education, initiated an education survey in 2011 with the aim of developing Ignatian pedagogy among teachers. He called it 'Unlocking the Future' and its aim is 'to support the renewal of Jesuit education in Zimbabwe so as to facilitate the attainment of quality education and practices in Jesuit schools in the traditions and standards of Jesuit pedagogy and ethos'. He noted at the time that we were responsible for eighteen schools with a total student enrollment of 10,000.

Theological reflection

A foundational practice Ignatius of Loyola gave to the Society of Jesus is the *Examen*. We have kept this Latin word as there seems to be no English equivalent. It is not the same as 'examination of conscience', although there are similarities. The nearest English rendering is the one coined by Fr George Aschenbrenner, 'Consciousness *Examen*', with its emphasis on reviewing a person's spontaneous behaviour in the light of the Spirit.[33] Socrates reminded us we should reflect on our life and there is nothing specifically Jesuit or Christian about this. But Ignatius taught us to pay attention to the movements of good and bad spirits influencing our lives and he made the daily practice of the *examen* a cardinal exercise for anyone serious about following Jesus.

Reflection is, of course, not just a personal exercise but one that is constantly used at the Society's corporate level. A good example of that was when Fr Weld, who succeeded Fr Depelchin in 1883, recalled all the Jesuits on the Zambezi Mission to Grahamstown for a period of assessment in view of the frustrations and failures the Jesuits experienced in their first years on the mission. And there were many

---

33 *Review for Religious*, Vol. 31, 1972/1.

moments even in the rush of activity in the first half of the twentieth century when the Jesuits paused to reflect. We saw how they favoured christian villages at first only to realise later they were unsustainable and there was an even better method of preaching the good news to hand: the outstations. Sometimes the superior had to put great pressure on his men to make them change their way of thinking, as when they dragged their feet over supporting Kutama as a Teacher Training School.

Yet, even when our reflection was corporate, it was inward looking. It did not embrace the wider political and social context in which Jesuits worked. Arthur Shearley Cripps, as we have seen, was an Anglican priest who struggled with great courage to defend African interests from the encroaching segregationist policies of the settlers in the early part of the last century. We saw how he approached the visiting Jesuit Provincial at Driefontein in 1931 looking for support, and Stephen Buckland tells us of 'the polite but fateful words' Cripps later recorded: 'they were very kind to me and charming but did not commend themselves to me altogether as to furthering Africa's horizons'.[34] The Jesuits in the 1930s did not appear to seriously question the political system the whites had established.

Change came in the 1960s with the lead given by Pope John XXIII and the Second Vatican Council when the Church moved from being inward looking and on the defensive, a legacy stretching back to the French Revolution and the Enlightenment, to an engagement with the modern world and all its 'joys and hopes, griefs and anxieties'.[35] This engagement led to serious reflection, especially in Latin America, on the political, social and economic aspects of the lives of people everywhere – not just Catholics. The Jesuits remained newcomers to this dimension of their mission and struggled to find their voice, which they finally did in the 32nd General Congregation of 1974/5.

But even then, our voice was one thing, our action another. I have already referred to Ian Linden. I remember being stung by the comment of his, already quoted earlier, in the late 1970s when he wrote of Silveira House, where I was at the time, as doing good work which was 'not immediately threatening' to the Rhodesian regime. This 'iron fist in a velvet glove' made me wonder at the time if we were

---

34 *Crossroads,* Zimbabwe Catholic Bishops' Conference Newsletter, April 1994.
35 *Gaudium et Spes,* op. cit.

really doing anything significant to bring about change.

Theological reflection has now become a standard tool that accompanies whatever we do. The Jesuits in Zambia started a centre in 1990 simply called the Jesuit Centre for Theological Reflection. At one point they tried to think up a more catchy name but they could not improve on it so it has remained JCTR. The centre was started by Fr Arul Varaprassadam, and then taken up and given intense focus by Fr Pete Henriot, who, for many years, had led the work at the Washington based Centre for Concern – a global hub for theological reflection in the 1970s. Pete scrutinised the situation in Zambia with his trained eye and what he wrote had civil society sitting up and taking notice. But it is one skill to be able to look at and diagnose the ills of society and quite another to suggest ways in which those ills can be put right.

Finally, and most challenging of all, it takes a particular kind of Jesuit leader to implement the fruit of reflection in the policies of the province. It may involve a 90 per cent turnaround or even a 180 per cent one. One person, there were others, I have held up in these chapters, was Terrence Corrigan, superior of the Salisbury Mission in the early 1960s. Corrigan had that unusual ability to simply say, 'let's do it'. In that vein he closed a recently purpose-built Jesuit novitiate and made it into a centre for leadership and development training, opened a new school for people denied access to quality secondary education and believed in the vision of his men who wanted to open a school for social work training and a programme for promoting credit unions. Without putting the label 'theological reflection' on the process by which he came to his decisions, he did the hard bit: actually making the decisions and seeing them through. Bishop Chichester was clearly another, especially with his work in founding the sisters' congregation and the seminary.

Silveira House, although 'not immediately threatening' the regime, did implicitly include reflection on the situation in Rhodesia and later Zimbabwe in its programmes. In the 1990s the centre issued around 25 short books reflecting on different aspects of life in Zimbabwe at the time. Staff at the centre also tried to promote the implementation of the findings of these reflections in the field, for example, in constantly adapting to the needs as they became clearer. There was a time when we approached the Tonga people around Binga to ask what kind of economic development they needed most. Fortunately, we tore up our preconceived plans when it became clear their priority was the preservation and promotion of their own language. We followed this up with, I think, great success.

Mukai/Vukani

The cry for theological reflection continued to be heard in the province as a whole but there was the ever-present danger of just paying lip service to it. A number of us thought a periodic magazine would help, and *Mukai/Vukani*[36] began in the 1990s specifically for this purpose. Soon, Oskar Wermter became the editor and publisher and he faithfully hammered away at the production year in, year out. He provided a forum for many people to try out their writing skills and reflect on the situation in Zimbabwe. I was one of them, and was later asked to write a 500-word theological reflection each week. Arkmore Kori, who worked in the research department at Silveira House, and Janice MacLaughlin later took the initiative to publish a selection of these in book form.[37] But those of us who tried our hand in this genre would admit we were not ruffling many feathers or stirring consciences. We did not make a noticeable impact. There was no Emil Zola among us.

I write this on a cold June morning in 2020, and one member of my community at breakfast today asked simply, 'is anyone writing about what is happening in the country at the moment?' He was thinking of a theological reflection on Zimbabwe under Emmerson Mnangagwa. Such a work would mean a description of the government's social and economic policies and their impact on the people. It would then go on to hold this information up to the light of the gospel and draw sharp conclusions. This would then be put into appealing words that have the power to move people. The early Jesuits were very insistent on this. There was no point in having hard facts and beautiful sentiments if you cannot touch people with them. You do not have to be a Cicero or a Martin Luther King, but a share in their gifts would help.

There is a thirst among us for this form of reflection leading to action. It needs research, reflection and prayer. We know the power

---

36 The name was proposed by Peter Mutsvairi, from Musana, who was a scholastic at the time and later left the Society.

37 D. Harold-Barry, *Beyond Appearances: Reflections on Principles and Practice* (Harare: Weaver Press, 2018).

of words from the example of great men and women. The greatest example I know is how Churchill through his words single-handedly stiffened the resistance of the British at the lowest point in the Second World War and turned their fortunes round. Autocrats routinely detest freedom of speech. It is one of the pillars of liberty.

Communications

We have seen how Ignatius encouraged his men to communicate regularly. 'Another special help will be found in the exchange of letters … through which they learn about one another frequently and hear the news and reports which come from various regions.'[38] As mentioned earlier, Jesuit reports, for example, from Canada in the seventeenth century are prized documents about the history of that country.[39] An historian, writing in 1916 about the reports the Jesuits sent to Lisbon from Mozambique in the same century, concluded their reports were, 'the clearest, best written, and far the most interesting documents now in existence on the country … Compared to the ordinary state papers, they are as polished marble to unhewn stone.'[40]

The early Jesuits who came to Zambezia in the 1880s wrote long letters and ample journals. They had a lot of time on their hands and so could provide this service for us and for a wider public who supported them. Later the *Zambesi Mission Record* was produced between 1898 and 1934 and this gave detailed reports of the activities on the mission. At the same time the English province produced an 'in-house' periodical, *Letters and Notices* which began in 1863 and is still going. If the ZMR is full of news, *Letters and Notices* is more a reflective journal and has an excellent tradition of taking pains to bring out the character of deceased Jesuits with all their lights and shadows. In recent years it has also included pieces on former Jesuits.

The English Province also ran a news-sheet for chaplains in the First World War, *Chaplains' Weekly*, which was so popular it was continued when hostilities ceased and it too is still produced, even if its title, in Zimbabwe, has been changed to the more mundane 'Province

---

38   Constitutions, Part VIII,1,9 [673].
39   Cf. the Introduction.
40   Festo Mkenda SJ, 'The Society of Jesus in Angola and Mozambique', in R.A. Maryks and J. Wright (eds), Jesuit *Survival and Restoration: A Global History, 1773-1900* (Leiden and Boston: Brill, 2015), p. 456.

Newsletter'. Since the Salisbury Mission and the Zimbabwe Province were offspring of the English (now British) Province their news and obituaries featured in these publications. In the 1970s Fr Richard Randolph started *Crossroads*, a news-sheet for the Catholic Bishops' Conference and this gradually morphed into the *Zimbabwe Catholic Church News* under Oscar Wermter in the 1980s. The driving force behind this paper, Oscar tells us, was Petronilla Chikambi Samuriwo, a professional journalist who took over the editorship, and under whom it flourished. Unfortunately, Petronilla died prematurely, aged forty-three. Mention has been made already, when treating of theological reflection, of *Mukai/Vukani* to which Fr Wermter also added *In-Touch,* a magazine of news on line. Wermter was also responsible for setting up the Communications Secretariat of the Zimbabwe Catholic Bishops' Conference with an office and full-time staff. This too is still operating, but today there is more emphasis on on-line productions and videos. Oscar, during the many years he devoted to media work, continually adapted his methods in response to evolving methods and needs. Nobert Rwodzi appreciates this but wishes the province would invest in a media centre. He laments our 'ugly website' and limited YouTube channel. He would like to see the history of the province recorded electronically, including the vocational and apostolic stories of the old Jesuits 'while they are still alive'.

Fr Nigel Johnson made a sustained effort to set up a community radio station, *Radio Dialogue,* when he moved to Bulawayo in 2000. There are many independent radio stations, both Church and otherwise, in Zambia next door but the Zimbabwe government resolutely refuses, even to this day, to allow independent voices to be heard. Johnson developed a number of ingenious alternatives to radio; he held open-air talk shows and mass-produced CDs with music and reflections on them that taxi and minibus drivers could play to their passengers, and that could be broadcast on short wave from outside the country. But without a broadcasting licence, options were limited.

Today the phrase 'Social Media' covers a wide spectrum of means of communication and there are many 'platforms', for example, *Jesuit Communications Zimbabwe, My Catholic Faith* and *SJ Community Contacts.* A question arises as to whether the insatiable appetite for instant news detracts from its quality. When a person is inundated with words, voices and pictures, these may blot out the opportunity to savour and reflect on what is seen and heard. The sheer quantity and range of news can anaesthetise one so that he or she is not touched by the most painful images. You can move from drug addiction in Seattle to deforestation in the last rain forest in Mexico to the Windrush generation in the UK – all in a matter of seconds. We have come a long way since our forefathers wrote their journals in their ox-wagons on a break in the journey to Old Tati.

When Oskar Wermter left the social communications department of the ZCBC (SocCom), his successor tried to continue to produce *Crossroads* but he gave it up after a while. Oskar then concentrated on Jesuit Communications (JesCom) which he set up to continue his work in communications, and he and his staff prepared to launch an independent radio station, *Radio Chiedza*. They invited people to discussions and public debates in the Catholic Centre, near the cathedral, and in the Dominican Convent. This is an on-going initiative by JesCom which hopes to start a local FM radio for Harare, to be called *Corah* (Community Radio Harare). It is part of a larger initiative, beyond the Church, to start a local citizens' radio. But earlier attempts like these have failed as the government insists on its own media monopoly and it remains to be seen what will come of this initiative.

Wermter also worked for the conference of Southern African bishops (IMBISA) where he wrote many documents to support their work. He also wrote a series of brochures on topical subjects, notably in his *Mbare Reports* covering the critical time he worked there and witnessed at first hand the way elections were run, the unrest resulting and the painful results of *Murambatsvina,* discussed in an earlier chapter.

JesCom is now run by Emmanuel Gurumombe SJ who has added to the activities already mentioned by taking some initiatives of his own, notably interviewing older Jesuits about different works of the Society in the country and live streaming church services during the Covid-19 lockdown, at its height at the time of writing.

These last two sections have dealt with communications and publications and a place should be found for Br William Lovell's devoted work in the Chishawasha printing press from the late 1920s to the late 1960s. Lovell went to Cape Town in 1926 to learn printing with the Salesians. On his return, he set up the Chishawasha Press which printed catechisms, hymn books, biblical texts, readers for schools and a variety of other works.[41]

'Intellectuals'

When I announced, back in Ireland in the 1950s, that I was joining the Jesuits the response I would often receive was, 'Oh, they're the intellectual ones.' And it is true, as I discovered, that there is a tradition in the Society of pursuing the pathways of the mind. Many other religious communities do likewise, but it is positively encouraged among us, even if there is a slight danger of a rift between 'academics' and 'bush missionaries'. Even before the early Jesuits arrived in the country, they were gleaning information about the language and the culture. Fr Hartmann's *Outline of a Grammar of the Shona Language* appeared in 1893. It was the first book ever published on the Zezuru dialect, and his *English-Mashona Dictionary* came out the following year. Fr Biehler's *Dictionary English/Ciswina* in 1906 ran to four editions and was only replaced by Fr Michael Hannan's *Standard Shona Dictionary* in 1959. 'One of the best planned dictionaries in any Bantu language',[42] the work of Hannan and his team was reprinted three times and a new enlarged edition came out in 1974. An appreciative review in *The Rhodesian Herald* was headed, THREE PAGES ON 'TO WALK' and indeed there are roughly 300 different entries on that one word. Hannan and his team also translated the New Testament into Shona, giving variants for the four dialects of *Zezuru, KoreKore, Manyika* and *Karanga*. It was used for decades and even today, when there is another more modern version available, there are those who prefer it to the new.[43] He extended this work to those parts of the Old Testament found in the lectionary of the liturgy. Wolfgang Thamm tells us his NT translation 'had the same effect on the Shona language as Luther's bible had on the German'.[44]

Fr Joseph Moreau, who later spent all his life in Zambia, wrote

---

41 Johanny, Diary of Chief events, St George's archives.
42 T.G. Benson, 'A Century of Bantu Lexicography', *African Language Studies*, 5, pp. 64-91. Quoted by George Fortune in his introduction to the second edition (1974) of Hannan's dictionary.
43 Dachs and Rea, p. 125.
44 Thamm, p. 75. Thamm actually wrote 'was said to have had' but when I asked him 'by who?' he replied, 'by me!'

two books in Shona in 1900: a catechism, that ran to four editions and a prayer book. Fr George Fortune's *Elements of Shona* (1965) is considered canonical, and Fr Des Dale produced short, easily accessible books on the language. For Ndebele, Fr Joseph O'Neil published a *Grammar of the Sindebele Dialect of Zulu* in 1913 which was still in use in 1961. He and Fr Charles Bick had published thirteen books on the language by 1918.

Dachs and Rea tell us, 'Between 1898 and 1928 the *Zimbabwe Mission Record* published thirty-five articles on African custom and beliefs.'[45] Francis Rea himself needs a mention as he was a first-class historian in his own right. Besides the *Catholic Church and Zimbabwe, 1879-1979*, he researched the archives in Lisbon and Goa and wrote numerous articles on the history of the Church and the Jesuits in southern Africa. Rea also taught at the University of Zimbabwe, then called the University of Rhodesia and Nyasaland, as did other Jesuits: George Fortune (linguistics), William (Bill) Butler (mathematics) and Michael Bourdillon (social anthropology). Fortune and Bourdillon later left the Society. Roger Riddell followed his undergraduate studies in economics at the then University of Rhodesia by becoming a key person in calculating the 'Poverty Datum Line' – an indicator of what an average family would need per month to live in dignity. The concept was that it would be continually updated but when inflation soared in the new century economists had no bearings on which to build their calculations. The PDL concept has been revived again in more recent years. In Zambia, the 'bread basket' – a similar calculation – may have been influenced by this research and it had a far more respectable sequence. It still appears in the *Jesuit Centre for Theological Reflection* bulletin which is produced regularly. Roger too later left the Society and has had a distinguished career in the linked fields of aid and development. He was appointed by Prime Minister Mugabe to chair the first economic Presidential Commission of Inquiry shortly after independence, which made an impact at the time but later got lost in the headlong advance of corner-cutting and corruption.

The intellectual angle of our work can attract students, and Nobert Rwodzi was one who was drawn to the Society by '*Mukai/Vukani* that I read during my university years. It was centred on faith and justice and that interested me.'

---

45 Dachs and Rae, p 127.

Liturgy and church décor

Leitourgia was the public worship in ancient Greece and, like so many concepts, the word was adopted by Christians, in this case to describe their way of celebrating the Eucharist. Justin, who died a martyr in about 165, describes how this was done. 'After the memoirs of the apostles or the writings of the prophets are read for *as long as time allows* ... the president offers prayers and thanksgiving *as best he can.*' [46] I put in italics phrases that, over the centuries, disappeared from our liturgical books as procedures became rigorously standardised. There was no room for personal initiative and the emphasis was on the exact following of the rubrics which were normally printed in red. Jesuit Ian Brayley, a noted Old Testament scholar and wit who taught my generation, used to say the breviary (prayer book) was 'divided into two parts: the black bits you had to read but not understand and the red bits you had to understand but not read'.

After the Second World War, there was a 'liturgical revival', a renewed interest in the sources and purpose of the liturgy, and authors such as Justin were dusted off and re-studied. A new wave of scholars challenged us to see that the liturgy was not just a set of time-honoured procedures, a sort of handbook of instructions, but a guide to a living event that could transform lives if celebrated imaginatively. I was astonished to discover in the archives a 1959 a letter from Fr Peter McIlhenny, secretary to Fr General's assistant, tentatively but forcefully suggesting that a renewed approach to liturgy could be 'a very sound basis for the re-education of the boys at (St George's) college'. He based his enthusiasm on his reading of Clifford Howell SJ's *The Work of Our Redemption,* then recently published, which became a source book for the liturgical revival. McIlhenny was writing in the context of the Jesuits cracking their heads over what to do about the growing gap between boys educated at St George's and the rest of the population of Rhodesia.[47] At the time, the Jesuits were even thinking of sending African boys to their schools in England to enable them to break out of the closed world of Southern Rhodesia which, he implied, St George's was condoning. 'There was a tendency for the mission to fall into two halves ... as the college is perhaps isolated

---

46 Justin 1st Apology Ch 67, 3.
47 McIlhenney to Corrigan, 8 December 1959, Box 26B/4.

from its *total* environment.' In the end the foundation of St Ignatius College was the route chosen.

In the 1950s, there was little awareness of the possibilities of liturgy in the countries from where the missionaries came. It was a formalised ritual where exact conformity to rubrics was prized over imaginative flexibility. In shaking the pillars of this particular temple, Howell seemed far ahead of his time. Besides, the missionaries worked in an environment where 'traditional religion was extremely strongly rooted. ... (its) ritual was visually more impressive than that offered by Christianity and also more directly linked to the specific needs of the people, especially in connection with agriculture'.[48] Looking back, it seems safe to say we were almost totally unaware of this. 'Missionaries found themselves at times judging converts by their outward behaviour and appearances, and condemning almost every detail of autochthonous (original, 'sprung from the land') culture as outward visible manifestations of the pagan inner person. Such an attitude baffled the local people and at times provoked stubborn resistance among traditionalists.'[49]

In the post Vatican Council II era there was a fever of liturgical experiment perhaps most notably exemplified by the Zaïre rite and the still popular *Misa Luba*. I once attended a Eucharist in Kinshasa according to the Zaïre rite where the priest and his many attendants, all dressed in the same colours, danced into the church to the sound of singing, drumming and the dancing of the whole congregation. The service then proceeded in a way that leant heavily on the cultural modes rooted in the lives of the Congolese. It took two hours, but even a foreigner could sense the people were absorbed by the dynamic of the event and time meant nothing.

In Chapter 4 we met Fr Roland Pichon in Chikwizo who, acutely aware of the power of liturgy, designed his church so that there was an 'Egypt' attached to the main building but divided from it by a 'Red Sea', a red curtain, which was opened only after the catechumens were baptised on Easter night and entered the body of the church to much dancing and celebration. Such imagination, alas, was drowned out by

---

48 D.N. Beach, 'The Initial Impact of Christianity on the Shona: The Protestants and the Southern Shona', in A.J. Dachs (ed.), *Christianity South of the Zambezi* (Gwelo: Mambo Press, 1973), p. 27.

49 N.M.B. Bhebe, 'Missionary Activity among the Ndebele and the Kalanga', in Dachs, p. 45.

other concerns of the Church in the 1970s in Rhodesia. It was a time when the country was cut off by war and sanctions from the influence of other countries in Africa. This had good and bad sides to it. The good thing was that we developed our own church musical tradition led by Gweru diocese, notably by Fr Joseph Lenherr of the Bethlehem Missionary Society who worked with Stephen Ponde and others. They replaced the harmonium with drums, *mbira*[50] and *hosho*[51] and Jesuit parishes followed suit. The down side was that developing in isolation meant we were not exposed to what was happening in other parts of the continent and were unable to share our experience with them. Br Ladislaus Bvukumbgwe was a widely respected composer and his work was carefully collected after his death by Fr Gibson Munyoro and placed in the archives.

The evolution of liturgy and its place in the mission of the Church is a live topic and, for example, when the Apostolic Nuncio to the United Kingdom, Archbishop Claudio Gugerotti, visited Campion Hall, Oxford, on 25 August 2021 to speak with the Jesuits in formation, he spoke, among other things, on liturgy, his previous field of study and how it offers a springboard for evangelisation.

Have Jesuits in Zimbabwe been imaginative with regard to liturgy? A similar question could be asked about our decoration of our churches. Considerable effort is put into finding the resources for laying the foundations, building the walls and putting on the roof. But, apart from the late Anthony Berridge and the one-armed decorator of Hermann Husemann's churches, Moses Manyanga from Masvingo,[52] who was also employed by Mark Hackett at Makumbi, I am not aware of any imaginative pursuit of church decoration. Even a church in a well-to-do parish like Our Lady of the Way in a northern suburb of Harare has a rather bare and cold interior with little to raise the mind and heart. Again, the Bethlehem missionaries led the way, and their church at Serima, which Evelyn Waugh called 'an African Chartres', was considered a most imaginative and attractive building.

---

50 A handheld hardwood soundboard, with a series of thin metal keys affixed to its surface.
51 A pair of gourds with seeds.
52 One of his works appears in the photo section of this book.

Finance

Modern missionary efforts have been largely supported by the home countries of the missionaries. Besides the actual provinces providing funds, Misereor, the German Catholic development agency for work in Africa, stands out as one of the largest partners – they do not like the word 'donor' or 'benefactor'. Many European and North American Catholic churches had similar agencies and throughout the twentieth century Africa benefited from this solidarity. It echoed the anxious concern of Paul in the early church for a collection to be made in the Corinthian church for the Judeo-Christian community in Jerusalem which seemed to be in financial straits.[53] Paul had a theological point to make. There were already strains between the Judaizers and the gentile churches and even among the Christian in Corinth there were factions. Disunity among Christians has a long history.

Interestingly perhaps, the early missionaries in Mozambique and Angola enjoyed no such substantial support from their home country. They were forced to be self-reliant and develop resources on the spot. Francis Rea tells us of the Jesuit estates *(prazos)* where the Jesuits farmed the land with the help of slaves.[54] Rea describes a fairly benign form of slavery far removed from the cruelty of the American south before Lincoln.

> In Zambezia the slave was fairly sure of being protected and fed and that meant much, because for the contemporary African murder and starvation were far more real than were the political theories of Locke and Rousseau. Some became slaves voluntarily. Mauriz Thoman thought that the work imposed on them was not very heavy; indeed, ten times less so than that imposed on the peasantry of Europe. Their master had to treat them with some consideration, because flight was easy and recovery impossible.

Nobert Rwodzi, while he was still a scholastic at Arrupe, makes the obvious point that once again Africa will have to learn to rely on her own resources:

> The Society in Africa is becoming more and more African in personnel and there is need for a deliberate move to invest in

---

53 2 Cor. 8-9.

54 W.F. Rea, 'Agony on the Zambezi: The First Christian Mission to Southern Africa and its failure', ***Zambezia***, 1(2), January 1970, pp. 46-53.

projects that generate capital for the training of our men. This could be in real estate. We have a lot of land but we are slow in thinking of having our buildings on such land out to lease and so generate income. It is possible that by the time we wake up, the land we have will be gone and, on that land, there is nothing for us.

Fr Chrispen Matsilele is part of a group working on a scheme to use the resources of the Jesuits in Zimbabwe to develop a more self-reliant church. But it is too early to do more than speak of the broad concept.

Archives and libraries

In the introduction to this book, mention was made of the Jesuit practice of writing frequent letters and reports. 'Ignatius himself learnt the Society's mission by what he found her doing.' We also, fortunately, had the habit of keeping these documents – even if they were just heaped in a cupboard somewhere. We, in Zimbabwe, were further blessed in having one or two outstanding Jesuits who took on the tedious – yet fascinating – task of ordering these documents and preserving them before the ants and rodents got to them. Some of these creatures were human and at least one Jesuit comes to mind who had a penchant for 'burning rubbish'. Dieter Scholz meticulously kept a collection of newspaper cuttings from the war years only to find, when he got back after years away working with JRS, that Anthony (Jeep) Davis had consigned the lot to the flames.

But a huge quantity of documents was preserved, catalogued and placed in 650 (to date) boxes. Fr William (Pussy) Rea and Fr Patrick (Pat) Lewis were the two giants in this task. Some of our ancestors wrote in tiny handwriting and their letters were often frayed and on the point of disintegration. Pat typed out a large number of these and bound them in easily accessible folders. A recent visitor to the archives, researching on the early years, photocopied some 3-400 pages on his mobile phone in a couple of hours. The task of digitalising the archives has begun.

The archives also house a huge quantity of photos, building plans, slides, CDs, historical and missionary magazines and so forth. There is a Shona saying, *Natsa kwamunobva, kwamunoenda usiku*, which, loosely translated, could be understood as, 'Know well where you come from, where you are going is unknown.' In my own experience, Jesuit novices are often excited by our early history – our glory years and our darkest – and it gives them a sense of identity about being a Jesuit.

Eddie Murphy, the chief province archivist, asks,

> Why should we keep Jesuit archives? There is more to it than recording history. As in our individual lives, we grow in awareness of where the Lord has led, and is leading, us. Our ministry has developed under the influence of the Spirit for the needs of the Church at any particular time and place. How that tradition developed is an integral part of our own discernment of where we are being led today. Our history is not just a record of achievements but of a process that continues to unfold, calling us to be sensitive to how God is at work today. Our tradition has more to do with a discerning awareness and less to do with the sense of accomplishment.
>
> Our interest in the past is about how our companions of old, discerned the needs of their day and set about answering them with creativity and generosity. In brief, we have no specific ministries but we do have a history of a variety of apostolates in education, implanting the Church in other lands, preaching etc. What we start with is a process of discernment based on the Spiritual Exercises that leads us to a service under the guidance of the Vicar of Christ.
>
> The history of our companions of the past inspires us by their dedication and helps us face creatively the situations of our day. It also helps us understand their failures and learn from our own. The failure of the first phase of the Zambesi Mission laid the ground for the success of the second. As Augustus Law lay dying among the shambles of the Nguni mission, he wrote these, his last, words in his diary: 'I do not think I could despair even if I tried'. We should not only remember the names of Richartz, Prestage, Moreau and Torrend, who founded missions that are flourishing to this day, but also Law, Depelchin, Terörde and de Vylder, who left nothing except their bones.[55]

Jesuits are equally keen on establishing libraries wherever they go.

---

55 Not quite true. These words of Eddie Murphy were written on 20 October 2021 in Lusaka and I have adapted and abbreviated them here.

When I first came to this country, I was astonished to see even the most remote missions, St Michael's Mhondoro, for instance, with its library. When we set up our four colleges in Africa for the formation of our younger members, a good library was always high on the agenda. Fr Edward (Eddie) Murphy gave roughly four decades to establishing or developing comprehensive libraries in Zambia, Kenya and Zimbabwe. The internet is challenging the hegemony of 'the book in your hands' and it is hard to predict the future of books. Publisher Irene Staunton of Weaver Press, has persistently published books in Zimbabwe through good times and bad, says:

> From one perspective, Zimbabwe has never had a book-buying population, (but) if you give someone a book, they will almost certainly read it. Chenjerai Hove, a well-known Zimbabwean author, once commented, 'when someone in Europe buys a book, they read it and it goes on a shelf. But if you give someone a book in Zimbabwe, it is read until it falls apart.' ... Zimbabwean culture is very social, and doing things together as a family is hugely important. Isolating yourself somewhere to read a book is not a very social thing to do. Sharing what has happened to you is more important than slipping away to read quietly by yourself.

When asked how interest in poetry and books could be stimulated, Staunton replied.

> If I was Minister of Education ... I would invest in libraries and I would encourage lots of activities in libraries: reading sessions, book club sessions, writing sessions, authors' visits, etc. You could do a great deal around libraries. You could make them very, vibrant cultural hubs.[56]

I am of the generation that saw the advent of TV, at first, as the death knell of films as we knew them, only to realise, on the contrary, that it freed up the cinema to expand its horizons. Can we imagine, for example, the production of *The Silence*, in an earlier age than our own? Maybe something equivalent will happen with books. Books will not disappear – as canals, for commercial transport, did with the advent of the railways.[57]

---

56 In an interview with A. Klother, Mediaforum 2/2006, <www.zimbabwenetzwerk.de>
57 I hear that canals are now being revived in the UK but this time for leisure.

Richartz House

As Jesuits grow older, sometimes also becoming infirm, they may need special care. In the past they were able to stay on at a mission or college and their needs would be met by the community. They would join in the life of the community as best they could and be in touch with local people. I remember, in the 1960s, meeting Fr Kaibach and Fr Esser at Makumbe in their declining years. Kaibach was still wearing boots and I suspect he 'died in his boots'. Neither of them, I seem to remember, had ever been home since they came out in the 'teens of the century. In chatting to Esser, I remember his saying he failed his *ad auds*[58] and he seemed to nurse an enduring hurt that he had failed the exams unfairly! If a Jesuit needed nursing, they might go to Nazareth House as Archbishop Markall did in his last years but this seemed exceptional.

By the 1990s, it was felt a more 'professional' approach to care for our old and sick members was needed. Also people were living longer and to die at 90 was no longer unusual. A house was built next to Prestage House and Fr Pat Lewis suggested the name, Richartz, after one of the great early members of the mission. Purpose designed, it provided en suite large rooms for six or more residents and was opened in 1998. I called on one of its first residents, Maurice (Bo) Rea, a rather blunt Canadian, and, trying to be positive, said, 'This is great. People can just pop in any time and visit you.' To which he replied, 'Yes, and they can pop out too'! Later, several more rooms were added and a full-time nurse and a team of medical assistants were employed. Dr Dianne Coots visits Richartz each week to check on the residents.

The old and infirm are now expertly served medically but the Covid crisis has underlined some questions that were beginning to be raised even earlier. Dr Coots told me she laughed when she saw the title of the St George's Centenary book, *Men for Others*. 'When will you learn', she said with a smile, 'to be men for each other?' Richartz represents a huge step forward in medical care but perhaps also a step backwards in 'a family spirit' – something that exists, or used to exist, in ordinary families.

Our older members are now cut off from the colleges and missions

---

58 A live exam in hearing confessions.

where they used to work and are unable to chat to people in these works and perform the function of a *sekuru* in any village, especially in interacting with the young. We know there are pressures in modern life that were not there before. Active members of the province are often too busy to spend time with the old or infirm and younger members are also occupied with their concerns. But there could be a way of preserving the best of the old ways while welcoming the advantages of the new.

12

Into the Future

The older I get the more I look forward to the future.

Richard Randolph SJ

From 1957, when the novitiate opened at Silveira House, Chishawasha, young Zimbabweans applied to enter the Society. The numbers were small to begin with and many did not stay. The novitiate moved from Chishawasha in 1964 to Mazowe and finally to Lusaka in 1969. By the 1990s, the Province of Zimbabwe was welcoming three, four, five or even six young men each year, and a high proportion of them came to stay. In the 1980s, the numbers were so small that no large-scale planning was going into formation with the exception of the theologate at Hekima College in Nairobi, founded in 1984. Philosophy was studied either in Europe or in Zaïre (now the DR Congo), at S Pierre Canisius, Kimwenza (Kinshasa), which had been established for philosophy and some branches of the human sciences in 1954. It was a venue that entailed anglophone scholastics spending a year learning French. This was a stop-gap arrangement and by the 1990s we had to crack our heads to set up an institution where the increasing number of English-speaking scholastics could study. I was responsible for Arrupe House at the time, where Anglophones from all over Africa did a year's course in French. We settled down in the old convent at St Anne's Hospital in Harare and thought we would be there for many years. As a sign of this we did major alterations to the chapel and Anthony

(Tony) Berridge spent his weekends painting its interior in 'earthen' colours.

But a major rethink unfolded and Cecil MacGarry, who had already been one of the driving forces in the establishment of Hekima, came to plan the morphing of this small venture into the new Philosophate, Arrupe College. To complete the picture, a French-speaking college in Abidjan, Ivory Coast, was founded more recently, so recently they have not yet decided on a name. It is still known by an acronym, ITCJ (Institut de Théologie de la Compagnie de Jésus).

When Arrupe started in 1994 there were twenty students from six countries. Fr Valerian Sherima (from Tanzania) was the first rector, assisted by Fr Fidelis Mukonori as minister. There was a planning team, and what stays in my mind was the decision to establish separate houses which could be some distance, a kilometre or more, from the central campus. The thinking was that both Kimwenza and Hekima, where relatively large numbers of scholastics lived and studied, reflected an older more institutionalised model. Living in a small family-size house with eight or ten people, at some distance from the campus, allowed a person breathe his own air and find his feet more easily. For Nobert Rwodzi, it was like a development of the novitiate where the novices 'could be doing different apostolates but we came back at the end of the day to sit around and share the fruits of these apostolates, encouraging each other and helping each other the best we could'. In the small communities, each one was responsible for his own budget, clothes, stationery, and gadgets. He also did his own laundry, and each small community took care of its own shopping, cooking, cleaning and the rest. If Jesuits are, primarily, their own 'formators', the more room they had to do this the better. In olden times one could hide in the crowd and never face even the smallest decisions. Some of my generation are incapable of cooking anything more demanding than a boiled egg.

So what attracts a young person today to become a Jesuit? Nobert Rwodzi answers that 'the Jesuits helped me to see what it is to be with the poor'. Tafadzwa Mandimutsa was drawn to the wide variety of works the Jesuits were engaged in: parishes, social centres, schools, chaplaincy and media work, 'all in a bid to bring people closer to God' and 'help them realise how close their Creator was to them'. Elphas Ndlovu singled out the hospital experience he had in the novitiate where he was 'doing works I never imagined doing; cleaning wounds, praying with patients, consoling the bereaved, counselling patients and cleaning the hospital premises'.

Nobert notes 'how different we were' as novices and yet still one body desiring to use our gifts to serve the people of God, and Lovemore Mashiri mentions being struck by the variety of Jesuits he met when they visited the missions. 'They were young and old and came from Germany, Poland and Ireland as well as Zambia and Zimbabwe and yet there was something that united us all.' The young Jesuits I spoke to mentioned the 'prospect of a new enlarged province fills some of us with some anxiety but the experience of Arrupe University is helping us to bond and live in harmony. We are already overcoming any fears we might have had about new environments and people who are different from us. And, as an international body we are well placed to respond to the opportunities of the digital age. We are already doing this through online classes.'

Another thing that attracted Mashiri was the way the novices were consulted about important issues. 'I receive the shock of my life at the sight of two men coming all the way from Rome to facilitate a discernment process for the Society's ten-year apostolic preferences. I began to realise that the Society is serious; it means business. We are involved, even as novices.'

We end this account where we began, with a province roughly equivalent in size to the boundaries of the Zambezi Mission approved by Leo XIII in 1877. We have seen the labours involved in occupying this space in order to be with the people and share with them the Good News and we have explored the processes by which the Jesuits pursued their goals. We have noted Pope Francis's adage, 'time is greater than space', and every Jesuit in this story has known that theirs is simply a contribution to something far greater than any individual or set of individuals. Looking back, we can see how far we have come. The present writer has tried to describe the achievements of the Jesuits who, together with a multitude of sisters, teachers, catechists and members of other religious communities, gave their lives to this task. He has also tried to record the weakness inherent in the 'dual' mission the Jesuits found it so hard to challenge. While describing this shadow side of the mission, which bore a legacy still affecting us today, he hopes he has been fair to the enormous generosity and imagination of generations of Jesuits in Zambezia. We can legitimately hope that time will heal the wounds that remain. They are, even now, far from the daily consciousness of people in Zimbabwe who have other concerns uppermost in their minds.

It is October, that tense season each year when the sky is charged with energy as the clouds push their way into the clear blue skies, bearing their promise of rain. Politically, our country is becalmed. There is nothing of substance to report. Our leaders seem to want to keep things as they are. They like it that way. Talk of change is just that: talk. And yet, below the surface, like the seed growing in the field (Mark 4:27), there is a seething swirl of expectation. It is as though we are back again in the early colonial days, when the old felt they had no other option but to resign themselves to the conquest of their land, while the young, eager to resist in the only way they could, grasped every economic opportunity open to them. We sometimes forget that the country was not 'quiet' between the first *Chimurenga* and the second. The whites faced a formidable challenge from black enterprise in the 1920s, as we saw in Chapter 6 above. Their response, as always, was to use force. For what else can we call the legislation, without consultation with the blacks, about land and labour in the 1930s?

As I write, the Spanish island of La Palma has erupted in fire and lava, filling the air with toxic gas and destroying homes and livelihoods. There is no way of putting a lid on a volcano whose time to explode has come. So it is with human societies. There comes a moment when they erupt and demand change.

Both the state and the church in Zimbabwe are quiet on the surface but seething within. This is perhaps easier to see with the state for its excesses are grist to the media's mill and need no discussion here. But in the church too, though restrained and respectful, there is distinct unease. Yes, we now have eight bishops and hundreds of priests and religious sisters. We have an impressive number of missions, parishes, schools, hospitals, clinics and other institutions – even a Jesuit university. But the stories we hear of the lives of some of our messengers of the gospel are deeply troubling. The worldwide church is reeling from the revelations of scandals caused by some bishops, priests, sisters and brothers. People dedicated to the service of Christ's mission to the world are actually blocking the Lord's message of good news from reaching people by the example of their lives. And we, in our local church and our local Jesuit province, are not spared from these universal viruses. We live in an anxious time which calls to mind Karl Rahner's words: 'The devout Christian of the future will either be a "mystic", one who has experienced "something", or he will cease to be anything at all.'[1]

Rahner is talking about a 'crisis' in the Church. A crisis is a moment of decision. What we are living in the Catholic Church today can be seen as a catastrophe when all the structures and ways of proceeding we were accustomed to come crashing down leaving us confused and dismayed. Or it can be seen as a moment of opportunity, a moment of purification, allowing us to focus on what is essential and discard the rest. This could be what Rahner means by experiencing 'something'.

The experience of retreat giving – listening to people speak of their inner struggles and their experience, or lack of it, of God, and trying to share words of guidance with them – convinces the present writer of the great thirst today for a deeper experience of life. And this can unfold into an experience of God, as revealed by Jesus. Despite everything, our local church is ready for this.

Fr Edward Murphy,[2] after reading these reflections, helpfully draws them together under three headings.

1. **The collision of cultures**, which underlay the whole story of the Zambezi Mission, meant that the missionaries came with a deeply Europeanised way of proclaiming the Gospel message. They failed to distinguish the Gospel values from the culture they themselves had grown up in. The result was they were asking the local people to accept a package where the gospel and the manifestation of empire were confusedly intertwined.

2. **A time of change**. During the later decades of the period this study has covered, especially the 1960s, 70s and 80s, the Church herself was going through great change just as most of Africa was grappling with the end of colonisation. The Vatican Council's emphasis on the Church, not as a hierarchy, but as 'People of God' all on one level, on 'inculturation' in language and custom and on local personnel taking

---

1 K. Rahner, 'Christian Living Formerly and Today', in D. Bourke (trans.), *Theological Investigations VII* (New York: Herder and Herder, 1971), p. 15.
2 In a personal email.

over authority, meant that the Church became more self-reliant at the local level and more aware of her own ability to be herself with her own national identity. For some older missionaries it was a time of uncertainty and confusion but for most, it was an exciting time when they could see all around them signs of new life and vigour.

3. **A moment of arrival**. As the old century drew to a close, a new generation of locally born Jesuits made their presence felt. Foreign born Jesuits, who had made the decisions for so long, now stepped aside. It was not an easy transition and the early applicants had to struggle with little companionship and few role models. It was often difficult to gain acceptance and find their place. Yet, in Eddie's words,

> As the rising generation began to take over the ministries of (the) province, they began to establish their own way of being Jesuits to their people. It is important, at this stage, that previous 'empires' be dismantled, that is, often works and projects established by an individual mission with the help of overseas funds. They must be downsized or dismantled to fit into a province plan. Time also will tell what becomes of them but the younger generation cannot be burdened with such, often individualistic, work.

-oOo-

I end on a note of hope. Elphas writes: 'I am presented with a lot of excitement and challenges. One can feel the pain and bitterness of the poor in Zimbabwe. Their cry is growing ever louder and falls on deaf ears. Children are born and raised in a broken environment filled with individualism, poverty, secularism and corruption. These are the people who need us now more than before. This stirs me to reflect on our mission and adapt it to the current needs of the people. And it gives me a sense of direction; to give hope and restore faith to the many who seem to be losing it.' And Nobert says: 'We should imagine ourselves as beginning anew, as erasing all our present apostolates from our mind and asking what apostolates would be of top priority? I have a feeling that the current crop of Jesuits has gone on slumber and forgotten the value of creativity and innovation.'

Provincial Leonard Chiti, in his letter to the new Province of Southern Africa for St Ignatius Day 2021, wrote:

> [I]nasmuch as we contemplate our roots in our past, so as to

sustain us in the present, we must also look to the areas of our lives where we need to undergo a conversion for the future. We are, after all, each of us sinners, called to be companions of Jesus, and each other. And what has been the quality of that companionship? We need to beg for the grace of conversion: as a body, as a community, and as a companion. I believe it is only with the eyes of the converted, that we will truly be able to see 'all things new in Christ'.[3] Only then will we truly notice the poor, the marginalised and the outcast around us; only then will we be able to discern the Holy Spirit's presence in our lives; only then will we be drawn to encounter Christ in each other.

Today, 25 November 2021, is the one hundred and forty-first anniversary of the lonely death of Augustus Law at Mzila's. He was attended by just one other Jesuit, Joseph Hedley, who was himself severely debilitated by malaria. The scene speaks to us of utter failure, the sort of failure the crowds witness on Golgotha.

---

3   This is the theme of the Ignatian Year promulgated by Fr General, Arturo Sosa.

Appendix

Jesuit Foundations in Southern Africa
1875-2021

1875	St Aidan's	Boys' school	Closed 1973
1878	Graff Reinet	Residence	Closed 1890

Zambezi Mission 1879

1880	Old Tati	Mission	Abandoned 1886
1880	Old Bulawayo	Mission	Abandoned 1886
1880	Pandamatenga	Mission	Abandoned 1885
1882	Dunbrody	House of Studies	Closed 1934
1883	Mopea, Quilimane	Mission	to Port Prov.* 1893
1884	Vleischfontein	Residence	Closed 1894
1886	Keilands	Residence	Closed 1909
1887	Empandeni	Mission	Closed 1889-94
1894	Empandeni	Mission re-opened	to Marianhill** 1931
1887	Stutterheim	Mission	Closed 1898
1888	Boroma	Mission	to Port Prov. 1893
1890	Fort Victoria	Residence	1901-09 temp. closed
1890	Salisbury	Residence/Cathedral	to Archdiocese 2009
1892	Chishawasha	Mission	

English Province 1894

1894	Bulawayo	Residence	to Mariannhill 1931
1896	Bulawayo	St George's College	moved to Harare 1926
1896	Gokomere	Mission	to Bethlehem*** 1947
1899	Umtali	Residence	to Carmelites 1946
1901	Bulawayo	Observatory	to government 1929
1902	Embakwe	Mission	to Mariannhill 1931
1903	Gwelo (Gweru)	Parish	to Bethlehem 1953
1905	Chikuni	Mission	to Pol Prov.**** 1912
1905	Kasisi	Mission	to Pol Prov. 1912

1906	Driefontein	Mission	to Bethlehem 1947
1908	St Joseph, Hama's	Mission	to Bethlehem 1947
1910	Katondwe	Mission	to Pol. Prov. 1912
1910	Kapoche	Mission	to Pol. Prov. 1912
1910	St Peter's, Mbare	Parish	
1910	Enkeldoorn	Parish	to Franciscans 1959
1911	Holy Cross	Mission	to Bethlehem 1947
1915	St Patrick's Bulawayo	Parish	to Mariannhill 1931
1912	Kutama	Mission/Teacher Training	to Marist Brothers 1939
1313	St Michael's Mhondoro	Mission	to Archdiocese 1978
1915	Gatooma	Parish	to Archdiocese 1964
1915	St Paul's Musami	Mission	
1915	Que Que	Parish	to Bethlehem 1953
1921	Umvuma	Parish	to Bethlehem 1946
1924	St Joseph's Semokwe	Mission	to Mariannhill 1931
1925	Visitation, Makumbe	Mission	

Salisbury Mission 1927

1929	Monte Cassino	Mission	from Mariannhill to CPS***** 1971
1929	St Barbara's, Manyika	Mission	from Mariannhill to Carmelites 1950
1929	St Benedict's, Chiendambuya	Mission	from Mariannhill to Umtali Pref 1953
1930	All Souls Mtoko	Mission	to Archdiocese 1962
1930	Silveira, Bikita	Mission	to Bethlehem 1940
1932	Triashill	Mission	From Mariannhill to Carmelites 1948
1936	Chishawasha	Seminary	to RCBC (ZCBC) 1975
1945	Highfield	Parish	to Archdiocese 1978
1948	Marymount	Mission	to Chinhoyi Diocese 2011
1951	Wedza	Mission	to Franciscans 1961
1952	Marandellas	Parish	to Archdiocese 1966
1953	Mangula	Mission	to Chinhoyi Diocese 1986
1953	Assumption, Rhodesville	Parish	to Archdiocese 1985
1956	St Barbara's Kariba	Parish	to Chinhoyi Diocese 1998

Appendix: Jesuit Foundations in Southern Africa 1875-2021

Sinoia Mission 1957

1957 Silveira House	Novitiate	Moved to Mazowe 1964 & Lusaka, 1969
1957 Holy Name, Mabelreign	Parish	to Archdiocese 2019
1958 Our Lady, Mount Pleasant	Parish	
1958 Sipolilo	Mission	Moved to Guruve 1980 to Chinhoyi 2002
1961 Garnet & Prestage House	Curia/Student House	
1962 St Albert's	Mission	to Chinhoyi Diocese 1998
1962 Sinoia	Parish	to Chinhoyi Diocese 1994
1962 St Francis Xavier, Braeside	Parish	to Archdiocese 2017
1962 St Martin's Chikwizo	Mission	Abandoned 1974
1962 St Ignatius	College	
1963 St Peter's Kubatana	School/Technical School	
1963 Karoi	Parish	to Chinhoyi Diocese 1993
1963 Mazowe	Novitiate, later pre-seminary	to ZCBC 1980
1964 School of Social Work/ Social Work Training		to University of Zimbabwe 2016
1964 Bindura	Parish	to Archdiocese 1978
1964 St Raphael's Chitsungo	Mission	to Chinhoyi Diocese 1995
1964 St Rupert's, Makonde	Mission	to Chinhoyi Diocese 2003
1970 Kangaire	Mission	Closed 1978
1970 Sacred Heart, Banket	Parish	
1970 St Boniface, Hurungwe	Mission	to Chinhoyi Diocese 2004
1977 St Kizito Murombedzi	Mission	to Chinhoyi Diocese 1998

Vice Province of Zimbabwe 1978

1978 Waterfalls, Harare	Novitiate	Closed 1983
1979 Mutorashanga	Mission	to Chinhoyi Diocese 1979
1980 St John's Alaska	Parish	to Chinhoyi Diocese 1990

Zimbabwe Province 1983

1990 Arrupe House	Juniorate	subsumed into Arrupe

		College 1994	
1994	Arrupe College	Philosophy & Humanities Under JECAM ******	
1998	Richartz House	Care home for aged and infirm	
2000	Bulawayo	Ingwe Studios	House closed 2010
2004	Emmaus	Guest House, Residence	

Zimbabwe-Mozambique Province 2014
Southern Africa Province 2021

* Portuguese Province of the Society of Jesus
** Congregation of Mariannhill Missionaries
*** Bethlehem Missionary Society
**** Polish Province of the Society of Jesus
***** Precious Blood Sisters' Congregation
******Jesuit Conference of Africa and Madagascar

Acknowledgements

Others have walked this road before me and the most recent account of the Jesuits in Zimbabwe is by Fr Wolfgang Thamm SJ. Thamm declares his 'is not a work of historical research but rather a story of the main lines of our history'. But then he goes on to do a good deal of research and produces a comprehensive, if brief, description of the 140 years of Jesuit presence in this country. The strength of his book is in informing us of all the major works even if it is done factually without much comment. Also, as a German, he reflects the enormous contribution of the German Jesuits to the mission of the Church in Zimbabwe.

Many others have written on the Jesuits in Zimbabwe or edited their letters. I have drawn on their labours and am hugely indebted to them. I have also invited Jesuits in active ministry today to read what I have written and comment and younger Jesuits in formation to share their thoughts. The books and sources I have consulted are listed here.

Let me mentions some names. First, Chiedza Chimhanda, who while serving as Provincial, asked me to undertake this work. Others who read the text or contributed were: Joe Woods, Roger Riddell, Roland von Nidda, Pauline Hutchings, Dieter Scholz, Nigel Johnson, Günter Gattung, Dominic Tomuseni, Lovemore Mashiri, Nobert Rwodzi, Tafadzwa Madimutsa, Elphas Ndlovu, Paul Mayeresa, Stephen Silungwe, Stephen Buckland, Admire Nyika, Pat Makaka, Lorenz von Walter, Eberhard Fuhge, Mark Hackett, Courage Bakasa, John McCarthy, archivist at St George's College. The list could go on. I am particularly grateful to Eddie Murphy for his encouragement and sharp critical comments.

And without Irene Staunton of Weaver Press who, with Murray MacCartney, have seen to the editing and production, this work would have lacked that meticulous and attractive presentation Weaver always gives us. Thanks too to Kevin Philip for the unusual maps, mosquitos and all.

I want to include Eye Specialist, Dr Sharai Shamu, whose great care of my sight enabled me to undertake this work in the first place and see it through to the end. There was a time when I thought my sight was deteriorating irretrievably but she brought it and me back from the brink and has continued to keep an eagle eye (!) on me.

This is not a comprehensive history of the Society of Jesus in Zimbabwe but a series of, what Fr General Adolfo Nicholas in another context, liked to call 'flashes,' that is, brief descriptions of significant developments which would give a sense of the whole story. I claim to do no more than that and so let me apologise to anyone who feels their presence or their work is omitted or too skimpily treated.

David Harold-Barry
Emmaus House, Harare
1 February 2022

Index

abandoned
    babies 308
    children 108
abductions 96, 101, 134, 154, 155, 157, 271
African
    advancement 266, 280
    Catholics 6
    Christianity 4, 284
    custom and beliefs 88, 321
    independence 19
    interests 80, 314
    nationalism 265
    people 73, 197, 220, 240
    religions 121, 243
    voice 80
African Women's Club see AWC
AIDS *see also* HIV/AIDS 241, 304, 305
All Souls 22, 127-128, 186-187
All Souls Mission 187
Allen, Alfred 59, 63
An Ill-Fated People 20, 80
Anglo-Zulu war 33
antagonism 187
anthropology xviii, 321
apiculture 308-309
archaeology 308, 310
archives xvii, 89, 94, 212, 230, 295, 326-327
Arrupe, Pedro 159, 176, 191, 196, 198, 216, 252, 273, 275-276, 294, 306, 310
Ashton, Thomas 71
assault 142, 284
astronomy 308
At Kalahari's Brink 71, 72
atrocities 17, 140, 154, 272, 277, 278, 311

AWC 165-166
Balling, Adalbert 71-72
Banket 132, 141-142, 144, 150
Barotse 51-52, 54, 56-57
Berridge, Antony 228, 232, 251, 324, 332
Berry, Jim 214-215, 225-230
Bethlehem Mission Society 84
Bethlehem Missionaries 5, 84, 182, 324
Bick, Charles 71-72, 321
Biehler, Edward 68, 320
Bikita *see also* Silveira 117
Bindura 97, 175
Blanca, Salvatore 13, 32, 38-39, 42, 47, 64, 83
Boers 37, 58
Book, Augustine 67-68
Brand, Coenraad 19
Brand, Quinton 208
Breaking the Silence 192-193, 277
British colonial administration 24, 207
British Defence and Aid fund 271
British South Africa Company (BSAC) 19, 67, 70, 73, 78, 79, 221
Bulawayo 40-47, 61-63, 74-75, 81, 86, 119-122, 126-127, 161-162, 201, 208-210, 302-303
bull sessions 39
Bullen, Josephine 70, 71, 89
Burrett, Rob 42, 62
CA 246
camels 81, 217
casualties 63, 208, 299
catechism 69, 94, 104, 156, 176, 320-321
Ndebele 71
     catechists 71, 86, 124, 143, 150, 333
     as teachers 85, 87, 123, 133
Catherine II 11
Catholic Ancillary Teachers of Rural Zimbabwe see CATORUZI
Catholic Association see CA

Catholic Church 7, 10, 25, 62, 66, 86, 201, 207, 212, 260, 266, 283, 296-297
    centenary 279
    compromised 5
    crisis 335
    headquarters 162
    mission 6, 12
    missionary work 33, 265
    state relations 265
    teachings 37
Catholic Commission for Justice and Peace see CCJP
Catholic Institute of International Relations see CIIR
CATORUZI 111-113
CCJP 140, 154, 172, 193, 249, 267-272, 277, 285, 287
CCP 295-297
Celts 8
Central African Federation 136
Chamberlain, Joseph 68, 76
chameleon
    approaching 70
    white 60
charism 114, 118, 196, 198-199
charismatic movement 114
Chichester Convent 188
Chichester, Aston Ignatius (Chick) 25, 109, 119, 122, 127, 133, 143, 178-189, 265, 315
Chidziwa, Joseph 76
Chief Chivero see Mhishi, Michael
Chikwizo, St Martin's 128-130, 323
Chimurenga 154
    first 1896-1897 73, 75, 80, 334
    second 1967-1979 154, 224
Chinhoyi 132, 138, 141, 181
    caves 151
    diocese 102, 159-160, 297
Chinhoyi Rural Training Centre 152, 157
Chishawasha 66-68, 71, 79-83, 85, 103-105, 127, 163-164, 171, 178-180, 257-259, 331

Mission 65, 68, 80-81
printing press 319-320
Chitsungo mission 149
Christian Church 22, 26, 124
Christian Community Programme see CCP
Christian faith 3, 28
Christian Socialism 14
Christian villages 69, 82, 122-124, 314,
Christianity 4, 20, 29, 106, 126, 157, 177, 195, 274, 296, 323
church and state 187
church decor 322
CID 225, 227, 245, 246
CIIR 247, 267-269, 272, 274
Civil War in Rhodesia (1976) 267
CJ 142, 228
Coglan, Sir Charles 171
commercial farms 102, 138, 251, 25, 257
commitment 6, 15, 24, 109, 205, 267, 282
communism 96, 169, 198, 243, 281
congregation
    constitutions for the 181
    for local sisters 180, 188, 315
    Mariannhill 117, 125
Congregation of Jesus see (CJ)
Conway, John 96, 97, 171, 210, 214, 287
Correia, Francisco Augusto da Cruz 28, 29, 30
CPS 85, 118, 125, 185
credit 247-248, 256-257, 259-261, 315
    agricultural 248
    unions 315
Criminal Investigation Department see CID
Croft, Gregory 230, 289,
Croonenberghs, Charles 17, 31, 34, 37-41, 48, 51, 59, 60, 64-65
Cuama River (Zambezi) 28
culture 18, 23, 38-39, 73, 122, 172, 176, 179, 181, 195, 198, 320, 323
    and charism 195, 199
    and traditions xix, 9, 25, 121

collision of 335
Jesuit 197
local 177, 296
of the Bantu 106
political 201
shift 31
Shona 116, 146
Zimbabwean 328

Da Silveira, Gonçalo 26-30, 67, 128, 133
Daignault, Alphonse 61, 66-67, 89-90, 308
Daignault, Charles 89, 103, 105-106, 174
dance 23, 31, 99, 112, 138, 156, 169, 211, 323
    Mashave 22
    ritual 106-107
Davis, Anthony (Jeep) 91-94, 99, 103, 226, 234-235, 326
De Mercedes, Dominican Sister 108-109, 180
De Nobili, Roberto 4
De Sadeleer, Frans 31, 35, 40, 43-48
De Vylder, Louis 31, 35, 37, 40, 54-56, 62, 63, 327
De Wit, Anthony 39-40, 42, 44, 56, 58, 62, 63
degradation 16-18, 176, 259
degraded people 15, 17-18
Depelchin, Henri 8, 30-34, 36-40, 42, 43, 49-59, 62, 64, 66, 119, 313, 327
disability 117, 306
disasters 48, 60, 125, 136, 224
Dominican
    convent 98, 184, 209, 319
    school 135, 162, 164, 174
Donovan, Desmond (Gussie) 95, 110, 289
Dove, John Thurston 119, 197, 219, 239, 243-247, 251-252, 255-256, 265
Driefontein 68, 83-84, 86, 124-125, 158, 265, 314
dual mission 7, 15, 201, 282, 333
Dutch Reformed Morgenster Mission 19
East Germany 131, 181, 281, 292

education
- African 85-87, 202, 236
- and evangelisation 124
- co-ordination 312
- for development 219
- girls 165
- higher 220
- Jesuit 78, 178, 233, 313
- multiracial 175, 204, 212-214, 221
- primary 220
- public 87
- purpose of 177
- religious 142, 217, 232
- resistance 2, 40
- secondary 90, 111, 315
- system 77
- with production 114

Education Bill 177
Embakwe 71-72, 86, 126
Embakwe Mission 72
Emergency Powers Regulations 271
Empandeni 60-62, 68-71, 75, 82-83, 86, 89, 123, 126, 309
Empandeni Mission 60, 68
Engelbrecht, Jan 37, 58, 83
Enkeldoorn 173-174
enlightenment 11-12, 178, 314
entomology 308-309
environment 23, 61, 152, 164, 199, 201, 211, 212, 217, 323, 333, 336
Eucharist 28, 94, 237, 322, 323
European farms 5, 138, 139, 148, 149, 152, 153, 157
evangelisation 106, 124, 129, 219, 295, 324
fighters 135, 269
- freedom 99, 228, 249, 266
- guerrilla 275
- liberation war 115
- recruiting 155

finance 152, 170, 222, 242, 245, 325

First World War 80, 126, 210, 317
football 12, 91-93, 99, 209, 226, 306
Fort Victoria (Masvingo) 81, 84, 117, 182
Franco-Prussian War 56
FRELIMO 135
French Revolution 12, 314
Frente de Libertacao Mocambique see FRELIMO
Fuchs, Karl 13, 31, 41-42, 62, 63

Gangarahwe 140, 141
gardeners 7-9, 13-14, 30
General Congregation (GC) 79, 199, 238, 264, 266, 314
German Catholic development agency see Misereor
German priests 126, 186
God xviii, 3-4, 21-23, 37, 78, 115, 293, 298, 311, 327, 335
    Creator 3, 72, 75, 332
    people of 333, 335
    will of 16, 46
    call 181
Gokomere 68, 70, 84, 117, 186, 310
Goodman, Lord Baron Arnold Abraham 24, 207
government 16, 243, 271, 274, 278, 299
    agents 96
    auxiliary forces 158
    colonial 15
    imperial 76
    interference 231
    policy 109, 213, 248, 253, 316
    regulations 88, 98
    Rhodesian Front 202, 212, 234, 240
    schools 111, 214, 227, 233, 291
    Shona system of 75
    Southern Rhodesian 206, 221
    training courses 116
    Zimbabwe 318
Grahamstown xix, 30, 32-33, 56, 58, 60, 64, 121, 184, 209, 231, 279, 313
Great War (1914-18) 80, 103, 208

GuBulawayo 31, 40-41, 44, 48, 57, 59-61, 64, 192
guerrilla fighters 275
guerrilla war 147
guerrillas 96-101, 110, 135, 149, 153-158, 214, 224-225, 227-228, 249-250, 269-270, 279-281, 290
Gwelo (Gweru) 74, 119, 122, 173-174, 182, 186, 204, 239, 324
Hartmann, Andrew 61, 66, 70, 72, 127, 178, 219, 320
Hatendi, Peter 3, 13
Hedley, Joseph 32-35, 41, 43-48, 59-60, 337
History of the Vashawasha 76
HIV 241, 303-305
HIV/AIDS 251, 303-305
Holy
    Inquisition 27
    Land 200
    Other 3
    Spirit 276, 327, 337
    Thursday 84, 145
    Trinity 139, 151
    water 4
Home, Sir Alec Douglas 24, 207
Hooy, Gerard 56, 63
human rights 72, 271
Hurungwe (St Boniface) 143, 157, 159
hymns *see also* songs 120
Ignatian
    ethos 115
    pedagogy 313
    spirituality 115
    workshops 298
imperial citizenship 5, 167, 168
impis 75
inculturation 176, 335
Independence 14, 61, 102, 111-112, 135, 147-149, 157-158, 191-192, 202, 225, 229, 278, 280
indunas 54-55, 61, 69-70, 74, 76
Industrial Training College 236

inferior 20, 106, 195
inferiority 22
inflation 102, 253, 321
influenza epidemic 1918 80
informal settlements 102
injustice of white rule 81
injustices 5-6, 213, 268, 283, 298
intellectuals 320
Internal Settlement 99, 101
Internally Displaced Persons 157

Jameson, Leander Starr 19, 68, 70, 74
Jesuits *see also* Society of Jesus 10, 15-17, 38-39, 78-79, 119-124, 176-179, 195-196, 201-203, 217-222, 241-243, 264-265, 279-283, 328-329
    British 213
    Brothers xvii, 67, 84, 210, 235, 296
    missionaries 13, 86, 121, 162, 276
    French 11
    German 67, 96, 131-132, 157, 290
    in Rhodesia 266
    in Rome 199
    in the late nineteenth century 2, 4, 8-9
    in Zimbabwe xx, 12-13, 70, 103, 200, 281, 295, 324, 326
    Lithuanian 181
    local-born 189
    of the Zambezi Mission 59, 62
    role of the 282
    schools 214
    Spanish 276
    Zimbabwean 197, 199
Jesuit Refugee Service (JRS) 267, 273, 275-277, 326
justice 6, 15, 22, 76, 133, 264, 284, 298
    courts of 74
    promotion of 79, 264
    social 232, 247, 266, 283
Justice and Peace Commission 218, 247, 253, 267, 278, 283

Kangaire Mission 150, 293

Kariba 62, 132, 136-137
Karoi 132, 138-139, 143, 302
Khama 33, 36, 75
Kimberley 33-34, 37, 208
Kroot, Bartholomew 56-59, 63
Kutama 82, 83, 86, 123, 132-133, 140, 143, 148, 160, 182, 184, 188, 220, 223, 235, 314
    College 94
    Training School 87, 88
Lake Bangweulu 30, 32, 50, 64
Lake Ngami 60
Lake Tanganyika 14
Law, Augustus 17, 32, 34-35, 38-41, 43-49, 51, 59, 62, 63, 65, 192, 256, 327, 337
LCBL 91, 113, 118, 127, 141, 143-144, 148-150, 175, 296
legacy 7, 23, 284, 314, 333
Lessing, Doris 24, 206
Lewanika, King of Barotseland 54-57, 64, 75
liberation
    struggle 96, 134, 157, 280
    war 5, 16, 115, 119, 145, 156, 157, 188, 193, 205, 210, 214, 215, 252, 266, 308
libraries 326, 328
life-giving processes 15
Lisson, Bernhard 134, 145, 147, 290, 292
Little Children of the Blessed Lady see LCBL
liturgy 175, 300, 320, 322-324
Livingstone, David 30, 35
Lobengula 30-31, 36, 40-44, 51, 59-61, 64, 69-70, 74, 117, 192
Lobengula, the Ndebele king 36
lobola 180
London Missionary Society 2, 33, 36, 40
Loubiére, Jean-Baptiste 82-83, 123-124, 184
Louw, Andries Adriaan 19
Loyola, Ignatius of xix, 2, 10, 21, 313
Lozi 50-51, 54, 56, 64, 75, 120, 164

Mabelreign 171, 172, 266

Macheke (Monte Cassino) 117-118, 125-126, 185, 188, 235
Magondi 291
Maisels, Israel (Issy) Aaron 271-272
Makonde 143-144, 146, 157, 289-292
Makonde (Magondi), St Rupert's 143
Makumbe 68, 95, 106-112, 115, 117, 133, 175, 180, 260, 329
    Centre 116
        Mission 106, 289, 290
        Children Home 108
malaria 13, 43, 50, 56, 62-63, 84, 127-128, 133, 337
Mandebvu, Hedrick 156
Mandela, Nelson 271
Marandellas (Marondera) 100, 174
Mariannhill 71, 117-121, 124-127
Marist brothers 83, 94, 220, 223
Marxism 96, 157
Mary Ward Sisters 159, 228
Marymount 132-135, 150, 158, 187, 229, 277, 290, 292,
Mashave 22, 146
Mashonaland 3, 61, 66, 73, 76-77, 79, 124-127, 162, 236
massacre 97
Masvingo 181, 186, 236, 325
Matabele 17, 33, 59, 126
Matabeleland 30, 40, 58, 60-61, 68, 71, 74-77, 119, 126, 260, 277
Matopo shrine 21, 76
McLaughlin, Janice 153-154, 157, 246, 252, 270, 272-273, 275,
    299, 316
mechanics 1, 7-9, 13-14, 30
meteorology 308
Mfecane 21
Mhangura 137
Mhishi, Michael *see also* Chief Chivero 103-104
Mhondoro 103-104, 143, 163, 250, 260, 263, 285, 328
minority languages 253
Misereor 30, 72, 152, 230, 235, 245, 252, 325
missiology xviii, xix, 288
Mission and Culture 176
mission farms 67, 69, 118

missionaries
> Catholic 3, 35
> German 103, 181
> Protestant 16, 17, 36, 50, 63

Mlimo 21, 75, 76
Moffat, Robert 16, 63,
monogamy 21
Monomotapa 29
mosquitoes 26, 68, 127
Mount Pleasant 172, 266, 273
Mugabe, Robert 14, 82-83, 88, 105, 133, 157, 167, 184, 188, 192, 229, 250, 270, 278, 321
Mukai/Vukani 316, 318, 321
Mupunzaguto, Negomo 28
murder(s) 18, 40, 95, 96, 98, 141, 192, 281, 302, 325
Murombedzi 82, 88, 140-141
Murombedzi (Gangarahwe, St Kizito') 140
Murphy, Edward 42, 327-328, 335
Musami 89-94, 96-99, 103-104, 110, 186, 214, 220, 248, 279, 281, 285, 287, 288, 290, 292, 306
Musengezi River 29
Muslims xix, 27, 29
Musodzi, Elizabeth 164-166, 169
Mutorashanga 139, 150
Mwari cult 21, 74, 75
Mweemba 49-55, 57, 62, 64
Mzilikazi, King of the Ndebele 16
Mzingeli, Charles 166-168

National Archives of Zimbabwe 41
nationalist(s) 225, 243
> fighters 19
> leaders 88, 245
> movement 192, 233, 243
> struggle 5

Native Commissioner see NC
natives 24, 74, 78, 107, 179, 206
> heathen 17

Nazareth sisters 185

NC 75, 79, 140, 180-181
Ndebele 4, 16, 21, 25, 41, 61, 69-70, 73-78, 104, 120, 126, 192-193, 278, 300, 321
Ndebele kingdom 9, 44
Nigg, Theodore 31, 34-35, 41, 48-49, 52-53, 62
nigger 74
Nkomo, Joshua 167, 192, 243, 270, 272, 273
observatory xvii, 265, 308-309
occupying space 13-15
Official Secrets Act 271
Old Empandeni 61
Old Tati 13, 119, 319
Our Lady of the Way Parish 172, 204, 324
ox-wagons 26, 64, 81, 319
paganism 27
paintings 31, 41, 112
Pandamatenga 37, 49, 52-59, 62, 67, 119-120
Paravicini, Pietro 32
passive aggression 19
Pauling, George 81
peace-building project 253
Pieper, Gerhard 134, 150, 293
Pieter Beckx 12, 30
polygamy 9, 21
Pope Francis 12, 121, 193, 242
Pope Gregory 4
Pope Paul III 11
Pope Paul VI 3
Pope Pius XII 187
Precious Blood Sisters see CPS
Presentation Sisters 148, 175, 185
Prestage House 329
Prestage Trust 59
Prestage, Peter 48, 56, 58-60, 66-67, 69-70, 75, 84-85, 89, 127, 178, 219, 327
primary school 111, 120, 268
    St Albert's 153

  St Edward's 148
  St George's 141
prisoners 1 00, 300-303
Protestants 13, 41, 50, 63, 202
pungwe 96, 97, 99
Que Que (KweKwe) 174, 204
race relations 24, 193, 202
racialism 15, 20, 61, 212, 283
racism 5, 129, 194, 206, 212, 213, 221, 235, 240, 268, 283
Racist Missionaries: An Obstacle to Evangelization in Africa 194
railways 5, 81, 329
Randolph, Richard 118, 318, 331
Rea, Francis xviii, 321, 325
Reckter, Helmut 139, 140, 159, 160, 297
reformation xviii, 3
Reformation, Enlightenment and Revolution 3
refugees 135, 140, 170, 186, 241, 273-276, 311
  Mozambican 229, 272, 277
regiments 74-75
religion xix, 3, 13, 18, 41, 60, 73, 76, 77, 115, 121, 178, 179, 216
  African 27
  traditional 2, 29, 177, 323
religious beliefs 3, 21, 29
remains
  of Chichester 188
  of Donovan 110
  of guerrillas 135
  of Kariba Dam workers 136
  of Law 48
  of Livingstone 30
  of victims' 193
RENAMO 135
resistance 2, 70, 213, 323
  Shona 73, 77
  to education 106
  to integrated sport 213
  white 19

Resistencia Nacional Mocambicana see RENAMO
    resourcement 199
retreats 115, 151, 216, 228, 244, 247, 252, 277, 310-312
revolution 3, 82, 100, 123, 166, 178, 205, 233
Rhodes and Founders 93
Rhodes, Cecil John 5, 61, 73, 74, 76, 77, 208
Rhodesian Bush War (1972-79) 267
Rhodesian Front 202, 221-222, 234, 240, 272
Rhodesian government 5, 168, 206, 230, 270
Rhodesian project 5
Rhodesian Security Forces *see also* security forces 281
Richartz House 329
Richartz, Francis 67, 68, 71, 78-80, 82, 103-104, 123, 140, 178, 219, 327, 329
Richert, Gregor 144-145, 147, 290
rinderpest 69, 104
rising 74-77, 82, 104, 164, 172, 182
    of Ndebele 4, 69, 73, 300
    of Shona 4, 69, 73, 117, 124
Rogers, Edward 219, 233-234, 238-242, 265, 304, 308
Rozvi dynasty 77
Rudd Concession 61, 73
rural credit 256
sacrament 170, 264, 296
    Blessed 9
    of Reconciliation 217
    of the sick 112
Sacred Heart 32, 40, 137, 141
Salvation Army 110, 141, 143, 260
Savings Clubs 140, 258-260
Savings Clubs and Credit Unions movement 219-220, 257, 259, 266
Savings Development Movement see SDM
Scholz, Dieter 5-6, 132, 135, 151, 160, 173, 267, 270-272, 277, 283, 326, 343
school 85-86
    academic 109
    carpentry 92, 143
    discipline 112, 114

    homecraft for girls 90
    technical 109
    industrial 91
    Jesuit 85
    mission 88, 95
School of Social Service (later Work) 234, 237-239, 242
School of Social Work 96, 197, 219, 238-239, 242
SDM 257-258, 260
Second World War 7, 131, 181, 186, 205, 210, 244, 317, 322
secondary school 19, 92, 127, 135, 220, 227, 266
    at Kutama 184
    at St Albert's Mission 153
    community 233
    for girls 109
    for people of mixed race 71
Secondary School Sacred Heart 141
security forces 99-101, 140, 154-155, 249
segregationist policies 16, 235, 265, 266, 283, 314
self-government 78, 207
Self-Help Development Foundation see SHDF 259-263
Selous Scouts 97, 98, 287
seminary 25, 125, 138, 171, 173, 175, 182, 183, 186, 188, 315
    minor 182
    preparatory 182
    regional 189, 266
settlers 16, 20, 24, 37, 61, 66-67, 69, 73-74, 76-78, 127, 141, 174, 202, 314
    Catholic 34
    European 280
    white 18, 61, 69, 78, 117, 124, 205
SHDF 259-263
Shepherd-Smit, Christopher 96-97, 288
Shingirirayi 306
Shona 3-4, 21, 25, 29, 44, 69, 73, 75, 77-78, 97, 100, 116-117, 120, 124, 146, 192-193, 250
Shoshong 33, 36, 63
Silveira House 14, 98, 171, 189, 219-220, 242-248, 250-252, 254-256, 299, 310-311, 314-316

Sinoia (Chinhoyi) 82, 131, 204, 302
Sinoia Mission 132, 138, 139, 147, 148, 152, 159, 271
Sisters of Notre Dame de Namur 85, 184
Sisters of Notre Dame see SND
Smith, Ian 14, 24, 129, 142, 172, 271-272, 274
SND 70, 71, 89
Society of Jesus xix-xx, 1, 10-11, 30, 42, 49, 65, 79, 121, 141, 194, 197, 205, 221, 264, 313
Society of Our Lady of Africa see SOLA
sociology xviii, 19, 239
SOLA 149
songs 35, 107, 108, 115, 120, 175, 303, 312, 323
Southern Rhodesia 89, 161, 178, 205, 206, 208, 233, 272, 301, 322
Southern Rhodesia African National Congress 192
Southern Rhodesia Trade Union Congress see SRTUC
Spenser, Edmund 18
spirit mediums 76, 135, 146, 164, 200
spiritual
    activities 4
    bondage 177
    conversation 200
    experiences 199
    hearth 132
    nourishment 244
    writings 195
Spiritual Exercises 10, 191, 199, 310, 311, 327
spirituality
    Ignatian 115
    Jesuit 307
SRTUC 167
St Aidan's 35, 38, 209, 231, 289
St Aidan's College 30
St Albert's Mission 96, 132, 152, 153, 158
St Barbara 136-137, 125
St Boniface 143
St Boniface Mission 228
St George's 68, 91, 161, 185, 187, 201, 203-222, 228, 234, 240, 303, 310, 322

St George's College 197, 204, 266, 274, 300, 309
St Ignatius 68, 203, 214, 215, 221-225, 227-232, 265, 276, 289, 311
St Ignatius College 18, 94, 108, 178, 191, 204, 220, 258, 309, 323
St Joseph's 50, 119, 124, 148, 150, 152, 158
St Paul's Musami 102, 222, 233, 234, 235, 238, 280, 286
St Peter's Kubatana 152, 220, 233-234, 237-238
St Peter's Training Centre 297
St. Rupert's Mission 145
Staudacher, Urban 72

Tati 37, 41, 47, 49, 54, 56-59, 61-64, 83, 85
TB sanatorium 107, 108, 113
Teacher Training College see TTC
Teacher Training School 87, 118, 314
Teacher/Catechist Training School 86
Terörde, Anthony 31, 33, 38, 49-53, 55, 63, 327
terrorists 97, 153, 268, 273, 274
Tertianship 191, 273, 293, 306, 307
Thatcher, Margaret 18
The Catholic Church and the Struggle for Zimbabwe 282
The Catholic Church and Zimbabwe 201, 321
The Grass is Singing 24, 206
The Man in the Middle 267, 272
The Propaganda War (1977) 267, 268
The Shield 108, 175, 186
theological reflection 282, 313-316, 318
Thomas, Martin 97, 104, 285
trade union 167, 235, 244-246, 252
traders 29, 36, 37, 40, 58, 60-61, 63
trades test 159
tradition xx, 9, 20, 26, 104, 121, 313, 320, 324, 327
traditional
        customs and religion 2
        herbs and roots 2
        legal procedures 18
        religious beliefs 29
training
        moral 86

teacher 86, 87, 90, 92
transformation 14, 71, 255
transformative processes 14
Treason Trial of 1956 271
Tshamatshama 43
TTC 83, 94, 95, 132, 184, 185
UDI 130, 204, 212, 221, 224, 266
Umzila's 43-45, 47-49, 51, 62-64, 256
Unilateral Declaration of Independence see UDI
university chaplain 297-298
University of Zimbabwe 19, 38, 65, 321
urban
areas 114, 227
    blacks 163
    businesses 261
    centres 94
    conditions 170
    dwellers 253
    life 165
    living 161
    parish ministry 161
    parishes 161, 295
    population 161
    tensions 161
    townships 169
urbanism 164

Vambe, Lawrence 19-22, 25, 75, 80
VaShawasha 19, 20, 25, 80, 81
Vatican Council 94, 128, 139, 199, 264, 266-267, 314, 323
Vervenne 49-50, 52-54, 59, 67
Vleeschfontein 57

Waddelove, Francis (Waddy) 140, 219, 257-260, 262-263, 266
Wankie (Hwange) 52, 62, 81, 119-120
war
    Rhodesian Bush see Chimurenga
    Second Matabele see Chimurenga
Watsham, Anthony (Tony or Seamus) 223-224, 230-231, 309

Wedza (Hwedza) 83, 98, 119, 140, 153, 182, 185, 214, 225
Wehl, Charles 43-47, 63
Weisskopf, John 49, 54, 58, 63
Weld, Alfred 8, 17, 30, 32, 33, 38, 39, 40, 43, 53, 57, 58, 61, 64-66, 313
white
    administration 61
    adventurers 74
    alien influence 25
    Catholics 98
    conquerors 4
    control 75
    decision-makers 172
    enemy 95
    farmers 151, 153, 156
    fear 206
    forces 73
    government 168
    hegemony 5, 206
    Jesuits 190, 281
    man 22, 24
    missionaries 4, 97, 274
    parish 172, 266
    people 179
    politics 243
    power 5
    presence 24
    Rhodesia 22, 23
    rule 79, 81
    settler 60
White Fathers (Missionaries of Africa) 50, 124
Whitehead, Edgar 104
whites only 203, 205, 213, 235
witchcraft 9
women
    as minors 180
    dignity and rights 166, 167, 263
    freedom of 181

parental consent 180
role of 167
rural 250
status of 181
success of 259

Zambezi Mission xviii, 42-43, 48, 56, 58-62, 65-66, 86, 89, 121, 131, 184, 313, 333, 335
Zambezi *see also* Cuama River 49-51, 54, 56, 86, 104, 119-121, 131-133, 162-163, 187, 218, 253
Zambezia 121, 317, 325, 334
Zambia 49, 54, 62, 121, 124, 130, 136-137, 151, 268-269, 273-274, 320-321, 328, 333
ZANLA 96-101, 110-111, 135, 153, 155, 290
ZANU 154, 167, 224, 243, 262, 270
ZANU-PF 116, 140-142, 154, 298
ZAPU 105, 167, 243, 270, 272
ZCBC 275, 319
Zimbabwe African National Union - Patriotic Front see ZANU-PF
Zimbabwe African National Union see ZANU
Zimbabwe African People's Union see ZAPU
Zimbabwe Catholic Bishops' Conference see ZCBC
Zimbabwe National Liberation Army see ZANLA
Zimbabwe People's Revolutionary Army (ZIPRA) 149, 272, 290
Zimbabwe Project (ZP) 267, 272-275, 277

www.ingramcontent.com/pod-product-compliance
Lightning Source LLC
Chambersburg PA
CBHW051554230426
43668CB00013B/1850